0/04

GOOD PEOPLE
in an
EVIL TIME

GOOD PEOPLE
IN AN
EVIL TIME

Portraits of
Complicity and Resistance
in the Bosnian War

SVETLANA BROZ

EDITED BY

LAURIE KAIN HART

TRANSLATED BY

ELLEN ELIAS-BURSAĆ

OTHER

Other Press
New York

Translation copyright © 2004 Ellen Elias-Bursać

Production Editor: Robert D. Hack

This book was set in 11 pt. Minion by Alpha Graphics of Pittsfield, NH.

10   9   8   7   6   5   4   3   2   1

Library of Congress Cataloging-in-Publication Data

Broz, Svetlana.
    Good people in an evil time : portraits of complicity and resistance in the Bosnian War / Svetlana Broz ; English translation: Ellen Elias-Bursać.
        p. cm.
    ISBN 1-59051-061-5 (hardcover : alk. paper)
    1. Yugoslav War, 1991-1995–Personal narratives.   I. Title.
DR1313.8.B76 2003
949.703—dc21

                                        2003013382
                                        Rev.

To Sonja and Ivan

Front Lines

Massacres, rapes, torture, concentration camps: The horrors of war beset Bosnia after it raised its flag of independence. Virtually every community suffered, but Sarajevo and a handful of others stand out.

1 Bihac
Holds out under siege until Serbs retreat in late 1995.

2 Prijedor
Serbs run a notorious concentration camp here following 1992 cleansing.

3 Banja Luka
Bosnia's largest Serb-held city and scene of extensive ethnic cleansing.

4 Tuzla
Fighting off the Yugoslav Army in 1992, the city becomes a symbol of free Bosnia and its major refugee center, growing from 160,000 to 900,000 people.

5 Srebrenica
Some 7,000 men disappear after a Serb attack on the UN-protected Muslim city in July 1995.

6 Zepa
Serb anti-Muslim atrocities in July 1995 lead to war crimes tribunal.

7 Mostar
The ethnically mixed city divides in the Muslim-Croat sub-war of 1993.

Dayton accord line
(2.5-mile-wide demilitarized zone)

Roads portrayed may be impassable due to wartime damage.

Elevations in feet

0   20
MILES
NGS CARTOGRAPHIC DIVISION

CONTENTS

ACKNOWLEDGMENTS

I owe hundreds of people gratitude for their help in writing this book, people who understood its purpose. Since I cannot thank them all individually, I will say that I owe the most to those who agreed in the name of the truth to bare their wounded souls again. My profound respect to those who helped me collect this material. The people most directly involved in work on this book deserve a special place: Mario Kamhi, for his enthusiasm and help in the field research and final preparations; my daughter, Sonja, for her boundless love and understanding, which spurred me on when it was hardest; Ellen Elias-Bursać, for her love, care, and perfect understanding in making the book accessible to readers all over the world; Uwe Kitzinger, CBE, for his colossal help and moral support; Thomas Butler, for his endless patience and assistance; Laurie Kain Hart, for her anthropologist's ear attuned to the universal message of these testimonies that happened to be found in the Balkans but could come from any region of conflict in the world; Judith Feher Gurewich, for her wonderful support; and Swanee Hunt, Jeff Spurr, Perry Klass, Larry Wolff, and Michael Sells.

Svetlana Broz

INTRODUCTION: WHY READ THIS BOOK?

The war in the former Yugoslavia is no longer in the headlines. The inside pages of U.S. newspapers carry scattered reports about economic crisis and ethnic tensions in Bosnia and Herzegovina and Croatia, where the war raged during the 1990s. Paddy Ashdown, High Representative of the International Community in Bosnia and Herzegovina that oversees the implementation of the civilian aspects of the 1995 Dayton Peace Agreement, has said that he expects to be the last such representative as BH makes the transition to self-sustaining statehood. What can testimonies like those collected here possibly mean to us at this date, when Bosnia and Herzegovina's problems seem remote, endemic, or, at the very least, not ours?

There is a long answer to the question, which the reader will discover in reading this book, and a short answer, which is that we need, more than ever, to know the limits and possibilities of human ethics during the terror and tyranny of war and to understand the truth about the causes of war. This is particularly crucial in regard to what have been called the "new wars" of the late twentieth and early twenty-first centuries: "ethnic conflicts," as they are labeled, that appear to involve neighbor-to-neighbor violence. Some have argued that these wars are the product of ineradicable "tribal" hatreds. Others point to the cynical use of ethnicized or racialized politics by individual leaders, or to global structures of inequality that lead to competition and polarization. Bottom-up or top-down? Or simply a question of thuggery? How do we answer these questions? We can begin by listening to the people who lived through the war tell us what happened to them. Political history will record how the politicians, intellectuals, professionals, and the military created the war; this book documents what people tried to do about it when it came to their cities, towns, and villages.

Unspeakable Crimes

The people we hear in this book were faced with a world in which unspeakable crimes not only went unpunished but were rewarded with glory, profit, and power. In these conditions, they were starkly confronted with the limits and possibilities of their own choices. The testimonies recorded here document acts of seemingly random brutality as well as erratic acts of protection, self-sacrifice, and kindness. Some individuals abused others; many more did not.

In this book the historic events of the war are described from the point of view of the immediate, fragmented experiences of those drawn into it against their will as the state of Yugoslavia dissolved and political leaders jockeyed for power. Those leading these mass annihilations produced reasons to legitimize and promote them: the idea of democracy was abused in the service of fascism as it has been so often in the twentieth century (Broz observes that all nationalist parties have the word *democratic* in their titles), and "self-defense" played its usual part as the mask of aggression. Why did this resonate sufficiently in the hearts and minds of some citizens to drive them to mobilize and engage in forms of violence? Which citizens in fact committed acts of violence and under what conditions? Who resisted—why, how? It is our responsibility to ask these questions. By the end of 2002, the International Criminal Tribunal for the Former Yugoslavia had documented a total of 7,000 war crimes committed in Bosnia and Herzegovina during the war. Given that the population of the territory at the beginning of the war was about 4.5 million, it is clear that "popular participation" in genocide was limited to a tiny proportion of the population.

Shock and Resistance

The testimonies describe ordinary people in Bosnia and Herzegovina who were surprised that the war could come to their towns, destroy their everyday lives, change their relationships with their neighbors, and ultimately change the course of their personal and collective history. It was a shock and they were unprepared. They remember the war as though it were a strange visitor: "The war began for me on 18 September 1991 . . . "; "No one believed the war would come to Sarajevo . . . "; "On the sixth of April 1992, a tank appeared in front of my building"; "We couldn't believe that the things happening everywhere else would start in Vareš . . . " People quickly discovered the reality of the danger. These stories describe the real quandaries and complexity of life in war.

War made the common projects of integrated communities impossible: collective house building, routines of sharing coffee, workplace solidarities. It was a sudden and violent reconfiguration of social life. People struggled against this radical reinterpretation of the world that was played out by power politics on their identities, bodies, and homes. Ordinary people tried to thread through the war step by step, seizing where they could an opportunity to help neighbors or friends, and resisting the myth that ethnoreligious differences make them enemies. This resistance was sometimes as small as the offer of a cup of coffee to a stranger and at other times as great as self-sacrifice.

The Capriciousness of War

The testimonies communicate the frightening capriciousness of war. It was impossible to know who might offer help, or when, or how, or—more importantly perhaps— why (a chance opportunity? sympathy? morality? ideology?). At the same time, because these testimonies demonstrate that people also very broadly resisted the premises and practices of genocide, they disprove the hypothesis that ordinary people produced the war to express their fundamental and long-standing antipathy to other ethnic communities. It is not plausible to suggest, after reading this book, that citizens used the war to pursue a long-desired but suppressed grass-roots separatism. Rather, they were shocked by what separatism produced—and desired. As one of the interviewees put it, "The politicians think one thing, the people think something else."

Yet we have evidence here of how the people are drawn into the sweep of the politicians' war. Complicity by the civil authorities complements the actions by military and paramilitary groups: people lose their jobs and apartments in an insidious erosion of rights; familiar places become strange to their inhabitants. Who was more dangerous? The people one knew? Or the people one didn't know? Some claim neighbors did the pillaging; others claim it was always outsiders. One woman tells us, "I was terribly disappointed in people during the war. . . . It was only the rare person who was consistent." A former friendship—even a superficial acquaintance—might mean that one received special protection in a camp; or, to the contrary, suddenly the war became the cover for a personal vendetta. Bosnia and Herzegovina is a small country. The alliances and antagonisms of past personal and family relationships are continually in play in these accounts of the war.

If the reader is baffled by the inexplicable advances and reversals of fortune in the stories, this truthfully imitates the experience of the narrators themselves. The rule of law has disintegrated. Civilians are trapped or empowered by their minority or majority status in an unstable landscape of war games. A neighbor declares that he can offer protection. Is this a boast, a ruse, a game of self-aggrandizement, a residue of systems of clientelism in local politics before the war? How much latitude for clemency might a conscript lay claim to under the eyes of his superiors? What devices do combatants employ to distance themselves from their own actions? A jail warden asks his prisoners (civilians trapped by their minority status), whom he knew in former times, "What are you doing in prison?" as though he does not know why people are being incarcerated. A commander asks the thug whom he has ordered to beat civilians, "What is going on here?" as though he were outraged by the very idea of brutality. The authorities who provoke and witness abuses pretend not to understand them. In a strategic use of true terror, they claim that violence is the result of spontaneous popular rampages.

In these conditions of capricious cruelty, it is impossible to devise a formula for self-protection and indeed the texts do not offer any such formulas. What they do show us is how it is possible to protect others. Most people had the power to expose or support a neighbor. There are clues here for each of us to consider concerning why and how some refused to be complicit in these systems of betrayal. Broz's book affirms that there is a latitude of personal action in war.

Fear

Reading these testimonies all together, it is possible for us to understand more clearly the intensity of fear, and the distortions of human action terror produces. The strategy of the aggressor was always to intimidate and implicate ordinary citizens. Fear is most powerful as a tool, the texts reveal, when it takes the form of a triangle. There is the aggressor, the victim, and then another victim. Perhaps the worst, too familiar version of this is a threat against a child or loved one. But the triangulation can, and did, take many forms.

Broz explains in more detail:

Some of my friends asked me why I included such a lot of testimonies from the same place—for example, Vareš—given that these people are saying the same kinds of things about the war. I wanted to stress that this is not the opinion of one person who was living in this place, but the opinion of the majority of the people. The Croats in Vareš did not want to leave their small town. So some Croatian politicians decided to inflict a terrible atrocity next to Vareš in Stupni Do, where their military and paramilitary units murdered thirty-eight women, children, and elderly people, all Muslims. The citizens of Vareš were watching this—because Vareš is on the top of the hill and Stupni Do below so they were all able to see this massacre. And they thought, "Oh my God, someone, in our name, has carried out this horrible atrocity, and now we have to go away; because all of us will carry collective responsibility for this." This was the goal of the genociders: they were circulating by car with the megaphone, warning all Croatians to leave town, then sending paramilitary Croatian soldiers, opening doors, telling the Croatians to leave, stealing their jewelry.

The most horrible crimes were deliberately done in the name of ethnic cleansing: ethnic cleansing was not a consequence but the objective of this war. This entailed the most obscene rape, torture, and murder of members of the other ethnic group with the intention of leaving surviving victims who would tell others what they had experienced, and frighten others into fleeing. This "cleansing" entailed the destruction of houses—so that people would have nowhere to return to—as well as cultural and historical monuments of the persecuted minority so that their history would be erased.

The Illusion of Solidarity Within Communities and of Antagonism Between Them

The testimonies speak through the very lack of consistency of behavior to the absence of a thoroughgoing popular idea of ethnic difference. "Nationalism," one interviewee tells us, "is everyone's excuse to steal and murder"— it is no special property of this or that group. One cannot count on one's own community to help one out in blackmarket conditions. The narratives do not coalesce into a dichotomous (or trichotomous) picture of Serbs helping Serbs, Croats helping Croats, and Bosniaks (Bosnian Muslims) helping Bosniaks on the basis of "blood." In fact, help and aggression come from various quarters. Sometimes it was outsiders who initiated the violence, sometimes it was insiders who panicked at rumors or were acting in self-interest or "choosing the side where they would be safest." Mirror-images of bearded, long-haired Muslim mujaheddin and bearded, long haired Serbian chetniks haunt the imaginations of civilians.

In retrospect, the interviewees are thankful to strangers and neighbors for help, but they also feel bitter toward all sides for making the war. They are no less bitter toward their "own" side. If there is a popular hatred here, it is of war itself. But it is certainly the case that over time this generosity wears thin. The victims of violence can excuse its madness as a plague for a short period of time, but the longer it goes on, the more it is institutionalized and repeated, the more they become disillusioned with human beings and with human nature, and the harder it all is to bear.

In Broz's later postwar explorations of whether or not a desire for revenge dominated the feelings of former victims, she found to the contrary a pervasive rejection of eye-for-an-eye ethics. This was true even in the case of Tuzla, where seventy-one teenagers were killed by a shell on the evening of 25 May 1995. When NATO bombed Serbia during its intervention in Kosovo in 1999, Broz expected to hear Sarajevans express some pleasure in this turn of the screw. But, she comments, "I didn't hear anyone in that city who was happy about the bombs falling on Serbia, though I did hear one man say, 'It's not so bad that the people of Belgrade get a whiff of what a cellar smells like, as long as no one gets killed.'"

Before the War? The Nature of Pluralism

The narrators frequently insist: we all got along before the war. From an outsider's point of view, like most generalizations, this is neither completely true nor completely untrue. In recollecting communal conflict, people tend to remember the prewar harmony of ordinary people. This is the case with Greeks and Turks remembering the period before the division of their populations in 1922; or with Hindus, Muslims, and Sikhs recollecting life before the partition of India and Pakistan in 1947. It is in many ways a true

observation, but it also eclipses some of the important prewar social tensions—for example, between city people and rural people, or between
classes—that characterize all societies. Just as resentment against commer-
cial classes in parts of Africa took the overt form of anti-(South-)Asian violence in the mid-twentieth century, political and economic inequalities in
the former Yugoslavia became ethnicized. The testimonies describe how,
for example, the prominent Muslim founder families of certain towns were
specifically targeted as members of the cultural elite, as well as how wealthy
or politically prominent Serbs and Croats were targeted. However, the testimonies also tell us that people did not divide up into classes of the more
or less enlightened. Educated people were no better behaved than others—
and arguably worse, when we consider the numbers of doctors, professors,
and clerics involved in the initiation and organization of violence.

Memories of the prewar period expressed in the interviews demonstrate
both sides of this reality of historical ethnic and religious identifications.
On the one hand, people lived side by side with others of different traditions, and at varying rates intermarried with them, erasing or subduing the
markers of difference in succeeding generations. "Yugoslav" was a primary
identification for many people, though probably unevenly in the cities,
towns, and villages and across various regions. Everyday activities were
constituted by a multitude of interactions—hospitality, common tasks,
civic involvements, god-parenthood, work, and so on—within and among
groups (to the extent that we can even say that groups existed). On the other
hand, distinct neighborhoods did exist in many localities, and people tended
in the majority to marry within networks of ethnic community. The testimonies reflect this duality: on the one hand, people recollect living all together in harmony in the village or town, making no distinctions between
people on the basis of religious heritage; on the other, people refer to traditionally distinct neighborhoods, or to different kinds of interactions
among kin versus neighbors; when war came, they expected that others
"would tell their own people first." But what is distorted by the retrospec-

tive lens of war is the fact that it is *normal* for both kinds of networks to exist in human societies. Sometimes the distinction between them is vague or obscured: the near and dear might be assembled on the basis of class, education, religious background, or neighborhood, but everywhere there is an assembly of the near and dear, and contrasted to this, the outsider. The violence of the war broke the sustaining interactions that connect this inside and outside world. Information about when to stay, move, flee, or fight became a privileged commodity theoretically restricted to certain parts of the social network. The testimonies reveal how individuals tried to re-connect those parts through the sharing of information, food, and shelter across the divides created by the war.

The State and the World

This book is not a political history of the war. (Readers will find the chro-nology of the conflict included after the Introduction helpful, and there is a list of recommended readings in Appendix III.) But we need to keep in mind a few key facts. The first is that while the war was not the result of ethnic antagonisms, the stakes of the war were very real indeed. What was in question for the political masterminds was control of resources: the material resources of territory and capital, and the political resources of nationhood in a world in which only nations in the form of states have a political voice. Europeans, and especially southeastern Europeans, often tell Americans that they do not understand what coexistence means in Europe, and that their broad, misty American ideas do not make sense in the con-stricted spaces and limited resources of their communities. In south and eastern Europe (and not only there) the state is an enormously important source of employment and goods. Access to those things is mediated by the people one knows. Control of those things is crucial for the education and advancement of one's children. The explanation of one's failures and the successes of others is often given in terms of privileged access to such resources. This is why the control of the state is so very important in social terms. There can be a sort of dearth of what, after political scientist Benedict Anderson, we might call "places to go" in life. The notion of limitless opportunity that Americans revere is not a widespread illusion in the former Yugoslavia. Coexistence, then, is the product of how people work with the physical and social relations at their disposal; it is not an ideology so much as a daily practice. It does not depend on whether or not people love their neighbors, but on how they are connected in the system that runs their world and on how their opportunities are organized. As Yugoslavia fell apart, it was not clear how the resources of the old states would be redistributed. The fighting was certainly not a "clash of civilizations" or an "interethnic conflict"; but it was not "fighting over nothing." As Broz writes, "It was territorial aggression, backed by the convenient ideology of ethnic separatism, which justified the crime of ethnic cleansing committed on orders from the politicians."

References to the crimes and failures of the international community appear throughout these testimonies. The greatest scandals were those associated with the safe havens established by the United Nations Protection Forces (UNPROFOR) at sites now infamous such as Srebenica, where civilians collected under the promise of protection and were abandoned to be murdered in the thousands by General Mladić and the Serbian military. It would be strange to reflect on the question of individual responsibility, as this book urges us to do, without also reflecting on the experience of Bosnians as they watched the international community, the world, make promises and betray those promises. The world might have been watching Bosnia and Herzegovina, in its self-protective, evasive, and limited way; but Bosnia and Herzegovina was also watching the world, and we see in these pages what Bosnia and Herzegovina saw. In the testimony "These Are Just Kids," a French UNPROFOR soldier plays a game with an escaping child: "One of the soldiers took a piece of paper, showed it to them and said, 'If you can guess which hand I'm holding the paper in, I'll take you to the other side.'"

The tunnel in Sarajevo, to which many of these accounts refer, might stand as the peculiar and ambiguous sign of the surrealist agreements of the war. In 1992 Sarajevo was surrounded. 1993 United Nations forces came to protect the airport runway under a special and controversial agreement with the Serbs who controlled the area. More than 800 people died on the runway under these conditions, as Sarajevans tried to escape from the starving city or to ferry food into it. So they dug a tunnel underneath the runway, five meters deep, 800 meters long. With their hands, eighty people working from both sides created a passage with a rail system inside and carts to carry the dead and wounded and supplies. It is said that there were five million passages through the tunnel in the war. It was as though a small vein was permitted to operate to keep the city on the edge of life, and for the inhabitants it was a vehicle of survival. It was also to the advantage of the black marketeers on all sides. It was to the benefit of the Serbs whose interest in sustaining the siege was not so much in conquest as in the strategic uses of Sarajevo in political bargaining, and in the steady erosion of the character of the city and Sarajevan pluralism. It was a kind of excuse for the international community to do nothing about the siege. No one destroyed the tunnel.

A Social Universe

This book can be read as a picture of a society in war, with all the depth of a full social universe. We learn about the social networks through which people survive when there is no public space and no public protection or resource. The interviews give us a picture of the cultural life of Bosnia and Herzegovina, for example, the rituals of hospitality, and the traditional obligations of the host to his guest that lie behind small exchanges in time of war. Above all, we see the importance of the home and the severity of loss of home. The stories reflect Bosnia and Herzegovina's historical experience: "Son, never close a door with your ass. Wherever you end up, always do good to others if you can. I can remember three wars. And remember this, you reap what you sow"; and they reveal the values of honor and status that count in normal social life. There are hints of the politics that operate behind the scenes—how and why certain people in positions of power obtain passes, escape, or are protected. The stories describe what money can buy even in times of war and occupation: escape, food, shelter, warmth, identity cards, transport, gas. People in Bosnia and Herzegovina make black jokes about that, as they do with everything concerning the war: "An American soldier came to Bosnia and Herzegovina for training. After six months he returned to the United States, confessing that he had passed nine exams of the course but failed the tenth. 'What was the one you failed?' they asked him. 'Well,' he answered, 'I really couldn't run, shoot, and carry a refrigerator on my back at the same time.'"

The portrait of life that develops in these pages is most vividly a picture of the excruciating details of war. Each of us will be struck by some different, resonant fragment of experience that suddenly sharpens our understanding: The lack of privacy during the siege illustrated by voices carried through an apartment building by empty water pipes. A boy who shouts, "Stop this war, it's urgent!" A woman who cannot light a fire for warmth or cooking because her neighbor is annoyed by the smoke, and she risks betrayal by him. New forms of common sense arise: If you were so lucky as to have some beans, you must also be lucky to have some winter shoes because one pair of winter shoes would be enough to cook one lunch of beans.

A Note on "Ethnicity" and on the Construction of This Book

It might not be immediately obvious to an English-speaking reader that the testimonies in this book are arranged in groups of three—a Bosniak (Muslim), a Serbian, and a Croatian testimony following one another in sequence. However, in the headings of each testimony, the people interviewed are not labeled by ethnic community. There is a reason for this. First of all, this structure can be only approximate in a society that until recently put little emphasis on religious background, and in which mixed marriages and secular identities were prominent. Identities are not what they seem: we read the words of a woman with a Muslim name who is a Catholic; of a man with a Serbian name who considers himself a Muslim; of a boy who claims to be a Yugoslav; of a child of a mixed marriage who switches identity halfway through the war. And then there are names that give no indication of an affiliation. The Serbs label a man an "Ustasha"; the Croats call the same man a "Chetnik." Identities are not fixed; they appear in context out of a confrontation, a challenge at a border, the sudden pressure to claim one name or the other ("During Tito's Yugoslavia I was a Yugoslav; now I am a Bosniak."). The strength of one person's identification with an ethnoreligious identity is different from that of the next person. A label reduces all of that to one dimension, to a way of summing up a person that is deceptive. So we leave it to the reader to discover the subtlety, the uncertainty, even the sense of play that has existed in these identities. The nationalist labels Croat, Muslim (or Bosniak), and Serb distort reality.

> For the whole time while fighting was going on, both in Grbavica, and later when I was living in the Muslim part of Sarajevo, I held on to my feeling of being a Yugoslav. I lived in the belief that all of us were Yugoslavs. Others would ask me, "So why aren't you out defending your Yugoslavia, if you are such a Yugoslav?" I didn't know whom I was supposed to be defending it from, nor where. I didn't know who was attacking it, or why. If I'd known, I would have.

The ordering of these stories in threes is not intended as an argument to distribute responsibility for the war indifferently among all sides or to level the differences among the communities in the actions of war. It is meant to demonstrate, however, that individual responsibility was a reality on all sides. The terminology we apply to people has the power of a weapon. Equally, when people reject nationalist labels, they engage in a form of resistance that is as significant as it is often unremarked. And here the irony is that it was not so difficult to make the transformation from one category to another if one could acquire the right identity card to establish oneself as a Serb/Croat/Muslim. It was difficult for the nationalists to recognize their enemy.

It could be said that nationalists by definition cannot "know" their enemies, because, in fact, they invent them. Though they are sadly not imaginary, these wars are in this sense wars of the imagination. How else—as Philip Gourevitch asks at the beginning of his book on the Rwandan genocide, *We Wish to Inform You that Tomorrow We Will Be Killed with Our Families*—can we explain the murder of innocent people? They have to be imagined as something else. Small children are not small children, but "Jews," or "Chetniks," or "Ustasha."

What, after all, is an ethnicity? "Ethnic" is defined by the widely used *American Heritage College Dictionary* as follows: "of or relating to sizable groups of people with a common, distinctive, racial, national, religious, linguistic, or cultural heritage." In other words, in popular American speech we use "ethnic" group to describe any group of people with a common "heritage"—which can mean just about anything. This twenty-first century meaning is relatively recent. "Ethnic" began its career as a word in English in the fifteenth century with the meaning of "heathen" or "pagan." By contrast to Christians or Jews, "ethnics" were social groups with their own tribal religions. In the eighteenth and nineteenth centuries, with the development of ethnology, or the comparative study of cultures, there was debate about what defined an "ethnos"—a distinctive language? customs? or "skulls, statures, and complexions?" In the United States, the concept of race is mingled with concepts of ethnicity. Rejected by most physical anthropologists as an imprecise and misleading concept from the scientific point of view (discrete "races" do not exist biologically), race is nonetheless widely used as a synonym for ethnicity to indicate particular population groups, generally thought of as distinguished by physical as well as social characteristics. But ethnic groups are not in any sense biological units: ethnicities are segregated by socioeconomic and political boundaries and are produced in the course of history through interactions with others.

Ethnicity, as anthropologists have documented, does not describe a fixed and consistent marker of human character, but the way people distinguish themselves from others by contrasting selected features of one group to those of another. An ethnic group could be constituted using the criterion of religion, or the criterion of skin color, or the criterion of language, or some combination of just about any factors imaginable. In the context of Europe, what we refer to as an ethnicity may also be called a "nationality"— confusing, sometimes, for the U.S. observer who thinks of nationality in association with citizenship.

Some outside observers have wanted to argue that the South Slavs— Croats, Bosniaks, Serbs and others in that geographical area—are all one ethnic group, by which they mean one racial/population group, indistinguishable by physical appearance, as though the war would be justified if they were distinct "races," and is illogical if they are not. But it is not nature (or "race") that creates ethnicity, it is history; and it is not ethnicity that creates war, it is the manipulation of ethnicity in the pursuit of power. The distinctions that were exploited as boundary-defining and fatal criteria in the context of the fall of Yugoslavia and the war were those of historical religious origin: Catholic (Croat), Muslim (Bosniak), and Eastern Orthodox Christian (Serb). Thus for the purposes of talking about the war, we refer to these groups as "ethnic groups"—they are not races, they are not isolated civilizations, they are not languages: they are political categories that have emerged from historical struggles.

Given that ethnic labels and their political valence can change so quickly in time—look at the list of terms in the U.S. for referring to people of African or Latin American origin—it will not surprise the reader that there are several terms in currency to refer to Bosnians of Muslim heritage. At the time of the war, the term most frequently used was *Muslim* with a

capital "M"—this was used by the Yugoslav state as an ethnic label distinguished from the word used for those who practice Islam as a faith, which
was *muslim* with a lower case "m." Currently, the term most prevalent is
Bosniak. In this book the term *Muslim* is generally used, as this was the term
used in testimonies in the 1990s. However, in the commentaries and ap-
pendices the term *Bosniak* will be employed. Similarly, some writers now
distinguish between "Serbians" as those living in Serbia proper, and "Serbs"
as those living in Croatia and Bosnia. (In this book, only the noun *Serb* will
be used, and *Serbian* is its adjective.)

A Note on Oral History

A testimony is not a record of facts, though it contains facts. A testimony in
good faith, however, is a record of truth. In testimonies people talk about
the heart of their experience, which is shaped by the moment in which they
are speaking, the person to whom they are speaking, and their sense of what
they want the world to know. The stories are not raw in the documentary
sense. They were selected, condensed, and translated. The reader reads—and
should read—such accounts with an awareness of this individuality, partial-
ity, and intentionality. The stories are diverse and individual. Different people
emphasize different parts of the experience of the war and the peace. A book
of oral histories does not aim to provide a summary of events or generalizations about this or that community, still less a "sample" or a "survey" of majority opinion. They do add up, though, as Broz shows us in her preface and
in her afterword, to a sensibility, a close reading of the experience of the conflict that prevents a calamitous misunderstanding of history.

Svetlana Broz

During Svetlana Broz's childhood in the 1950s and 1960s Federal Republic of Yugoslavia, the English-speaking world knew little of life in Eastern

Europe or the Soviet Union apart from the myths generated by Cold War politics. It was only in the 1980s, with the Sarajevo Olympics, with tourism in Croatia, and with glasnost in the Soviet Union, that this grim and gray profile broke a little with a glimpse of the reality of the vibrant society that was, in fact, the former Yugoslavia. That vision was almost immediately buried by a new set of myths generated by the outbreak of nationalist wars: the myth of the savage Balkans, the myth of ineradicable "tribal" hatreds, and a people, or peoples, resistant to the values of civilized society. Only a stone's throw from Paris, Vienna, and Rome, the former Yugoslavia was again cast as the dark part of the continent. The American public had access only to a media horror show of refugees and prison camps, the grandstanding of politicians, and ravaged landscapes. What was missing was the voice of the people who were suffering this catastrophe and who could explain to us how this new war in the heart of Europe was generated, prosecuted, and experienced. Like others who have been compelled to gather oral histories of war, Broz did not so much choose her task as was chosen by it, in her unique personal connection to the Yugoslav nation and Yugoslavian pluralism.

The evidence for pluralism that exists in these testimonies is connected to the particular history of Bosnia, because Bosnia's experience of Yugoslav history was determined, as Buturović's contribution to this book (Appendix I: Bosnia-Herzegovina: History, Culture, Ethnicities) shows, by a unique synthesis of different religious and imperial traditions. In some sense Bosnia was, in its development after World War II, the epitome of the project of a common Yugoslav nation, and that project was the primary objective of Yugoslavia's leader, Josip Broz, known as Marshal Tito, from 1945 until his death in 1980. Tito was Svetlana Broz's paternal grandfather. Broz was a living symbol for the people she interviewed of that nation-in-common that in retrospect resonated with peace and prosperity—even if not a liberal democracy.

On both sides of her family, like most Yugoslavs, Broz's life was shaped by the events of World War II. Broz never knew her maternal grandfather.

A partisan fighting against the Nazis and their collaborators in Croatia, he was killed before she was born. His body was never found. When Broz was a child, she went with her mother to visit the people who had last seen her grandfather before he was killed. She listened to their story of that last night, when her grandfather had come to the house of this couple to hide. Her hostess explained to Svetlana's mother: "I am ashamed. When your father came to the house, my husband brought him in. But I burst into tears. I was afraid: afraid for my family, myself, my children, that he might be discovered and all of us killed. Your father said to me; 'I don't want you to be frightened; I won't stay.' And so he left. And that night he was murdered and never seen again."

In this way Svetlana Broz knew from an early age about the merciless isolation of the choices war puts to ordinary citizens. Like others who have focused on resistance in wartime, she intends to show us that acts of altruism are not serendipitous errors but part of the normal repertoire of human action. "Because I am well informed, a lot of people think I'm irrational to be an optimist," Broz says. "They think, How can she know these things and be an optimist?" It is exactly—she would argue—*because* she is well informed that she can argue that hope is justified. "I want to be sure that those people who remained human beings are known. My interlocutors never generalized, never said that such and such a group is guilty, are perpetrators. Evil as well as goodness has a first and a last name."

Svetlana Broz was born, therefore, into the First Family of post-WWII Yugoslavia. Tito was a resistance leader and hero during WWII, then postwar head of state, and president from 1952 until 1980. Though she was born and educated in Belgrade and lived there most of her life until she left for Sarajevo in 1999, when she talks about her childhood it is not Belgrade or its political circles that she describes. Instead, her first memories are connected to the diverse origins of her family in the various parts of Yugoslavia. Her mother's mother was a teacher in small villages, and her first memories from before she began primary school are connected with rural Slavonia, in Croatia, where her grandmother was employed (she never remarried after the disappearance and death of her husband), and where Svetlana spent months every year. It was a flat, calm landscape, regulated by the rhythms of the agricultural year; Broz remembers a strong regional flavor, the special songs and clothes of the peasants—a distinctive but not then politicized regional character. Later, during primary school, she spent her summer and winter vacations in Bosnia, on the outskirts of Sarajevo in the village of Hadzici; her mother's mother grew up in a house next to the one she now inhabits. Broz's maternal ancestors came from Middle Europe during the Austro-Hungarian period and integrated into Bosnian society; in her house Serbo-Croatian, Czech, and German were spoken. Her grandfather Tito's mother was Slovenian, and his father was Croat. Her father's mother was Russian from Siberia. Broz was always happier in small places than in Belgrade. Her grandmother taught her to read and write when she was four and through books she discovered the world.

Despite the status of her family, Svetlana had the impression of growing up in a normal family. She was aware that Yugoslavia was an exception in the Eastern Bloc; that it was a relatively liberal state. Certainly like other Yugoslavs she was proud of this. But her life was not sybaritic: "Power is always connected to privilege; but I myself did not feel that way. On the contrary, I had to make more efforts to realize what I wanted, having this surname that might carry privileges. From the beginning of my primary school I had to know more than the other children. If I made one mistake I would have a lower mark than the others, because the teachers were making sure that I would not be favored as a member of this family."

Her mother was a physician with a specialization in internal medicine. Svetlana shared that experience of medicine with her mother, and later trained as a cardiologist, and her daughter, too, wanted to become a doctor, but her hopes have been discouraged by the poor state of education in postwar Serbia. Svetlana's father was employed in internal security. He retired in 1965 when she was ten; they did not discuss his work. Both parents were protective of her because of her surname, but as a young girl Svetlana wanted her autonomy, and from time to time they had arguments about travel or freedom. More serious, perhaps, was Svetlana's independence of mind; never a member of any political party, she began her own critical investigations of history when she was young:

> When I was growing up I was trying to figure out what was wrong in this society. There were some things with which I did not agree when I was young. One of them was that every manifestation of nationalism was forbidden according to law. People who publicly manifested their nationalistic ideas were prosecuted: especially those people who were in power in the republics and autonomous areas, who wanted a local power base. When I started to discover trials of people who were nationalist, I couldn't at that age recognize how this problem might be serious; and being young and favoring a free mind, I was against these trials, thinking that everyone should have the possibility to think in his own way. I was thinking only about free speech. It is also the case that advocates of freedom of thought—not nationalists, but simply people of the opposition—were sanctioned by losing a job and other forms of prosecution (though few were imprisoned); but there was a big difference with the nationalists, who were indeed imprisoned. It is clear to me now that nationalists were a greater danger to the state of Yugoslavia than I had thought.
>
> There was also expropriation after the war; equalization. Inevitably, that caused resentment. I was not in favor of this action. As usual, those who were in power took the best houses for themselves; but it is always the same: each war distorts the ethical situation and then it depends on the moral and ethical norms of each individual.
>
> My mother told me a lot of personal stories about passing through the postwar period. She was a student then in Belgrade. The division between Tito and Stalin in 1948 was the crucial factor distinguishing Yugoslavia from the other Eastern Bloc states; and if Tito had not made this decision, we would have been Romania. But people who were pro-Stalin, and innocent people

without any orientation to Stalin, were put in concentration camps; and this is not the way to deal with it, to be tortured in this way. Nobody was talking or writing about these camps. It was a kind of unwritten law. So I had to collect unwritten testimonies to discover what had really happened. There had been tremendous repression of those who opposed the government. It is amazing to me that people would talk to me, with my surname, when they had, in those camps, to pronounce my surname a hundred times a day: I thought they must be allergic to it. . . . But they recognized me as a young human being who wanted to have her own approach, not to abuse them.

There is no question about the importance of Tito to Broz's project, ideals, and access to information. When she decided to collect the material for this book, she was deeply convinced that people from all backgrounds in Bosnia and Herzegovina would recognize her as someone who could not, by definition, be nationalist, because of her association with Tito. This was her carte blanche to enter into the homes of her interlocutors. In a situation in which, as she puts it, people were "framed" by their names and surnames, she had a unique opportunity to exploit: "I was not scared that my interlocutors would not talk to me. The majority of them shared a nostalgia that in the period of Tito they lived a life of dignity without fear. They could sleep freely in the parks and mountains with unlocked car doors or in the field and that nobody would attack them. But now they had a fear about everything even if they had ten locks."

Svetlana's memories of the period before the dissolution of Yugoslavia echo the popular chorus: "We got along." Perhaps her version is stronger; in the cities integration among the various communities was more pronounced than in some rural areas, and Broz did not belong to any particular nationality herself.

After Tito died everyone was afraid of what might happen. After the first few months of confusion, we went on. Tito had made a presidential system to change each year: six republics [Croatia, Serbia, Montenegro, Bosnia and

Herzegovina, Slovenia, Macedonia] and two autonomous regions [Kosovo, Vojvodina]. The presidents changed year to year and sometimes we didn't even follow who was president that year. And people were not thinking in the categories of ethnic groups. They joined each other on their religious holidays. Orthodox were going to the Catholic Christmas Eves and vice versa and to Ramadan or Bairam. A minority of people were believers; the majority were agnostics, and didn't know to which ethnic group their best friends belonged. I heard a story last year in Prague about a couple who ran away at the beginning of the war from Serb-controlled Sarajevo. The woman had a name that might belong to any ethnic group, and he had a recognizable Muslim name. He was in danger of being murdered in that Serb-controlled area. So she got him a false identity card with a Serb name and they decided to escape with their children. They were married for sixteen years by then and they were driving in the car and he was scared and memorizing his Serb name and surname as there were all these checkpoints, going toward Belgrade—which was the only way you could get out—and at one point he asked her: "Can you tell me are you a Serb or Croat?" If the war had not happened, he never would have asked this question, or known.

Broz contends that the state after Tito could have survived without him had it not been for the ambitions of the politicians who took the stage and tried to become new Titos in their own right. Milošević (former president of rump Yugoslavia) is her case in point:

When he realized it was not possible to be a leader of all Yugoslavia in the way he wished, he tried to destroy it and construct a Greater Serbia and Greater Croatia. But it was a problematic project, as people were then living decently together. So they had to have a trigger mechanism for destroying the unified country. This trigger mechanism was not imminent in the country before, so that it could be easily exploited. They had to spend years creating a psychological level of fear that might incite war. And all of them used nationalism: They had no other tool and indeed they chose the most virulent tool.

Nobody can articulate what new system was implied in all this. They called it transitional—but transition to what? We are now in countries "in transition"—a euphemism for something no one knows. And everything was done on the basis of fear. They had to frighten the members of their own ethnic groups with the specter of members of other ethnic groups, and in this name they abused everything they could: history, the past, the myths.

Broz was still practicing medicine in Belgrade when the nationalist fever began to spread. In 1987 she watched Milosevic draw a thousand supporters at a rally and recognized him as a new Hitler in Europe. She argues that Milosevic was never a nationalist but only abused nationalism for his political purposes. He sacrificed more than 300,000 Serbs who were expelled from Croatia in political deals with Croatian president Tuđjman; there was nothing protective, she explains, about his attitude toward the Serbs.

The first multiparty elections in former Yugoslavia occurred in 1990 and parties oriented toward nationalism were intensifying their message. I was living in Belgrade, with a non-Serb name—I have many ethnic branches in me but hardly one Serb. In this period in 1990, I became somehow very alone in Belgrade, where I thought I had a lot of friends. And my daughter asked me, in this house where there used to be about forty people passing through every day, why no one came. And I told her that I was mistaken, that I was a friend to the people I knew. But it cannot have been the other way around since they had left me because of my surname, because I was not a Serb. When I asked my friends, Do you know where you are going, following the new Hitler in Europe? And they would say, "You are talking this way because you are not a Serb."

They were poisoned by the media; frightened now that these "non-Serbs" would murder them. And at a certain moment each of them started believing this story. When it was clear to me that those whom I thought were my friends defined me by what I was not—which is absurd, we learned from logic that this is not a proper way of making a definition—then I recognized that these people had been poisoned and I was very sorry about that. My daughter was very young at that period and she suffered a lot because she and her brother were recognized as members of Tito's family. They were tormented in their primary school by their classmates; so I had to change their schools and ask professors not to talk about who they were. My children early on recognized the injustice, the madness of society.

Broz was employed by the Medical Military Academy as a cardiologist. The Yugoslav People's Army began a process of eliminating non-Serbs:

> It wasn't hard to figure out what they intended to do; so I was fighting—not because I was worried, I could always find another job or leave the country; but I did not want to run away—I was fighting for all those sane people employed there and persecuted because they were not Serbs. I confronted the directors of the Academy, the Generals and so on, asking them: "Are you crazy? I too would dismiss half the people in this building—but not because they are not Serbs; only because some of them are thieves, or incompetent, or lazy, or immoral. You will destroy this institution because you will expel the best intellectuals"—which is what happened. I decided to stay and fight, and leave when I myself decided. I survived all those years from 1990 to 1999 and then I resigned with a day's notice.

She was warned by Serb colleagues that it was a dangerous situation. But she was surprised in 1990 when the plaque on her door disappeared. When she visited some of her colleagues she saw that instead of the usual plaques—everything had been in Latinica letters—they had written their titles in Cyrillic on paper. It was the first demonstration of their decision to be "Serbs."

Before 1990 Broz had not engaged in any special humanitarian work. When the first war began in Croatia, she stayed in Belgrade. When the war in Bosnia began, it was possible for Serbian citizens to enter Bosnia and Herzegovina through the border it shared with Serbia, using only an identity card. At the very beginning of the war, in the first six months, friends who were in the Serbian-held section began to call her and ask for medical help. She urged them to bring the sick to Belgrade where she could help them. When she was faced with the fact that none of them had normal, or even elementary, medical care—that they would die if they didn't come to Belgrade—she asked where the doctors had gone. She got the answer that they were now working as mayors of the municipality or politicians, and not working as doctors.

> And I became very angry that they were letting these people die. So in December 1992 I decided to go there, thinking—all of the patients they bring to me are Serbs—what about the others? I began working in improvised cardiology units in the villages. It was announced by local radio that I would offer a clinic. At the beginning they asked how many patients I could treat in one day and I said as many as I can. The first day I checked 110.
>
> I was traveling on the weekends: Friday noon I would pick up my daughter Sonja from school, and we would come back Sunday evening. Then it happened that people began to tell me their experiences. They were lying on the table naked and I would ask about their heart and they would say, "Yes, yes but let me tell you . . ." I discovered that they thought that I had a better chance of surviving this war than they had. Which meant for me that they thought that I had a chance to carry their testimonies. And it was important for them to leave a trace of hope for their children, for the future, as well as a documentary trace about goodness in this evil time. And when I recognized that, I asked myself, Do you have a moral right to ignore this need? If those people, in the first year of the war, when no one knew how long this war would last, made such a sensitive distinction between the perpetrators and those who kept their moral and ethical norms and who really risked something to help them, do I have the moral right to ignore those experiences? And that is why I decided to put aside my medical equipment and to travel through Bosnia and Herzegovina to find new stories.

Broz did not use the stories she heard in her clinic for this book; her professional ethics required her to keep those to herself. She wondered whether or not she would be able to replicate what she had heard in the clinic and if the stories she had heard there were in fact quite exceptional. To the contrary, she found it was easy to locate new stories. From 1993 until 1997, she used her vacation time and her weekends and free days for collecting testimonies while she continued to work at the Military Medical Academy. She had amassed more than enough for a book and was then transferring the audiotapes to computer when, in January 1997, someone broke into her house in Belgrade and stole the audiotapes, CDs, disks, computer, transcripts—in short everything that existed for the purpose of writing this book. A few tapes given to a professional typist survived but the great majority were lost.

Broz then faced the dilemma of whether or not she could return to the same people to take their accounts a second time. The recording of these testimonies was for each interlocuter a very painful experience; she could not imagine subjecting them to this process of intimate recollection a second time. She did not feel she had the moral right. So she began again, traveling to collect new testimonies. A second time she was convinced by her experience that there are thousands of such stories, always more to be found. Broz ended up with 9,000 pages of testimony.

Broz's interlocutors wanted to tell their stories; they were introduced to her through a growing network of people who had learned about her project. They were speaking to be published. One quarter of her interviewees initially asked for anonymity—primarily to protect those "good people" about whom they spoke. By the time the third edition was published in Bosnia and Herzegovina almost all of them asked to publish in their own names.

In these conversations, Broz found that emotions were not expressed by words.

> They expressed their emotions by body language, by long pauses, or trembling fingers, with a lot of swearing. If I wanted to include all that, I would have to include myself, too, my own sorrow. I did not want the book to be pathetic. I think that their pure testimonies are the best expression of what they want to talk about. And maybe it is really impossible to verbalize emotions; there was too much emotion to verbalize. I decided to put aside all those nonverbal expressions and to leave only their words; I leave the reader to understand the depth of suffering.

Broz's own relatives in Sarajevo suffered, and she observes through them the long-term effects of these experiences. Her uncle and aunt, with the rest of their neighbors, went every day during the war to wait in line at a pump for water.

> You can imagine how someone who is sixty, who lost forty-eight kilos of weight, handles this. They were two skeletons. Without any food, in the dark, and going seven kilometers there for water and seven back. Sometimes snipers were playing a game with citizens in Sarajevo. They didn't want to murder them, but they let them go for water, wait fourteen hours in line for water and then return home. In front of their homes, carrying ten or twenty liters of water—because they couldn't carry more, my uncle was thin and weak—and in front of the house the snipers shot the canister and all of the water spilled out, and he stood there weeping.
>
> In the first winter my uncle went to collect water to fill the bath and when he finished after two days and nights, he was sleeping in the corridor of the apartment, because the corridor was the most protected place in the flat—of course, because it had no windows. In the early morning my aunt was weeping and woke him up and he thought their son must have been shot through the window, and she said, "No, he is OK, but can you go into the bathroom," and he entered the bathroom and found a frozen bath full of water. From December to April it was frozen—the whole depth. It was less than 20 degrees Centrigrade below zero. They were sleeping for six months with their boots on their feet. After six months the water melted and they had water to clean their bodies.

This is not, however, how Broz finishes the story of the war. It is less interesting to her, and less important, that people are capable of criminality, and more significant that they are capable of ethical action. The example of the Jews in Sarajevo is striking; eighty-six members of Broz's companion's family were murdered in the Jasenovac concentration camp during World War II. In Bosnia and Herzegovina, the majority of Jews were exterminated during that war, under Ustasha and Nazi control. Broz's companion's father, uncle, grandfather, and grandmother survived in Sarajevo thanks to the

Muslims who kept them safe through the four years of the war. About 4,000 Jews remained after WWII thanks to Muslims, Serbs, or Croats who hid them, and at the start of the war of 1991–1995, 1,200 Jews lived in Sarajevo. About a thousand left in convoys and went to another country at the start of the siege. The 200 who stayed devoted themselves to rescuing and sustaining all Sarajevans; they used the massive support from around the world that came for the Jewish community to support all Sarajevans. For this reason, Broz included in this book the story of the Jewish Center, which continues to serve all Sarajevans regardless of ethnicity, "to show the readers that it is possible not to care about ethnic belonging." This community plays an important role in the normalization and recovery of postwar interreligious dialogue.

At the Jewish Center a group of men gathers to tell us stories about their community. Their illustrative legends stretch back into the expulsion of the Sephardim from Spain, to the mutual support of Muslims and Jews against abusive pashas of the Ottoman period, forward through WW II, their childhoods, and the war of the immediate past. Speaking Ladino, Spanish, Bosnian-Serbo-Croatian, and English, one of them says:

> I must tell you how it was before, before the wars. There was a Rabbi, and a Bishop of the Serbian Church, and they lived 200 meters distant from one another in Sarajevo. And every morning they would meet for coffee, and talk about what was going on, religious matters. One morning when I was about six, I was on my way to my primary school, and I saw my Rabbi and I wanted to go up to him to kiss his hand. So I approached him to do so, and he stopped me and he said, in Ladino, which we spoke, "Asinikiu"—which means, you see, little donkey—"beso los otros prin (kiss the hand of the others first, and then me)." That's Sarajevo before WWII, that's Sarajevo before this war.

When Broz moved permanently to Sarajevo in 1999, she felt that she was finally at home. Belgrade had lost its spirit—or perhaps soul is a better word; while Sarajevo, she felt, had saved itself despite suffering so terribly. She is critical of the Dayton Peace Accords that left in power hard-line nationalists in Bosnia and Herzegovina. "Eight years after the peace treaty was signed, international organizations in Bosnia and Herzegovina are still carrying out 'peace training' under impossible conditions, while nationalists remain in office and in power, and run their campaigns with the same slogan: 'Vote for us or you will be exterminated.' No matter whether you are talking about the victims or the perpetrators of the war, all of them are afraid they will be exterminated. It is a closed circle that can't be cut in such a way."

Bosnians are ambivalent about the role the outside world played and is playing in their affairs, although they are dependent on it to keep the war profiteers and nationalist politicians from reigniting the conflict. Catholic, Orthodox, and Muslim transnational religious organizations are attempting to dismantle the indigenous, mutually shaped religious practices and architectures in the image of their own fundamentalism. Saudi-style mosques, basilicas with sky-scraping campaniles, and Orthodox churches in imitation Byzantine style compete in the landscape against the subtler traditions native to Bosnia and Herzegovina. The rest of the world thinks it knows best. It is not easy to reclaim a pluralist civilization after it has been shredded by war and the divisive forces of global sectarianism.

A psychiatrist in Mostar who organized community-based mental health care after the collapse of the hospital system in the region observes:

> America did not understand our system of mutual respect before the war, and it will be a long time before America reaches that kind of tolerant system. Members of the international community come from abroad to "train" us. People who really had a consciousness of who we were before the war are of course insulted. We couldn't, in that past era, recognize each other by names or faces as members of this or that group. But now the prevalent illness of this postwar period is posttraumatic stress disorder around the question of identity. After the war it was a kind of predictable development that each person wanted to find his own "identity" as a reaction to what happened during the war. But they are conscious that they are the victims of political manipulation.

Time and time again Broz, like others in Bosnia and Herzegovina, speaks of the "normal" people and the "normal" way of thinking, in contrast to the criminals and the "mad" way of thinking. As one of the interviewees reflects, "We were doing fine in peace and then off we went to war. For a bunch of thugs." The people in this book talk about nationalism as a sickness. They call our attention to the continuum of violence that begins in the appeal to national rights and injuries by ambitious politicians and ends in the murdering of children jumping rope. They offer us their testimonies as part of an ongoing work not only of understanding but of changing history, and they ask us to be vigilant. The objective of this book is to shape the present and the future: How do people who have suffered in ethnically defined violence make it possible to live next to one another again? These testimonies are not just about the past: they constitute an attempt, through the spoken word, to lay the foundation of unity in a traumatized and segmented society. They draw a picture of the war that makes it possible to live in a multiethnic world. The testimonies are a part of the long process of reconstruction, which depends so greatly on the way in which we imagine ourselves and others.

Laurie Kain Hart

Haverford College

Haverford, Pennsylvania

CHRONOLOGY OF
THE CONFLICT

1918

Following the end of World War I the Kingdom of Serbs, Croats, and Slovenes is established.

1929

The kingdom is renamed Yugoslavia.

1941

Germany and Italy invade Yugoslavia and bomb Belgrade. Yugoslavia is partitioned among Germany, Italy, and Bulgaria. Establishment of the "Independent State of Croatia," which includes Bosnia-Herzegovina but not Dalmatia (annexed by Italy) headed by Ustasha party leader Ante Pavelić. A Serbian royalist resistance organization (the "Chetniks") takes form in Serbia led by Draža Mihailović. A communist resistance movement is also formed, led by Josip Broz Tito.

1942

Tito's Anti-Fascist Council of National Liberation of Yugoslavia (AVNOJ) holds its second assembly in Jajce, central Bosnia, and lays the plans for a future socialist federation of Yugoslavia.

1944

Tito's partisan army and Soviet troops liberate Belgrade. King Peter, in exile in London, recognizes Tito as head of the Yugoslav armed forces.

1945

Tito is the head of the government with the support of the Allies; his opponents do not take part in the first postwar elections. After his victory he establishes the People's Federal Republic of Yugoslavia and abolishes the monarchy.

1946

The new constitution of the socialist federal Yugoslavia recognizes six republics: Bosnia-Herzegovina, Croatia, Macedonia, Montenegro, Serbia, and Slovenia.

1948

Tito breaks with Soviet leader Stalin. Yugoslavia is no longer part of the Cominform.

1963

Yugoslavia is renamed the Socialist Federative Republic of Yugoslavia.

1974

A new constitution reinforces the rights and powers of the constituent republics of Yugoslavia, as well as its autonomous provinces, Vojvodina and Kosovo. It also recognizes the Muslims as a constituent nation within the new confederal form of government.

1980

Tito dies on 4 May.

1986

Slobodan Milošević becomes Serbian regional Communist Party president.

1987

Milošević, leader of the Serbian League of Communists, visits Kosovo Polje. He ostensibly goes there to hear at first hand the grievances of Kosovo's Serbs, but, instead of restraining their anger and attempting to reconcile their differences with their Albanian neighbors, he endorses the allegations of genocide against the "Serbian nation."

1989

Milošević addresses a million Serbs at Kosovo Polje on the 600th anniversary of the defeat of the medieval Serbian kingdom by Turks in June; five months later he is elected president of Serbia.

1990

January—14th Extraordinary Congress of the League of Communists of Yugoslavia collapses with the walkout of the Slovenian delegation, due to the Serbian delegation's resistance to reform.

September—Adoption of new Constitution of the Republic of Serbia. Vestiges of autonomy of Kosovo and Vojvodina effectively ended.

1991

June—Slovenia and Croatia declare independence and the Yugoslav army attacks Slovenia.

July—The Yugoslav army announces withdrawal from Slovenia. Yugoslav (Serbian)-Croatian skirmishes going on since early 1991 escalate into war between Croats and rebel Serbs, backed by the Yugoslav army, in Croatia.

September—Formal opening session of European Community–sponsored conference on Yugoslavia, chaired by Lord Carrington, a former British Foreign Secretary. Leaders of Serbia, Croatia, and the Federal Army (JNA) sign cease-fire agreement with Lord Carrington. UN Security Council resolution (UNSCR) 713 places an arms embargo on the whole of the former Yugoslavia.

October—Bosnian parliament issues memorandum on sovereignty. Serbian leader, Dr. Radovan Karadžić, declares this could lead to war of extermination, and Serbian delegates walk out. Serbian deputies in Bosnia proclaim Assembly of Serbian Nation.

November—Former US Secretary of State Cyrus Vance and Lord Carrington meet Serbian President Slobodan Milošević and Croatian President Franjo Tuđman and Yugoslav Defense Minister Veljko Kadijević in Geneva. Further cease-fire agreement signed.

December—Serbian autonomous regions of Croatia proclaimed as Republic of Serbian Krajina (RSK). Germany recognizes Slovenia and Croatia, with diplomatic relations to be established as from 15 January 1992. President Alija Izetbegović requests UN peacekeepers for Bosnia.

1992

January—Bosnian Serbs declare establishment of their autonomy within the republic, effective from date of international recognition of Bosnia. European Community recognizes Slovenia and Croatia.

February/March—Referendum on independence is held in Bosnia. Majority of Bosniaks and Croats in favor, the majority of Serbs boycotts it. The United Nations creates a Protection Force (UNPROFOR) initially designed for Croatia, headquartered in Sarajevo.

March—Fighting in Bosanski Brod and Neretva Valley between Bosnian Serbs on the one side and Bosnian Croats and Bosniaks on the other.

April—Paramilitaries from Serbia massacre Bosniaks in the Bosnian town of Bijeljina. Serbian militants open fire on thousands of peace demonstrators in Sarajevo, killing at least five and wounding thirty. Siege of Sarajevo begins. European Community recognizes Bosnia. The Assembly of the Serbian Nation of Bosnia-Herzegovina proclaims an independent Bosnian Serbian Republic, which was later named "Republika Srpska." Bosnian Serbs step up ethnic cleansing campaign in eastern, northern, and northwestern Bosnia.

May—Mortar attack on bread line in Sarajevo kills seventeen people. Ratko Mladić named leader of Bosnian Serb army, formed in the wake of the withdrawal of the Yugoslav army from Bosnia.

June—UN peacekeepers take control of Sarajevo airport, enabling the start of the aid airlift.

July—Serbian assault on Goražde. Water and electricity cut off in Sarajevo.

August—Foreign correspondents report the existence of Bosnian Serb–controlled concentration camps. Three years later, the International Criminal Tribunal for the former Yugoslavia (ICTY) will indict nineteen persons for confining more than 3,000 Bosniaks and Bosnian Croats under inhumane conditions in the Omarska camp near Pijedor and also for killing, raping, sexually abusing, and mistreating the prisoners. In Sarajevo, a marketplace massacre kills fifteen persons.

September—UN Security Council approves resolution 776, agreeing to the expansion of UNPROFOR into Bosnia, where it was mandated to facilitate the provision of humanitarian aid throughout the region by protecting convoys run by the UN High Commissioner for Refugees (UNHCR).

October—UN Security Council approves resolution 781, introducing the no-fly zone (NFZ) for all military flights over Bosnia.

November—Exodus of Bosniaks and Croats from Jajce. UN convoys reach Tuzla after seven-month Serbian encirclement. UN Secretary General Boutros-Ghali, in besieged Sarajevo, states that conditions in the city are better than ten other places in the world.

1993

January—Cyrus Vance and Lord Owen produce Vance-Owen peace plan, creating ten largely autonomous provinces in Bosnia based on ethnic mix, geographical and historical factors, communications, and economic viability. Deputy Bosnian premier Hakija Turajlić shot and killed at Serbian roadblock while traveling in a UN vehicle convoy. Clashes between Croat and Bosnian armies in Gornji Vakuf. Srebenica-based Bosnian forces kill Serbs in Kravica.

March—General Philippe Morillon, commander of the UN forces in Bosnia, makes a personal stand to stop Srebenica falling to Bosnian Serb forces.

May—Thorvald Stoltenberg, a former Norwegian foreign minister, replaces Vance as UN representative and cochairman of ICTY. Summit meeting in Athens between all Bosnian leaders and Croatian and Serbian presidents. Karadžić signs Vance-Owen peace plan. UN Security Council approves resolution 824, declaring that the Bosnian capital, Sarajevo, and also Tuzla, Žepa, Goražde, Bihać, Srebenica, and their surrounding areas, should be treated as safe areas by all parties concerned and should be free from armed attacks. Bosnian Serb referendum on Vance-Owen peace plan and independence: The plan is rejected (96 percent against). UN Security Council also approves resolution 827, establishing the International Criminal Tribunal for the former Yugoslavia, tasked with prosecuting those accused of serious violations of international and humanitarian law.

June—In Sarajevo, fifteen people killed and eighty wounded in mortar attack during a soccer game. UN Security Council approves resolution 836, mandating UNPROFOR to defend the UN safe areas and occupy key points on the ground in those areas.

July—A Bosniak-Croat war rages in the Mostar area where there are reports of the existence of Croat-controlled concentration camps. In Sarajevo, twelve persons are killed by mortar while lining up for water.

August—Croatian Democratic Community (HDZ) proclaims the Mostar-based Croatian Community of Herceg-Bosna a republic. Bosnian Serbs and Bosnian Croats accept new Owen-Stoltenberg proposals on a union of three ethnic republics in Bosnia.

September—Bosnian Assembly votes for the Owen-Stoltenberg proposal, but only if territories seized by force are returned.

October—New Bosnian government: Haris Silajdzić appointed prime minister. Croat massacre of Bosniaks at Stupni Do.

November—The historic bridge in Mostar is destroyed during Croat-Bosniak clashes.

December—Yasushi Akashi, a former Japanese diplomat, becomes UN Secretary General's special representative for the former Yugoslavia.

1994

January—Cease-fire between warlord Fikret Abdić's forces and Bosnian army.

February—Mortar shell kills sixty-eight people and wounds over two hundred in Sarajevo market. European Union backs use of NATO air power if necessary to lift Bosnian Serb siege of Sarajevo. At UN request, NATO agrees to authorize air strikes. There is an agreement between Bosnian Serb Republic and Bosnian government to a cease-fire in Sarajevo, negotiated by Lieutenant-General Sir Michael Rose, commander of UN forces in Bosnia.

March—Bosnian government and Bosnian Croat leaders tentatively agree to form a federation. Bosnian Serb Assembly rejects Bosniak-Croat Federation and demands that sanctions against Serbs should be lifted.

April—Bosnian Serbs shell Goražde, a UN safe area. In response, NATO planes bomb Bosnian Serb armored vehicles. Akashi holds talks with President Milošević and Bosnian Serb leadership in Belgrade, securing a cease-fire agreement on Goražde.

May—In Vienna there is an agreement between the Bosnian government and Bosnian Croats, setting the Bosniak/Croat Federation at 58 percent of Bosnian territory; it divides the federation into eight cantons. In Geneva a meeting held under the aegis of the Contact Group (of Britain, Russia, US, France, and Germany) calls for a four-month cessation of hostilities. It calls for negotiations, on the basis of territorial division of 51 percent for the Bosnian Federation and 49 percent for the Bosnian Serbs.

June—Draft Memorandum of Understanding on the European Union (EU) administration of Mostar initialed ad referendum by enlarged EU Troika and Bosniak and Bosnian Croat sides.

July—Hans Koschnik of Germany inaugurated as EU administrator of Mostar.

August—Bosnian Serb Assembly rejects Contact Group peace plan. Yugoslavia's President Milošević announces a decision to sever political and economic ties with Bosnian Serbs because of their rejection of the peace plan.

September—Pope John Paul cancels trip to Sarajevo for security reasons.

December—Former U.S. President Jimmy Carter visits Sarajevo and Pale, headquarters of the Bosnian Serbs, and announces a cease-fire agreement.

1995

January—Four-month truce takes effect in Bosnia.

February—International Criminal Tribunal indicts twenty-one Serbs for genocide. Bosnian Serb leaders refused to allow extradition of anyone. The Federal Republic of Yugoslavia rules that alleged Yugoslav war criminals must be tried there.

May—Mortars rock Sarajevo as truce expires and eleven persons are killed in the suburb of Butimir. Serbs raid UN–monitored weapons collection site. In response to high levels of shelling and shooting, Lieutenant-General Rupert Smith, UNPROFOR commander for Bosnia, calls for air strikes, but he is overruled by Akashi. Bosnian Serbs raid UN arms collection points, and, in response, Smith orders bombing of an ammunition depot near Pale. Bosnian Serbs shell Tuzla, killing seventy-one people, and take UN forces as hostages.

June—The Bosnian Serbs release UN hostages. The US House of Representatives votes for unilateral lifting of arms embargo.

July—Bosnian Serb forces move into the Srebernica safe area overrunning UN posts and capturing UN troops. NATO air strikes. Bosnian Serbs threaten to kill UN hostages. The Bosnian Serb forces take Srebrenica; they bus the women and children to Kladanj, and send the men on a trek to Tuzla, which results in a massacre of several thousand Muslim men. UN and EU demand Bosnian Serb withdrawal from Srebrenica. UK, US, and French representatives deliver ultimatum to Ratko Mladić, commander of the Bosnian Serb army: attacking Goražde or putting UN lives at risk would lead to extensive air strikes. Bosnian Serb forces enter Zepa. The International Criminal Tribunal indicts Karadžić and Mladić for genocide and Milan Martić (self-styled president of Serb Krajina) for war crimes. The US Senate votes to lift embargo on Bosnia if UN decides to withdraw or Bosnian government requests UN withdrawal. Tadeusz Mazowiecki, the UN Special Rapporteur on Human Rights, resigns, saying he could not participate in pretense of protection of human rights. Abdić declares himself president of the Independent Republic of Western Bosnia.

August—Croatia launches a successful offensive in the Krajina region, causing 150,000 Serbs to flee eastward toward Yugoslavia. NATO agrees to use air power to protect safe areas. Bosnian government forces gain control of Abdić's stronghold in the Bihac region. A Bosnian Serb mortar attack kills thirty-seven civilians in Sarajevo. NATO warplanes wipe out Serbian artillery, ammunition, and command sites around Sarajevo. Meanwhile, US diplomat Richard Holbrooke begins pushing a peace plan.

September—Bosnian, Croatian, and Yugoslav foreign ministers meet in Geneva and agree on basic principles including that Bosnia-Herzegovina would continue its legal existence with its present borders. Twelve-hour pause agreed to in the NATO/RRF strike campaign to allow for US envoy Richard Holbrooke, General Mladić, and President Milošević to conclude a "Framework for a Cessation of Hostilities Agreement." Bosnian, Croatian, and Yugoslav foreign ministers meet in New York and agree that Bosnia will have a central presidency, parliament, and constitutional court. Provision is made for holding internationally supervised elections.

October—General cease-fire in Bosnia-Herzegovina is declared, but fighting continues, especially in western and northwestern Bosnia.

November—Beginning of the peace negotiations on Bosnia-Herzegovina in Dayton, Ohio, leading to an agreement on the end of the war, and on new political institutions for Bosnia, between the presidents of Serbia, Croatia, and Bosnia-Herzegovina. The ICTY in the Hague indicts the leader of the Bosnian Serbs, Radovan Karadžić, and General Ratko Mladić for being responsible for the mass killings in Srebenica.

December—The Dayton peace agreement is officially signed in Paris by Slobodan Milošević, Franjo Tuđman, and Alija Izetbegović. Bosnia-Herzegovina and the Federal Republic of Yugoslavia officially recognize each other. The peace agreement calls for a Bosniak-Croat federation and a Serb entity within the state of Bosnia-Herzegovina. United Nations transfers authority in Bosnia to the NATO-led international force (IFOR).

1996

January—Presidents Tuđman and Izetbegović sign a cooperation agreement in Sarajevo. NATO's forces begin foot patrols in the tense Serb-held suburbs of Sarajevo to try to reassure people whose home areas are due to revert to the control of the Bosnian government. After three and a half years of interruption the telephone lines between Bosnia and Herzegovina and Federal Republic of Yugoslavia are reestablished. Croatian-Bosniak relations still remain tense in Mostar. EU administrator in Mostar, Hans Koschnik, warns he will not allow Mostar to become a Balkan Berlin. He threatens to withdraw EU aid if violence persists between Croats and Bosniaks. The Bosnian parliament elects its first postwar government. The Bosnian government adopts a draft on amnesty, which the Bosnian Assembly should enforce as a law at its next session. The amnesty refers to all members of paramilitary forces in Bosnia who have not committed war crimes and to all Bosnian Army deserters.

February—The Bosnian Serb Army withdraws from Sarajevo, and most of the 50,000 Serb inhabitants leave the city for the Republika Srpska or Yugoslavia.

March—Many mass graves containing several thousand bodies are discovered, among others in Prijedor (northwestern Bosnia), Brčko (northern Bosnia), and in the area of Srebenica. The existence of approximately 190 mass graves is known, of which sixteen contain more than 500 bodies.

April—Some 30,000 persons are reported missing in Bosnia-Herzegovina, 3,000 in Croatia.

May—The International Criminal Tribunal for the Former Yugoslavia (ICTY) indicts the Bosnian Serb Duško Tadić for the killing of numerous Bosniak and Croat civilians in the detention camps of Omarska and Keraterm in northwestern Bosnia.

July—The ICTY issues an international warrant of arrest against the leader of the Bosnian Serbs, Radovan Karadžić and General Ratko Mladić, who are charged with having committed genocide and crimes against humanity in Bosnia-Herzegovina between 1992 and 1995.

September—Parliamentary and presidential elections in Bosnia and Herzegovina. In the parliamentary election the three national parties are reelected: the Bosnian Party of Democratic Action SDA—the only party that has candidates in both the Bosnian-Croat Federation and the Republika Srpska—(BH: 37.9%; Bosnian-Croat Federation: 55%; Republika Srpska: 17.8%), the Serb SDS (BH: 24.1%; Republika Srpska: 54.4%), and the Croat HDZ (BH: 14.1%; Bosnian-Croat Federation: 23%). In the presidential elections, President Izetbegović wins the majority of votes to become the leader of the three-member presidency. The other two presidents of the rotating chair are Momčilo Krajišnik (Serb) and Krešimir Zubak (Croat).

November—In its first trial the ICTY sentences the Bosnian Croat, Dražen Erdemović, to ten years in prison. He is found guilty of killing 1200 people in Srebenica in July 1995. As long as the Republika Srpska refuses to co-operate with the ICTY, it is being denied financial aid for reconstruction.

December—The UNHCR and the Western states agree in Geneva on the repatriation of Bosnian refugees. End of the EU mission in Mostar. While it has promoted the reconstruction of the city through mobilizing financial aid from European countries, it failed to overcome the political and ethnic division of the city. Muslim citizens have almost entirely left Croatian West Mostar.

1997

January—Bosnia's multiethnic parliament meets for the first time and appoints a cabinet.

February—Bosnian government declares that the siege of Sarajevo is over.

1998

March—The UN Security Council adopts resolution 1160, condemning the excessive use of force by Serbian police against civilians in Kosovo.

1999

March—International peace monitors evacuate Kosovo, as Yugoslav forces build up and launch offensives against Kosovo forces. NATO airstrikes begin against Yugoslav forces in Kosovo. By the end of the month NATO Secretary General Javier Solana directs initiation of broader range of air operations against targets in Yugoslavia, to allow NATO commanders to intensify their action.

May—The UN War Crimes Tribunal indicts Milošević on charges of crimes against humanity.

June—Yugoslav forces begin to withdraw from Kosovo. NATO Secretary General announces bombing campaign has been suspended.

2000

October—Milošević concedes defeat in the presidential elections in September and steps down as president.

2001

February—The UN war crimes tribunal at The Hague sentences three Bosnian Serbs to long jail terms for systematically torturing and raping Bosniak women in the early 1990s. The verdict marks the first time the tribunal has called rape a crime against humanity.

June—The Yugoslav government hands over Milošević to the UN war crimes tribunal.

July—Milošević makes a defiant appearance at the UN war crimes tribunal and says it is an "illegal" body set up by his Western enemies. He refuses to enter a plea, which the Tribunal treats as not guilty.

August—The UN war crimes tribunal finds Bosnian Serb General Radislav Krstić guilty of genocide for his role in the massacre of thousands of men and boys in Srebenica. Krstić sentenced to forty-six years. Three senior Bosniak generals indicted to face war crimes charges.

November—The UN war crimes tribunal charges Milošević with responsibility for Serb atrocities in the 1992–1995 Bosnian war.

December—Milošević refuses to plead to charges of orchestrating genocide by Serbian forces in the 1992–1995 Bosnian war, deriding the indictment as a "supreme absurdity."

2002

February—Milošević trial opens as prosecution presents its case against the former Yugoslav leader. UN chief prosecutor, Carla Del Ponte, accuses Milošević of being "responsible for the worst crimes known to humankind."

2003

February—Biljana Plavšić pleads guilty to war crimes before the ICTY and is sentenced to eleven years in jail.

Alexander Kitroeff
Haverford College
Haverford, Pennsylvania

PREFACE

When I was in my last year of medical school in 1979, I was studying for an exam in surgery, and part of the material I covered was on surgery during war. I admit that at the time I was absolutely certain, at least as far as my country was concerned, that I would never need to use this material.

Twelve years later, the bugles of war sounded in Yugoslavia.

All you could read about in the papers or hear in any conversation when the hostilities broke out were the horrors of war. Every day for three years I heard only words speaking of the evil. Those rare writers who wrote politically unbiased texts were every bit as obsessed with the horrors of war as those who were busily blasting the horns of the great princes. I found that friendships of many years did not survive because all some people could do was wrangle over whose contribution to the evil was greater. And this in the cosmopolitan city of Belgrade.

In every unfortunate conversation with my deaf, former friends, I began to feel as if the slightly crazed European metropolis where I was born had become a beehive where every bee was busy at work building its own segment of the hive, feeding it not with pollen but with hatred, carefully stored.

Believing that there was nothing human in that madness, I started going to the combat zones, first as a doctor, to see if I might be of help to those who were suffering. Treating people of all three religious traditions, I felt their need to open their souls and tell me, shyly at first, what had happened to them during the war. From these brief stories on cardiology wards, I realized how thirsty people were for a truth that was subtle and nuanced where the shells were falling, in a way that it wasn't in Belgrade or in the worldwide black-and-white coverage.

These first sparks of hope that there might be human goodness even in this greatest of evils, regardless of the God a person prayed to, stirred in me a desire to set down my stethoscope and take up a tape recorder to record authentic stories of people of all three ethnic groups.

The working title of my future book, *Good People in an Evil Time*, was, also, my most concise question to my interlocutors.

I admit it was hard to earn their trust. The conditions these people lived in were awful. They were first in ruined houses, damp cellars, with shells blasting nearby, and then they'd go from there to strange houses, often in unfamiliar neighborhoods and towns, where they were bombarded by the sickening rhetoric of the national leaders on the need for national homogenization, every bit as disturbing as the exploding shells. They were too scared to allow their names and the names of the people of other backgrounds who had helped them survive to appear in print. Many requested anonymity to shield themselves and their saviors. This was telling proof of how strongly they felt surrounded by intolerance and exclusivity. I had to respect their need for privacy. Thus a dagger (†) next to names or initials in the testimonies indicates that those people wished to keep their identity private. The names of those who committed the atrocities are authentic. No one requested privacy for them.

My interlocutors talked to me about their experiences with people of a background different from their own. In conditions such as these, stories of goodness are not, indeed, suspect. Overall, the onus for the veracity of each of the stories rests with the person who told it.

The language that people used depended on how educated they were. My interventions were limited to the shaping of language and style. The facts and quotations are authentic.

A careful reader may well note how few really emotional descriptions there are in these stories. There were almost none. While I listened, I had the sense that people kept their emotions under lock and key somewhere deep inside, perhaps even in their subconscious. Their trembling voices, interrupted by quiet, barely audible sobs; the huge gaps between words while they garnered the strength to continue talking, flooded with feelings that stole their words; their curses to vent their tension—all these remain recorded on the original audio cassettes. Their eyes, faces, the trembling hands with which they held a glass or lit a cigarette are etched in my soul. Each reader should feel his or her way to the depths of anguish and joy.

Human goodness is something we take for granted under normal conditions. Often enough we don't even register it. In evil times, when someone's survival depends too frequently on someone else's respect for moral and ethical norms, only against a backdrop of countless horrors does goodness gleam like a pearl in the sand, plucked from a shell at the bottom of the sea.

Someone had to dive to find those pearls and string them into a necklace. Without them, the evil that individuals committed will hold in thrall all of us who were born in this part of the world. This is a place where so many honorable and noble people live. No one speaks of them. I believe that the time will come when every criminal will answer for what he or she did. The question is, Will the deserving people reap just rewards for their goodness and courage? What rewards can there be for those who lost their lives for refusing to acquiesce to the bestiality and mindlessness around them, and insisted on protecting people of other backgrounds? No army or government can give them the credit that is their due. Streets or city squares won't be named after them. Their names will endure only as long as the lives they saved, and, perhaps, the survivors' children. Future generations should have a way of knowing that good people did, indeed, exist.

I covered 7,500 kilometers one winter during the war along the icy roads of Republika Srpska, searching for stories. My perseverance was rewarded: I recorded more than a hundred testimonies.

I would have completed the book in 1996 had those who objected to its publication not moved to stop me. Something happened that I might have expected while I was in the combat zone in Bosnia, but hardly in the center of Belgrade: my home was robbed and most of the material I'd collected was stolen. This did, indeed, slow the publication of the book, but it did not prevent it. To the contrary, it was proof that even the raw material had value, though the value, apparently, was all the greater when the recordings were stolen and hidden.

I spent yet another postwar autumn driving 6,000 kilometers around Bosnia and Herzegovina, and finally recorded enough material to complete the book.

There are an equal number of stories in this book from Bosniak, Serbian, and Croatian interlocutors, interwoven just as their lives and fates in Bosnia and Herzegovina were interwoven. This is a collection of individual human stories from the areas I managed to visit. The tragedy of all the peoples living there is far too great to fit into any one book. Any generalizations based on this material would abuse the sincerity and suffering of those who had the strength to speak of their experiences.

My fundamental motive that guided me in this project, even when I faltered, was the desire to reaffirm goodness as the ultimate postulate at a time of prevailing evil, and spiritual and material destruction, when a human life is worth no more than a bullet. This goodness, I believe, will be the foundation for the future of all three ethnic groups in the land of my ancestors.

The good people who mustered the strength in the most terrible of times to testify to the goodness of others, and all those who had the courage, without asking what price they would pay for their own acts of goodness, are the most durable guarantee of the truth of that motive.

Dr. Svetlana Broz
Sarajevo 2003

TRANSLATOR'S NOTE

This book is about people crossing ethnic lines to lend one another a hand. If English-language readers are to have a clear sense of what these brave people did, they need to know the ethnic group each person was from. Readers from the republics of the former Yugoslavia have various ways of figuring out the nationality of the people described in the stories by looking at names, religion, and, sometimes, place. For this reason I inserted the occasional explanatory word, saying, for example, "my *Serbian* neighbor," rather than "my neighbor." This allows the English-language reader to know explicitly all that the native reader knows implicitly. It is, however, ironic that a book about transcending the bounds of ethnicity for the sake of a broader, more inclusive humanity must focus so much on ethnicity in order to be clear.

Readers should keep in mind that the testimonies, often an hour or more in length, were first recorded by Dr. Broz. Then she condensed the taped version into a written story, and I translated the stories into English. It is only fair to recognize the number of filters between the person who gave his or her testimony, and the English version you have before you.

The Kokkalis Program at the Kennedy School and the Minda de Gunzburg Center for European Studies brought Dr. Broz to speak at Harvard in November 2000. At the end of her talk, Uwe Kitzinger leaped to his feet, saying he wanted to read her book in English and would do all he could to help her publish it in the United States, and I stepped forward, pledging to translate it. The collaboration has resulted in the formation of a new circle of friends and colleagues who have touched, and changed, each other's lives. Special gratitude to Mario Kamhi, Uwe Kitzinger, Laurie Hart and Thomas Butler, Ljiljana Cook, Perry Klass, Senad Pečanin, Cynthia Simmons, Jeff Spurr, and Larry Wolff.

Ellen Elias-Bursać
Harvard University
Cambridge, Massachusetts

PRONUNCIATION KEY

The letters ć (*Teslić*) and č (*Foča*) are both forms of ch (ć, a softened t, is pronounced like the ch in *much* [soft "ch"], while č is a fuller ch sound, like the ch in *chocolate* [hard "ch"]), while the letter c (*Vraca*) is always pronounced as ts. The š (*Šamac, Vareš*) is the same as the English sh, the ž (*Užice*) is pronounced zh. The j is always read as a y (*Jugoslavija*), while the đ (*Srđan*) is the equivalent of the English-language j sound in *joke*. There are occasionally words such as *Brčko*, which appear to be missing a vowel or two; in these instances the letter r serves as a partial vowel, allowing the pronunciation: Birchko. There are two alphabets used in Bosnia and Herzegovina, known as Latinica and Cyrillic. See glossary entries.

THE
TESTIMONIES

CAN YOU COUNT ON YOUR NEIGHBORS?

TOLD BY SALIH DELIĆ

The Village of Donje Baljvine near Mrkonjić Grad

November 1998

I was born in 1934 in Baljvine and have lived here in this tiny village my whole life. Serbs have always lived here in the upper stretch of the village, about a half a mile from us. Throughout the history of Baljvine, Serbs and *Muslims have never taken each other to court over land disputes, though our fields have always abutted each other's.

The local Muslim men never married *Serbian women from the village, because for generations we were taught that would be wrong. They feel like family to us. Our boys do sometimes marry Serbian girls, but usually from other towns.

I was seven years old when World War II began. I remember that even then there was solidarity between the local Muslims and our neighbors, the Serbs. That kind of feeling is a tradition in this village.

Baljvine is probably the only village in this whole region that wasn't burned during World War II, because the neighbors protected one another.

* First mention of terms and places defined in the glossary will appear with an asterisk in the text.

3

For a while back then there were *Ustasha forces in the area and some of the men serving in the Ustasha were Muslims. A German man named Karlo ran a hotel in town, and next to it stood the Ustasha barracks on the banks of the Vrbas River, though those barracks are underwater now. Once Ustasha fighters came to our village to torch Serbian homes. The Muslims rushed out of their houses and raised barricades on the street. They wouldn't let anyone by.

"If you feel like torching houses, start with ours. Only then, with theirs. You aren't touching our Serbian neighbors," they told the Ustasha.

"Why won't you let us by?"

"We all get along just fine here. We won't let you hurt them. Once you've torched all our homes, you can go burn down theirs, not before."

"If you are all so crazy about each other, you can have your Serbs. We'll leave you be," the Ustasha replied, and left.

Meanwhile some Muslims went off to the Serbian village of Bočac to warn the people there to hide because the Muslims wouldn't be able to protect them all. The Serbs got out of Bočac in time. The Ustasha did torch their homes, but the people's lives were saved.

After the Ustasha retreated, then the Chetniks came, but none of our Serbian neighbors would let them attack the Baljvine Muslims. In that war and now in this one we have all survived pretty well.

There were Serbs and *Croats in the *Army of Bosnia and Herzegovina, just as there were Muslims and Croats in the Serbian army, and Muslims and Serbs in the *Croatian Army, depending on what seemed best for each person. Everyone was blinded by the politicians and it was hard for people to figure out which side to join; each of us chose where he thought he'd be safer.

When the Serbs and the Muslims had to retreat in the face of the advancing *Croatian Defense Council forces [HVO] was when all hell broke loose.

We'd invite each other to weddings, *slavas [saint's days], Christmas or *Bairam feasts, funerals, and other occasions. We even visited each other when there weren't particular occasions. Ours really were good neighborly relations. And so they are today.

The mosque was built before I was born, but I remember the stories my grandparents told about how Serbs donated money to the project and helped raise it. Today our mosque is the only one that wasn't demolished in the whole territory of *Republika Srpska.

There was no *Orthodox church in our village so the local people had to travel about ten miles to the nearest place of worship. In 1990 a Muslim delegation requested of the municipal president of Mrkonjić Grad his approval for a project to raise an Orthodox church. The president of the municipality was amazed.

"Why would you Muslims be asking me for permission to build an Orthodox church?"

"We have our mosque, but the Serbs have no place of worship. We feel this is disgraceful and we have come to right this wrong," they answered.

The permit was issued quickly and construction began immediately on the church. All of us pitched in. I, myself, made a modest contribution, and the younger men helped in the building, though it was interrupted by the outbreak of war. We could never have respected ourselves if we hadn't pitched in to build the church. The church was finished this year.

I stayed here throughout the war. There were about 200 Muslim households and roughly the same number of Serbian ones. We got along just fine. We lived normal lives: the school was open, buses ran, the only thing was that we had to ask for permission from the authorities to leave the village because there were Serbian checkpoints where people didn't know us Muslims personally. It often happened that they'd stop a Muslim from here and ask, "Where are you from?" When they heard we were from Baljvine, they'd say that we could pass. They let us by because they knew we live in harmony here.

When the war began our Serbian neighbors gave us weapons. Baljvine was within the territory of Republika Srpska, and that way Muslim and Serbian boys could patrol around the village at night so that no one from outside could get in and set fire to someone's house. If that had happened everyone would have wanted to know whether it was a Muslim or a Serb who had set the fire. No one would have considered that it might have been an evildoer from Herzegovina or Croatia. Rumors like that could have led to awful things, as they did in so many other places where extremists from somewhere else would sneak in and start the bloodshed, and then blame the local people. We didn't dare let this happen, so we patrolled the village side by side.

No one was able to poison our good relations at any time during the war. There was no one who so much as slapped another person, let alone anything worse than that. If it hadn't been for evil descending in the form of the Croatian Defense Council forces on Mrkonjić Grad, we would never have even felt the war.

In mid-June 1992 a local Serbian man heard some noise in the woods on the hillsides above the village and heard someone call out: "Halt! Halt!" He knew that the Serbian lines were a couple of miles away, and as soon as he thought he'd heard the words "Here are the *HOS [Croatian Guard Corps] fighters," he came running down through the Serbian part of the town to let them know that Croatian forces were about to descend. That instant all the Serbs fled in terror to Bočac.

An hour later the rest of us heard what was going on. All of us who had weapons went up the hillside to intervene. But there was no one there. A few minutes later the captain of a Serbian unit from Banja Luka appeared. Astonished by the fact that we were prepared to defend the abandoned homes of our Serbian neighbors, he was infuriated with the local Serbs, and went straight to Bočac.

"You should be ashamed! The Muslims were there, ready to defend your homes, and you ran away," he glowered at them. They picked up and came straight home, once they figured out it had been a false alarm.

For a year and a half, the police forces of Republika Srpska were stationed in the village for our safety. We provided them with food, accommodation, and firewood. When they saw there was no need for them to stay, and when the front moved further away from Baljvine, they packed up and moved on.

Baljvine has no natural springs of drinking water. From time immemorial people have believed that this means they shouldn't work on Thursdays. They believe that working on Thursdays might bring on bad weather that could kill someone or ruin crops. So that is why Thursday is a day of rest in our village for the Serbs and for the Muslims. The military police couldn't figure out why it was that we shared the same day off.

In 1992 General *Talić of the Republika Srpska army came through the village. He held a meeting at about 11:00 one night. He told us, at the time, "You Muslims cannot stay here with the Serbs."

I guess he was testing us. Šaban Habibović, the village president, replied, "As long as the army leaves us alone we'll have no trouble with the Serbs. We aren't afraid of our Serbian neighbors. They won't harm us."

Talić asked Šaban, "If that is really true, Šaban, do you dare go over into the Serbian part of the village?"

"Sure. If you want me to, I'll walk from one side of the village to the other."

"In front of whose house would you dare to stand and call the owner out?"

"I'll stand in front of any house you say."

"Then you walk in front of me and stop where you like," Talić told him.

Šaban walked to the part of the village where the Serbs lived and called a man by name who rushed out in his pajamas, "What's wrong, Šaban? Something happen? You need help?"

Šaban's escorts hid in the dark so the man couldn't see them, and from there they eavesdropped on the conversation.

"I had to come. I need help."

"Say the word, Šaban. What can I do? Just let me throw some clothes on. I'll be right back."

When Talić overheard the conversation echoing through the night he stepped forward and said, "God help us! You Muslims aren't Muslims, and you Serbs aren't Serbs! You must be from somewhere else. In that case, go right ahead and live together if that's what you want!"

Talić and his men left, and that was how we lived until the bad days came and hit us and the Serbs alike.

My son hadn't served in any of the armies. He was obliged to report for a *work detail at a village across the lake, on a farm run by the Republika Srpska military. When there was work to do, he worked, and otherwise he was free. They never forced us Muslim men to go digging trenches on the front lines. Other people did that. The people from our village worked on the farm because we were good workers. When the Croatian *shells began pelting the area the members of the military who ran the farm told the young men, "Boys, you've eaten, now get going and stay close to the woods. Go wherever you want, but get out of here fast."

The only people who lost their lives during the whole war from the area around Baljvine were two Serbs killed on the front lines. Not a single person from our village lost his life.

On 15 September 1995, Serbian soldiers woke us up at four o'clock in the morning and told us, "You've got fifteen minutes to get away. Take only what you need. Any of you with a cart and horse get behind your horse and go through the woods toward Bočac. The Croatian Defense Council forces are coming!"

They'd already told the Serbs, so they had started evacuating before we did. Good God, of course they would tell their own people first, but they did tell us in time, and we were able to make it down into Bočac.

Bočac is a Serbian Orthodox village where there were no Muslims living at all. We spent four days there under a bridge. The local people treated us decently. The first night there was trouble when two soldiers from the Serbian forces came over to us and demanded that we give them five of our girls. They needed them, they said, to roll up their blankets. You never know what young men are capable of doing, because they aren't grown yet. Some wretches had no understanding for their own fathers, so how would they have any for me? They started provoking us.

"What do you need our girls for at this time of night? Why do you need to roll up blankets now?" we asked, scared.

We called the police right away, and the police stopped the soldiers. In the morning the people of Bočac activated their system of *civilian protection, and while we were staying in their village they kept watch over us and guarded us.

"Build yourselves camp fires to keep warm, and get some sleep, those of you who can," they told us.

They brought us bread, cookies, milk . . . We had babies with us, twins, fifteen days old, who were given a quart of milk each day. The doctor from the local Serbian military unit stationed there stopped by daily to visit the elderly people among us who were infirm.

On our fifth day there, buses were arranged for us and we were taken to *Tešanj. All we had to pay for was the fuel. There were no attempts at provocation, no one pulled any of the men *fit for military service into a different group the way they did in other parts of Bosnia. The Serbs in charge knew we would never turn against them. When we arrived in Tešanj they found us places to stay.

I later moved with my family to Bugojno where I stayed until 8 February 1998, when we returned to Baljvine.

The village was completely destroyed by Croatian Defense Council units. Not a single house was intact. The only building they left untouched was the mosque. After the war everything had to be rebuilt. At this point more Serbs have returned than Muslims have because their homes weren't as badly damaged as ours were. They were the first to come back and the first to recover.

International organizations have financed the rebuilding of homes. By now twenty-five houses have been reoccupied in the Muslim part of the village, and thirty-nine are being renovated, as well as a lot of Serbian homes.

When I first came back with my son, who is twenty-two, it was cold, windy, the house was in ruins, mud everywhere.

We repaired the house thanks to donors from abroad and with the help of our Serbian neighbors, whom you can see outside even today helping their Muslim neighbors rebuild. This morning they brought us potatoes, cheese, milk, and freshly baked bread.

"Hey, why have you brought so much!" I asked them. "You've barely enough for yourselves."

"Whatever we have we'll share. As usual."

FRIENDS AND STRANGERS

TOLD BY ZORA UDOVČIĆ

From Novska, interviewed in Bosanska Dubica

January 1996

I used to live in the town of Novska, in Croatia, with my husband and two sons. At the time the war broke out my husband and I had jobs, and our eldest son was way down in Bileća in southern Bosnia completing his obligatory military service, while our younger son, fifteen, was in the middle of secondary school.

Each day the situation was getting worse in Novska so I sent our younger son away to stay with my sister in Zenica, central Bosnia, over his summer vacation.

The way the boundaries had been drawn in Socialist *Yugoslavia, Novska was part of Croatia. My husband and I felt more and more insecure there as Serbs, and this came to a head in October 1991, when a neighbor, a Croatian woman, came to our apartment terribly worried to tell us, "You must leave Novska right now. They have started taking Serbs away to a camp! They are arresting people in their own homes!"

I started packing the essentials, but my neighbor stopped me, saying, "It's better if you don't take anything. They're stopping people and arresting them on the street if they suspect they are trying to get away. You'll be too obvious if you're carrying a suitcase."

"If I leave everything behind, I don't know what I'll do. We have no money for the trip," I said.

My neighbor hugged me, and while she sobbed and kissed me, I felt her push a rolled-up bill into my hand.

"I can't help you more than that. I wish you all the luck in the world," she said as we parted.

We walked out of the apartment, terrified. I had nothing but my purse and in it all our documents. I clutched the fifty *German marks note she'd given me.

We managed to get out of town unnoticed, and made it all the way to the region of Baranja, on the border between Croatia and Serbia, where we lived as refugees in a village until April 1992. Our younger son spent that whole time in Zenica because we thought he'd be safer with his aunt, since we had no income.

As soon as we realized, what with the experience we already had, that the war was about to break out in Bosnia as well, my fear for our younger son became unbearable. Whenever I pleaded with my husband for him to go and fetch the boy, he'd tell me, "There is no way that I, as a man liable for military service, can go. I would never make it to Zenica or back here with our son. They'd pick me up somewhere along the way."

My maternal instinct overrode my fears. I myself set out for Zenica to bring my son back. I managed to hitchhike to *Tuzla in central Bosnia, but from there I couldn't go any further. Buses were no longer running along the sixty miles between Tuzla and Zenica, and taxi drivers refused to go. Desperate, I sat down on the sidewalk and burst into tears. A stranger came over, a middle-aged man, and asked, "What's wrong, ma'am? May I be of help in some way?"

"I cannot believe there is no way for me to get to Zenica. My son is there. He is only fifteen and I must get him out," I told him, looking up with hope.

"Well, I have to say, ma'am, that you really are asking the impossible! There are barricades up every few miles from here to Zenica and there are armed men at every checkpoint. That is why no one dares drive you."

I sobbed miserably. The man walked slowly away, his head bowed.

At least a half hour passed. I was still sitting there. Who knows what I was waiting for? I knew I could not go back without my boy.

Just then a car pulled up in front of me and at the wheel was that same stranger who had explained to me just a half hour before that I was asking for the impossible.

"Ma'am, get in. I'll do what I can to help you," he called to me.

I sat in the car, as if hypnotized. Tuzla was further and further behind us. I listened to the stranger's voice.

"I'll try to get us over on special transport roads that run through the woods. Maybe they don't have barricades up in there yet."

All I could say, over and over again, was that I had to reach my son. I never even asked the stranger for his *name or where he worked.

Early that evening we pulled up in front of my sister's house. When they caught sight of us at the front door, they were overjoyed. My sister said, "Have a seat and tell us how you got here. I'll put on some *coffee."

I looked over at the stranger who, shaking his head, answered, "We haven't the time for that, ma'am. We've got to get back to Tuzla before dark. Take your son's things and let's go!"

In the car my son and I talked about everything that had happened in the year since we'd last seen each other.

Every once in awhile I'd remember that the stranger was in the car with us when I'd catch sight of his kindly eyes as he drove without saying a word. I never noticed that we'd already driven straight through Tuzla. Intoxicated by the joy of being with my son, I was startled by the stranger's voice. "Ma'am, this is as far as I can go. The Serbian barricades are just beyond the next curve in the road. You'll have to do that part on foot. I'll be heading back to Tuzla."

On my way out of the car I thanked him, and asked, "How much do I owe you?"

"Nothing, ma'am. Your happiness and your son's are all the payment I need."

As my son and I walked toward the Serbian barricades, I turned to watch the car speed toward town.

It was only much later that I put two and two together and realized that the stranger had had to stop before the barricades because he was not a Serb.

We lived in Baranja until the moment when we heard the tragic news: our older son had been killed in the fighting in Knin.

We had no kin anywhere in Serbia, and we needed to bury our boy. They'd sent us his body. We decided to bury him in Bosanska Dubica, not far from Novska where we used to live, and to move there ourselves.

After the funeral all my days were the same: I'd stand from early dawn to late night by his grave.

My husband stayed with our son in Baranja so that the child could finish the school year, but I couldn't tear myself away from the graveside.

My next-door neighbor, a Muslim woman named Esma, used to come up to the cemetery every evening, take me by the hand, and tell me, "Come on, Zora, come down to the house to rest. Tomorrow you'll come back."

She'd take me down quietly, respecting my grief. When we got to the house I'd find dinner on the table that Esma had made me. When I stubbornly refused to eat, her husband Daud would tell me, "You have to eat. You'll lose your strength and get sick."

Life had lost its meaning for me. In desperation, I tried to hang myself three times in the stable. Each time Esma and Daud stopped me. Like shadows they kept watch over me and followed me everywhere. The third time as Esma was taking the noose off my neck, she said, "Zora, you must think of your younger son. He needs you. I know the pain must be terrible, but you have no right to leave your boy with no mother!"

The terrible war lasted so long that my son, who had turned eighteen in the meanwhile, was called up to serve in the army of Republika Srpska. He fought in western Bosnia until September 1995, when Muslim and Croatian forces occupied that territory.

His fellow fighters who returned weren't able to tell me whether my son had been taken prisoner or had been killed. There was not a single word of news. Then one morning they called me into an office at the municipal seat where I was working and said, "Zora, there is someone on the phone for you from Vienna."

I didn't know a soul in Vienna. The first thing that came to mind was that this was some kind of mistake. When I picked up the phone I heard a woman asking, "Hello, is this Zora Udovčić?

"Yes."

"I'm calling from Vienna. You don't know me but I have a message for you: your son is a prisoner in a camp near *Mostar in Herzegovina. He is not wounded, he is well and he says hello."

I don't know how long it took me to get out the words, "I'm sorry, but I must ask you: how could you know all this from Vienna?"

"I wanted to give you the news of your son first because I know what it is like to be waiting in expectation. Now I can explain the rest. My brother who lives in Mostar gave me the message for you because he's working now at that camp. He got to know your son who gave him your work number and asked him to let you know he's alive. My brother couldn't call from Mostar because there are no phone lines working between Mostar and Dubica, so he asked me to call you from Vienna. What matters is that your son says he loves you and to wait for him!"

Both of these strangers were Croats.

The war is over now, and I am waiting for my son to come home from the camp, and I'm feeling better now.

CAPTAIN MIĆA

TOLD BY STJEPAN BRADVIĆ

The Village of Križani near Tuzla

November 1998

I lived in a small village near Tuzla with my family until the war broke out. I was fifty-nine when it started. In May 1992 young people from the village got organized, and, armed with hunting rifles, they kept watch as civilians. My son was with four other boys on 21 May in the morning near the next village, when they stumbled on some fifty *Chetniks, Serbian fighters, who took them prisoner.

I went with an older relative of mine to ask the men to release our children. As soon as we showed up they took us prisoner, too, saying: "Now we'll slaughter you, too. You are Croatian Ustasha, all of you."

That same afternoon under an armed escort they had the seven of us walk to another suburb of Tuzla. When we got there they beat us. They called their headquarters at Požarnica from there and ordered, "Send a truck and five soldiers. We've taken seven Ustasha fighters prisoner."

Young men leaped from the truck and kicked, punched, and smacked us with their rifle butts. Then they herded us, bruised, into the truck like cattle. We had been so badly beaten that we were barely conscious. That evening they took us to the headquarters where they chased us down off the truck and beat us again, and then dumped us into a room. I kept passing out from the blows to my head. The next fifteen days I could hardly eat. Armed soldiers guarded us every night until 11:00. Then a man named Captain Mića came in, wearing a uniform. It was the first time I'd ever seen him. He looked us over and turned to the soldiers. "What have you done to these people?"

"Nothing. They beat themselves."

"Get out!" he ordered. When he was alone with us, he said, "Get up. On your feet."

All of us pulled ourselves up somehow, except me. Two others helped me stand. He gave us chairs.

"What's wrong," Mića asked me.

"They beat me. I'm having trouble breathing."

He wouldn't let anyone near us that night so they wouldn't beat us. The next morning he had us moved to a cellar in Požarnica where we spent twelve days. That was at a time when Požarnica was being shelled from our village, so they beat us every day. The Chetniks would come in and say, "Here we are, holding you alive, and your people are shelling us!"

Seeing that they'd kill us soon if they kept this up, Mića had us moved to a village near *Bijeljina. As soon as he left they started beating us there, too.

We were lying bloody and broken on the floor when Mića stopped by to check on us.

"What's wrong?"

"They keep beating us and beating us. They won't give us anything to eat."

He had us moved yet again to another village near Bijeljina to a *school building of some sort, where we were better off. We had food there and beds. There was a specialist Croatian fighter named Mijo held at that camp with us. He was about fifty. I was standing fourth from him in line when they asked him, "Why did you rape a Serbian woman?"

"I didn't, I swear I didn't! I speak four languages. I was training Croatian troops, but I don't know anything about rape."

Three soldiers started beating him right in front of us at six o'clock that evening. They took turns. When he couldn't get up any more they shouted, "Stand up!" Since he couldn't stand, two of them made him and the third kept clubbing him with his rifle butt. They smoked whenever they took breaks, drank brandy, and talked about all sorts of things. They tortured him until midnight.

In the morning one of the three soldiers who had beaten him walked in. "Stand up, you Ustasha!"

Mijo didn't budge. The soldier kicked him and saw he was dead. He took out his billy club and screamed, "Why did you murder him, you bastards!"

He beat us with his club. We ran outside to get away from him. It was raining . . .

When a committee of three Serbian officers came to investigate the case, the soldiers reported, there, in front of us, "He killed himself. Bashed his own head against the wall."

A truck came to take the body away and bury it. They chose my son and two other Croats to bury him. My son told me, when he came back, "They took us to the place where they dump refuse from the factory to bury him there. We'd dug up a layer about the depth of the shovel, and I was digging deeper when I heard a voice behind me: 'Throw him in and shovel a little dirt over him.'

"'I haven't got enough dirt to cover him. Shouldn't we dig deeper?'

"'Cover him with what you have. Otherwise I'll kill you and bury you in there with him!'

"We sprinkled a little dirt over him and came straight back."

We were guarded at one of these detention places by a young man from Požarnica who was certainly no older than twenty-five. I knew his father and his grandfather, Andrija.

When two drunken soldiers, one of whom I knew, barged into our room one night and wanted to beat us, Andrija's grandson wouldn't let them. "Don't you dare. I am on guard here. Captain Mića ordered that no one's allowed to hit them."

"I'll slit their throats," said the bloodthirsty boy whose father used to work with me. I thought they'd kill him, they were so infuriated, both of them. They only withdrew when he drew his gun.

That young man would bring us bread that he tucked under his uniform, and cigarettes, canned food, whenever it was his turn to guard us. He talked normally with us. He knew that our only fault was being born Croats.

Buses kept bringing in new prisoners. Women and children were separated and taken off somewhere. There were about 1,500 of us in the warehouse, and there was nowhere near enough room. We had to crouch next to each other. There wasn't enough space to lie down. We spent about a month there. The horrors started again: they beat us daily. I thought none of us would survive.

We weren't beaten by the sentries on duty. Once I asked one of the sentries if I could go out to the bathroom, and I saw ten people with their throats cut lying on the ground behind the warehouse. I could barely walk back in.

At night they'd take out the Muslims they meant to murder; they'd come along and kick someone and say, "Stand up!" None of them were ever seen again. By morning, when the sun came up, they'd already been taken off somewhere.

Every morning three or four men were taken out who hadn't survived the beatings. I don't know where they buried them all. They never shot anyone. All those young men were always drinking while they beat us. When they wanted to beat one of us Croats they would blindfold us so we couldn't see who it was beating us. I didn't know any of those men.

A committee inspected the prisoners, Muslims, in Batkovići concentration camp, and one of the members of the committee was a doctor. When he got to us Croats, bloody and swollen from our beatings, the doctor said, "No point in examining you. After all, we'll kill all of you because you are Ustasha."

"Doctor, please, couldn't you give us something for the pain?" I moaned.

"No medicine for Ustasha. You all of you deserve to die!" the doctor answered and walked right by. He gave medicine to the Muslims.

They brought in a Croat who had been beaten and had some twenty stab wounds. I bound his wounds up with my own shirt that I tore into strips. When they saw me helping him, the soldiers chased me away.

"Anyone coming near him will be shot. Let him suffer and die."

I crept over with water and washed him. While I was at the camp he recuperated a little. I don't know what happened to him after I left.

Once they named thirty-five prisoners in the camp from Batkovići for an *exchange. The seven of us from my village were among them. We got as far in the bus as the Serbian side of the front line, where they made exchanges, and waited there for three hours but no one showed up on the other side. One of them ordered me, "Hey you, old man, walk over toward the other side. Here is a white flag. Go about a quarter of a mile and see whether any of your men from Tuzla are there." He gave me a scrap of paper with someone's name written on it. "If they brought this man from Tuzla for the exchange, I'll give all of you for him." He punched me in the head a few times until I was all bloody. "This is your big chance to run. Go for it. But we'll slit your son's throat if you don't come back."

I made it over to the Army of *Bosnia and Herzegovina trenches. They called, "Come over this way, man, now that you've made it this far alive! Surrender to us!"

"I don't dare! They've got my son up in that bus. They'll murder him!"

"They'll kill all of you no matter what. At least this way one of you survives!"

"I can't, they've got my son! If they have to murder them all, let them kill me, too!"

When I refused to surrender, one of them shot at me. Bullets were zinging all around my feet. It is pure chance that I wasn't hit. I heard them shouting, "We'll be the ones to kill you, then. You'll never make it back alive!"

I ran back to the bus carrying the white flag. When I made it back, an officer asked, "Are you alive?"

"Yes," I could barely answer. Then he turned to his soldiers: "Put him into the bus and no more beatings. Tell the driver to turn the bus around. We don't want our own men slaughtering them."

I heard the Chetniks shouting: "Are you kidding? An exchange? Forget it, pull them off that bus, let's murder them right here in the woods."

As soon as I got up into the bus, the soldier told the driver, "Hurry, turn the bus around and make it snappy! Captain's orders. Get out of here with these people. The Chetniks are going to murder them!"

After about an hour the officer caught up with the bus and stopped us. "People, get out here. There's a water fountain. Have a drink, relax."

He pulled out two packs of cigarettes.

"Anyone who smokes, have a cigarette. Catch your breath, cool off, and then we're going back to the camp."

It was St. Peter's day, an Orthodox holiday, and really hot. They took us back to Batkovići. Dinner had already been served. Hungry, exhausted, and scared, we lay down, wordless . . .

Ten days or so after that first aborted exchange, just when they were serving us lunch, someone called me and my son from the door. The Chetnik who was the worst with the beatings led us out. "Come over here. A guy from Tuzla wants to see you."

We found Captain Mića there with six soldiers. He told them to go out of the room and leave us. He got up and shut the door and windows. "I had to get out of the hospital to check up on how you are doing. So nobody kills you." After a brief pause he asked us, "You want to go home?"

"Do we! How could we not want to go home? But what about the other five?"

"Ivan, your son from Tuzla asked me to bring you back no matter what it takes."

I was speechless. I had no idea Mića and Ivan knew each other.

"If you can let all of us go, then fine. But if not, we won't go by ourselves. Let them murder all of us," I answered.

"Fine, old man, if that is the way it is. I'll see to it that you are all released tomorrow."

The next day, 15 July, Mića called all thirty-five of us. They took us by bus, and he rode with us. We stopped in front of a checkpoint barricade and waited in the bus. Some Chetniks from another town showed up and wanted to beat us. Mića ordered his soldiers: "Guns at the ready! If anyone comes close, shoot them. I have brought these folks this far and I'm not going to let anyone hurt them now. I mean to hand these people over alive."

No one dared come near. He had no idea what had happened to us during that last exchange.

On the other side, the prisoners who were there to be exchanged were already waiting in trucks. Mića released us first so that we could go over to the other side, before those men had started to cross over toward us.

"Go now to your own army. Let them look after you. I can't protect you any more," he told us when we said good-bye.

IF YOUR OWN WON'T
TAKE YOU, I WILL

TOLD BY SEAD R.†,
Displaced Person from Bratunac

Story Told in Tuzla

November 1998

I was born in 1970 in Bratunac along the *Drina River, by the border between Bosnia and *Serbia. I'd finished secondary school and was working for a private entrepreneur, a Serb, who treated me very decently. In April 1992 my mother, brother, and sister-in-law left Bratunac out of fear of flooding, rather than war, when Murat *Šabanović planted explosives at the hydroelectric dam. They went to Tuzla, and Father and I stayed to see to the chores to be done and to look after our apartments. At that time strange things began to happen around Bratunac: *paramilitary troops with men we'd never seen before began coming and taking people from their homes. You could see by the insignia on their cars that they belonged to the Serbian paramilitary group called the *White Eagles. They were *Arkan's and *Šešelj's men, and when they took the people away they'd break into their homes and loot and steal, and hijack people's cars.

---

†Throughout the testimonies, a dagger indicates a person who requested anonymity.

23

You could hear shooting all over town early in the morning of 11 May. We didn't know what was going on, so we decided to assemble the entire neighborhood at a neighbor's house. The shooting was getting louder just when we saw a big group walking down the street, their hands raised up above their heads. We didn't know where these people from the neighboring streets were being taken. The column of women, children, and the elderly, seemed endless. One of our neighbors suggested, "They are probably taking them somewhere out of town. I've had it with this uncertainty. Let's join them."

Some of us were against it, and we stayed in the house. Soon we heard them kicking in the front door, which we had locked. The column kept passing by. There were three women and seven men in the house. All of them were the same age as my parents. The first to come into the room was a young man in a uniform, professionally equipped: he was wearing a bullet-proof vest, he had several hand grenades on his belt, and had a gun and a pistol. He cocked the gun, and ordered, "No one moves an inch. You so much as twitch and I'll shoot!"

We all froze just as we were. Several boys came running in after him who couldn't have been a day over thirteen. They were all wearing the top half of old police uniforms.

One boy glared at me with loathing, probably because I was a Muslim, since we'd never seen each other before. A *scorpion gun with a silencer dangled from his oversized sleeve. He lunged at me, speaking in a Serbian accent, "Empty your pockets onto the table!"

He took what little money I had on me, and then he studied the registration card for my car. "Where's the car?"

I'd driven my car over to the home of a Serbian friend of mine, a car mechanic, a few days before. We had taken it apart in the garage and taken out the seat, as if he was getting ready to paint and repair it. That was how my car was saved.

"They've already taken my car," I told him.

"Who took it?"

"I don't know who the people were. They stopped me on the street, forced me out, and drove it off."

"Why didn't you give them the registration?"

"I had it on me, but they didn't ask."

He took my license and slipped it into his pocket.

I answered his next questions. He asked whom I'd voted for, and said, "I know, you voted for Izetbegović." Then he asked, "Why didn't you try to run to the woods?"

"What would I do in the woods?"

"If you'd fled, you and I would be facing off right now around some beech tree, and I wouldn't be maltreating you here in your own home."

I chuckled at that, thinking how cruelly right he was. He forced me to take off my socks, and then he pointed the scorpion at my toes and asked, "So, do you think I'll shoot?"

I was scared. I didn't know what to answer.

"Come on, I should. One toe more or less won't make any difference to you," he said to scare me.

"Who is your father?"

In the next room he tortured my father to make him admit where he kept his money and his gold, thinking that we were in our own home. He put the scorpion up against my father's temples, forced him to lie on the floor, and kicked him twice in the head with his army boots. During the hour he spent with us, the column had disappeared down the street. Finally, they took us out of the house and said, "Walk down the street with your hands in the air."

They followed us. We watched as our Serbian neighbors ran into their houses. I was surprised by a construction engineer a few years my senior. I caught sight of him holding a semiautomatic gun, wearing an army shirt, with a black cap on his head. He was running down the steps out of a Muslim house. Trapped by our eyes he tugged the cap further down over his face.

They brought us out to the stadium where there were already several thousand men, women, and children. All of us sat on the grass and waited. No one had any idea what was supposed to happen next.

After three hours I could hear them parking trucks and buses. We still had the hope that they might be taking us somewhere.

The people who had gotten there earlier had their documents on them.

"Dad, I wish we'd been able to bring our documents with us," I said to my father.

"Who cares about our documents. Let's just try to get out of this alive," he answered.

One of the people on the security detail around the stadium was a colleague of mine, a truck driver whom I'd helped back when the war began in Croatia because he, as a Serb, had not been able to drive there. I called out his name.

"Pero!"

"What are you doing here?"

"What sort of a question is that?"

"I had no idea you were here in Bratunac."

"What else can I do? Where could I have gone?"

"Why didn't you get in touch with me earlier?"

"Obviously I had no clue what was going on."

"OK. Do you have any cigarettes?"

"Nothing."

He took a couple of packs of cigarettes out and gave them to me. I felt a little freer. "Is your car here?"

"What good will that do you?"

"Our documents got left behind at a neighbor's house when they made us leave . . ."

"Wait here a minute."

He came back after a quick exchange with some soldiers.

"Come with me."

He took me, under his arm, across the playing field. There were many people who thought he was going to murder me. Even my father thought as much because he hadn't seen us talking.

We walked back to the house where they'd taken us from. He pushed the door open with his foot and asked if I knew where I'd left the documents.

"Sure, on the table."

"Go in quick and bring them out. We can't stay a second longer than necessary because they are going from house to house now and searching."

I ran in and grabbed our documents.

"What the hell is going on?" I asked on our way back.

"Believe me, I don't know any more than you do."

"What will happen to us?"

"I have no idea," he answered, though later it turned out he had known everything.

I didn't dare ask him for help, figuring there was no way out of the situation. I sat next to Father and handed the neighbors their documents. You could hear bursts of rifle fire. They pushed us through a gateway that was twelve feet wide. I said to Father, "Excellent, at least we're going somewhere."

I didn't see what was happening in front of us. At the exit I realized they were pushing the women and the children to one side, and the men to the other.

"This doesn't look good," I said.

Some of the elderly men were making it over to the side with the women and children. I told Father, "You go over to the right. I haven't a hope. At least you save yourself." He was against it but he managed in the end. They loaded them right into buses and trucks and drove them off. I had no idea where they were headed.

Once the stadium was emptied there were about 420 of us left. The Captain commanded: "Line them up and bring them over to the hall."

I knew he meant the Vuk Karadžić elementary school hall, near my house. I'd been able to hear the moans of people being tortured and murdered in there for the last few days. A young man wearing a camouflage uniform looked us over, one by one. When he stood in front of me, he asked, "Sead, is that you?"

"Yes."

"Where the hell have you been?"

"I'm right here."

I didn't recognize him what with the uniform, the terror, but I began to feel a spark of hope.

"Don't you recognize me? Don't you remember how you used to roll me and my brother around in the mud here when we were kids? Now you'll get a chance to see how a Serb hits back! I'll see you in the hall!" he said and walked off, and my spark of hope was snuffed.

On my way into the stadium I saw Pero and called to him in despair. He waved, nothing more. By a short cut he got to the doorway before us and there he signaled me to be patient.

They herded us into the hall with the butts of their rifles. There were a lot of people who had been beaten and were all bloody, lying on the floor under the basketball hoop on the left side. We were crowded onto the right side of the hall, in the most impossible positions. Nine people suffocated that first night. Everyone who stepped across the white line on the floor was murdered. They tortured and murdered some of the people right there in front of us, some in the dressing rooms, and some they took out to the hangar.

A boy told a friend of mine whose father had been a hunter for many years, "I just moved into your house and I found this bullet. Where is your gun?"

"That bullet is from the hunting rifle my father used to have. I handed it over as soon as they asked."

"Where is the gun," the boy repeated, striking him with his rifle butt. Then they carved crosses all over his body, put out their cigarettes on his skin. At one point they cut him from ear to ear across the throat, but they didn't actually slit his throat, on purpose. Later he told me, "I was expecting, when I felt the blood dripping down my chest, that I'd start to gurgle, but I didn't . . ."

They didn't maltreat me physically but it was bad enough watching what they were doing to other people: making them lick up blood, eat paper. They'd choose whom to murder with a bouncing basketball. One of Arkan's men whom they called the "Macedonian" forced a kid who was never a nationalist, a boy scout, to kneel on the parquet floor while he bounced up and down on his back and beat him, shouting, "Faster, faster!"

Suddenly he yanked out his pistol and shot the kid in the back of the head. The boy's head sprayed all over the floor, and his murderer said, "Boy, what a rotten horse," and kicked him, dead, over into the corner.

There were Serbs who were calling the names of several people and taking them outside. One man from the Vihor factory saved six people's lives that way while we were thinking he was taking them out to their execution.

The man who remembered me from childhood called on me a couple of times, "Would you clean my gun for me?" he asked, and went on, "What would you do if I gave you a gun? Would you shoot me, or your own people?"

Soon after that one of my neighbors called me, "Sead, go outside."

I thought, "My time has come." The ones who went out either didn't come back and you'd hear bursts of shooting out there, or they'd come back in beaten, heads bloodied, a sock crammed in their mouths. My childhood acquaintance said, "The time has come, Sead, to find out what you have done to the Serbs!"

There were four soldiers on either side in the corridor. They barked, "Shut that door!"

I shut the door and leaned on it. They were holding metal rods they'd pulled out of smashed school benches. While I was thinking how they were about to murder me with those rods, Pero came, cocked his gun and said, "No, not him. Leave him to me!"

I couldn't figure out what was going on. I thought, "My friend will be the one to murder me. I guess it was meant to be."

"Come over here, you Muslim bastard," he screamed.

I walked by the soldiers but didn't feel a single blow. He kept screaming, "You damned Muslim! Don't you try to escape, a bullet will find you!"

He led me right over to the passenger door of his car and shoved me in. Sivi, another guy I knew, sat in the driver's seat. He put a gun down between the two of us. I tried madly to figure out what to do. He closed the door and turned the key in the ignition. Pero stayed outside, and tapped the window with his gun.

"Get him out of here."

Only then did I realize that they were actually saving my life.

"Where do I take you?" Sivi asked me.

"I don't know. Nowhere is safe now. Can you get me out of Bratunac?"

"That I can't. Bratunac is crawling with man hunters. Where to?"

"Take me to the store where I worked," I said, figuring that I'd find Braco, whom I used to work with, there. As I was getting out, Sivi called over his shoulder, "I've done what I could. Good luck!"

Braco put me in his car, "Sead, where can I take you? If I take you home, they'll find you there and murder me and you."

"Take me to the river. I'll swim across the Drina and get into Serbia."

"You can't even get to the Drina. The riverbanks are thick with soldiers."

A convoy of the prominent Muslims of Bratunac was forming in front of the local mosque. At the municipal headquarters they had been given passes with fake Serbian names so they could make it into Serbia. Some of them later showed up in Tuzla, others went down to Macedonia.

Halfway into town we ran into Ibro, a Muslim, driving his wife and mother-in-law. Braco flashed his headlights. When Ibro stopped, he asked, "Where are you headed?"

"We're going to Zvornik. I got a pass."

"Take Sead, will you?" Braco asked him.

"Believe me, I don't dare. I barely managed to get this pass for us."

"Take him, you have one more place in the car!"

"I don't dare, I really don't," he said, his voice trembling. He started his car and left.

Braco sat back down and said, furious, "Look, if your own won't take you, I will."

I had no idea how we were going to get across the bridge when there were two checkpoints, one on the Bosnian shore where we were, and, across the river, another one on the Serbian side of the Drina. Braco clenched his teeth and drove straight for them. As he was driving he pulled out his *ID card and tossed it into my lap. "From here on in you are me, Dragan Matić."

"Hey, wait a minute, they'll want to see your driver's license and they'll ask for my ID. They'll see we have the same name!" I blurted, terrified, right before the bridge.

"Gee, I hadn't thought of that," he mumbled, confused.

I gave him back his ID card just as we pulled up to the first checkpoint. Braco decided. "You be Dragan Petrović."

"Hey, what's up? Where are you going?"

"To Ljubovija," he whispered, hoarsely.

At that moment the policeman leaned into the car and saw me and recognized me. "Where are you taking him? Are you crazy?"

"I am taking him across."

"Do you realize what you are doing?"

"Get off my back. I have enough problems of my own."

"I'll let you pass, but the Serbian checkpoint on the other side won't."

"You let us pass. We'll figure something out when we get there," Braco told him softly.

"Go ahead, but I never saw you," said the policeman shaking his head.

And he told his colleague to move the car that was blocking the bridge in the middle.

As soon as we came off the bridge on the other side we were met by the police of Serbia. The policeman asked for Braco's registration and my ID.

"I left mine in my car," I answered calmly.

"What is your name?"

"Dragan Petrović."

"Where are you headed?"

"We are going to Ljubovija."

"What for?"

"We're going to visit our girlfriends," Braco said, trying to sound convincing.

"Shut off the car, get out, and put your hands on the roof," ordered the policeman.

I don't know who was more scared of the two of us while they searched us next to the car. Braco breathed a sigh of relief when he heard the saving voice of a policeman he knew.

"Braco, is that you?"

"Sure is."

"Let the man go. I know him. This is the tenth time today he crossed over to Ljubovija."

As we were getting back in the car the policeman added, jokingly, "Don't you go helping any of those greens [Muslims]."

"What good could I do them? You can see for yourself what is going on! I'd be better off murdering them than driving them," he answered resolutely and tried to drive off, but he was so terrified that he turned the key in the ignition when the car was already making an awful grinding sound, and turned on all four blinkers instead of the headlights.

Let's get out of here, I prayed to myself.

Braco left me to stay with his friend Boro in the nearby town, and went back to Bratunac to see if he could manufacture a fake ID for me with a Serbian first and last name.

"You stay here and don't worry about a thing. We'll figure something out," Boro calmed me down as he brought me into his house.

Braco spent all night till dawn searching for a way to make an ID, but in vain. In the morning he set out to pick me up and drive further into Serbia. As he was crossing the Drina bridge he saw an ambulance whose driver he knew pretty well. He stopped the man and asked him, "Where are you going?"

"I'm off going up to Serbia. I'm taking my mother to the hospital," the driver explained, but Braco looked into the van and noticed a girl he knew, a Muslim girl, sitting back there. That made him bolder.

"I have a friend staying near here. Could you take him, too?"

"No problem," answered the driver, uneasy about Braco's discovery. Everyone was keeping it from one another that they were helping people.

When I got into the ambulance I saw the girl. She had a pass for the name Rada Savić. I added "and Rade" on the pass next to her name. From that moment on we were brother and sister. We quickly cooked up a story that we were from Srebrenica where the Muslims had murdered our parents and torched everything we had, and that we were trying to get somewhere where we would be able to live.

Once we made it to Serbia we weren't sure where to go from there. We decided to cross back over into Bosnia to the town of Bijeljina where I had a cousin living. From her house I called her father, who was a bus driver. He found a colleague, a Serb, who drove on the *Belgrade-Tuzla line.

"Would you drive my son to Tuzla?"

"Of course I can. I'm from that area and I know all the men patrolling at the two checkpoints along the way," his colleague replied, readily.

At the bus stop in Bijeljina he greeted me with a grin, "Come right in and sit down. This will be a breeze." When he saw I was scared, he said, "Put this coat on. You'll be the ticket collector."

There were only two travelers in the whole bus. No one was traveling from Belgrade to Tuzla at that point. We passed the checkpoint at his village and at another without a hitch and pulled into Tuzla.

That was the last bus to drive from Belgrade to Tuzla. The next day chaos broke out in Tuzla.

Later in the war I got in touch through amateur radio operators with my friends who saved my life. We talk regularly on the phone now. I still haven't had a chance to see Pero and Braco, but I can hardly wait to hug them.

OUT OF THE HELL
OF MOSTAR

TOLD BY ZORICA BALTIĆ

Refugee from Mostar, interviewed in Banja Luka

December 1995

I used to work as a history and geography teacher. Just before the war broke out my husband and I retired, and we were enjoying the pleasures of a nice apartment in the center of Mostar that we had earned with our forty years of work.

Our children had grown and left Mostar, following their own lives.

The most awful tragedy happened to me on 2 August 1992. That night we were woken by the noise of someone smashing in our front door. My husband ran out into the hallway and that same moment I heard a burst of gunfire. The scene was horrifying: he lay on the floor riddled with bullets, covered in blood that was splattered all over the walls. He was dead. I heard footsteps pounding down the stairs. I stood there powerless over the dead body of my husband. I was completely alone. All the other tenants in the building had heard the gunfire and my scream, but no one came to help. Miserable, I tried to get into the neighbor's apartment. I banged on the door but no one opened up to me. A married couple who lived on the floor below me heard my cries and came up. They were Muslims. They took me to their apartment and I

35

spent the next three nights there. They never by word or gesture suggested that I was a burden to them, though I'm sure they were afraid.

That same day when my husband was murdered, a Croatian acquaintance of ours, Anđelko, came to see me. He had been our neighbor in Konjic years before. I could feel the pain in his voice as he expressed his condolences.

None of the people I knew dared to organize my husband's funeral. Anđelko did. He paid the funeral fees, took my husband's suit for them to dress the deceased in, and arranged for the funeral that was held two days later at a spot set for us by the Muslim-Croatian government. Anđelko was the only family friend who came.

A taxi driver refused to drive us to the place where the funeral was to be held so I had to ask a stranger on the street if he would drive us. He did. The workers at the funeral parlor, gypsies and Albanians, agreed, at Anđelko's request, to open the coffin so that I could see my husband one more time. The four of us lowered the coffin into the grave. During the brief funeral we were in danger of being murdered because there was gunfire all over town.

After the funeral I was afraid of sleeping in the apartment alone that night. That fear drove me to ask several friends if I could sleep at their places, but they refused to have me.

That evening I went to see Anđelko. He and his wife, Olga, received me so warmly. They let me stay there that night, and that helped me feel that there was a ray of hope for me. Their nobility kept me from losing all my hope in other people.

The next day I ran into Ivica, a Croat, a teacher by profession, who had done his training in my classroom. He recognized me on the street and took my hand. He brought me back to his house. I made the acquaintance of his wife, Kamila, a Muslim woman who was a judge. Both of them did all they could to ease my pain, grief, and fear. During the next twenty days they had me over to stay at their place fourteen times. I felt secure there. Ivica told me that nothing bad could happen to me there, and Kamila sympathized with what I was going through. For the first time I felt like a human being, not a hounded beast.

When I didn't know where to turn I decided to see a doctor. Ivica took me by car to see a friend of mine, Dr. Meliha, a Muslim woman who was head of the psychiatric ward of the Mostar hospital. Meliha tried to advise me about what I should do with myself. I think she feared I might try to take my life. I asked her if she would help me by writing a doctor's order with which I could leave Mostar for further treatment, but at that point it would have been impossible. Meliha suggested that I stay in the hospital in her ward, but I was afraid, because there was a man working there whose brother-in-law was a HOS commander. That man wanted my money, apartment, and everything I had in return for getting me to Italy or Austria.

One day Meliha introduced me to a doctor, a Muslim woman, whose husband had been a friend of my husband's. She was head of one of the hospital wards and agreed to keep me in her ward. First she explained that I must never get up out of bed because someone might suspect I was healthy. She did not hang a temperature chart at the foot of my bed.

When my son managed to get a message through to me that he was alive, she was the only one who knew of it. We wept together while I wrote him my answer. She was a true doctor, a humanist and a wonderful person.

Thanks to the kindness of these people I survived the horrors of Mostar during the war and managed to get out.

A LONGING TO PAINT

TOLD BY ĐURO FIŠER

The *Grbavica part of *Sarajevo

October 1998

I moved from Croatia to Bosnia at the age of five and that was where I grew up. In 1986 I graduated from the Sarajevo Art Academy. It had been my lifelong aspiration to work in Sarajevo as an art teacher. Unfortunately, this did not happen, so two years after I was done with school I took a job in northern Bosnia where I worked until the war broke out.

In April 1992 I came to stay with my mother, who had been given an apartment in Grbavica, a part of Sarajevo, and I have been here ever since.

Because of problems I was having with my cervical vertebrae, I had been operated on at the Military Hospital seven years before the war broke out. My disability freed me from work detail and I didn't have to fight at the front.

When everything began in Sarajevo I had no idea what was going on, but even later, what happened made no sense.

The *Yugoslav People's Army raised barricades on 1 May between my apartment building and the Miljacka River that runs through downtown Sarajevo. Our street became the front line. Sometimes I would spend the night in one state and wake up in another. Often I didn't know where I was. In the end I was a foreign citizen in the Yugoslavia that used to be my country.

The man in charge of the work detail came to my house one day and asked, "Why aren't you with us? Can't you work?"

I explained that I had been operated on. He said, kindly: "That's fine, then. Have your mother bring me the medical papers. You stay right here in bed and don't you worry."

Milutin, a Serb, was our first neighbor to stop in. "Hello, how are you? Have you enough to eat?"

Since the war had caught us completely unprepared, we had food only for about three days. Milutin went home and brought us back flour and whatever else he had so we could share it with him.

My mother was a true logistics expert; she looked after an elderly gentleman who lived in the building across from ours. Every time she left the building she was in danger of being shot by a sniper, but because of the financial straits, since only the two of them received pensions, she had to venture out if she was going to feed all three of us. In three and a half years I didn't leave the building more than three times.

Fata, a Muslim woman who lived near us, dodged sniper fire to run to the library and bring me books. Thanks to her, during the war I read so many books that I probably could have earned a second university degree.

The soldiers who slept in our building knew I was here, but no one came to rob us. Mother was the one who had to lug everything, from food to firewood and water, and I didn't dare help her, even with the things I might have managed.

Miroslav, a Serb from Sarajevo who was a special fighter in the Vikić unit, somehow made it over to Grbavica to help out his parents. His apartment in downtown Sarajevo had burned so he broke into an apartment near us and moved in. We met him when he came, at someone else's urging, to ask my mother if she could clean for him. He was willing to pay her.

Mother was terrified because he seemed so intimidating with his bushy beard. She didn't dare turn him down for fear he'd murder her, so she rushed to clean the apartment all at once. When he got back from work, he told her, "Sit down a minute and take it easy."

She looked at him, surprised, and saw tears in his eyes.

"Look, ma'am, this isn't our war. It isn't your war. I helped some people and now I'm in trouble. I've got to get out of here."

He was a man who helped everyone, not just Serbs, which was why he was having trouble with his fighting unit. They told him he'd be murdered if he kept it up. He took off and went to Bijeljina, which is on the Bosnian border with Serbia. Whenever he came back to Grbavica he never passed up the opportunity to stop by and see how we were faring.

My most glorious moment was when Tasa, a Muslim friend, brought me what I needed for painting. Who knows where he'd gotten a hold of it all.

"It'll help the time pass more quickly for you if you paint," he said, simply, as if he knew that the war hadn't quenched my desire to paint.

This part of town was under Serbian control so that made it easier to get a hold of some things. That was how I got a package from a Muslim friend of mine, who lived in Germany. He sent it via Novi Sad in Serbia. For the first time in three years I could relish the fragrance of oil paints. The package included all the other essentials we needed so badly.

I received humanitarian aid just as everyone else did, despite the fact that I was blacklisted. Our kind neighbor, Milutin, always went with Mother to help her carry the packages home.

DEATH IN ANOTHER MAN'S GRAVE

TOLD BY FAIK KULOVIĆ, Chemical Engineer

Sarajevo

October 1998

On a hot summer's day in 1992 I was standing in front of the building that housed the Sarajevo Center municipality command headquarters. The shimmering stillness of the baking air was shattered by exploding shells. Each one dropped into my consciousness and blasted it to pieces. I looked skyward hoping its purity would help me bear the pain.

I don't know whether it was because the sky was the same color as my friend Zoran's (whom we called by his nickname, Koki) eyes, or whether childhood was my escape just then. But the image of our tattered trousers, which we brushed off whenever we got up out of the dirt, our childhood when we never could figure out which of us was stronger, now stretched clean across wounded Sarajevo.

Kaleidoscope-like, the images of our boyhood and youth flickered by, one after another. We were inseparable for twelve years. After every quarrel, neither of us ever victorious because we were equally strong, we'd go home together, giggling at how silly we'd been.

We'd spent our evenings as students together, too. How was it that I hadn't thought of him until now? The months had slipped by. Daily, vol-

41

unteers, Serbs and Croats, too, were coming to me at headquarters to help defend the city, and I didn't know where Zoran was.

With reluctance I looked back from the blue expanse to the hills around the city and cringed at the thought: "Is it possible that Zoran is up there in the hills with the Serbian forces? It can't be that the story of which one of us is the stronger is going to be resolved this way, when we are forty-two years old? Where else can he be except up there, if I haven't seen him for such a long time?"

The explosion of a nearby shell brought me back from that wrenching stab of doubt and sent me back to work.

I forgot Zoran again. For more than a year I never looked up at the sky, or perhaps the ruins of my city were burying all my memories.

One day during the second autumn of the Sarajevo tragedy, when I was out on the street again in front of headquarters, I spotted five soldiers of the Army of Bosnia and Herzegovina walking behind a coffin bearing a Serbian name and a cross. They were going to a nearby graveyard. One of the soldiers stepped out of formation and came over. No, I wasn't wrong: it was Zoran. I was so overcome I could barely speak.

"Good God, Zoran, where have you been until now? Come, sit down, let's catch up."

"I can't, Faik. I am on my way to bury a fellow soldier who died in combat with the Croatian Defense Council forces near Vitez," he answered softly.

"OK. But on your way back stop by for coffee."

While I waited for Koki I had enough time to despise myself and the things I had thought about him. How could I even associate him with the men up in the hills who were shelling their own city? Just because he was a Serb? Impossible. That never meant anything to him or to me. I waited impatiently to tell him. Only by telling him could I rectify my wrongs.

A blast reverberated from the graveyard they'd gone to and roused me from my reveries. I sent a soldier to find out where the shell had hit. He was gone too long. When he did come back, he told me, "The shell fell on the cemetery. There are casualties, some wounded, some killed."

The fear mounted with every step as I hurried toward the cemetery. I searched for Koki among the wounded, but found him only when I looked into the freshly dug grave where they'd laid his fellow soldier to rest. He was flung across the coffin, his back to the light. I called his name, but it was no good. His eyes were open but they saw no more.

Shrapnel from a shell fired from the Serbian positions had murdered him.

NEIGHBOR, COME BACK!

TOLD BY PERO SIMIĆ

Refugee from Gradačac, interviewed in Modriča

December 1995

I lived in Gradačac with my wife and two children in our family home. We had friends among Muslims and Croats. My family and I are Serbian. Right before the war began my wife and daughter went off to visit relatives who lived outside town.

I was working as a fireman at the local factory and I stayed on the job once the war broke out. My son and I were assigned to a work detail from day one. During the first year of the war we received pay, and after that, rations. No one ever forced me to work under fire.

During the years of the war, those who knew me were evenhanded, even though I am a Serb. The colleagues I worked with at the factory used to go down to the cafeteria and bring up food for themselves and for me, just so that I wouldn't have to run into trouble by going down there myself. When Gradačac was being ethnically cleansed, no one forced my son or me from our jobs, nor did they throw us out of our house, and no one looted our home.

I got sick in 1995. Two members of the committee for prisoner exchange, neighbors of mine, a Croat and a Muslim, stopped by on 6 December with joyous news.

"Pack your things, you are going out on the exchange."

"Hey, I can't believe my ears," I shouted.

"We know you're sick and that you can't manage packing and getting to the border on your own so we've come to help you and drive you there."

When we got to the place where the exchange was to happen, the two of them carried my bags because I didn't have the strength.

There were a lot of Serbs who paid someone to take them over the front lines to get out of Gradačac, but I experienced having my neighbors tell me, when we parted, "Get well soon and come right back."

As they said these words one of them handed me ten marks and the other twenty, because they knew I was broke.

My son stayed on in Gradačac. He is still working at the factory. People from all three ethnic groups work there.

A CLEAN STREET

TOLD BY SLAVENKA MUHIĆ†

Bosanski Šamac

December 1995

Twenty-five years ago I married Adil, a Muslim, though I was a *Roman Catholic. To that happy marriage our daughter, Sena, was born. For decades we lived happily in Bosanski Šamac, and had friends who belonged to all three ethnic groups, without any prejudices. We visited one another for the religious holidays, which all of us honored. In the center of town there was an Orthodox church, a Catholic church, and a mosque within a few hundred feet of each other. No one was bothered by the other church's bells or the *muezzin's voice calling to prayer. I was proud of my town because of that cacophony, which sounded sweet to me. When someone built a house, everyone who had the time to spare would come to the building site to help so that the job would get done sooner.

Serbian authorities took control of the local government at the very start of the war. Regardless of the fact that we all knew each other, the ones in power changed in the way they treated others. All those who were not of the Orthodox faith found themselves having to leave the town or bow down to humiliating orders from the authorities, which summoned them to a work detail.

Sena was nineteen years old when the war began. She was summoned to clean streets, but I couldn't accept that. The only solution I could see was to get her out of town. I went to see a neighbor, a Serb, who often traveled to Serbia.

"I have come to ask you to take Sena with you in your car to Belgrade. But I have no money," I said.

"Don't worry. I'll take her to stay with relatives of mine."

"What will happen if they stop her on the border crossing?" I asked.

"I'll do all I can to keep that from happening, but if I fail I certainly won't leave her there. We'll come back together."

The next day they left. That same night my neighbor came to tell me, "We made it into Serbia. I put Sena on a train there. She arrived safe and sound at my relatives' place in Belgrade."

Sena spent four quiet months there. Soon after she left I received a summons to report for a work detail. I was supposed to work in Obudovac where the Serbian army was quartered because that was where the front line was. I was terrified at the thought of what might happen to me there. It was tough to imagine a Croatian woman among Serbian soldiers who were fighting against Croats at the time. My first reaction was, "I won't go. Better they shoot me here."

A long-time Serbian friend of mine, Sima, heard of my troubles. He came over to our house and said, "I will take you personally to Obudovac. You can be sure you won't have trouble. It is better for you to do your eight days of work than for them to arrest you."

The next day he drove me to military headquarters where he learned that I'd been assigned to work in the kitchen. He brought me into the place I was to work and all the soldiers he met there, he told, "This is Slavenka. Please look after her. She is on a work detail for the first time." As he was leaving he advised me, "Just tell them you are a member of my family."

He left, and there I was, miserable, with those complete strangers.

They were surprisingly nice. They invited me to have a cup of coffee with them. My hands were trembling so, I couldn't lift the cup. The next day while I was washing army pots and plates a soldier came over and said, "You have a visitor."

I turned and saw Sima.

"I am going to die of fear here, Sima!"

"I told you you've nothing to fear. Has anyone been rough with you?"

"No. They are all very nice, but I'm still petrified."

"Please, hold out for these seven days. I'll work to see that this doesn't happen again."

When they called me to a work detail the next time, I was sick. Adil was digging trenches on the front line for his work detail. Sena was in Belgrade. Sima took the doctor's diagnosis to headquarters to explain my absence from work.

That man intervened to shield me from humiliation countless times. He did not give up until he found a place for me to work at the central accounting office.

While Sima was away at the front they came for me and forced me to clean the street. The part of town I was supposed to clean was where the shop was that Sima owned. With broom in hand I turned a corner and stopped, in awe. The whole street was already spic and span.

At the other end of the street Sima's wife, Fatima, a Muslim woman, waved to me. She was standing in front of the shop and beckoned me over.

"Tell your fellow sufferers to come into the store."

All of us street cleaners sat and drank coffee with her, and though she never said as much, we knew that Fatima had cleaned the street for us.

LITTLE MOSCOW

TOLD BY ZEHRA GOZO

Mostar

November 1998

Thirty percent of the marriages in Mostar are between people of different ethnic backgrounds, and the city brandished this fact like a shield against all the nationalist madness that reared its ugly head in the early 1990s. That great proof of how much love there was in my city made us all feel sure that nothing horrible could happen among the people who lived there.

During the Second World War the Serbs of Mostar were under terrible duress; they were taken to camps. Muslims saved them and hid them, especially in the part of town called *Donja Mahala, which is why they often called it "little Moscow" (a haven for the resistance).

In spite of all this, the war did begin in the spring of 1992 with an attack by the Serbian army that fired on the city from the surrounding hills. We lived in uncertainty because we had no idea what was going on.

Most of my neighbors hid in the cellar of a large building. I stayed with my seventy-five-year-old mother in our house on the left shore of the *Neretva River. Since my brother was forty-four years old, he was often obliged to serve on guard duty.

49

On the night of 8 May, when the shell blasts were becoming unbearable, I decided that we were going to go with the people. Let whatever happens to them happen to us.

In the morning we realized that all the Muslims had gone somewhere during that night, and no one remembered to call us, what with all the commotion. We stayed behind with our Serbian neighbors, who started crying when they saw us, "Now we know who are our friends. Everyone else has abandoned us, but you stayed!"

The Yugoslav People's Army entered the city on 12 May, and the next day they began to inquire about whether there were any Muslims left. They talked to us nicely, even though they knew we were Muslims, and they tried to put us at ease, saying, "Don't you worry. You will have everything: electricity, running water."

Soon they started burning houses.

On 19 May the army summoned Serbs over the radio to prepare to be evacuated to the town of Nevesinje.

Our traditionally good relations with Serbs were what determined our decision to join them. We believed that in that way we would be getting out of hell.

The Montenegrins, who were loading seven Serbs from our street into a truck, let the three of us get on, as well as a married couple who were also Muslims, because they didn't know we weren't Serbs. Our neighbors did not betray us. The Montenegrins drove us to a village next to Nevesinje. Mirko, one of our neighbor's brothers, took us to his summerhouse where his relatives were also staying. They made us coffee with milk and reassured us, saying that while we were with them nothing bad could happen.

Mirko put us up in a Muslim summerhouse. He visited us every day, brought us food from his house, until he registered Mother and me with the *Red Cross. He took care of us until 17 June.

Then the Serbian army retreated from Mostar and chaos erupted in the village. The Serbian forces that had surrounded us began shooting.

The local people fled in their cars, and we were left alone. We lost contact with Mirko. A Serb we didn't know brought us, lost, into his home from the street.

"I'll find a way to get you safely out of here," he told us.

That night Serbian soldiers threw bombs at Muslim houses and plum orchards. Everything was smashed, roofs collapsed, glass shattered . . .

In the morning an elderly Serbian man came by and told our host, "What are you waiting for, get out of here and save yourselves!"

We realized that we were a threat to the man's life. He no longer knew what to do to help us. We set off on foot across the fields, detouring the villages of Nevesinje to a village further on where we spent two days, but Serbian forces drove us from there as well.

Local people we didn't know who were both fleeing took us onto their tractor. We stopped by a canal. Along its slopes men had placed posts they had fashioned from felled trees, and had stretched sheets of plastic and tarpaulins under which 700 Muslims were staying who had been expelled from six of the villages around Nevesinje.

Serbs from the nearest village who had been minding herds of livestock on a hilltop came running up on the fourth day and urged us with agitation, "Run, some other forces are on their way, torching villages!"

People scattered in all directions in a panic. No one waited for anyone.

The three of us managed to climb up a hill. Our legs sank knee-deep in mud. My brother and I dragged our mother along no matter what it took. The elderly had less strength and often were left behind where they were later murdered. The stronger and more capable people climbed up the steep hillsides and collected on the hilltops. Some of them proposed we set out toward Mount Velež. Others said, "Shells are falling there!"

"We have no time to quibble," a man with a deep authoritative voice decided. As if following orders, or so it seemed to me, each person set off in a different direction. People went in smallish groups with someone they trusted.

We weren't familiar with the terrain. I had thought it didn't matter that we were splitting up and that the paths all led to a crossroads where we'd be assembling again. About thirty of us went by mistake in the wrong direction. After great effort we reached the other side of Velež Mountain. There they were shelling Muslim villages and people were fleeing. Below us we could hear the whispers of the people fleeing . . .

The people we were traveling with gave us an ultimatum.

"You can continue along with us only if you leave your mother behind. All of us will be murdered because of her. Either you leave her, or you stay with her and the rest of us go on without you."

We decided to stay with our mother, even if it meant we'd be killed. We spent forty-seven days here, totally alone. For twenty-five days we hid in a depression in the ground and slept in the rain. It was the rainiest June I can remember. Mother was sick. Her teeth chattered. My brother found a hut after many days and we hid there. We collected twigs and made a fire to warm up a little. We had no food.

One day we caught sight of cows. At first we thought they were ghosts. They were going out to pasture and we didn't have a chance to milk them because their udders were empty. We hoped we'd have better luck that evening, but they obviously went back by some other route.

The only good thing was a spring of water nearby.

As the days passed I grew weaker, I kept throwing up and could no longer walk. I started to lose my sight, my joints swelled, my legs were black and white, my hair fell out, my fingernails started peeling off . . .

Mother kept trying to bolster our spirits by talking about how nice it would be once we got home, even if we had to live in a basement storage bin.

In moments of weakness my brother suggested we turn ourselves in, but we wouldn't hear of it. His wife and children were on the *Dalmatian coast. He kept urging me, "It would be best for us to turn ourselves in. Let them murder me. At least you'll be alive and you'll explain to my children what happened."

"It is better to die than give up," I answered him with my last ounce of strength.

I often heard him crying, "Is this how it's going to end? Will I never see my children again?"

"Look, we've never done anybody harm. I don't believe it is our destiny to suffer like this and die. There must be a way out," I kept repeating with faltering conviction.

We survived for forty-seven days with no food. When we came home I weighed eighty pounds, my brother, 106.

On the last day of our ordeal my brother went off to bring back water and firewood.

"Don't carry wood back. If no one finds us we'll die today or tomorrow anyway. Don't burden yourself unnecessarily. Bring only water," I pleaded with him.

"All right, I'll fetch some water," he said barely audibly and crawled off toward the spring.

The hut was out of sight in a sheltered spot but the spring could be seen from above. When he'd climbed up he caught sight of three men. He knew they'd seen him and he figured, "I have nowhere to run. If I try to escape they'll catch up and murder me." He came over to them slowly. He saw they were wearing uniforms with Chetnik insignia, black bandannas and *beards. They were quiet. He figured they probably were not alone.

"God help you," they greeted him in unison.

"God help you, too," he answered, petrified with fear.

All three of them showed their shirts and on the inside were the insignia of the Army of Bosnia and Herzegovina, the Muslim forces.

"What is your name?" they asked him harshly.

"Muharem."

"How come your name is Muharem?"

"My mother is a Serb and my father a Muslim," he explained, stuttering, while another four came over to join them. He could tell by the look in their eyes that they didn't believe him.

From their conversation he learned that up on Mount Velež Serbian soldiers had murdered the father, mother, sister, the sister's two daughters, an uncle, and an aunt of one of the men.

"Do with him whatever you want. He's yours," they said to the man, who asked, "Are you alone?"

"No, I'm not. I am here with my mother and sister."

"Take us to them."

"Don't murder them, please," he moaned.

I saw them as they were coming toward us through the fog. It looked as if there were more of them because I was seeing double. One tree looked like a whole forest to me. I told my mother some soldiers were coming.

"I don't care. Let them come," she answered listlessly.

"What is your name?" they asked me.

"Give me something to eat, I'm starving."

"What is your name?"

"I'm starving."

"I'll give you food, just tell me your name."

"My brother went off to get water. Don't kill him," I pleaded, not seeing him among them.

"Don't worry, your brother will be here in a minute."

Several soldiers came up with my brother, who told me, "Show them our papers."

"You know we haven't got any," I lied, trying to protect him from the strangers.

"Don't make things worse, please, give them our papers," he coaxed, and then he shook them out of my purse.

When they looked them over, they noticed, "You don't look like yourselves at all. Last year lots of Serbs got their hands on three ID cards, one for each *nationality. How can we believe that you really are the people in these pictures?"

One of them picked up my job pass and asked, "What's this?"

My brother brought him over my ID card so that they could compare them.

"This looks fine," they decided. We were so relieved.

"Now let's see whether you can walk," one of the soldiers told me and helped me up. I took a step and stumbled.

"You'll recover. We'll be moving on in four days. Wait here for us. We are going into the village. We'll bring you some food tonight."

Completely numb with hunger we had no strength to get excited. My survival instinct made me practice walking. I had no sense of direction. I was nearly blind. My brother led me by the hand, and I held a walking stick in the other.

They did not come back that night. We heard the pounding of a battle going on in the distance. We had no idea what was happening. My brother was desperate, "They'll be killed, and then the enemy will search the area and find us and murder us."

Our saviors did come back the next day around noon. One of them was wounded. They'd brought us fruit salad and juice. They had potatoes as small as walnuts.

"We have a wounded man with us. We have to keep going so his leg won't get infected. Get ready to go with us," they hurried us along.

By evening we had climbed up to the highest peak of Mount Crvanj, Zimomor, which is at an elevation of over 5,700 feet. It was very cold. The fighters hopped from foot to foot, massaged each other, and picked the ice off.

We spent three days traveling. They put Mother on a horse because she couldn't walk. She screamed with pain because there was no saddle.

She kept slipping. They'd push her back up and she'd slip again. They also lifted the wounded man, who had been hit by a *cluster bomb in the leg, up onto the horse using an unrolled tent and he groaned with the pain as well.

We would stop so that someone could scout out the area. Then one by one they would take first my mother across, then the wounded man, on the horse. My brother and I would catch up with them on foot. I held his trouser belt and limped along on a shepherd's staff.

We boiled up the potatoes they brought. They had a few cans of sardines. We were careful with food. In the morning we ate a little of the sardines, and in the evening we'd drink a little juice.

They were soldiers of the Army of Bosnia and Herzegovina who were looking for survivors from their region in order to evacuate them.

On our way we came across a valley where a lot of raspberries and strawberries were growing. People picked them and brought them to me. Images began to come back into focus as my vision improved . . .

The fourth day they brought us to a field hospital. The doctor examined us and hooked us up to an intravenous line.

From there they transported us to Konjic where we arrived on 11 August. Here I heard the voices of people saying, "Why did you bring them here? They'll die tomorrow." I heard them say of my brother, who was in his forties, that some old guy had been brought in who was eighty and who was at death's door.

Dragan Andrić, an officer of the Army of Bosnia and Herzegovina who had dispatched soldiers into the hills to save the lives of people who fled the fighting and were wandering, lost, inquired if I had seen any Serbian military or paramilitary troops while I was out there.

I was so exhausted and furious that I replied, "All Serbs are Chetniks as far as I'm concerned!"

"No, they are not. I am a Serb but I'm no Chetnik," said this man, who had saved us, calmly.

After thirteen days of treatment and recovery they returned us to Mostar.

The Muslim couple who had fled Mostar with us had no strength to go on beyond the village where we first stopped. They hid for days until finally their fear and the constant uncertainty prompted them to surrender. On their way to the police station they had the luck to run into Mirko, who told them, when he heard what they were planning, "Come with me. Your treatment will be different than if you go there by yourselves."

He took them out of the village by car without stopping at the police station. They were terrified because they couldn't guess what it was he had in mind. Only when he drove up to the *line of separation by the town of Stolac and told them, "Now you can go on foot into your own territory" did they realize that he wasn't turning them in, he was saving them.

Mirko is about sixty years old. When we were fleeing I didn't see him. Recently I went back to Nevesinje to see him. He didn't notice me. I watched him from a distance while he was working, but I didn't dare approach him because I knew that the town was still run by hardliners. Politicians think one thing; the people think otherwise.

Mostar was not a fortunate city. On the symbolic date that the whole world had been celebrating for nearly fifty years as Victory Day against Fascism, 9 May 1993, a war of Croats against Muslims began.

In November, at the door of what was left of our apartment that had been hit by sixteen shells on the eastern side of town, a young man appeared, a Muslim, who wanted to know if we were still living here. When he learned that we were, he said, "A mutual friend of ours from Croatia called me. He wanted to know if you were alive and well, and whether you are needing anything and was there anything he could do to help you."

"Can you read him a letter from me when he calls again?" I asked, delighted by the visit.

"I'd be glad to," the young man replied, and came that afternoon to pick up the letter. In it I asked our friend to visit a cousin of mine, a child, whom he had taken to the Croatian coast in April 1992.

He did go and find the boy, brought him food, and when the combat stopped he arranged for the boy's papers and returned him to Mostar.

At the border they asked, "Are you going back to Mostar with your son?"

"Yes, there is no more need for him to be in Croatia," my friend answered, accepting the child as his son.

Thanks to the efforts of Zoran Mandelbaum, president of the Mostar Jewish community, the first packages and humanitarian aid began to arrive in my part of town. I got packages from Croatian friends from the western side of Mostar, and from Dubrovnik.

A HOSPITABLE HOME

TOLD BY RADOJKA UMIĆEVIĆ

The Village of Čađavica near Bosanski Novi

January 1996

I've lived for sixty-nine years in my native Čađavica. In September 1995 the campaign of the Muslim army was threatening the territory of my village and the relocation of the Serbian positions, and this meant the retreat of the inhabitants from the village.

My children and grandchildren quickly threw the necessary things into a tractor trailer. Before they left the village my granddaughter raced into the kitchen where she found me sitting, and blurted, in a panic, "Come on, Grandma, hurry up! What are you doing here? All of us are already up on the tractor!"

"Children, go on without me. I survived the last war in my own house, and I'll try to get through this one, too. If it is fated for me to die, let it be on my own doorstep."

"But, Grandma, you will be all by yourself in the village! No one is staying behind but you!"

"So be it. Don't worry about me, my child. Every person is born alone and dies alone."

My granddaughter kissed me and ran, with tears in her eyes, out of the house.

Two hours after the sounds of the last tractors had passed I heard shouts from the orchard above the house, and then all you could hear were the steps of people climbing up the stairs. I sat motionless at the table. The door burst open. I saw two people in the doorway in uniform, holding weapons.

"Is there anyone in the house, grandmother?"

"No one's here but me."

They went upstairs and came down soon enough, cursing. When I saw them holding a rifle my family had forgotten, in their panic, to take, I understood why they were so angry.

"Whose weapon is this?" one of them asked.

"Go on, get rid of it. That is a hunting rifle," his comrade answered for me.

"Where are your children, Grandmother?"

"They got away in time."

"Are there any men in the house?"

"What sort of a home would this be without a man?" I answered. They exchanged glances and laughed.

"Fine. But you shouldn't be drinking coffee alone. Is there enough for us?"

"This is a hospitable home. I'll find some coffee," I said and got up and made them coffee. They sat at the table. When I put the cups in front of them they announced in unison, "We won't have our coffee unless you join us."

I brought coffee for myself as well, sat with them and asked, "Where are you from, boys?"

"We are from the village of *Otoka. Do you know where that is?"

I knew that it was a village near *Bosanska Krupa, only ten miles from mine.

"Is there anyone else, Grandmother, here in the village?"

"I don't know, boys, but I believe no one else stayed."

"You are probably right. Our men don't seem to be shooting."

"Well, you didn't shoot at me, either."

"And why would we? You didn't offer any resistance, even though you did have a hunting rifle in your house," they said, chuckling.

Later that afternoon, after they'd gone around the village and seen for themselves that there was no one there but me, they came back to my house and said, "We will stay here at your house, if you don't mind. You sleep upstairs. We will be in the kitchen."

I spent that night remembering stories I had heard since the war began in which Muslims tortured and murdered Serbs whom they came across in the villages they'd taken, about how they torched their houses and barns and desecrated graves.

These men were about forty years old. They were younger than my children. The war had not erased the grin from their faces. They behaved toward me as if they had come to my home for a normal visit as guests. They never raised their voices when talking to me. I knew that if our people came back to the village and found them there I would not allow anything to happen to them.

The next few days another dozen or so middle-aged soldiers came into the house. All of them behaved extremely well. They happened upon me once in the yard when I was carrying firewood.

"Didn't we tell you, Grandmother, that you mustn't ever go out on your own? Our people are in the hills around the village. One of our snipers might shoot you!"

"I didn't have any more dry firewood," I said.

"You tell us where it is and we'll bring it in. Whenever you need something, we'll go with you. Please don't go outside and walk around by yourself."

One morning I saw flames burning at the other end of the village.

"Why are you burning houses? Someone will be living there tomorrow," I asked them angrily.

"Grandmother, we had to do something. We don't burn any houses. We set fire to some straw to show people we're here. Our men are watching from up above and it's getting to be time for us to go back," said one of the soldiers, sighing.

"You're right, Grandmother. Someone will live here again. Just not us," added a second.

They asked me to make them coffee they had brought me themselves, not allowing me to use up my own. They never would start drinking theirs unless I joined them with my own cup.

Their men were at the cemetery. They didn't desecrate anything. They just showed me the names of all the people they knew.

"Those were upstanding, fine people," they said.

They asked about the local people whose names they knew.

"Give my regards to Dr. Kepa if you ever see him. I'd rather have a chat with him than with God," one man said.

On the fifth day one of them gave me a piece of paper.

"What is that? I don't read."

"The name of our unit is written down here. Who knows where the war will take us tomorrow? Maybe men from one of the other units of the Army of Bosnia and Herzegovina will come to your house. If that happens, show them this paper. It reads: '5th Corps, the glorious 511th BBT, and from the other side, the 266th from Otoka—the wolves 1st light glorious N8 Infantry—22 September 1995,'" one of them said, and another continued, "You see, Grandmother, it doesn't matter that you don't know how to read. Keep this note handy. If you need it, let them do the reading."

The next day there was firing at the lower end of the village. The soldiers leaped to their feet.

"There you go, Grandmother, your people are back! Don't hold anything against us!"

They ran out of the house. I heard familiar voices as they vanished into the distance. "This war sure is stupid."

The other cursed loudly.

BIG SHEPHERDS WITH
A LOT OF SHEEP

TOLD BY DR. ANTE JELIĆ

*Vareš

November 1998

I was born in the town of Vareš where I finished elementary and secondary schools. I graduated from the Sarajevo University School of Medicine in 1981. I got a job right away at the Vareš Medical Center where I worked until 3 November 1993.

That was when a lot of horrible things happened in Vareš. I was fired. I was one of those who couldn't believe that the things happening everywhere else would flare up in Vareš. We all went to the same school, worked, lived, and socialized with each other. We thought that we would never have to leave town.

Between 15,000 and 20,000 Croats arrived in Vareš, refugees from Kakanj, on 13 June 1993. I visited these people and did what I could to help them. They were all telling me, "All you Croats will be *expelled, too."

"That can't happen here. There is no situation which could force the people of Vareš to leave their town," I answered them, adamant.

It soon became clear that I was wrong. One of the most difficult days in my life was on Saturday, 23 October 1993, when a terrible massacre happened in the village of *Stupni Do where mostly Muslims lived. The people who lived there had gone to school and worked with my father. Friends of mine lived there, too, people I was close to.

In the morning, about 8:00, when I was about to go out to buy a loaf of fresh bread, you could hear sirens and gunshots and soon there were shells exploding. My daughter clung to me and said, frightened, "Tata, don't go out, please!"

"I won't, dear. It's better to be hungry."

It was hard for me to see the flames and smoke rising over the village on the edge of town. I didn't know what was going on. I had lived in our building with my wife and two daughters for more than four years. My neighbors all stayed indoors that day . . .

The next afternoon a representative of the Red Cross municipal organization in Vareš came to announce: "You must come to the hall of the secondary school."

"What will I do there?"

"There are Muslims being held prisoner there."

"Why?"

"Your guess is as good as mine. All I know is that the people holding them prisoner are calling for a Croatian doctor."

It bothered me that they were asking for a Croatian doctor. There were other doctors around besides me. I had no idea what was going on. When I got there I was appalled. In a hall no larger than 1,500 square feet there were some 250 Muslims between the ages of seventeen and seventy being detained. I knew them all. These people needed help and I was powerless. I felt miserable.

They were being guarded by uniformed members of the Croatian Defense Council forces whom I had never seen before. Later I learned that these soldiers had come from *Kiseljak, Kakanj, and Fojnica. They beat the prisoners and were maltreating them. The prisoners begged me in whispers, "Doctor, stay here as long as you can. While you are here they won't beat us."

I had some medicine on me and I handed it all out. They asked me to measure their blood pressure. I put the cuff on some of them five or six times just to stay in the hall as long as I could. I was shivering with fear. I couldn't even see what their blood pressure was in the state I was in. I stayed in the hall until 10:00 that evening, when finally a member of the Croatian Defense Council forces came over to me.

"What are you doing here, doctor?"

"Your men asked me to come," I answered calmly, masking my fear.

"You have nothing left to do here. Get out!"

As I was on my way out a soldier kicked me in the behind. When I got home I told my wife, "I am afraid that we, too, will have to leave Vareš."

A colleague who had been to see the prisoners came to the parish office. Moved by what she'd seen, she asked me, in tears, "Ante, what can we do?"

"I am going to bring them whatever medicines I can find. I don't know what else we can do," I said and found the parish priest, who greeted me with the words, "Take anything you need from what we have in the way of medicines stored at *Caritas for those poor people." He greeted me at the door with five cartons of cigarettes. "Take this to them, let them have something to smoke."

When I brought the medicine and cigarettes to the prisoners they told me, desperate, "Look, doctor, put the cigarettes away and take them back. We'll be beaten even more if we are found with them."

Looking at what the Croats were doing to the Muslims, and knowing that the Serbs and Croats and Muslims all treated each other the same, I realized that the late President Josip Broz *Tito was right when he said, "Cherish brotherhood and unity as your dearest possession."

It was hard for me to face how much evil there is in people, when they can beat and maltreat others so terribly.

After that Sunday I went to work at the emergency center. All the Croats were called up on 30 October and that was when the Croatian Defense Council forces called me up, too. That was the first time I held a rifle, though

I never shot it. I had never served in an army because I'd been in a car accident at the age of twenty-seven. When I was younger I had felt bad about not being able to serve.

They took me to a place where, before the war, there had been an intermunicipal teaching center. A medical team of a doctor and two medical technicians was providing first aid to wounded fighters. I stayed there until 2 November. At about 3:30 A.M. I saw there were fires raging on the mountain above Vareš. I heard the firing of guns but I didn't know what was going on. I couldn't find anyone to ask from the Croatian Defense Council officers' corps, so I called the emergency care station in Vareš over the phone. No one picked up. Only the next afternoon did a man at the emergency care station in Vareš pick up the phone. He was someone who had retired before the war.

"There is no one here, my dear doctor, but me."

"How come, Pero? Where is the on-duty doctor?"

"All the Croatian staff fled to Brezik this morning."

"What do you mean, Brezik? Brezik is around on the other side of the mountain!"

I was in Vareš within a half hour by car and there I found a horrible situation. A large number of people, mostly Croats, had abandoned the town carrying only a bundle, each of them. Children were crying and calling to their parents. There were people trying to push their way onto the packed buses and trucks. When I tried to get to my apartment I noticed people gesturing that I must be crazy.

"Why are you going into town? All of us Croats are leaving Vareš!" they told me.

I took my wife and children from the Vareš apartment. We went all of us together into town and spent the night at the emergency care center. That night the Croatian Defense Council forces called on all Croats to leave town because apparently there were Muslim fanatics, *mujahedin, coming who would slit people's throats, maltreat them, burn down houses, and rape women. Very few Muslims were still in town at that point after the earlier Croatian cleansing. Since my daughters were seven and nine years old, I figured it best for us to leave. The next morning we left Vareš. My mother-in-law went with us.

Driving in a sedan with only four gallons of fuel we joined the long line of cars and following goat paths and back roads we left Vareš. We were moving in the direction of Serbian territory but we had no idea where we were headed. The next day we reached a village in Serbian territory. There were Serbian civilians here who knew me. They stopped the car and asked, "Doctor, will you get out of your car? We have a sick child. Could you take a look?"

I did have some medicine with me so I got out and examined the child. Afterward, Croats berated me, "You were crazy to pull out of line. You've lost your place."

We got to Trideseti, a spot near a Serbian village. I had been there before for vaccinations. People knew me and I knew them. There had never been anything unpleasant between us. We stopped. We didn't know where to go next. The local people came to us and asked, "Do you need food and clothing?"

It was cold though it hadn't started snowing yet. The people were feeling so much fear and uncertainty that they didn't notice hunger or the cold.

That first day of that awful journey I saw a group of Chetniks wearing black uniforms, with long beards, fur hats, and skulls on their insignia. They fired off guns and shouted, "We are going to Vareš! We'll set Vareš ablaze!"

We spent that night in the car. In the morning I heard that many of the Croats who had spent the night in their cars had suffered. Members of the Serbian fighting forces had dragged them out, beaten them up, and taken everything that was theirs, even the cars. No one touched me. Dado, a local man, came over.

"Doctor, it would be better if you didn't stop by the road. Something nasty might happen to you. Come to my house. Leave your car."

"Dado, I'm worried someone will damage my car if I leave it," I answered.

"In front of my house no one will dare touch your car," he answered firmly. Dado gave me a sleeping bag and took me to his barn. My wife, daughter, and mother-in-law slept in the car. That night even more Croats lost their cars. In the morning it started raining; it got cold. Around noon I saw a Serb in a uniform who asked me, "Do the two of us know each other?"

"I don't recall," I answered.

"I am Milan from Ilijaš. Where did you work?"

"In Vareš."

"Are you the doctor?"

"Yes."

"See? We know each other. What are you doing here?"

"I'm waiting."

"Go ahead. I'll follow you."

I was so relieved. I figured I wouldn't have any more problems because we were coming up on a checkpoint. Milan told the soldiers at the checkpoint, "This is a doctor. Let him through."

I started to sing in the car, I was so glad. There was a lot of mud on the road and there were long waits. A friend from Vareš who had been working in Germany for twenty-five years was stuck there at Trideseti. His car was taken and everything in it. The Serbs in uniforms took all his money. He said, with resignation, "Now when we get there they are going to put all of us in jail. You, too, will end up with no car."

I couldn't believe him.

By that evening we had made it to a village on the road from *Ilidža to Kiseljak. That was the first time I'd seen a sign for the new Serbian part of Bosnia: Republika Srpska. They had set up a checkpoint there and it was a border crossing. It was raining. The children were crying . . . They made us get out of the car. "You will have to leave the car here," a Serbian soldier ordered.

"Why?"

"It isn't running properly."

"What do you mean it isn't running properly? The car is only two years old. There has been no gasoline available so I haven't gone more than 3,000 miles with it. Can't you see it's brand new?"

"Shut up. Proceed on foot."

I saw that Republika Srpska soldiers were taking other people's cars. A bus came from Kiseljak, a town held by the Croatian forces, and picked up all the civilians. When it started off for Kiseljak, some members of the Croatian Defense Council forces drew up a list of all the men on it who were fit for military service.

The women, children, and elderly men were let off the bus in town when we got to Kiseljak, but the men fit for military service were taken down to the police station where they held us for two hours. Then they loaded us on a truck. I didn't know where they were taking us until I found myself in a prison with barred windows. There were about thirty of us there. I heard that there was another prison nearby where there were another forty Croats. I couldn't sleep that night. No one beat us. I felt sick when I heard members of the Croatian Defense Council forces saying, "We're going to go beat up some Muslims, steal their blankets, and bring them back for you."

I didn't want a blanket. It was raining so hard that a quarter of the ceiling collapsed on us, but luckily no one was seriously hurt. I had my doctor's bag and there were bandages in it, so I bound up those who had been injured. Some of the people there had taught me in high school, there were workers there, too, businessmen, engineers. I didn't see a single medical doctor. I kept silent because I didn't feel like talking. About noon, I said, "I can't stand this any more. I have to go outside."

I started to pound and kick the door and bars. A young member of the Croatian Defense Council forces appeared.

"What do you want?" he snarled at me angrily.

"I have to go to the bathroom."

"Shit and piss in your pants," he spat at me scornfully.

"You should be ashamed! Have you no respect for your elders? I am at least ten years older than you. I am a doctor. There are people here suffering from prostate problems and who must go to the bathroom every half hour. And you are not letting them," I shouted, furious.

After a few minutes another man appeared at the door in uniform.

"I am the warden of the jail."

"I am Ante Jelić," I responded, looking straight at him.

"The doctor?"

"Yes," I answered tersely.

"What are you doing in prison?" he asked me, amazed.

"I was wondering that myself," I answered bitterly.

"Would you rather leave?"

"You ask! And these people would like to leave, too."

"They will have to stay awhile."

"Then I'm not leaving either," I answered, feeling my face burn. "Look, you must see to their basic needs," I went on, with more restraint.

"OK, they can use the facilities," the warden mumbled, taken aback, and took me to his office. I sat down and lit a cigarette.

"Sir, I have never felt more humiliated and more miserable. I am sitting in prison and I have done nothing wrong."

"Doctor, these are the Kiseljak barracks. There is a field hospital here. Would you work with us?"

"I don't know where the field hospital is."

"If you agree, I'll take you there," he offered his help.

I saw a colleague of mine, Dr. Dodik, there, a man I'd worked with in Vareš.

"Where have you been? Your wife was here a little while ago with your brother-in-law. They were looking for you. They have no idea where you'd disappeared to. They went off to see your sister."

My sister had moved to Kiseljak three years before the war and had found a job here. I knew her phone number so I called her from the field hospital and told her where I was.

"We'll be right there to get you," she answered, elated.

"Why don't you stay here and work. We don't have enough doctors," my colleagues from the field hospital asked me.

"I can't work yet. Right now I'm simply not able. I have to go to my sister's to eat something, take a shower, get some rest."

"Will you come back tomorrow?"

"I'll come back tomorrow."

My family had found accommodation in Kiseljak with an elderly woman. The woman put my daughters and wife up in the larger of her two rooms, and she slept with my mother-in-law in the smaller one. After my times on duty I would sleep in the room with my wife and daughters. We were miserable. After thirteen years of marriage, all that we had built together was gone. We were living off the mercy of others. All sorts of thoughts raced through my head. On 10 November the local authorities informed me, "Tomorrow you must go back to the village of Daštansko to defend Vareš with the Croatian Defense Council forces."

"What will I do there?"

"We know what you'll do," they answered in surly tones.

The next day it was Serbian soldiers who escorted us in their transport vehicles to the line of separation. When we reached our final destination I experienced, as did many others, all sorts of humiliation from the Croats who had stayed in Daštansko.

"Traitors! Why did you leave? You were too cowardly to defend your town with us," they taunted.

They immediately took me to a makeshift medical center at the barracks where there were people who had been slightly wounded, whom I treated. We stayed in an old building without running water or facilities. The center had been set up in an unfinished building. There was straw on the floor and stretchers on which twenty to thirty patients and casualties were lying. I didn't know what all this shooting and murdering could possibly be for. I often thought that I'd be happiest if a bullet hit me and killed me instantly. Then I'd start to think of my daughters and my wife. I was mired in all the hopelessness. I escaped into the work I'd been trained to do.

While I was escorting the wounded to a hospital in Serbian territory, in Blažuj, I managed to stop in and see my family while on the road from Ilidža to Kiseljak. After a short visit in Kiseljak we would go back again through the territory of Republika Srpska. I hate the divisions—the new borders within Bosnia and Herzegovina. The unity in diversity in Bosnia lent it its true beauty for centuries. Suddenly they were all working on each making his own little fenced-in pen where he'd hold his sheep. I was sickened by the big shepherds with their sheep . . .

Around Christmas I organized a chess tournament. I wanted us to mingle and forget about the war for a few minutes.

New Year's came. There wasn't a lot to do with the wounded, so the staff of the medical center sat and chatted with the military police. We each had a glass of some brandy someone had brought. Around nine o'clock a soldier of the Croatian Defense Council forces came in who had been slightly wounded in some earlier fighting.

"I want to go to Kiseljak to be with my family," he hissed, drunk.

My colleague who was in charge of releases and sick leave for wounded fighters said, "There is no need for you to go to Kiseljak. We can change your dressings here. You are not that badly hurt."

"You haven't seen the last of me! I am going to bring a hand grenade right in here and put it on your table!"

He quickly came back and did as he'd said.

"Don't do it," they ordered him.

The soldier took the grenade, yanked out the ring and put it back on the table. There were a dozen of us in the room at the time. Everyone fled through the two doors. I didn't even know what a grenade was. I sat there, bewildered, only six feet from it. I tried to put my hands up to shield myself when it exploded. I felt a light blow to my left arm above the elbow. Not everyone managed to get out. Four of us were still in the room.

"We've been hurt," my colleague moaned.

There was blood everywhere. We went down to the makeshift emergency ward for first aid. I felt something warm oozing down my leg. I didn't feel too well. I took down my pants and saw I'd been hit. They cleaned my wound and then I could see it wasn't serious.

"You will have to go to the Blažuj hospital," my colleague Dodik told me.

"There are probably people who are hurt worse. Take them first," I said through clenched teeth.

"Don't be ridiculous. You must go, too."

At the Serbian border crossing I saw Leka, whom I'd known from Vareš.

"Doctor, what's wrong? Why are you wounded? Who shot you?" I dismissed this with a shrug, which was supposed to mean that he was asking too many questions.

"Lift the cross bar! A wounded doctor coming through!" shouted Leka to his fellow fighters.

I said to the driver, "There is a God! We couldn't be with our families for Christmas or New Year's, but now we'll see them after all."

"What do you mean, Doctor? We are headed for the Blažuj hospital. We can't go to Kiseljak now."

"My injuries are not very serious. There is no point in me staying in the hospital. If I manage to get released from Blažuj we can go to Kiseljak and see our families."

My colleague, Dubravka, was on duty in Blažuj. Her husband, an excellent orthopedist, had operated on me in 1985 when I had had a fracture of the left thigh. She recognized me and asked, "What's wrong?"

"A grenade."

Once she'd examined the injury, she said, "Colleague, you can go back. You were lucky. It isn't bad."

"I would like to go to Kiseljak to visit my wife and kids," I said.

"Sure. With an injury like this there is no reason not to."

"I'll need written permission so that my driver and I can pass."

"You will get your permission."

That was when my wife and I agreed, though we had received letters of guarantee from family and friends from Croatia and Germany, that we wouldn't move away. Instead we wanted go back to Vareš as soon as the opportunity arose. After twenty days or so I had to go back to Daštansko. We agreed we would split our on-duty time between there and Kiseljak.

I spent April and May 1994 in Kiseljak. In late May a military policeman named Kockica came to get me.

"You must go back to Daštansko. There are no doctors up there," he told me.

"Can you take me back to my apartment in Vareš along the way? I saw it last six months ago."

"Sure I can, but don't stay long. You know how things are there."

I couldn't get into the apartment because the door was locked. I told the driver I had to see my friends, a Muslim family, the Karamehićes. It was their daughter's birthday that day.

The driver was pleased. "That's fine, Doctor. True friends stay friends. Call me whenever you need a hand. I'll always help you as much as I can."

I went to see our friends Selima and her husband Satko. Satko, was the first to catch sight of me. He ran out and hugged me. We shook with sobs. We couldn't say a word for the first fifteen minutes. Satko was the first to speak.

"Dear Ante. How are the children? How is your wife?"

"They are great, Satko."

"Why don't you bring them here to stay with us in Vareš. Whatever we have to eat, they can share. What we have they will have."

"I'll go to Kiseljak and get them as soon as I'm able and I'll bring them to Vareš. If I can't bring them to our apartment, I'll bring them to you. Since I'm still obliged to serve in the army I must go on with the Croatian Defense Council forces."

That same day I told my colleagues at the medical center of my meeting with my old friend.

"He is only pretending. Don't believe him," they commented, because Selima and Satko were Muslims.

"The man is not pretending," I said with certainty.

"You mean to say you would really entrust your family to him?"

"You know I would. With joy."

I went to the commander and asked him, "Could I take a car, when I have a free moment, to Kiseljak one evening to pick up my wife and children? I want to take them back to Vareš."

"If I were to tell you you couldn't, you'd ignore me anyway. Go ahead. If anyone asks, I don't know anything about it."

Up on Perun I was a member of a Croatian team involved in exhuming and identifying corpses of Croatian Defense Council fighters who had been killed in clashes with the Army of Bosnia and Herzegovina. I met Muslim friends there from Vareš who had stayed in town. We walked back to town. They were the parents of kids I'd treated, the most healthy population, school-aged children.

"Doctor, may I kiss you?"

"You may. And let me kiss you, too."

I was given a car on 4 June and, thanks to my driver, without a hitch I brought my family to Vareš. When I got back to work, I ran into the disapproval and rejection of my colleagues. One of them asked me, "Why did you take your wife and children back to Vareš? You should not have done that until all the other Croats came back, too."

"We will never see the day that all the Croats come back. If we wait that long, no one will ever go back. My family is happy. They are staying with friends," I said, victoriously.

The next few days they wouldn't let me visit my family.

In mid-July 1994 I managed to get down into Vareš, but I was given an escort from the Army of Bosnia and Herzegovina: an armed policeman who was constantly by my side.

When the director of the local polyclinic saw me, he came over, hugged me, and said, "Ante, I need you like never before here. There is no one who can work with children. You must come back and work here."

He immediately called the mayor and announced joyously who was there to visit.

"What is he doing here? How did he get into town?" asked the mayor.

"He is being escorted by one of our policemen."

"There is nothing for him here. He must leave at once. There is no work for him in Vareš," snapped the mayor.

When I heard of the mayor's reaction I asked the director, "Do you suppose he could order this policeman to arrest me?"

"Don't you worry about a thing. As long as you are in the polyclinic no one will dare do a thing to you. You can stay here as long as you like."

My meetings with my colleagues moved us to tears. Everyone was thrilled to see me but I still felt like a prisoner. I didn't know what would happen when I stepped outside. Would they take me to jail, or back to Daštansko? A military policeman at the doorway asked me, "Is there something wrong, Doctor?"

"Your colleague is escorting me everywhere and he says that I have to go back now."

"Kid, you are dismissed. I'll escort the doctor," he said to his younger colleague.

"They told me I had to stay by the doctor's side."

"You don't have anything to do with the doctor any more. I will take him from here," he ordered.

I used to bring him medicine from Caritas. He knew that my wife and children had found an old house in Vareš and had moved in there.

"I'll take you to see your family. No one need know where you are."

While I was walking through Vareš, I felt uncomfortable because friends were stopping me and asking, "What's wrong, Doctor? Do you have to go back over into Croatian territory?"

"Yes, I do."

"They are taking you?"

"That's right."

In front of the house he stopped, looked left and right, and said, "There's no one around. Go in. But don't stand around outside. That way you'll avoid any trouble."

When I finally did decide to move back to Vareš, the president of the Croatian Defense Council municipal organization came to me and said, "You can't go back."

"Oh, I'm going. I am not taking anything of yours from here with me. I will take only what I have in my head and my stethoscope, blood pressure cuff, and fax machine. You can't stop me."

"You must stay with us. When all the other Croats go back, then you'll go back, too. Vareš is being run by the Muslims. It has nothing to offer you now."

I did go back, despite his words, to the town where they told me that the politics had changed and that I wouldn't be able to work.

Thanks to the help of Serbian, Croatian, and Muslim friends, I started working at the polyclinic on 9 June 1997. I am the only Croat there, but I have no problems. My patients still trust me.

UNCLE MARKO

TOLD BY NURA MEHMEDBEGOVIĆ

Sarajevo

October 1998

I used to call Professor Ciglar Uncle Marko. For awhile my nickname for him was "japek," which means "father" in the Zagorje dialect of Croatian, but the word sounded so odd that I kept having to explain it to everyone.

My father gave me life, but the man who brought me back from clinical death three times, saved my life with his own breath, and revived me from unconsciousness eighty times, and, furthermore, a Croat from the Zagorje region, who helped me, a Muslim woman, has really been more than a father to me.

Both of us lived in the Grbavica neighborhood of Sarajevo. We knew each other and socialized from time to time.

Just before the war broke out I had to undergo an operation on my head. The nature of my illness made me dependent daily on shots without which I couldn't have lived.

It happened that at the beginning of the war I was staying completely alone in my apartment. My husband had been working abroad and couldn't

get back, and my daughter and son-in-law were working as interns in
*Travnik.

On 6 April 1992 a tank appeared in front of my building. I didn't dare
leave the apartment alone. Everyday I was succumbing to stress: the neighbors would find me unconscious on the stairs, and whenever I came to I
would be at Uncle Marko's.

In the autumn of the first year of the war it was clear that even under
the best of circumstances I would be evicted and end up on the street.

One day that autumn I set out to go and see Uncle Marko. I lost consciousness in front of his building and they carried me to his apartment.
He gave me a shot and left a neighbor looking after me while he went off to
intercede on my behalf, because I couldn't travel. He went from one Serbian
office to another pleading with them not to evict me. He asked this of the
president of the municipality, who told him openly, "My dear professor, I
loathe Muslims intensely. You were my professor. I got an 'A' from you
and I can't refuse you anything. She can stay on in your apartment but she
must not go out or be seen."

There was a night when I was doing very poorly and Uncle Marko said,
"You shouldn't sleep in your apartment any more. Sleep here at my place."

I was relieved, because I had a terrible fear of solitude. What with my reputation and my Muslim name, as well as my illness, I didn't believe I'd survive
the war. That day everything shook, the window glass and the glasses in the
cupboard all rang from shell blasts. The two of us made barricades of books
in the kitchen, we lined the pantry with books and also the balcony door.

I was on a special list of people to be murdered. They searched for me
for two months. Even though the mayor knew where I was, he mustn't have
told them because they didn't catch me, even though I was there all the time.
The hunt for people continued. There were even neighbors in the building
who were trying to find out where I was staying.

The people who were after me resented me because I came from the
venerable Muslim family who founded the town of Bijeljina many cen-

turies ago. They banged on my Serbian friend's door. "Is there anyone still alive from this family? We must find this Muslim woman and kill her immediately."

"I don't know where she is," she said tersely, but she was the only one who knew whose apartment I was staying in. After they left she came running over to tell me.

They asked Boro. He searched the building from one end to the other until he found me that evening. "My dear, they are out to murder you, and I can do nothing to help. Be careful!"

After that awful moment I collapsed into bed. Those were horrible days, nights, terrors. I would wake up screaming.

My guardian angel was always at my side, with so much warmth, humanity, and goodness. He never found it hard to take care of me. If I couldn't sleep, I would try to be as quiet as possible, hoping that maybe his hearing was poor. But he came to check on me at all times of day and night, lighting a candle to check and see if I was sleeping. He'd sit by my side and make us coffee over a candle flame.

I remember when I first experienced clinical death: I saw myself on the bed, I saw Uncle Marko with huge tears rolling down his wrinkled face. He gave me artificial respiration and massaged my heart. I looked down at him from above and called to him, "Uncle Marko, I'm fine, nothing hurts any more, I'm feeling great, don't be sad!"

When I came to, I saw him wet with tears and asked, "Why did you fight so hard and massage my heart?"

"How do you know? Oh, child, what matters is that you're alive."

I was alone in the apartment in 1994 when a space heater without a glass shield tipped over and burned my leg, which produced a phlegmona. He took a man aside from the neighborhood and told him, "Nura is in trouble. If we don't take her to Kasindol to the hospital, she is going to die today."

They made an incision on my leg at the hospital and I spent the next six months tied to an armchair. Uncle Marko changed my dressings daily.

At that point my body swelled up and there was danger I might choke. To save me from choking, he tied my head with a rubber strip to the back of the armchair.

He slept for years in the same room where I slept so that he could hear if I started to choke or stopped breathing. He didn't dare sleep lying down, but slept sitting so that he wouldn't fall too deeply asleep because he feared he wouldn't hear me gasping to breathe. More than once when I started out of sleep, I woke to see him over me, watching me.

We had no wood at that point. We baked bread at a friend's house in a little pan. Uncle Marko came to the apartment one day and said, "An elderly woman ran into me downstairs and told me that she has been taking her meals at a local food kitchen but she has had no bread to eat for three days. Do we have any bread to give her?"

I looked at our little pan. It was what we had to last for four days, but she hadn't tasted bread for three days. I saw his eyes and asked, "Can we give her this loaf?"

He took her the loaf of bread, a happy man.

Once the professor was walking along the street when he heard two women he didn't know talking among themselves. One of them complained, "You know, I haven't a crumb of salt to salt my dinner."

He walked back to her and asked, "Ma'am, is it true that you haven't any salt?"

"I don't."

"Wait here, please."

He went up to the apartment and took two pounds of salt and brought it to her.

During a blizzard he watched a woman from the neighborhood dragging branches to her apartment so she could warm herself. He went off to petition on her behalf so that when piped gas was introduced it would be installed in her apartment.

When an acquaintance of his told him that she knew of a woman with two small children who had nothing to eat, he pulled a whole sack of flour out and carried it down the stairs to give to a woman he didn't even know.

To be a Croat in Grbavica, which was a Serbian part of Sarajevo, and to do things the way he did, was more than brave.

Because of my terrible headaches I had to be given a brain scan so that they could see whether my tumor was returning or not. The authorities in Grbavica did not want to issue me a permit so that I could cross the *Miljacka River into downtown Sarajevo to have the scan done.

Uncle Marko went from one official to another and pleaded with them, until finally, thanks to the fact that he was a physical therapist who helped everyone who struggled with problems of rheumatism, which there was quite a lot of during the war, he managed to secure my permit.

The person who issued the permit asked him on the morning when I was scheduled to go, "Is she coming back?"

"Of course she'll come back," the professor answered.

"Who will guarantee for her?"

"I will."

"Sign here. And I should tell you that this is no formality. You are putting your life on the line for her return. If she doesn't come back at the agreed-on time, you will be shorter by a head."

"I consent," answered the professor.

"Are you on a work detail?"

"No, I'm not, I'm over eighty years old."

"Well, you look pretty chipper. You'd do just fine in a work detail," said the man harshly, wielding his power over human destiny.

I went over and had the scan done. Only then could I taste freedom. I spoke on the phone with my daughter for the first time in more than two years. No one in my family could believe that I was willing to go back to Grbavica. They all put pressure on me to stay. When I was getting ready to go back, after only two days of freedom, they all asked, "You aren't going back there, are you?"

"Of course I am," I answered them.

"What's drawing you back?"

"Maybe you don't know, but I know. You can't even begin to imagine where it is that I'm going. It's Dante's hell."

There was a spell of silence.

"Where do you think I'd be living, where would I sleep?"

"Where everybody else lives and sleeps," they answered.

"You go ahead and sleep where everybody else sleeps. I am going back to be with my Uncle Marko. He put his head on the chopping block for me, and now I'll do the same for him. Even if I were to know a thousand percent that death awaited me at the border, I would cross it gladly, entirely aware I was doing something the man deserves. A life for a life, and kindness for kindness. There can be no other way to live."

I was supposed to be back at a certain time. At the very edge of the bridge I lost consciousness. When I came to I was stricken with panic because there was no wheelchair on the other side. I shouted so loudly that *IFOR [the NATO-led international force] soldiers carried me across the bridge so that I wouldn't be late.

Uncle Marko was there waiting. I asked him, "Did you think, even for a minute, that I wouldn't be back?"

"No, I knew that you'd come back on your hands and knees if you had to."

He told me his life's story during the sleepless nights of the war. Before World War II he'd lived in *Zagreb, he was married, and he had a son named Marko. There was a proclamation that those who were able should take in a child from an orphanage that was run as part of a convent. He went right off with his wife and they found a little boy who had a distended belly and inflamed eyes. The nuns told him, "No one wants him because he is so sick. Since you are a doctor, maybe you will save his life."

When they brought the boy home, all that he knew was that the boy's name was Žarko. The boy got well, finished secondary school, and went on to study medicine. When he set out to search for his family he learned that he had two sisters and that his last name wasn't Žarković that they had called him because of his first name, but Čučković. He is married and has two children. He works in Zemun as a doctor and always keeps in touch with his Uncle Marko, whom he visited with his wife right before the war broke out. He sent me the medicine I had to have all through the war.

Uncle Marko is Žarko's father just as he is mine. He has the three of us now for his children: a Croatian man, a Serbian man, and a Muslim woman.

SARAJEVO TOGETHER

TOLD BY VELIMIR MILOŠEVIĆ, Poet

Sarajevo

October 1998

Sarajevo, a city that stays together. That is how it has always been since time immemorial, since these people have been living here. A city a child can hug when it spreads its arms. Sarajevo fits snugly in the palm of your hand. The hand swings and the grains scatter in handfuls, human handfuls. Scatter they did down the slopes of Trebević, Vratnik, Bjelava. Wherever the grains fell, houses sprouted, gardens flourished, and in them, the people, Sarajevans. Old-time Sarajevans. And the young people of Sarajevo wherever you look.

Sarajevo, a heart nestled in hills.

Everything is close at hand here. Each house leans against the next and the gardens bloom and spill over into each other. It is only a few steps from church to cathedral, cathedral to synagogue, synagogue to mosque. All that was precious in life was worked into this marvelous shared mosaic. That was the luxury and the wealth of the times we had. And so it was until the years of the war, this vile war which tainted everything.

"Bad, bad times are coming," people started saying, and they drew closer together. Sarajevo was fuller than it had ever been. Good was drawn to good while evil pummeled the city from all sides. All at once, the city, forcefully and fearfully, was battered and wounded from without, and ravaged and smashed from within. The good, noble people, the innocent souls, the honorable people of Sarajevo who remained in the city were shocked. They relied on one another. That was how it was at first. And that was how it mostly was, right through the war. People like that sought each other out through the troubled daily life and ordeals of the war. They sought each other out and lent one another a hand. They helped each other as much as they could. That was when Sarajevo began to look like a handful of goodness: like yet another handful scattering grains citywide, handfuls scattering grains of humanity, just as they did in the days when life was so beautiful.

How can I start to talk about the terrible devastation of goodness when, despite all the chilling, horrible attacks of evil and malice, there was so much goodness still in this city, enough for all of us? We cherished every single crumb of that goodness in order to survive, every scoop of flour, every single onion, every can of food, every cup of cooking oil in order to light a tiny ember in the choking darkness of the war. That is why there will be no words here about Evil—may its home be far from mine. The words here will be of goodness and good people.

It is those people I mean to talk about. Good people and good neighbors. Because it was neighbors who held Sarajevo together. They took care of one another through many hard times, and in these, the hardest of times. One neighbor kept another neighbor going, held him so he wouldn't stumble, fall, so fear wouldn't break him or darkness swallow him, so he'd make it through, so he'd outlive all the pain and the horrors, all the blindness, ugliness, and all the evil.

When the shells began blasting around us, we found ourselves in cellars. The cellars were mildewed, dank, dark, and cold. It was hardest for me to see the children.

"Mama, I don't want to go down there to the cellar," a child once said. Later those words became the title of a book.

"Stop this war, it's urgent!" shouted a boy.

That shout soon became a groan. It was painful and chilling for me to watch the children around me. They were helpless, I was powerless. One day I brought all my children's books down to the cellar, my picture books, pencils, watercolors, notebooks, coloring books, paper: let them read, let them draw, give them peace, let them forget the war if only for a few minutes.

"There you are, divide these up. Read, talk . . . Keep them, I don't need the books any more . . . Just be sure to share."

And share they did. You couldn't tell who was a Muslim, who was a Serb, or who was a Croat. They were a marvelous flock of children, a little childkind all their own. They were that way and they stayed that way all through the war. Only children can do that. Children ought to take us adults by the hand and guide us through life.

When they'd read the books, they started putting on plays, little performances, in the cellar. The grown-ups were delighted. There was still coffee then, so we drank it together, there was tobacco so we rolled cigarettes together and passed them around. Someone would bring down a little fried bread or a bite of something else. The grown-ups learned how to share from the children. The cellars became wondrous human empires. Goodness reigned. The bit of good from little people for the greater good of all of us.

During those days there was a taxi driver cruising around Sarajevo, the likes of which Sarajevo had never seen: Mile Plakalović, a magnificent humanist. The time of evil and hatred stirred such a vast and powerful goodness in him he'd never known he had. His taxi went where no one dared set foot. He transported the wounded, picked them right up off the sidewalk. He gave children chocolates, clothing, brought food to the elderly and the disabled. He never asked what someone's name was or who was who. He loved children and flew to meet them. His taxi, dented, riddled with bullet holes, looked heroic.

"Just put your head down, my poet, and we'll be on Dobrinja in no time flat," he'd say to me.

While everything around us was blasting. Smashing, whistling.

"Put your head down. If you only knew what all has thundered by this crazy head of mine."

And so it was that we brought children gifts, held poetry readings. I would feel happy, but only briefly.

"How do we get back, Plakalović my man? The shelling hasn't let up. It is worse up here than it is down where I live, in Mojmilo."

About neighborhood again, about neighborly spirit—and bread.

In the chilly spring of 1993, with no electricity, no running water, no firewood or heat, many people around the Alipašino Polje part of Sarajevo were coming out of their apartments and finding sheltered spots around the base of the high rises to light a fire and cook; if there was anything to put in the pot, that was shared, too. I used to run through these kitchen hideouts on my way to Mojmilo, and I'd hear voices, "Neighbor, neighbor, greetings . . ." Two or three women and children would beckon to me.

"Come and join us, there is enough for all of us . . . Greetings . . . You are one of us . . . The youngsters love you . . . And we oldsters love you, too." Out of the hot pan, just off the fire, they'd give me potato strudel. It was useless to turn them down. I had to take it, and the pastry warmed my hand all the way to Mojmilo—warmed my hand and my soul.

That was how I felt when I got a call from Rešo Arifhodžić, an actor.

"Come out in front of your apartment building. Our friend Sejo has some cans of food for you . . . He got a hold of them so he's sharing . . . There is enough for you and for me."

That was how good Sejo Arslanagić, the actor, a man who gave thousands of performances for children in bomb shelters and cellars, was sharing "survival" with the poet who went around with him to see the children in all those shelters.

That was what Nađa Mehmedbašić did, too. She was a fine journalist who dedicated all her time to children during the days of the war. It was as if she could always tell whether I had enough to eat. She'd be in touch from somewhere out there in the dark and fear, and bring a little something so I'd "get by." She, or her wonderful son Enko Mehmedbašić, the well-known writer and comedian. Amir Ferizović did the same. He had been known before the war as a bookseller, a bibliophile. He lost all he had in the war. During the war he sold cigarettes, tobacco, papers, lighters . . . And whatever he earned, he gave to children, poets, actors, journalists. "All of us are orphans," he used to say. "We are the Party of Orphans."

And those things made it better for us, easier to bear, we were brothers and we looked after each other.

There are countless examples. My memories take me far afield. I'll never finish my story. There is no end to the goodness or stories about it. There's no end, in other words, to Sarajevo and its people. And there were such good people in those saddest and ugliest of times. That gave hope to the city for it to pull through, to survive, to overcome the evil and pain. The "Party of Orphans" would win.

Whatever people had they brought out into the streets. The streets and sidewalks of Sarajevo became trading centers, markets, shopping centers. Food, belongings, clothes were bartered. And the prices! A pack of cigarettes was the unit of value. We traded whatever we had. It was such solidarity, such human understanding, a great human community never seen before. We were all the same, all equal, all one family: one destiny—the destiny of the luckless. That was how this city lived, breathed, held on; day by day stretched into—enduring.

I remember one thing that happened. Of the hundreds of stories like it, I'll tell this one. The outdoor "market" along Alipašina Street stretched along the sidewalks half a mile, all the way to Mojmilo. A person along the way could see and hear just about everything. For a few days I had been seeing a couple of younger people who were displaying for sale a small, new typewriter. They looked discouraged and troubled, sad and cold. They stood by the typewriter, it seemed, despairing that there would be anything they could trade it for. On the third day they turned to watch me, as if they were expecting something, or asking. I couldn't resist and I went over.

"Poet, this machine is for you . . . No one wants it, no one needs it . . . Maybe you need it." That was what they said, and something turned to ice inside me.

"We are in the same boat, my friends, I have nothing to pay for it with," I said, ashamed, humiliated, the way I was feeling then.

"Twelve pounds of flour," the woman stammered.

"Even ten will do," her husband added. But I held my silence, a deep and bitter silence. Not even a stutter. I couldn't leave without saying anything, so I said, "I could never give you ten pounds of flour for that fine typewriter . . . It would be a disgrace, a pittance, it would be inhuman."

They misunderstood what I meant, and said, "Look, give us whatever you've got. Our kids are starving."

Again, deaf and dumb, miserable and aching, I continued, "Up on Mojmilo I have about twenty pounds. I don't know how I got all the flour and I can't even remember where all I collected it. If I were to bring you all that flour, it still wouldn't be right, it wouldn't be decent. You wouldn't be happy and I wouldn't be the poorer for it. It isn't flour we live from. But if you want, I'll bring it."

They trembled, and I ran all the way to Mojmilo. I had squirreled away a pound of flour here and a pound of flour there. I measured one heap after another. I set aside four pounds for myself, and took them the rest. When I stood before them with the sack I must have looked to them like God himself. Lord, what a glow I saw in the eyes of those two people. I will never forget those eyes, those faces, the gratitude.

"Here's your flour . . . But this arrangement is good only until the war ends . . . And when this evil is done I will buy your typewriter properly . . . Then it, and we, will be worth more . . . All the best."

The two people came to life, breathed trembling, grew wings, and flew off to their kids.

There, those would be my little tales of Sarajevo and its neighborly spirit and breath, my minuscule, tiny memories amid the huge events which kept this city and these people alive in the unequal battle we fought against evil.

Sarajevo together, as it was, so it is now, and so it always was. That spirit of Sarajevo and the people of Sarajevo will never die. There, you see, it was worth living. Evil and evil people all around us, at every step of the way and on all sides. And only a handful of good people and goodness held this city together. So that what was left of life wasn't scattered to the winds.

It was worth living and finding, amid the hell, those paradise dwellings of people and goodness. You could find it in Sarajevo. Despite all the powerful bad and evil things that happened everywhere and on all sides, in some places more, in some places less, goodness happened here.

That is why I knew that I wouldn't lose myself and I wouldn't lose this city and some of the people in it. Before the war my wife Saida's mother, Behija, a wonderful person and a noble spirit, loved to say, loved to have it heard, "My son-in-law is Montenegrin." She was a Bosnian Muslim, and her son-in-law was Montenegrin. I remembered that when I was dodging bullets, running to see Saida's frail, elderly aunts, I would always have a little basket in my hand with a pound or two of rice, or a cup of sugar. And on my way back I'd be holding the basket again. Aunt Bisera or Aunt Hafa would have set aside something of her food, to help us get by. "Take care, son, this will pass," they would say, tears in their eyes.

While terrible things were being written about mixed marriages, I spent the three years of the war with my friend Iva Lukas in my dark apartment, with no electricity, no gas, heating, running water, food, with nothing. Whenever it was dangerous to spend the night there we hid and slept on the floor of Hajra, a teacher, a Muslim, whose only son had been murdered and her husband Ante, a Croat, had died just before the war. She felt the need and a deep desire to give me and Lukas a sense of security, to help us find peace and respite in her little apartment. There were countless cases like that in Sarajevo. You don't forget things like that. It will give birth to a new goodness, a new beauty, a new love, a new life. A new Sarajevo full of wonderful little and big neighborhoods and neighborly customs and relations. Without that life would not be life. We all know that.

Sarajevo, a heart nestled in the hills. When will you start to beat again the way you always did? For here everything could be held in the palm of your hand. A few steps from City Hall to the Old Serbian church. Three steps from the church to the Beg Mosque. From there, three steps to the cathedral, only a couple of feet. And from that place to the synagogue takes no more than a quiet little stroll along the banks of the River Miljacka. We walked around that map in those terrible days of the war, moved, walked, survived.

And on we must walk!

Sarajevo

A SARAJEVO MOSAIC

TOLD BY SERAFINA LUKIĆ

Sarajevo

October 1998

I lived with my daughter, Tatjana, and grandson on the twelfth floor of a high rise. When the Serbian army surrounded Sarajevo, Tatjana was immediately fired from her job because she was married to a Serb whose last name she carried.

Although I was a teacher of the Serbo-Croatian language and literatures, born in Sarajevo, the war found me completely unprepared: I had only enough food in my apartment to last for less than a week. At that point, even though I was a Croat, I had never heard of the Catholic charity organization Caritas.

Those were four horrible years of starvation in which I fought to keep my brother alive as well. He was disabled and lived alone in the *Marijin Dvor part of Sarajevo. My older daughter was also very ill. I tried to get ahold of enough food for her and my son-in-law. I went through a terrible time in the hungry, empty city, feeding the six of us who lived in three different parts of town.

When I was a young woman I'd been a mountain climber. My knowledge of plants was handy, at least at first, while there was still a little electricity. I'd make them all sorts of dishes using a little oil and the plants I'd foraged: yarrow, radicchio, and lamb's-quarter that grew by sandy places.

The building used to be inhabited by Serbs who moved away, and refugees moved in. They were given heating stoves as a form of *humanitarian aid when the electricity went out. They didn't give me a heating stove since I was an old-timer. Maybe it bothered them that people called me Sara.

I found a metal can on the street which I used for heating water on the terrace when I'd gather twigs under the trees. The smoke bothered my new Muslim neighbor, who came to the door, pointed a gun at me, and said, "If you light that fire again, I'll kill you!"

"Look, we have a little child here . . ." I tried to explain what he already knew.

"I told you, I'll kill you," he cut me off coldly and left. I didn't dare heat up that little bit of water to warm the two-year-old girl. During the winter the child came down with a serious case of pneumonia.

The first person to come to my aid was a Catholic nun I'd met on the street.

"Do you know whom I might turn to for a little food for my granddaughter? She is not even two yet, and she is hungry and sick," I asked her.

"Come with me, ma'am," she said kindly, and took me down to the Catholic church in Marijin Dvor and gave me some milk for the child and food, and later pills instead of food.

Enver Šehović, commander of an Army of Bosnia and Herzegovina unit, which had its headquarters near my building, must have seen me wandering around in the streets looking lost. He didn't know me but he said, "Come by headquarters this evening."

When I showed up he took me to the kitchen and told the staff, "From now on you will give this lady three portions of food every day."

For about a month and a half I received warm, cooked food in a pot, and three slices of bread. Although there were six of us, it sure meant a lot . . .

I watched the soldiers chopping wood out in front of headquarters. A young Muslim man noticed me poised to gather up the wood shavings. He came over and handed me the core of a stump.

"Go quickly with this so they don't catch you," he advised me softly.

Just around the corner I ran into a soldier. "Where did you get that stump? Did you steal it from headquarters?"

"Oh, no, son, I found it," I lied, to protect the young man.

In those worst, most difficult days I spied a potato on the street. I leaned over, unable to believe my eyes that someone could drop such a treasure, and took the potato that had been half run over by a cart. A man I didn't know was crossing the street and came over. He invited me, "Ma'am, you should come tomorrow at noon to the Jewish community center."

The stranger on the street introduced himself to me the next day. "I am Albert Abinun. They call me Cicko. I work in the kitchen. Wait, please, for us to serve dinner and then we'll see what I can do for you."

Every day at the end of their dinner, Cicko gave me everything that was left over. Overjoyed, I would trot around town carrying my family the cooked food. Nada Levi gave me milk for my granddaughter whenever there was any. Ela Kabiljo gave me clothes for the child. No one ever asked for my name at the Jewish Center. I believe that they never knew I was a Croat, because it made no difference to them at all.

Under the crossfire of snipers, while the bullets were whistling everywhere, I ran to bring my brother food in Marijin Dvor. I heard the squeal of brakes and saw a taxi had stopped in the middle of the intersection.

"Get in, or both of us will be killed! Where are you going? Are you in your right mind?!" the taxi driver asked me when I scampered into the car.

"I have two sick people to tend to in different parts of town, my brother and my daughter, and I have to bring them food," I explained.

Later I learned that the driver was Mile Plakalović, the famous Serb who transported people around Sarajevo throughout the *siege free-of-charge;

he picked up people who'd been hurt or murdered by shells or *snipers and took them to the hospital.

That man always drove me whenever he saw me, and he never asked me for my name. Sometimes he even took me to a bakery where he would pick up bread that he was taking somewhere. He always gave me a whole loaf of fresh bread!

I will never forget the fragrance of hot bread that warmed my cheeks while I hurried to take it to feed all the members of my family who were always waiting for me, famished.

WHATEVER HAPPENS TO YOU WILL HAPPEN TO ME

TOLD BY HAMDO FATIĆ

Vareš

November 1998

I was born forty-eight years ago in a village near Vareš. In 1974 I earned my degree at the Sarajevo University School of Forestry. For twenty-four years I worked in Vareš and that was where I was when the war broke out.

There was a terrible tragedy for Muslims on 23 October 1993 when Croatian troops known as the *Maturice, brought in from Kiseljak, committed a massacre in the village of Stupni Do. They murdered thirty-eight innocent people and destroyed the entire village. As a rule it is always someone from somewhere else who comes in and commits the foulest evil in order to achieve a certain goal. Part of the plan was to burden the Vareš Croats with a sense of collective responsibility and the fear of Muslim retaliation for the massacre. That way the Croats would be forced to move out of town. The Croatian forces needed them as manpower elsewhere and the Croatian leaders also knew they didn't have military forces strong enough to hold Vareš.

That morning my wife told me, frightened, that something strange was going on outside. Muslims were being led through the town with their hands in the air, they were being beaten with rifle butts, kicked, and hit.

We lived in an apartment building that numbered thirty-five apartments. Only three of the families there were Muslim. The rest were Croats, with three or four Serbian families, of which two had already fled earlier.

Our next-door neighbor, Zvonko, tried to leave the building. Since the Croatian Defense Council sentries stationed by our building could see he was a Croat from his ID card, they ordered him back to his apartment. They wouldn't let anyone move freely around town.

My wife went right to Zvonko and asked him to hide me in his apartment. Without a word he welcomed me and our neighbor, Osman. We hoped they wouldn't look for us in there.

Another neighbor learned we were hiding in the building and organized our own guard duty at the entranceway. They took a table out, chairs, and beverages. There were always a dozen or so neighbors there. Their idea was to keep thugs, whose only interest was looting, from getting into the building. Once they'd cleaned out what there was in the Muslim apartments, the thieves would turn to the apartments of the more prominent Serbs and Croats. All they cared about was money. The neighbors stuck together. By not telling anyone where we were hiding, they saved us.

A few minutes after I'd gone over to Zvonko's, three members of the Croatian Defense Council forces were already in my apartment. Later, my wife told me what happened. They took all the money she had. They held guns and knives at my children's throats. They wanted to cut my wife's finger off and her ear because she was so scared it took her a long time to get off her wedding ring and her earrings.

No one knocked at the door to the apartment where we were hiding so we spent four quiet days there. The second night we asked our host, "We heard that they are looking for the rest of the Muslims from town. They have lists. They are missing about 100 people. Thugs are now even going through Croatian apartments. If they find us here, do you realize what will happen to you?"

"Don't you worry about that. Whatever happens to you will happen to me. There is no one to mourn my passing. I am a bachelor."

Vareš had not been tainted by nationalism. We were one of the last communities to feel the horrors of war. We had all hoped the war would pass us by. There were a few extremists in the Croatian Defense Council forces who supported expansionist policies. They were the ones who mobilized all the men in town.

They took the third Muslim in the building to jail with his son.

Although he was disabled, our host was required to serve on guard duty somewhere, even though he was not an active member of the Croatian Defense Council forces. He was forty-five years old. In the evening he came home weary and told us that they had buried four people whom the Maturice had murdered: a grandmother who was ninety-two years old, two Albanian Muslims, and a fifty-year-old man. Our neighbor had participated in digging the graves.

On the fourth day Zvonko brought a Muslim to the apartment whom we knew the Croatian forces were searching for in Vareš. Osman and I were afraid they'd happen upon us when searching for him. There was an empty apartment next door to mine belonging to some Croats who had left Bosnia for the city of Rijeka in Croatia. A relative of the family's had the key and she let us in. We spent the next three days there. From there our Croatian friend Damir drove us to the *UNPROFOR [UN Protection Forces] headquarters that was located in Ponikve and which was taking in people who were fleeing. He drove our entire families there. We stayed four days at Ponikve.

Afterward they transported us in trucks through Vareš and across the Croatian Defense Council lines to Breza, which was in territory held by the Army of Bosnia and Herzegovina forces.

There were many Croats who took part in saving Muslims and getting them to UNPROFOR and the territories under the control of the Army of Bosnia and Herzegovina.

On 3 November the Croatian Defense Council forces retreated from Vareš. That night when the Croats made their exodus from here the electricity went out, and megaphones were blaring around town. There was horrible shooting. There were other ways, as well, to intimidate the local Croats and get them to leave.

I was president of the Red Cross, so with my colleagues from Breza I came into town to see what the situation was like and what I could do to help. When I came back to my apartment I found that none of the Croats had stayed in my building. They had gone with the Croatian Defense Council out of fear of reprisals.

Later Damir had to seek the protection of UNPROFOR when the Army of Bosnia and Herzegovina came in. Then I was able to help him.

I had problems with the Muslim authorities because of my help to Croats who were protected by UNPROFOR. I brought them food, clothing, blankets . . .

Zvonko went to the town of Daštansko where about 2,000 Croats stayed with the Croatian Defense Council forces. After three to four months they started coming back to Vareš. Someone else had already moved into his apartment.

SAFE IN A
MUSLIM'S APARTMENT

TOLD BY STANA ČANČAREVIĆ

A Refugee from *Zenica, interviewed in *Modriča

December 1995

I married a man in Zenica and lived there for a full twenty-five years. I was employed in the kitchen of a general hospital. I socialized with and worked with people from all three ethnic groups.

The Yugoslav People's Army pulled out of Zenica on 15 May 1992. Immediately after that the mujehadin came in. They were foreign Muslim soldiers who occupied all of Zenica. They looked scary, with long hair and beards. They wouldn't even let Muslim girls wear short skirts or go out with their heads uncovered.

On the first floor of the hospital where I worked was a ward for disorders of the eye. The mujahedin who were wounded and treated here used to bow and pray several times a day. I would get a chill every time I saw those scenes. We worked in shifts. When a wounded mujehadin came into the hospital he always would ask who was working in the kitchen. Whenever he heard that I was Serbian he'd refuse to eat the food from the kitchen. He requested canned food and nothing else.

In contrast to the disturbing and bizarre presence of the mujehadin in the city and at the hospital, I will always remember my colleagues, women, for the way they persisted in protecting me from our boss, who was a Muslim extremist. He was always goading and threatening me. Whenever that happened, at least two Muslim women would take my side and stand up for me.

Once, a colleague of mine who was from Croatia grabbed a knife and turned on me, screaming, "I will murder all Serbs and slit their throats!"

While I stood there, helpless, confused and terrified, a Muslim woman stepped between us and said, "Kill me first."

In the building where we lived our next-door neighbor was a Croatian woman who had been calming us for months, saying, "Nothing bad will happen to you. Don't leave town!"

In December 1992 another neighbor, a Muslim woman, was waiting for me at the door of my apartment when I came home and said, frightened, "Come into my apartment."

"What happened?" I asked once she'd shut the door.

"You must flee the town immediately. Army of Bosnia and Herzegovina forces are searching the buildings and taking all the Serbs to a camp!"

Scared, I asked, "What should I do? My husband won't be back from work until later this evening."

"You stay here in my apartment because no one will look for you here, and I'll bring the things from your apartment that you'll need."

She packed the things up I asked for and brought them over to her apartment, and took part of her things to our place so that no one would notice that something was missing. I was on pins and needles until that evening when my husband was coming home from work. They had kept him on his job because all the younger and more capable Serbs had been taken off to dig trenches.

My neighbor met my husband at the door to our apartment. She sneaked him into her apartment.

During the night she found a friend, a Muslim, whom we paid 600 German marks to take us out of town. On the road he drove us along we were stopped at five places by Muslims manning barricades. At every checkpoint they searched our bags.

They always asked the same question, "Where are you going?"

"We are going to see our daughter who is married in the next village. We are bringing her her things," I answered. The man who was driving us confirmed that this was true.

Six of the checkpoints were controlled by Croats near a Serbian village. They kept insisting we go back to Zenica but it turned out that Serbs were assembling here who wanted to cross over onto Republika Srpska territory. We learned that an exchange was being organized and would take place on this very spot.

After seven days of waiting the Serbian officials permitted a convoy of Croats to be exchanged for a convoy of Serbs, the largest until that time, which numbered 1,500 of us.

THESE ARE THE BALKANS

TOLD BY ILIJA ČOVIĆ
*Konjic

November 1998

My whole life has been tied to Konjic, a little town halfway between Sarajevo and Mostar, from my memories of childhood, to my youth, marriage, children, and employment in the same city. Since the early 1980s I have been working as a driver for the company Konjic-Trans.

I was thirty-five years old with a wife and six children when we went to war with the Serbian forces. Since it was written in my *wartime assignment that I am a truck driver, I spent the entire war behind the wheel, except in periods when I was interned in a camp. I would drive goods from the bolts and screws factory up to Germany, and would bring back humanitarian aid for this region.

I often drove food for the *Čelebići prison camp where Serbs were held who had been taken prisoner by the Muslims. All my Serbian colleagues were taken to the camp from their homes where they had actually been arrested rather than captured during military action. Their only fault was that they were Serbs. Since I found this unacceptable, while they unloaded my truck I would sneak them cigarettes, a bottle of cognac or brandy, salami, and bread so that the prison guards didn't see because I would have had problems if they'd caught me "abetting the enemy." But they were my friends and fellow workers with whom I'd worked for years and I'd never felt they were my enemies. Today I can sleep peacefully because I know that there is not a single Serb who was held in the Čelebići camp who can say that I was ever inhumane to anyone. If there was someone I couldn't help, at least I did him no harm.

I also drove flour to the *Silos Camp in Tarčin where Muslims were holding imprisoned Serbs. Once about thirty Serbs came over to unload the truck. I did not know any of them. Near to us there was a man selling packs of cigarettes for one German mark per pack. I pulled out thirty marks and bought the cigarettes from him. He didn't know who I was. When I gave each of the incarcerated men a pack of cigarettes, they were all of them elderly people, one of them began to cry. Their guard, at that moment, happened to be a decent man whom I knew by sight, so I dared to do it.

The man who'd sold me the cigarettes grumbled, "If I'd have known whom I was giving them to, I'd never have sold them to you."

"All that matters to you is that you got paid. Who I'll give them to is none of your business," I answered, horrified by the amount of evil and hatred there was in him. I went off and bought bread and salami and handed that out, too. I never knew how to hate people, even when I had plenty of reason to, later. At that point I didn't even dream that I, myself, would soon be in jail.

When a gallon of diesel fuel was 200 German marks here, I was the first to put a tank trailer on my truck and go off to Herzegovina. Four transport vehicles of the UNPROFOR Spanish battalion escorted me to Čapljina and back.

Two pounds of sugar was seventy German marks and coffee cost 150 marks. Later I went to bring back food with my colleague, Muhamed. Then a human life was worth less than a bottle of cognac. I would say good-bye to my wife and children, never knowing whether I'd be coming back alive.

A big sack of sugar cost 7,000 German marks and I could smuggle five of them back in the cabin of my truck on one run, without being noticed, but I never did because it would have been dishonorable to make money off of someone else's misfortune. I could have gotten rich, but I didn't.

I handed out flour to Serbian families because people were starving. My friend, a Muslim, always entered the sack as "torn" in the books even though he knew full well where it was headed. And that was during a time when Serbian forces were shelling us from the hills!

I didn't care about the money. All I cared about was that my family was alive and well. I taught my children that at all costs they must never show disrespect for people of other faiths. Before the war people here used to celebrate Catholic and Orthodox Christmas and the Muslim feast of Bairam. We visited each other for these holidays and respected each other.

Now I have nine children and we are expecting our tenth. The child's godfather will be Brother Ivo, the best monk in the world, who is loved by Croats, Serbs, and Muslims alike today in Konjic.

The house of my first neighbor, Rasim, is only fifty meters from mine. In June 1993 he shot at me from his balcony once when he was drunk. I was out in front of my house and it never occurred to me that he was trying to murder me until I saw the bullets flying all over the place. I hid behind my tow truck and I was lucky that he was drunk and his aim was bad and that he was firing from a military issue M-48 gun instead of an automatic weapon.

In late July 1993 Muslims who were my neighbors and colleagues took me in for what they said was going to be a conversation. I brought along a blanket just in case and it saved me, because in fact they were taking me to prison at the Musale sports hall because I was a Croat and for no other reason.

My wife was about to have a baby just then. The same neighbor, Rasim, who had tried to murder me, took her to the hospital. After a few days, on 2 August, she had a boy, our seventh child. Robert is the most introverted of all the children, and I often say that that is because he was born at a time when people hated, rather than loved, each other.

While I was at the camp I found my close friend Bora, a Serb, who had been there for months. He had been beaten so badly that he couldn't walk. Three of us had to take him to the bathroom. For five days there'd be no bread for us. They gave us rice in hot water, we slept on the bare concrete and some people were so exhausted they couldn't even move. Many succumbed to the physical maltreatment and hunger. A normal person cannot even begin to imagine such abuse. When representatives of the International Red Cross came, the camp authorities hid some of us so that I still don't have a document proving I was held at the camp at all, though I have at least 500 witnesses who were there with me. The camp authorities hid the people who had been abused the most severely, the ones they singed with red-hot pokers, to conceal the traces of their crimes. There were brave people, however, like Dragutin, who told the Red Cross committee the names of the people who were alive, but hidden. Who knows whether they would have survived had they not been registered then. Because of that Dragutin paid the price for his courage with gruesome beatings as soon as the committee left.

I spent only a month at the camp. During that time I lost twenty-five pounds. With all the hunger, our wives used any avenue they could find to send us food through Muslim acquaintances, sometimes lard and chitlings only because they believed the Muslim guards wouldn't eat them because they were *pork. But the fight for survival was stronger than religion. Those guards who had a soul brought us the packages and we'd share our food with them, but the ones who had no soul took our packages home. They never maltreated me.

Neighbors who had influence intervened with the authorities at the camp to release me because I had never served in Croatian forces, and, on the other hand, I had six children at home and a wife who had just borne our seventh.

My boss had no idea I'd been taken prisoner. When he heard, he came to the camp and asked me, horrified, "Why are you here?"

"What kind of a question is that? It looks as if this is a time when it's more normal for me to be in a camp than at home," I replied. He called in all his favors and had me released. Otherwise I would have stayed there for at least another half year, which was the average stay for those who survived.

There was no food in the house when I got home. Whatever had been there while I was incarcerated had been stolen. People I knew had searched my house seven times.

Muhamed secretly supplied my family with food and looked after them. At that point a 200-pound bag of livestock feed cost 1,500 German marks. He didn't come out to the camp but my oldest daughter, who was twelve years old, spent all day standing by the camp fence clutching food for me, in hopes that someone would take mercy on her and let her give it to me.

After I got out of the camp I was stubborn and stayed on living here. Croats during the war criticized me for helping Muslims. Afterward it was Muslims who imprisoned me in the camp. I still feel overt discrimination at work only because I am a Croat. Here maltreatment is a way of life. After the war ended in 1996 they threw three bombs into my yard, and luckily killed only two sows.

Most people during the war had nothing to eat, just as I didn't, regardless of their faith. At such times it meant a lot to me when one of the Muslims greeted me on the street and stopped to ask how I was doing. It hurt me when people I'd known well before turned their heads from me or called me an Ustasha, people I used to think of as friends.

Serbs from my area suffered terribly at the hands of Muslims. A friend of ours, Spomenka, survived this torment with her husband and made it to Konjic. When it was *Serbian Orthodox Christmas, regardless of how little we had, we did what we could to scrape something together and mark the holiday to cheer her up.

Once I used my last five gallons of diesel fuel, worth at that point 1,000 German marks, to transport hay for a cow belonging to a friend of mine, a Muslim, which otherwise would have starved. Although it would have been cheaper to buy a new cow, it was a way for all of us to get milk.

When they searched my house looking for weapons I didn't have, angry when they hadn't found anything, they took my cross off the wall, threw it on the floor and stamped on it. They may have stamped on the cross but they could not crush my faith. Seven times they searched my house like that.

I was disgusted by the people who carted stolen goods from the homes of other people and I always wondered what it meant to them, when they could never know when they went to bed whether they would wake up alive. I often prayed to God to let me die, for a shell to fall and put an end to my pain, so that I wouldn't have to watch all that.

I began to think I should keep a diary, but I was scared of what would happen if they found it.

I'm not sorry, today, for what I experienced. If I'd been living abroad at that time I never would have believed that any of it could happen, that there was so much evil. Then again, if all people were evil, even the sun wouldn't warm us with its rays.

When I drove in a convoy that crossed to Sarajevo for the first time through Serbian territory, we were told that we would be covered by world television stations because it was the first passage by a convoy. Intentionally I stayed behind, knowing I'd certainly see someone I knew. And so it was: at the first checkpoint held by Serbian soldiers I saw a good friend of mine and jumped out of my truck to say hello.

He was standing in a group, so I said, "God help us, heroes," and handed him a bottle of Stock brandy. Good cheer erupted on all sides and while I hugged and kissed my buddy, an astonished man of color from UNPROFOR who had been sitting with me in the truck and guarding me with his gun, said, "I don't understand any of this. We are separating them and they are kissing."

"This is a brother of mine, a Serb. You don't get it, do you? These are the Balkans."

We know the Muslim faith frowns on the consumption of alcohol. So when we arrived in Sarajevo and a colleague of mine took a swig of something to quell his fears and stepped out of his truck holding the bottle, I told him, "Shame on you. You know it isn't polite for us to drink here."

Just then I caught sight of a Muslim I knew. The man was tipsy. He exclaimed, "Oh, come on! Whatever gave you the idea that drinking is frowned on here. Hand me that bottle!"

When he'd had a sip, he said, "Cheers, brothers!"

THE FIRST PACKAGES

TOLD BY HAŠIM BAJIČ

Sarajevo

October 1998

I worked as a taxi driver before the war in Sarajevo and supported my wife and two children. My younger son was nine months old, and the older one was seven when the war began. My family and I are Muslims.

I was thirty-eight during the first year of the war, when my right leg went numb, and I had to be operated on twice. Between the operations I suffered a stroke. After the second operation I was in much worse shape. Since then I've had difficulty speaking and barely can walk on crutches.

While I was in the hospital, every day I'd watch another taxi driver tirelessly bringing the wounded to the hospital. I learned that his name was Mile Plakalović.

When a colleague of mine, Raja, came to visit me at the hospital, I told him, "I'd like to meet Mile. I want to shake the hand of the man and tell him how much I admire him."

Mile kept bringing in the wounded, but he didn't come up to my room. I left the hospital having lost any hope that I would see him again.

The front line in the Sarajevo neighborhood of Zlatište ran 350 feet from our house, which was on the Muslim side of the border. My wife would go

111

with our older boy to gather branches in the woods so that we would have something for heat. Our border guards often stopped her and she'd have to throw all the bits of wood onto the ground in order to put her hands in the air. She'd come home with our son, her eyes full of tears.

"Won't they even let us get firewood? Is that a sin?" the two of them would ask me, and I didn't know what to say.

When she learned that they were giving out milk at the mosque, my wife sent our son to wait in line. The boy came home in tears.

"The mullah won't give me any! He says we have no right to milk, even if my little brother is only a year old, because I never come to the mosque."

There were days when my children had nothing to eat.

It was all we could do to survive until 1995 when the Catholic charity Caritas began to give out powdered milk without asking you what your faith was; all they asked for was a child's birth certificate. My children, Muslims, got milk from Caritas, a Catholic charity, but not from the mosque!

This was a time when parents and brothers most often weren't able to help their nearest and dearest. In 1993 I was bedridden and we had no income. That was when the scarcities and the hunger were the worst. Nettle soup was a luxury we set aside for the children.

One of those starving, freezing January days in 1993, Mile Plakalović appeared at our door. He was holding a package full of food.

"Good day, good people," he said simply, and put the package on the table.

My wife burst into tears.

"Hašim, I heard that you asked to see me while you were still in the hospital. Don't hold it against me that I didn't have the time then. There were a lot of wounded citizens who needed my help."

From the package he brought us it was clear that he knew his former colleague, now an invalid, was in very bad shape. I don't know whether he realizes that without his help we probably would not have survived the war. We had nothing in the house when Mile walked in with that package full of sugar, oil, flour, cigarettes, coffee, and treats for the children. From his first visit I felt that I was not forgotten and alone. He came often and brought us whatever he could. Aside from food and clothing, he brought sweets, which delighted the two little boys.

And Mile brought us wood.

He came at New Year's with a friend and brought the boys gifts. These were the first gifts they had ever received. In them were sweets and children's clothing. All that winter they were dressed from head to toe.

Mile's photograph stands even today, three years after the war, on our table. His visits are a holiday for all of us.

WE STAGED OUR OWN KIDNAPPING

TOLD BY LJUBICA VIDOVIĆ

Refugee from Sarajevo, interviewed in Banja Luka

December 1995

Just before the war broke out I was living with my husband in Sarajevo, where we had both retired. Before retirement I worked at the electricity distribution company and my husband worked in the police. We, both of us Serbs, had an apartment in a building where Croats and Muslims lived. Our friends and colleagues from work belonged to all three faiths. My sister, with our eighty-year-old mother, lived in another part of town.

No one believed that the war could come to Sarajevo. When the war did, nonetheless, begin and when the city was divided, our apartment ended up in what became Muslim territory. Before the Serbs lost their phone lines, my former directors and a colleague of mine from the office, all of them Muslims, used to call regularly and offer me help.

A friend of mine from school days, Majda, a Muslim, too, visited us daily.

During the first year, real wartime chaos and anarchy reigned in the city. Different gangs, most of them Muslim, terrorized the city by robbing, maltreating, and often enough murdering Serbs.

A man named Boško lived upstairs from us. He was a Serb and had been the director of the Bosna auto company. One night we heard a group of men breaking into his apartment. They beat him up brutally and said they'd throw him out the window from the seventh floor. They took him to jail that night. Without knocking, a group of young men barged into our place and started searching. Two of them went to the kitchen where my husband was and one of them struck him. I ran in just as the man was getting ready to hit him again, but another man prevented him. Surprised, the thug looked at his colleague, who told him, calmly, "Stop! No one will hit this man while I am here."

My husband and I were scared and surprised, and the startled thug quickly heard why his friend had stopped him. "When I was sixteen years old I was locked up for stealing. They were roughing me over until this man came in. He wouldn't let them hit me and was decent to me."

Then he turned to my husband and said, "You are a good man. I promise that none of our guys will bother you. We came over because of a report from a neighbor of yours. She told us you were going out onto your balcony at night and sending flashes of light to signal to soldiers in the Serbian army to show where they should shell. We aren't going to be in this part of town all the time, so you can't count on us to help you, but I urge you to find a prominent person to protect you because it could happen that someone shows up and murders you."

They left politely.

We were afraid because we didn't know who to turn to, since Majda had been taken in for questioning for her help to us.

Sadik and his wife Kira, a Muslim couple, lived on the fourth floor in our building. We knew them by sight, but I decided to turn to them for help. When they saw me at the door, they invited me in. I started to cry, and Kira said, "Don't you worry."

Sadik continued, "We outnumber the extremists. We will get through this. The two of us will help you any time you need help, but you must make sure no one else finds out."

Once I'd calmed down, thanks to how understanding they were, Sadik suggested, "Tie some string to a can. If you feel you are in danger during the night, lower the can to our window. That way you'll be signaling to us and we'll call the police immediately. They will protect you."

At that point the UNPROFOR troops had arrived in Sarajevo and the official police forces really were protecting those Serbs who could reach them for help. After that night we began sleeping more soundly. Members of *Juka's gang came into our apartment twice more. They barged in one night when my husband and I had already gone to bed. We heard the footsteps and men's voices in the living room and both of us ran out of the bedroom. I saw three men wearing uniforms and carrying weapons. One of them wore a cross on his chest, which gave me reason to hope that he was one of the Croatian Defense Council men. They never did Serbs any harm, at least no one I knew. That man signaled to me that I should follow the other man, who was walking into our bedroom. I caught him laying rounds of ammunition on our bed just as I entered the room. I shouted, "Take back your ammunition!"

Since he hadn't been able to plant the rounds of ammunition on us, they searched the place from top to bottom. When they were leaving they explained that someone had reported us for keeping weapons in the apartment.

In the summer of 1993 they kept trying to get my husband out digging trenches. Sadik protected him, and even had him distributing humanitarian aid. He saved two more Serbs the same way.

I ran into a colleague of my husband's, a Muslim who was working for the police. "Come right down and use our phone to call your mother while I am on duty," he said.

One day, after a phone conversation, just as I was leaving the police station, a car hit me on the street. The driver wanted to take me to the hospital but I was scared of him. Semiconscious, I kept repeating that I wanted to go home.

Two days after the accident I was feeling awful. My sister took me to the hospital. I recognized one of the doctors there, a Muslim who had treated me earlier. While making his rounds he told me, "You had a concussion. You are in pretty bad shape, but you aren't safe here at the hospital because you are a Serb. I think it would be best if you went home."

"What should I be doing while I'm home?"

"For the next three months you should rest, because there could be serious complications."

After two and a half months of bed rest at home, a friend of ours came with terrible news. "A shell has fallen on your sister's house. She is wounded and your mother has lost both her legs."

"Is my mother alive?"

"Yes, thanks to a neighbor, a Muslim, who carried her to the hospital, as badly hurt as she was, in his arms."

The doctor who operated on her came over to me in the orthopedics ward.

"Your mother is recuperating well. She will be going home, much improved."

The head doctor on the ward, also a Muslim, said, to comfort me, "In six months your mother will be walking again, using artificial limbs and crutches."

Thanks to such careful treatment, my mother left the hospital after a month. Although she was eighty-three years old, her wounds completely healed. Several months later she was walking, just as the doctor had said.

Because of the degree of my mother's disability, the two of us sisters were given permission by the Sarajevo authorities to move from the city. They did not give my husband permission, however, and I couldn't leave him behind. One day he came back from the police station, delighted.

"A fellow I used to work with will issue me the permission I need to go to Visoko."

"What will you do there? Visoko is in Muslim territory," I said.

"They explained that the only way for me to get out of here is for Serbian fighters to kidnap me off the bus in Čekrčići."

"In that case, Mother and I will go with you."

"They told me that if the kidnapping doesn't work I'm likely to be murdered."

We agreed on getting out this way, no matter how dangerous it was. Kira and Sadik saw us off, crying. A friend of my sister's, a Croatian woman, was at the station to say good-bye. She gave me 700 German marks when we parted.

In Čekrčići it took two hours of convincing between the Serbian fighters and the UNPROFOR soldiers, who wouldn't let us off the bus. Finally they let us go, as long as we signed a statement that we had gone with the men of our own volition.

AN OLD HAND AT THE UNDERGROUND

TOLD BY ANICA ZEČAR

Sarajevo

October 1998

I lived in Grbavica for more than forty years. My husband and children were frightened at the first shots. In vain I tried to explain, "A bullet you can hear isn't going to hit you. It's the one you don't hear that gets you."

The best idea was for everyone to go up into Serbia, to a town on the Romanian border, those first days, while it was still possible. I told them when they left, "You go right ahead and don't worry about me. I was in the *Partisans and an underground fighter and I did fine. I am not afraid of anyone."

I stayed alone and I wasn't afraid. I always made sure I was clean and nicely dressed. That way the neighbors wouldn't have to fuss too much if someone murdered me.

There was no one on the first four floors except me; all the rest had moved away. Above me lived a mixed couple. She was a Croat and her husband was a Serb.

Grbavica was under the control of Republika Srpska. I was the one to communicate with the soldiers who patrolled the area, because there wasn't

119

anyone else around. I never gave my last name. I was Anica to everyone. There were five neighbors who had stayed in the building and were in hiding—a Muslim, a Croat, a *Kosovar, and two Serbs—and I told everyone else they had fled. I gave Huso the Serbian name of Radovan, I gave the Kosovar another Serbian name: Ilija. Whenever soldiers buzzed me from the front stoop so that I'd open the entranceway door for them, I'd call out, "Radovan, could you take that pot off the stove so our dinner doesn't boil over?"

That way the men would know to hide in the elevator shaft. I saved them all. None of them was hurt.

Once three soldiers were looking for a doctor who lived on the seventh floor. The doctor's father was a Serb and she'd managed to get her husband, a Muslim, out. When I saw the three soldiers I said, loudly so that the men I'd hidden would hear and keep quiet, "Boys, the doctor lives on the seventh floor, in case you'd forgotten!"

I found someone to draw up Huso's papers with a Serbian name, and with them he made it to Serbia. I even managed to look after his apartment even though they kept coming and asking me, "Are there any Muslims and Croats here?"

"No," I told them, although I am a Croat.

"Whose empty apartments are these?" they questioned me.

"Brothers of yours who moved away," I answered, though the apartments had belonged to Muslims. In Grbavica, up until the last days of the war, the thugs who came around were mainly looting apartments rather than *squatting in them.

When they searched my apartment, Ismet was lying in my living room wrapped in a blanket between the bed and the wall. They didn't find him.

Once they opened the hood of my car and were poking around in the motor. I called down from the balcony, "What are you looking for, boys?"

"The rotor." That was the name of the part I had removed from the motor so that it couldn't be started. Then they asked me about Huso's car. "Whose car is this?" I answered, "That is Mr. Radovan's car."

"Where is he?"

"I'm not his commander that I know his whereabouts."

"How old is this Radovan?"

"I don't work at the Registrar's office. I've got no files on anyone. How should I know how old he is?"

They laughed and gave up. That was how I protected my neighbors and their property.

The next time they came with a tank. There were fifteen cars parked in front of the building, one of them mine, green, the pro-Muslim color. They asked me, "Old lady, whose car is this?"

"Mine," I answered.

"Nice color," said the soldiers and crushed all the cars but mine. That car survived the war.

I have Parkinson's disease, so I was paralyzed for a year and a half until a neighbor of mine, a pharmacist, brought me Artan. Thanks to the medicine I was able to move again after taking it for a month.

When all my window glass was broken, a neighbor of mine, a Serbian woman, went to the American embassy and got them to reglaze the window for me.

Two Serbs sent me food whenever they could. My Croatian neighbor, Josip, received all the packages meant for me and brought them.

Ismet was the one who helped the most. He has a wonderful wife. For two years we had no electricity or heat. Ismet found a stove and all of us on the seventh floor used it. Sick as I was, I couldn't carry anything, so poor Ismet carried hundreds of cooking pots up and down. They baked bread there and he was always bringing me some. He moved out of Grbavica thanks to a neighbor who paid the Serbs who helped him get away with automobile tires and a kilim rug. All the neighbors helped each other.

Ismet has gone on helping me in many ways. As soon as *reintegration went into effect, he came back and immediately saw to it that I got a phone line.

When the doctor's mother was murdered by a sniper while she was hanging out her wash on the balcony, the doctor moved away. Four widows were left in the building.

Maybe it will sound odd that I'm jumping back, for a moment, to the time of World War II, but I think that nothing that happens is coincidence. At that time I was given the assignment, as a member of the *Communist underground, to go to Varaždin, a city in northern Croatia, and work there as a maid for a German Nazi agent, Jajčević, in order to see who came to visit him. Every morning when I came to clean his apartment I would find a lot of food on the table left over from Jajčević's nightly parties. I gave all the food to a woman who had two children and lived in the same building. Only after the war did she show me a hole in the wall of a room that she had concealed with a cupboard. All during the war she had hidden a Jewish friend of hers there.

When I went to the bank in Varaždin after many years, that woman's daughter was working as one of the tellers. She recognized me. She left with my bankbook for a moment and quickly came back with an elderly gentleman who was her boss.

"Let me introduce you. This is the man you fed in 1942." As she introduced us, the gray-haired gentleman wept.

Ana Klak, who works at the Jewish Center in Sarajevo, has been helping me ever since reintegration. Their organization, Bohoreta, enrolled me in a program for aiding elderly, ailing, and lonely people . . . Nothing happens by chance.

SET YOUR MIND AT EASE

TOLD BY AHMET GOBELJIĆ

The Grbavica Neighborhood of Sarajevo

November 1998

Nino, a Croat, had a son who was a warrant officer second class in active service in the military in Belgrade. When the siege of Sarajevo began, his son called and asked him, "Why are you still in Sarajevo?"

"Your Yugoslav People's Army is shelling us, son."

"You must be crazy! That can't be true!" his son snapped, and for a long time they didn't speak to each other, until both understood what was happening to the other.

Uncle Nino used to tell other people he was a Serb because he lived in Grbavica, which was under the control of Serbian forces. When he was asked what his slava (Saint's day) was, he'd quickly say, "St. Nicholas."

Whenever he could, he'd stand by the entranceway to the high rise where we lived, trying to prevent looting raids. One night he tried to stop Lazo, a policeman known as the "hatman," asking him where he was going.

Lazo fired his gun off by Nino's ear and walked straight past him. In the pitch black darkness someone kicked our door and banged on it with gun butts, shouting, "Open up! Come out all of you in there with your hands up."

My family is Muslim, but we were born in all different parts of the former Yugoslavia and feel ourselves to be *Yugoslavs. As we were coming out, someone flashed a flashlight in our eyes. "Good evening. I am Lazo, a cousin of Juka Prazina's. Anyone giving you trouble?"

I knew his cousin Juka Prazina was the leader of a Serbian gang in Grbavica, but my mother hadn't heard the man's words. She was born in Serbia but she had a Muslim name: Nura.

"Son, I didn't hear a word you said. I was born in Niš," she said, "and I'm Serbian."

Lazo didn't ask for her identification card. He glanced at my long hair and beard which made me look just like one of those bearded Serbian fighters.

"Let's see your ID."

He read: "Ahmet Gobeljić, born in Niš on 5 May 1951." Without a word he handed me back the ID. Then he asked my brother, Hasan, for his. His stated that he was born in Peć, in Kosovo. Our father had been an army officer so we had moved from base to base as children. Lazo asked him, "Are you a Kosovar?"

Because he couldn't tell which Lazo would think was worse, his being a Kosovar or a Bosnian Muslim, my brother wisely kept his mouth shut.

Hasan wore prescription glasses, and Lazo, despite the dark, wore sunglasses. He took Hasan's glasses off and tried them on, but when he saw they were prescription lenses he quickly gave them back.

He pushed his knife into Hasan's mouth, asking, "What do you think? Have your local Muslims been up to anything around here? Where is the basement? I want to check to see if they are keeping something in the basement."

After this abuse he demanded that we hand over everything we had in the apartment to the army. The list of things he wanted included sanitary material. We thought he meant soap and toilet paper. He meant first-aid equipment.

Poor Nino, who did all he could to help his neighbors throughout the war, still has a buzz in his left ear since that night.

We had a big grocery store in our neighborhood. The manager, a Muslim man, used to be a friend of my father's. When the war started, all we had in the house were four pounds of flour and two quarts of cooking oil. Until July 1992 no one had looted the store, probably because it was right on the front lines so no one dared come close. During April I stopped by to see the manager because soon enough we were left without any flour at all.

"As you can see, business is lively. All out of flour," he shrugged.

In early May, Uncle Nikola, a Serbian man, someone I had said hello to in passing but didn't know well, rang at our door: "Neighbor, here you go, it might come in handy," he said and left a half-full sack of flour at the door.

When the grocery store finally was looted, I watched the thieves lug out tons of flour. It was just that the manager preferred not to sell me any.

That July, that first year of the suffering, Nikola succumbed to grief, unable to muster the strength to watch what was happening to his neighbors. My brother buried him following all the *Serbian Orthodox rites.

There were no problems during the war among the neighbors in our high rise. Before and during the war we kept up good neighborly relations. In other cities there were stories of Muslims reporting on a Serb for helping another Muslim.

Our whole high rise, mostly apartments assigned to people who had worked in the army, enjoyed the protection of our neighbor, Milan, a retired Yugoslav People's Army officer.

In October 1992 four Chetniks walked into our apartment wearing the typical Chetnik fur hats and insignia. We didn't dare lock our door and it wouldn't have helped anyway because they would have kicked it down. I was with my mother, while our brother was off on his work detail. They introduced themselves as soldiers from the Knin *Krajina region who had come to Grbavica to help the Serbian army. The last one to come in locked the door behind him. I don't know why they came, but they searched the whole place. Since they found no money, jewelry, or weapons, one of them lunged at me with his knife, but another of them said, "Don't slit his throat. Come on, let's take them up to the top of the building and push them off. That is what Alija *Izetbegović's men do to our White Eagle paramilitaries whenever they nab one."

All the neighbors from the other apartments heard the ruckus and noise, but no one dared come out to protect us. Our neighbor Milan found the courage, put a cardboard box over his head so no one in the community could recognize him, and ran off to the police station.

"Some thugs are after my neighbors!"

He did not say "my Muslim neighbors," just "my neighbors."

It was a matter of seconds. In their quarrel about whether to slit our throats or push us off the roof, it was looking more and more as if they'd settle on slitting our throats. Just then the police arrived and banged on the door.

The soldiers looked up. They were surprised by the unexpected courage of a person who would dare bang on the door, and they wanted to see who it was. They went over to the door and one of them called, "Who is it?"

"Open up! This is the police!"

I couldn't imagine where the police had come from, but only then did I realize that I might have been murdered. It was so incredible to me that someone could slit my throat or murder me over nothing.

For the whole time while the fighting was going on, both in Grbavica, and later when I was living in the Muslim part of Sarajevo, I held on to my feeling of being a Yugoslav. I lived in the belief that all of us were Yugoslavs. Others would ask me, "So why aren't you out defending your Yugoslavia, if you are such a Yugoslav?"

I didn't know whom I was supposed to be defending it from, nor where. I didn't know who was attacking it, or why. If I'd known, I would have.

The soldiers, curious, unlocked the door and saw the police, who ordered them, "Hand over your weapons and come with us."

"We aren't giving anyone our weapons," they protested.

There was a struggle, but the police did disarm them and take them away.

We got out of Grbavica alive thanks to a man I knew who saved a lot of people during the war. As soon as he'd heard what had happened, he said, "Look, it doesn't matter that I am on the side of some sort of Serbian thing. There are no ideals that would allow me to stand by while someone abuses and murders my neighbors, friends, and fellow citizens."

He took us down to the Trades Center and said, "Walk slowly across Vrbanja Bridge. I have told my guys not to shoot. Let's hope yours don't either."

When I got to the bridge, my fear evaporated. I wasn't afraid of a Chetnik bullet hitting me in the back of the head or a Muslim bullet to my forehead. All that mattered was that there would be no more knives held to my throat. Crossing the bridge meant stepping out of the Stone Age. There was no more waiting for footsteps on the stairs, and the screams and cries for help of those they were taking away who knows where.

After we crossed over from Grbavica into the part of Sarajevo that was under the control of the Army of Bosnia and Herzegovina, I joined that army. Then I dubbed myself the Combat Fighter from Niš. My beard and long hair had saved my life that one time in Grbavica. At that time my fellow fighters were amused with the colorful association to a genuine Chetnik.

In the spring of 1995 I was on guard along the worst section of Pijaca Street, behind the refrigerator warehouse. At the end of the shift I turned toward Suljo, who was on guard 150 feet from me. He took off his cap to scratch his head. As I walked toward him the two of us heard a voice, "Hey, you Muslim, put your cap back on! You don't want your head scorched!"

Suljo looked over at me thinking it was me, making a joke, but when he saw my expression he knew that he'd been wrong. We realized it must have been a sniper who had had it with the war and guard duty just as we had.

I'm sure the same thing bothered him that bothered us: What are we dying and murdering for?

I joined the army to save my life. I have never subscribed to this idea of a free, independent, integral Bosnia. I'm not interested in it today either, because all of it is a big lie. There is no democracy. Even here all they care about now is Islam.

A BALKAN SPY

TOLD BY BORKA MAKSIMOVIĆ

The *Vogošća part of Sarajevo

November 1998

I was born in Donja Vogošća where I grew up. For six and a half years I worked as a teacher, and for the last ten before the war at the *Holiday Inn, on workers' safety issues, once I'd completed my graduate studies.

When the war started I was in Sarajevo where I had an office and a small apartment. I thought I'd stay even though I'm from a Serbian family because I was figuring that there would be no fighting in the city itself.

In late May 1992 I thought I'd like to see my parents, so I walked from downtown Sarajevo out to Vogošća. Only once I was in Vogošća did I see the first shelling of homes and understand the danger. Vogošća was becoming a part of Republika Srpska.

With the siege beginning there was a shortage of food in Sarajevo, so I crossed back into the city carrying five baskets of food and shared them among my friends.

Friends of mine, Serbs from Vogošća, asked me to visit a Serbian man at the Sarajevo city hospital who had been seriously wounded in the leg in the early days of the war. I didn't know this man myself, but I took the obligation upon myself since his wife had killed herself before the war and he had two daughters. I visited him at the hospital. At that time the danger to Serbs in Sarajevo was horrendous. Four men with guns were guarding the poor man in his bed. As soon as I came in they surrounded me and asked, "Why are you visiting him?"

"The man was wounded, he is a widower with two children. I don't care what his nationality is. I have a moral obligation to visit him because I promised I would," I answered.

Two neighbors from the Ciglane part of town had driven me to the hospital. All three of us were arrested there. They grilled us with questions. They pored over every single scrap of paper in my purse. In the end they talked about taking me to jail, but, who knows why, they changed their minds and released me.

Ciglane was a new, elite neighborhood, and many of the people who lived there had a university education. This didn't help them at all in terms of their behavior.

"Chetnik-lover," people often called after me, and many other insults.

Milisav Janiz, whose father was Serb and his mother Muslim, took his mother's last name, Buturović, at the beginning of the war since he was living in downtown Sarajevo that was under Muslim control. He uses that name even to this day. I don't know whether the fact that he kept reporting me to the authorities was to prove his loyalty, but because of his groundless reports that I was pro-Chetnik and his accusations that I was flashing signals of light to the Serbian positions in the hills from the balcony at my office, that I was an undercover traitor, I was brought in eight times for interrogation and six times they searched my apartment. The police behaved more decently than he did. At least they told me my neighbors were reporting on me.

Once they took me to a school in the Vratnik part of Sarajevo. I heard later that that was where they had taken Milorad Ekmečić, in the same way. While I was going down the stairs blindfolded I could smell the mildew and I thought they were taking me to a firing squad to be shot. When they unbound my eyes I could see I was in a cellar with a lot of people. In the end it turned out to be nothing but an ordinary conversation after which they took me home again.

People from the local branch of territorial defense in Ciglane also brought me into a large glass building that looked nothing like the sort of space paramilitary units usually held.

After similar searches, in early July 1992, some three months into the war, some people who had moved into town from Vogošća, the brother of a colleague of mine with his wife and son, reported me to the authorities because my whole office was full of retail merchandise from a business I had been running before the war. The authorities jumped eagerly on the report. They brought me in for questioning and then took me to jail. A man named Boris took me to the jail with the crudest of excuses. "Let's lock her up. Her life will be safer behind bars."

That man had already committed quite a few crimes at that point but no one reacted. It was a time of anarchy when people did whatever they felt like doing.

I spent seventeen days in the Central Prison. Every night they beat the prisoners brutally. Everyone held there was a Serb and anyone who felt like it came and beat and abused them. The thugs would come in, saying, "A shell fell, let's go beat up some Chetniks!" and then they'd vent their rage and beat prisoners unconscious. In the cell with me was a Serb from Ciglane whom they beat so badly that he was still moaning and calling for a doctor at dawn. There were no doctors. In the morning they found him dead. He had succumbed to the beating. During my stay another Serb was murdered the same way.

They used to say that the Central Prison was like a fancy hotel compared to the prison down at the Victor Bubanj barracks. I don't know if I can even imagine what happened to the Serbs who were there.

After seventeen days I was let out of prison thanks to what was almost a private exchange: they got four of their men back from Vogošća in

Republika Srpska in return for me. Who knows how much longer I would
have had to stay there and whether I would have even gotten out alive if
they hadn't done that.

When I got back I found my place had been looted. Everything I'd had
was gone. The people who took me to jail took absolutely everything.

I had only the blouse and skirt I was wearing. No one reacted. Ismet
Bajramović *Ćelo, who was in charge at the headquarters, one night appre-
hended the people who'd ransacked my place. He detained them for questioning but they would not confess because the value in question was considerable.

I got back to Ciglane and collapsed with exhaustion. I had no energy. I
was hungry and had nothing to eat. I didn't have a single German mark to
my name. At that point we weren't being paid salaries at the hotel, and got
only two servings of soup per day.

I wanted to keep living in Sarajevo. I figured the madness couldn't last
forever.

I went out to Vogošća to see my parents because my father was ill. I was
there for three days and then came back to town. I brought a car full of food
and gave it to my friends in Sarajevo. All of them were hungry. After awhile
I heard my father had died.

The old management kept telling me during the siege that they hoped
I'd stay working at the Holiday Inn.

Many of my Sarajevo Muslim friends asked me to help their parents,
brothers, and cousins who were being held in jail over in Vogošća because I
knew the warden of the jail there. I couldn't resist the pressures, so the
Sarajevo police drove me once out to Vogošća because I wanted to do
something worthwhile even if it meant risking my life. The snipers were ordered to hold their fire. They brought me as far as the Traffic Controllers'
School. I had to go the rest of the way into town on foot because since Vogošća
was being held by the Serbian authorities, the Sarajevo police couldn't drive
me all the way there.

I went to the Vogošća jail to intervene on the behalf of these innocent
people who had done nothing wrong. If you wanted to do anything hu-

mane, you would immediately be accused of being a spy working for the other side. So the authorities took me in for questioning. One colonel questioned me at the Serbian military barracks. He labeled me a traitor and a spy and I could not shed those labels the whole time I was there with the Serbs, who prevented me from going back to Sarajevo in December 1992. I went to UNHCR [UN High Commission for Refugees] headquarters in the Ilidža part of Sarajevo to ask them to help me to cross back over into Sarajevo, but the Serbian authorities refused to issue me a document I needed because they had branded me as spying for the Muslims.

On the other hand, whenever I tried to go to Belgrade, guards at the checkpoint were forbidden from letting me pass because supposedly I was going in order to rat to the people in Belgrade on what the officials were up to in Vogošća.

Appalling murders were happening in Vogošća. There were people taking away innocent Muslim civilians and killing them. Absolutely no one blinked an eye, as if they were slaughtering a rooster, not a man. I couldn't stand by and watch it all in silence, so I went to the police station where there were people who really shouldn't have been there because they were unprofessional, untrained, and cared nothing for justice. I reported to them the first and last names of the murderers who I knew to have committed crimes. When I realized the police weren't lifting a finger to stop the murders, I went to the Pale Serbian headquarters to find Dragan Kijac, the man in charge of state security. I found his deputy and told him openly what was going on in Vogošća. I could tell by his reaction that he was surprised, that he hadn't known. He called in the man responsible for Vogošća state security and ordered him to investigate my allegations. That man summoned me to his office for a talk when I got back to Vogošća and wrote everything down, though I can't believe that if he was living here he didn't know what was going on since I, an ordinary citizen, knew all about it. After that, nothing changed for the better.

I think that the Serbs were undone by bad government. Unprofessional, ignorant, greedy barbarians are not qualified to lead people. The way they began was exactly the way they ended. The straw that broke the camel's back was when Serbian authorities began encouraging Serbs who had been living in the suburbs that rimmed the woods around Sarajevo to move out. These people who were convinced to leave their own homes ended up moving into Muslim houses that had been destroyed, even though the international community was supposedly guaranteeing their safety if they had stayed in Sarajevo. I am terribly bitter. I am first angry at the Serbian leaders, and then at everything else.

I have the impression, based on my own experience, that all three ethnic groups did more or less the same things. Robbers and thieves declared themselves commanders and did whatever they felt like. Many Serbs were murdered in Sarajevo and thrown into a pit and almost no one speaks of it. Everything has been hushed up because all information comes via TV and radio that are government controlled. The pits above Bentbaša, Kazani, were full of innocent Serbian victims. There were some courageous Muslims who did write about them. One such writer had to flee abroad. And Senad *Pećanin had trouble because of this. In time the fate of these innocent people was easily hushed up in a monstrous way. It seems to me that even the Serbian authorities weren't interested in cooperating with the international community to uncover these crimes. It is as if they didn't even care about the thousands of their fellow countrymen who were murdered. Their logic boggles the mind: "So why did these Serbs stay on in Sarajevo with the Muslims? They got what they deserved." Those Serbs fled the city and took with them the police, the army, the weapons, and then they fired on Sarajevo for four years, abandoning tens of thousands of their fellow Serbs in the city to pay the price of their atrocious politics! Only those Serbs who stayed throughout the worst of it in Sarajevo, and survived, know what anguish and humiliation they suffered.

There were few people on both sides at the time who had the courage to help others, especially if those others weren't of the same ethnic background, because that meant that they would at the very least be proclaimed traitors to their own people.

Muhamed worked for the Sarajevo police and the whole time he did whatever he could to help anyone he could help. He knew my brother was a colleague of his and that he was saving the lives of Muslims in Vogošća as much as he could. Once I got out of jail, I had an even worse reputation than before to deal with. Muhamed shielded me with his authority, saying only the nicest things about me. Who knows what would have happened or whether I would have survived at all if he hadn't been there.

I cannot forget Sabahudin, who was director of the Holiday Inn in the summer of 1992 when I was released from jail. He knew that I had lost everything I owned, so he asked me immediately, "Tell me what you need. Do you need money? Do you need any kind of documents? I will do anything I can for you."

Three years after the *Dayton Accords were signed, in 1998, I am living with my mother and brother in Donja Vogošća. Only six or seven Serbian families stayed on after reintegration. We are having a very rough time. I lost my job in Sarajevo. Though I won my dispute in court, the new hotel administration has not let me come back to work.

A neighbor of mine, a Muslim woman, and I were attacked in my woods nearby by a Muslim refugee with an ax when I tried to stop him from felling the trees. I reported it to the police, brought suit in court . . . Only now is the situation beginning to improve some. These authorities are powerless because they function according to the principle of "Don't touch him, he is one of ours," rather than the law. Unfortunately, as far as I can tell, the same goes for all three sides, and it is getting harder and harder for people to bear because it has been going on for such a long time. We can only hope that soon the rule of ethnic lunacy will be replaced by the rule of reason and law, so that honorable people, on all sides, can live with dignity, as they deserve.

SAVE THE CHILD

TOLD BY MORIS BIBER

*Laktaši

January 1996

With my mother, when I was a two-year-old child, I moved across the *Sava River from Croatia to Laktaši in Bosnia. In my heart I carry my childhood, school days, friends of all faiths, and my love, all of it bound up with Laktaši. Right before the war I married Mirzeta, a Muslim woman. After three years of the mindless violence and death, a son was born to us in 1995. Our joy at the triumph of life over ethnic blindness was shared by friends of ours, Serbs, who came to congratulate us.

I have committed myself to this area. The town in Croatia, where my father and two brothers live, is not far away. But someone drew a terrible line, called the front. Weapons spat across it from both sides, with the purpose of expelling or murdering the other side.

I fought from the first day of the war in the army of Republika Srpska. Once during a lull in the firing, in a trench in Slavonia, a fellow fighter asked me, "How can you shoot at your brothers and father?"

"I'm hoping they aren't here. And if they are, isn't that what we call fate?" I mused aloud.

136

It was not something that people talked about much. We all had the same goal in the trenches: survival. No one seemed to hold it against me that I was from Croatia. When I turned to someone for help I was never turned away. Many Serbs helped me as much as they could.

After we married we rented an apartment in the home of a Serb named Jovo. Before the war I was working so I had been able to keep up with my rent payments. When I donned my uniform, Jovo said, "I know you have no money. As long as the war goes on you don't have to pay for rent or electricity."

While I was at the front, our baby got sick a few months ago. The doctor prescribed something but Mirzeta couldn't afford to pay for it. She left the pharmacy with the baby in her arms, crying. She ran into our landlord, Jovo.

"Mirzeta, why are you crying?"

"I can't afford to pay for the baby's medicine."

Jovo took money out and gave it to her.

"Look, don't cry. Go back in and get what you need for the child."

SHELTER IN A SHOP

TOLD BY LEJLA TOPČAGIĆ

*Bosanski Šamac

December 1995

I was 19 years old when the war began. My father, a Muslim, was summoned by the Serbian authorities to dig trenches, and my mother, a Croat, and I were called to a work detail, cleaning streets.

For the first year I didn't dare set foot outside the house in *Šamac, the town where I was born and raised.

When I received the summons to report for a work detail, my mother said, "I won't hear of you cleaning streets."

Thanks to a neighbor, a Serb, I was able to get away for four months and stay with his relatives in Belgrade. Even after that time there was no reason to believe that the war would be over soon, so I came home. When I got back to Šamac the town authorities were after me every day. The same humiliation was waiting for me: street cleaning.

A friend of my parents, Sima, a Serb, dropped in one day for a cup of coffee. "I've opened a grocery store. Would you like to work there, Lejla?"

"Of course," I accepted at once.

"To free you from the work detail, I'll have to pay your health and retirement benefits," he explained.

I was overjoyed to be working but I hadn't expected to receive a full salary, because under the conditions at that time no one was paying benefits for anyone. After a month Sima handed me my first earnings: "Nice job. Keep it up."

In May 1995 Croatian shells fell on Šamac. A friend of mine let me know that I'd been put on the list for a work detail again. At that moment Sima happened to be out on the front line in Obudovac. I felt completely helpless. My mother sent me to a nearby village and then she reported to the authorities, knowing that she, too, was on the list. She explained to them that I had gone with Sima to Obudovac. The next day Sima asked my mother, "Where is Lejla?"

"I lied to the authorities that she was with you, and packed her off to the village. This is no longer a question of pride, but survival. I'm terrified that she'll be murdered because they are forcing us to clean the streets while the shells are falling."

"You were wise to do what you did. We must protect our children. Go right ahead and tell them Lejla's with me."

Every single night the police came to the door to check and see whether I was home. After four days Sima came to pick me up in the village. "I'm bringing you back to Šamac. This has to end. It's going to kill your mother."

He took me to the store, "Open the store and start working the way you always do. I'm off for a word with Mirko Lukić."

After his talk with the man who was head of the municipal government Simo sent a soldier to tell me, "Sima wants you to know that you're all set. No one will bother you any more."

And so it was. Thanks to Sima, no one harassed me any more.

I am still working at his store.

THE FRAGRANCE OF *LILIES

TOLD BY ZORAN BLAGOJEVIĆ

Tuzla

November 1998

I was born in Tuzla, graduated from secondary school there, and it was there I chose to live and work. I was 22 years old when the war hit this region. Even though I come from a Serbian family, I immediately joined the Army of Bosnia and Herzegovina. My unit had very difficult tasks before it, often in enemy territory. Shoulder to shoulder fought Muslims, Croats, and Serbs. The Muslims were the majority; the Serbs and Croats comprised a fifth. All of us had the same idea, the same motive, the same goal: to defend our city and our state.

Before we went into combat the fighters were always under terrible psychological strain. Each of us knew just how hard the task before us was going to be and we were aware of the likelihood that some of us would be killed and some would end up invalids. We all thought maybe it won't be me, and you could see that hope in everybody's eyes.

Early in the morning on 13 August 1992, when we set out on a planned mission on Mount Majevica, we were all of us in good spirits because we were very motivated to occupy a position from where the enemy had been

140

shelling Tuzla. At moments like that we always joked, asking one another, "What will you do if you end up losing a leg? You just got married. Will your wife want you back like that?" That was how we shook off our jitters and our fears.

We crawled toward enemy trenches for about an hour. The day before on that route we had cleaned out a *minefield so that we would be able to creep up on them unnoticed. It turned out, however, that we had been noticed. They had buried new *mines in a different order after we left. We stepped into the minefield without knowing this, and the first to stand on a mine was Mehmed. He was actually relatively lucky because the mine only set fire to his leg. He screamed with the pain. He got burns that kept him in the hospital for a month. Bimo, born in Tuzla, stepped on the second mine. Jozo activated the third. After the first mine blast the Serbian army opened fire on us. There was panic and disarray in the ranks. Many of our men began to retreat. Bimo was the one who had the most composure at the time. Half-cursing, half-shouting, he called to Mešo: "Stop screaming like a woman! Be a man, clench your teeth and shut up!"

We carried the wounded to the first spot where it was safe to walk standing up. When we carried them to our trenches to members of the infantry unit, the news of how our group had run into trouble sent them into panic. They all wanted to know who was hurt, who'd been killed.

That was when my school friend, Elvir, was killed, a guy we all remembered for the boundless serenity he carried inside him. He was a great and noble fighter although everyone who knew him was surprised by that because they figured that serenity and courage didn't usually go hand in hand.

Danijel, whom we called Dance for short, was eighteen and a half. He was still a kid and behaved as if he didn't take the war seriously. Whenever we went into minefields before that day, he was always impatient, waiting for us to de-mine the field. Instead he'd go scampering across like a squirrel and shout to us, "I haven't got the time to wait."

He was brimming with youthful vigor, and that was how he died, that day, saving Paša. Paša had gone to sit by a tree, and Dančе saw that he was about to sit right on a mine, so he jumped over and pushed Paša off. Paša stood up and stared at him, surprised.

Dančе pulled the mine out and showed him, "Take a look at what you were about to sit on." He was starting to say something else, but that moment he was struck by a bullet in the neck and it killed him instantly.

In the midst of all the distress, Bimo, who had just been wounded, began to sing and his song was stronger than all the voices, all the shouting, and the gunfire. He sang a song written during the war: "The fragrance of lilies spreads across the fields," and for us it meant the lilies in the Bosnian coat of arms. There was suddenly a hush as if the fighters on the enemy lines were surprised and had stopped shooting. Out of the tomb-like silence the song caught on. Meša was the next to pick it up and then everyone was singing. As we sang we retreated, carrying away the wounded.

Bimo's and Joza's legs were amputated below the knee.

Bimo had grown up in town. He loved hanging out at a little café called "6." The day after he was wounded, when I stopped by the hospital to visit him, he asked me, "Zoko, I have one wish. Take me down to the '6.'"

I asked his doctor whether it would be all right, but he said, "Don't even think about it."

"Is he dying?" I asked, unnerved.

"No," said the doctor curtly. I decided to take Bimo to the café anyway. He was as happy as a kid when he got there.

After fifteen days they let Bimo out of the hospital at his request, even though his wound wasn't clean or healed yet. He spent his time at home with his little eight-month-old son and his wife. He often came to the unit and was a source of moral support for the fighters. He told us that what had happened to him wasn't all that bad. And people accepted him, even without his leg. He didn't want us going into combat afraid of what might happen. Even today I can't be sure what sort of traumatic effect his wounding had on him. If he was traumatized, he sure never showed it. A year later, in May 1993, I lost a foot when I stepped on a mine in the *Brčko area and I know that it bothers me. I never could understand how Bimo was able to encourage his friends and fellow fighters the way he did.

At that point in Tuzla there was a shortage of medicines and prostheses. Bimo fashioned himself an artificial leg. He took a wooden bowl and lined it with sponge and gauze. On the outside curve of the bowl he screwed on a table leg and to that he attached a wooden shoe form he'd gotten from a cobbler.

Two months later a team of French orthopedists and prosthetists came to Zenica. It was their plan to start producing the first prostheses in Bosnia and Herzegovina. Bimo was one of the first who was supposed to go and have an artificial limb fitted. He was euphorically happy. Ten days before he left he was already counting the hours and minutes before he'd be able to settle this key question.

Ten amputees set out in a van on 20 February 1993 to drive across Central Bosnia from Tuzla to Zenica. I am sure Bimo was singing with them, then. On a risky stretch of the road above Kladanj, they were hit directly by a shell shot from large gun and all of them died instantly.

Just when we all thought the war was over for Bimo because he would never wear a uniform again, this man, full of life, died so tragically, only thirty years old.

SANE CHILDREN

TOLD BY JANJA PANTIĆ

Vareš

November 1998

I graduated from the Sarajevo Teachers' College in 1962 and went back to my home town at the age of twenty-two to work as a teacher in the secondary school.

We lived as one soul in Vareš until 23 October 1993, when the tragedy of the Stupni Do massacre happened.

That day there was a strange atmosphere in town. There was a feeling of terrible tension in the air and in people. The worst for me, as a Croat, was watching our Muslim neighbors being herded down the street. I saw friends of mine among the people. I tried to help them but I really felt helpless. I was devastated by the knowledge that members of the Croatian Defense Council forces had turned our school, a place where children are supposed to learn and to enjoy each other's company, into a prison and place to torture innocent people. Later my colleagues and I had to clean the school of the traces of their criminal acts so that we could resume our work there as teachers. Even today I can see those horrible sights.

The hell the Croatian Defense Council forces created lasted for twelve days, which felt more like twelve years. Desperate and helpless, appalled and ashamed of the amount of evil, more than anyone could ever dream of, I kept a diary. From those fragments of sentences perhaps you can get a feeling for my suffering at the time.

"23 October 1993: Is it possible? Maybe this nasty game can be stopped. Love is disappearing. Everything human is disappearing. My native town reeks of ashes. I am terrified for my Muslim friends. I am terribly sad. I want to help, but how? My hands are tied, but I would like to proffer a hand to my friends who are even sadder than I am. How can those faces brighten? I don't know. I only know that they have been humiliated. I sympathize and suffer with them. As a person I, too, have been humiliated . . ."

"24 October: another day has dawned but with no sun. Is there any future for normal people? I have no words left! . . ."

"26 October: a meeting with friends in Majdan: what joy!

"From Majdan I can see into Stupni Do . . . On my way back I meet a student of mine. It is so hard. I cannot look him in the eyes. I heard that his brother was murdered. His brother was a student of mine, too. The men who torched Stupni Do went on to loot Vareš . . ."

When the Croatian Defense Council forces retreated, they left the Muslims they'd captured locked up in the school. Chaos hit a second time because this time such a large number of Croats left town out of fear of retaliation. Again I watched the columns of men, women, and children, this time Croats. I was miserable. I had resolved not to go anywhere, as had my husband. We felt that no matter where we went, we would no longer have our home. We decided to stay, although I thought we would be the only Croats to stay. We nearly were.

That night when the people of Vareš were leaving I found my neighbor Jozefina and her son. Her sister quickly came with her friend, a Croatian woman, and her Muslim husband. We sat together through the night, six desperate people, uncertain of what the new day would bring. The town seemed deserted. We were waiting for the arrival of the Army of Bosnia and Herzegovina.

The next day about noon we realized that we weren't alone after all. We found two Croatian and one Serbian Orthodox family in the next entranceway over in our building. We felt a little better. Around noon we went off to look for Jozefina's brother. He had stayed with his wife and mother-in-law.

Soon we were informed that we would have to find shelter. That was when things got really crazy. We didn't know where to go, where to hide. We went to the school where some of the Muslims still were who had been held there. They had been freed by UNPROFOR forces who were protecting them. Our meeting with those people was really hard. Among them was a close friend of my husband's. They greeted each other. I found a colleague I had worked with. He looked awful. Regardless of the evil done to him by members of "my" people, he had the strength to continue to think of me as a friend.

After we'd spent two nights in the school we came back to our homes. Many of the apartments in our entranceway had been looted and ransacked. Ours had gotten by unscathed, thanks to a Muslim neighbor who had taken the name plate off our door which showed our last names, and had written "Muslims" on a scrap of paper and stuck it there. After that we spent many days together, looking after each other and helping out.

After a few days, two colleagues of mine and I reported to the municipal headquarters for a work detail. We cleaned out the school and hoped that we might start working again. But I only started working in March of the next year. We were all back at the school again: Tinka, Pero, Muhamed, Dragan, Zdravko, Nada, Lena . . . Together again, Serbs, Croats, and Muslims. And we will do fine together, just as we used to. We realized that we are better off together. We socialize among ourselves and try to make our life more pleasant.

My husband, as a Serb, had some difficult moments. He sat in the house waiting until finally the police came to pick him up because he hadn't shown up for a work detail. They didn't harass him, they didn't even say anything nasty. To our surprise they gave him an excellent job. He worked at the municipality. He would go around to all the abandoned buildings and offices with Dževad and Borko. Again it was a Serb, a Muslim, and a Croat together. They issued permits for offices. He worked with Salih, too. They got along pretty well. The war was still going on. That was in 1994. A year later he retired.

Everyone in Vareš asked me, "How did you, a Croatian woman, dare to stay in town with your Serbian husband?"

"Why shouldn't I have stayed? I never did anyone any harm," I answered.

By the time the war was over, most of the children attending school were from Muslim families. I think there were only five children of Croatian parents there when they conducted a survey and asked, "Which of your teachers is the most realistic, and which is your favorite subject?" To my great delight the children chose me. That was the nicest proof that our children are sane and untainted by ethnic prejudice.

AS LONG AS I'M HERE,
DON'T WORRY

TOLD BY ABID KAHVIĆ

Ilidža, a Suburb of Sarajevo

November 1998

At the start of the war the Serbian police in Ilidža demanded that Muslims and Croats be evicted from their homes. Despite the fact that I am Muslim, I decided to stay in my apartment with my wife and twelve-year-old Samir, my sister-in-law's son who was orphaned at a young age so we adopted him. We hid him in the apartment. All the Serbs in the neighborhood knew he was there except Nikola Vukičević, whom I was hiding the boy from.

I didn't want to get in touch with anyone.

My daughter, Šefka, and her husband and two children were living in another part of town that was under Muslim control.

A friend of mine, Sreto, who had a house in Blažuj, also a Serb-controlled area, called me at that point to ask if we needed anything.

"Nothing but cigarettes."

"Even if Karadžić were at the door, my friend Bido would never go hungry," he announced publicly, and for that he suffered repercussions, but he did bring us a package, which, aside from cigarettes, contained cooking oil, beans, and flour. For the next fifteen days we weren't hungry.

148

A Serbian neighbor of mine, who still lives in our building today, told my wife one day, "Rather than bother you, I thought that from time to time I might toss cigarettes and whatever else I have onto your balcony." He often asked, "Is anyone giving you a hard time? Write my phone number down and call me any time you need help."

Luckily no one touched us during the first Muslim attack against Ilidža in May 1992. The attack was directed at Ilidža and Hotel Srbija from Hrasnica and Sokolović Kolonija. Many young Serbian boys were murdered at the time and all the fury was vented on the local Muslims who had stayed. Voja, a friend's son, ran into our apartment.

"Quick, come up to our place!"

We did what he said and he hid us there, and then he went down and gave the Serbian soldiers at the entranceway food so that he'd be in their good graces and urged them not to search his apartment. When they wanted to shoot at our windows, Voja stopped them.

We hid Samir in our apartment under the book case. He was often down in the cellar and we'd bring him food. Once when he came up to our place to eat, Serbian police barged in and found him.

"Who is this and where did he come from?"

"I am the child's guardian," my wife replied.

"Let's see those guardianship documents."

She was so terrified she couldn't find them.

"Look, we believe you this time, but next time you'd better hide him because anyone else will take him away."

Afterward we hid him in the wardrobe and the cellar. Our neighbors, a Serbian couple, asked if their two sons could hide with Samir. They spent their time together in the cellar, storage shed, or wardrobe. My wife brought them food.

Another Serbian neighbor of ours reported them to the police when she saw them coming up to eat. The younger boy hid in a barrel on the terrace, but they found the elder boy, took him outside, and beat him up. They brought him back in to change his clothes because he was all bloody. His mother explained, in tears, "I didn't raise this boy to shoot at people! You wouldn't let him work but you want to give him a gun!"

They took him away, and their younger son managed to hide for a few more days but finally he reported for the army on his own, fearing for his brother's safety.

I was able to walk freely around Ilidža until the day when the White Eagle paramilitary unit arrived. They stopped me on the street, demanded to see my identification papers, and took me down to the police station.

A Serbian man I'd known from before came over and asked me, "What happened?"

I didn't know why I'd been brought into custody. He went over to the young men and said something to them. After that he drove me back to my place and said, "Uncle Bido, I don't want you leaving your apartment. You can see what these times are like. I don't know whether I'll be there to intervene next time."

Until 8 August I didn't so much as step out onto the balcony.

When we were being shelled all the people living in the apartment building except me went down to hide in the cellar. One of them told my wife, "Don't come down with us to the cellar any more. We don't want to have to look at your kind down here."

The next few days word got around that someone was sniping from our building. My wife pleaded with me, "Bido, come down with me to the cellar. We don't want anyone claiming you are the sniper."

With trepidation I went down to the cellar where I was greeted by my neighbor's voice. "Bido, as long as I'm here, don't you worry. You enjoy the same rights I do. When I'm not around, keep your eyes open."

Until we left Ilidža my wife was still able to move freely around the town, always on the lookout for cigarettes. Ljubo came into a supermarket one day and asked Dana at the cash register, "Are there any Muslims in here?"

"No, there aren't," Dana answered, though she knew my wife, and my wife was there.

Then Ljubo threatened, loudly, "Don't sell them anything, no matter how much money they offer."

When humanitarian aid was being distributed at the supermarket, it was my wife's turn after waiting for four hours in line. Behind her stood a Croatian woman married to a Muslim. They told the two women, "No bread for you."

After that we decided to try and cross over to Hrasnica, another Sarajevo suburb, which was under Muslim control. We were having no success at organizing our passage out until 14 August 1992, when a friend of my son-in-law's, a Serbian fellow, appeared.

"How are you managing? Are you able to get by?"

"It's getting tougher and tougher. Can you help us cross over into Hrasnica?" I asked him.

"Of course I can," he said, and with the help of a comrade of his he brought us as far as the line of separation at Hrasnica, and said, "Don't be afraid. If someone starts shooting at you I will shoot them. I'll cover you."

He gave me the keys to his apartment in Hrasnica and he stayed at my place in Ilidža.

When I found his apartment, I saw that someone else had already moved in, so I went to the apartment where my daughter and son-in-law lived. That very day they had been wounded by shell fragments. Their apartment was in a shambles, the food ruined, so we were hungry our first fifteen days there.

After they were wounded, our daughter and her husband and children managed to get out to *Split in Croatia where they were taken care of in a hospital, and later they went to stay with Croatian friends of ours. When the trouble started between Croats and Muslims they moved yet again to another country, where they live today. In August 1998 when I went to visit them I saw my third grandson for the first time, and he was already five years old.

We had hoped that things would be better for us in Hrasnica, but they weren't because the same principle reigned, except here they were persecuting Serbs.

We spent four months in a cellar with our Serbian neighbors, Slavica and Milenko, like one family. We shared everything down to the last crumb because there was nearly nothing to eat.

We were in the cellar when a Serbian man we knew, Vojo, came in, beaten black and blue, with only one shoe. "Please, hide me!"

We all got into trouble with the Muslim military police for protecting Vojo. He was on a work detail with Milenko. They cleaned the streets, dug trenches on Igman Mountain, chopped wood . . . It wasn't easy for them.

We are still good friends today.

After the Dayton Agreement was signed and reintegration started, I went back to Ilidža and found my apartment burned and destroyed. There were ten automobile tires still burning in it.

I found Sreto in Blažuj in his home.

"Bido, I'm going to have to leave. People keep shouting after me, 'Look at the Chetnik who stayed behind!' At least you know I was never a Chetnik."

He sold his house and moved to Valjevo, in Serbia.

Vojo and Milenko stayed on to live in Hrasnica. The authorities wanted to arrest them but I wouldn't let them. Later everyone let them be.

DIVIDE EVERYTHING IN THIS PACKAGE IN HALVES

TOLD BY JOKA ČORBIĆ,
A Refugee from *Gradačac

Modriča

December 1996

I lived with my husband and daughter in Gradačac before the war. At that point the two of them left town. I stayed behind in the apartment out of fear that a squatter might take it from us.

I didn't know at that time what it meant to be in a war. Soon I was sorry I'd stayed, because I couldn't even get through to my parents, whose house was only a couple of miles from mine.

Until the war I was surrounded for years by people of all three faiths with whom I communicated normally, and I never experienced anything unpleasant. In the four-story building where we had our apartment, the tenants were also of all the different faiths.

When the shelling of Gradačac started, we used the bomb shelter together.

At first I was afraid that someone might attack me as a Serb, because all of us in the town were being shelled from Serbian positions. But no one ever held it against me.

Once a Muslim neighbor brought over his package of humanitarian aid.

"Would you please divide everything in this package in half?"

I did as he'd asked, though I didn't understand why. My neighbor took half for himself.

"All of us are human beings. You, too, need to eat. This is for you."

Even then while it was still possible to move freely around town I was too afraid to go out. No matter whom I asked to bring me something, no one refused.

The authorities started searching apartments in the buildings where Serbs lived. One day they came to my place. I was expecting they'd search everything, but they were very polite. They asked, "Are you holding any weapons?"

"No," I answered.

"Where are your husband and daughter?"

"They aren't in town," I said, and went on. "Are you searching every single apartment?"

"We aren't searching every one, but someone reported you had weapons at home."

They didn't take anything, said a few more polite words in parting, and left.

All day on 10 July 1992 the town was shelled. The next day an evacuation was organized for the women, children, and elderly. Buses and trucks came to get us. They didn't ask anyone about their nationality. They said that we should bring some food and a blanket and they took us to a neighboring village that was full of people who had been brought there from all over. They explained that anyone who had someone to stay with could go on to Tuzla. I had some friends and cousins in Tuzla so I decided to go there in hopes that I'd find it easier from there to get into Serbia. Tuzla was an area under Muslim control.

It was only when I got to Tuzla that I realized that Serbs weren't being allowed to leave town. A friend of mine paid someone to be taken out of Tuzla, but I had no money. My husband had taken what money we had when he left with our daughter, and what gold I had I'd left with my mother in her village. I had a few coupons on me and some spare change. I stayed in Tuzla at the home of Milenko, commander of the local police, even though he was a Serb. The women and children were left in town, but most of the men had gone off to fight. I didn't know too many people there.

I ran into Tadija, a Croat who had worked with my husband at the same factory. He wanted to know immediately where my husband was.

"He got out of Gradačac in time with our daughter," I answered.

"Thank God he got out! I'm overjoyed. Tell me whom you're staying with and what I can do to help you!"

Tadija helped me a lot. His wife was working at the hospital, and got me fifty blood pressure pills. They were able to travel freely from place to place and go to their village. Whenever they were getting ready to leave, Tadija would ask me, "I'm off to the village. What are you needing in the way of food that I can bring back?"

He brought me whatever they had.

After a month and a half in Tuzla, Milenko asked me, "Would you like to join your husband and daughter?"

"I'm dying to see them," I answered, delighted.

"Here is the phone number of a man who is working in the Committee for Exchange. Give him a call and ask him to put you on the list for exchange. Tell him that I sent you." I could tell from the name that the man was a Muslim.

There were twenty-six of us on the list.

On the day set for the exchange, Milenko went with me, and along the way he told me, "When we come to the place where the exchange is supposed to happen, we'll pretend we don't know each other."

We waited a long time because the Muslims who were supposed to be exchanged for us didn't show up on time. Milenko managed to make arrangements so that the elderly and sick could cross without waiting.

When it was my turn to cross over I gave him only the most discreet possible nod as my good-bye.

THESE ARE JUST KIDS

TOLD BY LJILJANA ZITA, Lawyer

The Marijin Dvor part of Sarajevo

November 1998

Marko was a gifted young athlete, a runner. The coach had high
hopes for him. Like so many other children in Sarajevo he was burning to
do something for his city when the siege began. There were a lot of lonely,
elderly people living in the Marijin Dvor part of the city and they needed
food brought to them. Four days after celebrating his fifteenth birthday,
on 7 August 1992, Marko was on his way home with his Muslim friends
after they'd finished their shift of delivering food. They were already quite
close to the building where we lived, just after noon, when first one shell
exploded, followed immediately by two more.

When the first shell hit, I felt instinctively that my child had been hurt.
I ran barefoot out in the street and found Marko, injured. Already people
were trying without success to get him into a car, although the hospital was
only some thirty feet away. They managed to lift him onto a cart and push
him to the hospital. The first to leap to his aid was a policeman who was
working for security at the hospital.

His friends were only very slightly hurt, but Marko had been hit in
his right thigh by shrapnel from the first shell and had a compound fracture.

There weren't very many people wounded that day in our part of town, so my son was the first one into the operating room. At that point the doctors still had enough medicine and blood for transfusions for the injured.

I was crying in front of the operating room and pleading for them to save my son's leg because he was a runner. It was an impulsive reaction, and today I see things entirely differently: what mattered was to save his life. At that point all I could think of was that he was a runner who had a wonderful future ahead of him in sports, and life without his leg would be impossible. Today, when I work with disabled children, I understand that life always has meaning.

The operation took more than four hours. When he left the operating room, Dr. Nakaš showed me and my husband that the leg was warm.

"The first eight days are critical, but we are hoping that everything will work out."

After three days they were sure they had saved his leg. He could wriggle his toes. Drs. Fazlagić and Nakaš had worked a miracle: they had reconnected all his nerves, but there was still major damage to his muscles and because of that he would not be able to run, which they explained immediately to Marko and us.

Marko didn't seem to mind much. He stayed in touch with his friends from the club and the coach, Mirsad Bojić, who wanted to help him in a truly humane way. He put Marko on the list of athletes who would go to Montpelier for the Mediterranean Games. The coach was hoping that he could work out physical therapy for Marko in Izmir, Turkey. If he could get him out of Sarajevo to Dubrovnik, where Marko's grandmother and grandfather lived, he could recuperate in their home under more normal circumstances.

My husband and I gave our permission in writing that we agreed to let our son try to leave Sarajevo. The only way to leave the city was to run across the airport runway. At that point we weren't thinking about what might happen to him. The runway was constantly lit and exposed to sniper fire.

When he came back, Marko described for us what it had looked like: four of them ran across in the first group with a guide whom they called the "rabbit." As soon as they got across, a machine gun they referred to as the "sower of death" opened fire from the hills, so the next group had to wait until the machine gun fire died down. When things got quiet again, the next foursome ran across, including Marko and the team doctor. They were blinded halfway across the runway by the spotlights of an UNPROFOR armored car so they were forced to lie down on the runway. The French UNPROFOR soldiers pulled them into the armored car. They were lucky that the doctor knew how to speak French and he explained to the soldiers that these were members of an athletic team representing Bosnia and Herzegovina, and he showed them the kids' Olympic passports. It was entirely up to the good will of the soldiers whether they would send the teammates back to where they'd come from, or take them across the runway.

One of the soldiers took a piece of paper, showed it to them and said, "If you can guess which hand I'm holding the paper in, I'll take you to the other side."

The doctor was lucky again! He guessed! They took them over to Sokolović Kolonija, and later they crossed Igman in trucks, and got to Čelebići by van. At this point they were stopped by two men. One of the men was holding a baby in his arms and asked them, "Please take us to the Jablanica hospital. You are our only hope. Our child is sick."

They let them in the van, but an Army of Bosnia and Herzegovina patrol showed up and threw out the father and child, apparently because they were Croats, cursing, "You will not transport Ustasha."

While they were checking the passports, a Bosnia and Herzegovina army soldier cocked his gun and pointed it at my son, because Marko was a Croat.

The coach, who was a Muslim, stood in between the soldiers and Marko and said, "Look, these are just kids. You'll have to murder me before you kill Marko."

Then a second soldier came over who was in charge of the patrol and told his comrade, "Drop it. Let him go. Come back with me."

The group continued on its way toward Jablanica. Somewhere between Čelebići and Konjic a Croatian sniper hit the driver in the leg. The wounded man had such composure that he managed to drive them to the first house, which served them as a place to hide until an ambulance could come for him. They got a new driver from the Army of Bosnia and Herzegovina who drove them into Jablanica that first night where they were held for the next eighteen days.

During that time Jablanica was under Muslim control and was being run by an infamous fellow by the name of Zuka. Children whose names were not Muslim were in hiding from him. Marko was with two other boys who had the same problem. They made up Muslim names and used them instead of their own in conversation while they were there.

They slept in improvised conditions at a store where they found double-decker beds. Local people even brought them mattresses. The ones who didn't have a bed to sleep in slept on shelves.

In the same building above the store, there were U.N. observers, members of the *Spanish battalion, and at first everyone felt safer because they were close at hand. That lasted until the day when a jeep full of mujahedin cloaked in kerchiefs arrived in front of the building. After a few minutes they came out carrying weapons, helmets, and bulletproof vests that they had taken from the observers, and then they sat in a UN vehicle and drove away.

When the others saw what the mujahedin were able to do to members of the UN, no one felt quite so comfortable any more.

The Army of Bosnia and Herzegovina finally permitted their passage, but they had to wait, then, for permission from the Croatian Defense Council forces.

After fourteen days spent in Jablanica, one of the Bosnia and Herzegovina army officers said, "Since you are a burden to us and you are eating our food, at least you can pay off your debt by carrying food and water two or three times a week out to the fighters in the trenches."

The boys had no choice, so they did what they'd been asked to do, side by side with their coach, who wouldn't let them out of his sight.

After the eighteen days in Jablanica they had to come back to Sarajevo and run back into town across the runway.

Marko left for Split on the last official convoy of children and the elderly in December 1993.

A "*Rose" of Sarajevo, marks left by an exploding shell

A FLASH OF LIGHT THAT
IS SHINING STILL

TOLD BY DR. ZLATKO HRVIĆ

Mostar

November 1998

On the right bank of the Neretva, in the part of town they call *Western Mostar today, I spent my youth and all my years of work. I have not accepted the terminology of "east" and "west," nor do I intend to.

Born in a predominantly Croatian town, forty-two years before the war, my first and last names do not suggest that I am a Muslim so I was not so marked in these strange times. To others my name and background suggested far more that I was a Croat, and as far as I was concerned I had never cared one way or another. I only speak of it now because of the determinants of this story.

I was working at a hospital in a village near Mostar at a time when the Serbian forces first shelled the whole town, including the hospital. Luckily none of the 220 patients was injured. I remained with two technicians. We had no support staff or even cooks. They had all fled. We waited, expecting the army to take the hospital. I made my peace with the fact that I'd be taken prisoner. We were resolved to stay and to behave as normally as possible when the army came in, despite the fact that we were not happy about it.

Suddenly I saw an ambulance hurtling toward the emergency entrance. Before the van had fully stopped, my colleague, a Serb, jumped out and said, very upset, "Quick, get in the ambulance!"

"What's happened?"

"Get in the ambulance and don't ask. By the time I explain it all, it will be too late," he blurted, pushing me into the van, slamming the door, and running back into the building.

When those of us in the ambulance got down to the Buna River we saw thousands of soldiers. There were military units, paramilitaries, police from up in Krajina, White Eagles . . . You couldn't tell who was who. Looking at all the commotion I realized that my colleague had come to extricate me at the very last moment.

The first question the Serbian soldiers asked him when they found him in the building was, "What are you, a Serb, doing here?"

The ambulance was barely able to make its way through the chaos on the road and finally we had to stop because we couldn't get past the throngs of soldiers. At that moment I noticed a friend of mine near the van, wearing the uniform of a Krajina (Serbian) policeman. He lived in Mostar and had land and a house on the Buna River, just outside of town. I had known him since we were children, but in this situation I had no idea whether to speak to him or not. It was a big test for me: I was torn by the question of whether to pretend not to see him. He resolved my dilemma for me when he spotted me. As if nothing strange was going on, he asked, "So, what brings you here? What are you up to?"

"I'm on my way home from duty at the hospital," I answered through the open window, outwardly calm.

"So, what's keeping you?"

"You can see for yourself that I can't get through."

Without a word he walked in front of the ambulance and moved the soldiers aside several hundred feet. When he had brought us through the bottleneck he patted me on the shoulder and said, easily, "Hey, take care. Stop by. Come over when you've got the time."

My throat tightened and I couldn't say a word. All I could think was that this might be the last time I'd see the Buna.

When the Serbian troops retreated from Mostar I kept on working at the hospital. I had no major problems although the war had been going on for more than a year. I experienced all the horrors just like everyone else. I was just as exposed to the daily shelling and sniper fire but I was not personally at risk, I was lucky.

A person can accept life like this in hopes that better days will come. But just when we were the most hopeful of things getting better, undreamed of horrors happened instead.

The conflict between Croats and Muslims, a horrible one for me, started in this town in practical terms on 30 June 1993, though objectively it had been going on for a month and a half before that. That was the day in the western part of the city that all the Muslim men between the ages of fifteen and sixty-five were taken off to camps. The building where I lived was no exception. At some point that night they rang at my door. I opened to two armed young men.

"Hand over your ID card," one demanded. The other glanced at the card, and commented, "Didn't I tell you he was a Croat?"

Thanks to my first and last name and my place of birth that didn't make my ethnicity apparent, they passed me by that most horrific night of my life. The screams and moans, the calls of the children and women who were left without their fathers, husbands, and sons echoed all night through the neighborhood where I lived. I do not know how I made it to morning. I kept thinking that I should go out into the street and tell them to take me to the camp, too, though I have to say that at first I did prefer the fact, as any normal man would, that I didn't have to experience such horrors.

In the morning I decided to go out, in hopes that I could make it somehow to the hospital. I couldn't stay hidden in my apartment, waiting for the next round of soldiers to show up at the door. I kept thinking that my white doctor's coat I always wore would be some kind of shield. In fact, that was the hope I clung to. A person at such moments fixates on a totally irrational detail like that. For me it was my white doctor's coat, but when I stepped out of my building I saw an awful scene: around me on all sides swarmed armed soldiers of the Croatian Defense Council forces, many of whom were my closest neighbors, young men I saw every day. I stood there, frozen to the spot, and waited for one of them to arrest me. Nothing happened for what seemed like an eternity until I happened to notice a neighbor who was just at that moment unlocking the door of his car. I stood there, mute, and watched him. I didn't suggest with a single gesture that I was hoping he might help me. He decided himself, came over, and asked, "What are you doing here?"

"I was on my way to work," I answered clumsily.

"Get in, why don't you? I'll give you a ride," he asked, his voice trembling.

"Do you know what you are doing? You have daughters. You may be in trouble for this. Think first," I warned him in a whisper.

"It is because of my daughters. Our children grew up together. For the rest of my life I'll never be able to look them in the eyes if I don't help you now."

His invitation was like a flash of light for me, brighter than the flash when a shell explodes, a flash that is shining still today. I think that I was one of the few who experienced something like that during those days.

It seemed to take forever to get to the hospital, though it wasn't far from my home. We didn't speak a word. We were probably thinking the same thing. If they'd stopped us, the two of us would have been in the same danger and we'd share the same fate. Perhaps his would have been even worse, because he was trying to save one of the enemy! The Renault was shaking so much with our fear that I thought everybody else on the road could see it and they'd know and would stop us and pull us both out of the car. I wasn't as fearful for myself as I was for my neighbor. We were lucky. We went by countless sentry posts but no one flagged us down. When we stopped in front of the hospital I invited him in for a cup of coffee. He signaled me with a light wave to be on my way.

I watched him through the window. For a full fifteen minutes he sat motionless in his car, unable to drive.

Later I learned from my wife that he went right back to tell them that I'd gotten safely to the hospital, which meant a kind of freedom for me. He offered to bring my wife and daughters to stay at his apartment so that he could protect them until I was able to come back.

I stayed at the hospital for a week, thanks to colleagues of mine. One of them wrote an order for me and my wife to attend a congress in Zagreb, and set aside an ambulance for us in which we made it to Split with many difficulties.

Now I am working in the eastern part of Mostar because I have no choice. Personally, I do not accept this division. There is only one Mostar.

ONE GOOD TURN
DESERVES ANOTHER

TOLD BY RAJKA BOŠNJAK

Sarajevo

November 1998

I lived in the Grbavica part of Sarajevo with my husband, Dragan, who is a Croat, in a high-rise dubbed the "shopping center" on the sixteenth floor. My background is Serbian. Above us Biljana *Plavšić, who became a Republika Srpska leader, used to live with her mother. The two of them moved out of their apartment together on 22 May 1992.

Immediately after that, on the night between the 23rd and 24th of May, three and a half floors of our building burned between their apartment and ours. We spent the next fifteen days at Dragan's brother's place. While we were still at the shopping center a neighbor told me, "Be careful. You shouldn't try to get out through *Vraca. You won't be able to get through."

I couldn't leave my husband. When our apartment burned I felt it would be best if we fled to the old part of Sarajevo, the center of town. At that point in my wildest dreams I couldn't have imagined all the things that would happen in Sarajevo.

Fleeing as the Serbian troops marched in, we registered at the territorial defense office in the Hrasno part of the city. I was afraid because I

166

had never officially changed over my documents to my married name, and my maiden name was Serbian. They asked us where we were headed. We said we were going to Dragan's company. We were looking for his Muslim friend.

"He went home," they told us.

We went to look for him where he lived with his wife and his daughter and grandson. There we heard he had gone off to his weekend cottage in Otes, where we finally found them. They greeted us with such warmth, gave us clothing and fed us, and let us take baths. We spent fifteen days with them.

When the Serbian forces took Otes, their daughter, with her husband and child, came to join them in that two-room apartment, so we left and went to Dragan's company, where we slept in his office for a month and a half on a cot. We ate once a day. During that time Dragan's colleague, a Muslim woman, brought us each a roll every morning and she took our laundry home with her to wash, because I had nowhere to wash it myself.

Later we moved to an apartment that a colleague of Dragan's, who had left for Belgrade, offered us. He brought us in and showed us where everything was. He even left us some food. He said, "Use everything as if it is yours. I will be staying with my sister and brother and I'll drop by from time to time."

That was the last time we saw him, and Dragan told me later that his friend had left for Belgrade.

It was cold in the apartment. There was no electricity or heat and we didn't have a stove. Keeping out of sight of snipers, we'd roam around the streets and scavenge anything that might burn, even old shoes. We brought home what we'd scavenged, burned it, and cooked whatever we had, usually rice and beans. Anyone who had beans was living in luxury. Beans are as good as meat. Anyone who had money bought himself a stove, but we didn't. We didn't have any money. I had two gold rings, which I traded for eight pounds of flour.

A neighbor, a Muslim woman, stopped by one evening at the apartment and told us, "When it gets dark, come over to my place with Dragan. I'll give you a stove. Just so the other neighbors don't see. There are some of them who haven't got a stove yet, and they'll be angry that I gave one to you, you being new here."

Dragan and her son brought the stove down to our place as agreed.

We were overjoyed. That happened right before the 1993 New Year. We made a fire and I cooked a little something, so that we could warm up and eat something warm. It was a holiday for us but it didn't last long, because a neighbor came quickly to the door. He lived upstairs in the attic, and said, "My apartment is full of smoke, something's burning!"

We had only just felt the warmth of the stove when I had to take a pot of water and douse the fire.

We slept in the hallway because the apartment was on Tršćanska St. and snipers kept sniping from the Jewish cemetery.

At the time we moved into the Tršćanska St. apartment, hunger was already quite widespread. I'd brave the sniper fire to forage for weeds so we could survive.

One day I heard that Caritas, the Catholic charity, was distributing aid. I asked Dragan, "What do you think of me going to church? Maybe Caritas will give us something?"

"No point in trying. You are a Serb and even though I am a Croat, both of us used to be communists. We have no right to that aid," he said brusquely.

"At least give me your ID so I can try," I pleaded, but he was implacable.

One morning in March 1993 a neighbor told me they were giving out milk at Caritas. The busybodies in the neighborhood scared me with stories that the priest was asking, "Why did you go and marry someone of another faith? Time to reap what you sowed."

I was longing for a cup of milk; we were eating nothing but weeds at the time and we were thrilled whenever we had enough grain to bake bread.

That evening I said nothing to my husband. When he fell asleep I stole his ID card from his pocket and replaced it with his passport, which was left over from before the war, unused.

I resolved that night that I'd go to Caritas in the morning. Let them say what they wanted, they wouldn't kill me. I was very excited when I stood before the door to the parish office, thinking, "I should knock and say 'Praised be to Jesus' but those are words I've never uttered in my whole life, like 'God help me.'"

When I went in, I said, "Praised be to Jesus."

"Praised be his name. Sit here and wait a moment while I finish with these people and then I'll be right with you, ma'am," said Don Luka Brković, the parish priest in Marijin Dvor.

Preoccupied with my thoughts of what kind of a "ma'am" I could be when I didn't know which I was more, hungry or filthy, I jumped when the priest sat down next to me, and asked, "How can I help you?"

"Let me explain, sir. I am a Serb. My husband is a Croat. We were communists before the war, and now we are nothing, we are refugees from Grbavica. I heard that you were distributing milk. My husband and I are starving. If we qualify as members we would be very grateful, and if we don't, my apologies for taking up your time."

"Since you are so honest, I'll be glad to do all I can," Don Luka said gently, with a smile, giving me a slip of paper that would allow me to get two pounds of powdered milk.

The forgotten fragrance of cooking milk astonished Dragan when he asked, from the door, "Where did that come from?"

"The priest gave it to me."

"What priest?"

"I signed up at Caritas," I said. He stared at me in disbelief, not knowing that his ID was with me.

We were members of Caritas for three years after that. We got food and help at the Marijin Dvor church whenever it arrived. They never kept us separate from the rest of them. The two of us literally survived thanks to their help. I will never forget their kindness.

During 1994 all the neighbors had natural gas piped in. Each gave from 300 to 500 German marks for the cost of installing the pipes. We had no money to pay for it. A year passed and we were still out collecting paper, bits of wood, trash to burn.

One day three of Dragan's friends came by. One brought some screws, another some pipe, another a vent. They brought a gas man with them who didn't charge anything. They improvised the hookup and finally we, too, had gas. That was an experience for me! That was the life! When I lit the gas flame and sat down I'd say to myself, "Could this be happening, that you are sitting and getting warm and you can cook dinner?" Until then it was always: if I had the beans, macaroni, or rice, then I'd have nothing to burn. If I had the fuel to burn, I'd have no water. If I had the fire and the water, there'd be no food. Something was always missing, and often enough I didn't dare go out looking for what I was missing because of the snipers who were always shooting at us.

One evening we were very hungry. Dragan asked me, "Do you have anything?"

"A neighbor gave me a handful of macaroni in a paper bag. I don't know where it's from or if it's any good."

There was no electricity. The only light we had was from an improvised candle. We'd pour a little water in a glass, and, if we were lucky, a little oil, which was a rarity; I'd make a wick out of cotton. I cooked up the macaroni without oil, salt, or pepper, because I had nothing. I rinsed them out with only a little water because I didn't have enough of that either, and served them onto the plates. Dragan stared into his plate, which he could barely see, and asked, "Where did you get pepper?"

"I didn't pepper them," I answered, a little surprised.

We brought the candle over and found we were looking at a heap of worms.

There was a knock at the door one evening, and when I asked, "Who's there?" a voice said, "The military police." I opened the door and saw two men in the dark, one of them in uniform.

He asked, "Do you recognize me?"

"No," I answered, scared until I could see in the dark that they were good friends of ours from before the war.

"We came to take the two of you out for a drink," they announced.

At that time Sarajevo was burning: explosions of shells were rocking the city, sniper bullets whistled through the air.

"I'm not going out there and getting murdered. Dragan can go with you if he wants," I said and started to cry.

"Why are you crying?" they asked.

"How can I do anything but cry?" I answered, sobbing even harder.

"Is it that you're hungry?" they suddenly realized.

"We are, we're starving. We haven't had bread for three days."

"Is this possible!?" they protested in unison.

"It certainly is possible. Please, don't tell Dragan. He'll be angry that I'm complaining."

"You'll get a sack of flour when Dragan gets back," they said, and left.

An hour later my husband came back with a fifty-pound sack of flour. That meant more to me at that point than if they'd brought me a sack full of golden ducats.

Before the war I had worked in the place I am from, in a restaurant up on Jahorina Mountain. Sadik showed up to work, a young man with no experience. He had been born in *Višegrad. He was much younger than me and at first he had no skills. The staff and the guests always teased and harassed him. The director wanted to fire him many times because every time Sadik saw him, out of fear he would drop the tray of drinking glasses he was holding. I protected him because he was an honest village boy. I could tell because I was from a village myself. We worked together for twelve years. I would cover for him during the Muslim feast of Bairam so that he could go home to his family, and he would cover for me over the St. John's Saint's Day so that I could join my family's *slava*. We trusted each other: we'd leave the cash register to one another, uncounted.

The day before the war began, I left the night shift. Because of the barricades I couldn't get back to work any more, but I have never been sorry that I ended up where I am.

My brother, who is nineteen years older than me, told me, right before the war, "If war should break out, you are welcome to come up and stay with me on Jahorina, but, God help me, Dragan cannot come with you."

"How can you say that?"

"I wouldn't be able to protect him."

"How could that be possible? During World War II our mother saved so many Partisans from the Chetniks. She hid Vukica Grbić for forty days in the stable with her child, and she got Muslim women to trade their traditional trousers for skirts so that the Chetniks wouldn't slaughter them. Can it be that I am hearing that my very own brother can't look after me and my husband?" I asked him angrily. We no longer spoke, because the war had divided us. I couldn't forget that the whole length of the war, but after the war I had to admit to my brother that he was right.

"I was angry then, but now I can thank you. I had no idea at that point of the quantity of evil we were going to be faced with."

My whole family lives on Jahorina Mountain. I told them to their faces, "I was born here, I worked here for twenty-two years, but I can't live with you here any more."

In mid-September 1993 I was visiting with a neighbor in the next apartment. When I came home, another neighbor said, "Oh, Rajka, a tall boy was looking for you carrying a big suitcase. I'm not sorry he didn't find you, but you can bet I'm sorry about that suitcase. He took it with him."

My neighbors had eyes only for the bag, how big it was, and who was bringing what in it. I thought for a long time of who it might be. My youngest brother was tall like that, so it occurred to me that maybe he had escaped from somewhere and found me here. Then again, I thought, "What good would it do him to come here. He's a Serb, and they'd grab him and take him to jail or murder him." All sorts of things went through my mind for that hour until someone knocked at the door. It was Sadik standing in the doorway, pulling a suitcase on wheels.

"If I hadn't found you now, I was thinking out there on the street in front of the building that I would have given the bag to the first grandmother-aged lady I came across. I'd explain to her that I couldn't take it back with me all the way to Pofalići."

"How could you have given it to just anyone? You'd be sinning against your soul! I would have waited for you all day long if I'd had a suitcase that size," I answered, laughing.

He told me how the war had trapped him and his brother in Sarajevo where they were drafted into the army. His mother had gone from Visoko to Pofalići where she moved into an abandoned Serbian house which had a little garden. He had no idea what had happened to the rest of his family who had been expelled from Visoko and scattered.

"My mother remembered, and told me, 'Sadik, you know how much Rajka meant to you back then. Don't you go forgetting her now' and she sent you whatever she had. Unpack the suitcase, please. I need it," he said.

When I opened the bag, I couldn't believe my eyes. If my mother were alive today and had packed me a bag, she wouldn't have packed it with as many things as Sadik's mother had. Everything in there was rinsed and clean. I took out a layer of green beans, a layer of potatoes, a layer of parsley, carrots, pears, apples, zucchini, everything we were longing for. We had forgotten what was like to eat potatoes. We didn't know what vegetables tasted like any more.

That last spring of the war you could buy lettuce and scallions at the marketplace. Once I went down to the marketplace, longing for vegetables, at the risk of being shot by a sniper. I told the person selling the vegetables, "Two pounds of lettuce, please, and some scallions, but I have no plastic bag and I have no money to pay you."

"No need to pay, ma'am," he said, and packed the vegetables up in a new plastic bag. Happy, since the war had made us all crazy, I walked quite a ways from the marketplace driven by one thought alone: I hoped the snipers wouldn't kill me before I got to my apartment. I had just happened to notice that written on the plastic bag in large letters was the word: BELGRADE. I quickly took my blazer off and covered the bag with it. The snipers could have murdered me just for the bag. I ran home as fast as my legs would carry me.

In late 1995 the woman who owned the apartment, who had gone off to Serbia at the start of the war, knocked at the door. I saw how she was trembling when I opened the door. All she could say was, "It's me, Duška."

"Come on in. Don't be afraid," I told her and hugged her when she'd stepped into the front hall.

We had a little something at that point, which Dragan's sister had sent us from Sweden. I was pleased that I could offer her juice and coffee.

"Can I see how the apartment looks?" she asked.

"Of course you can," we answered.

"Can I take some of my things back?" she asked anxiously.

"Well, all of it is yours. We came here empty-handed. Everything we had burned up in our apartment."

"I'll just take a few things that are mementos from my mother," she said softly, as if trying to explain. We understood each other as if we'd been sisters. That evening she hadn't brought a bag or a suitcase with her, so she just took a few items of clothing. Dragan walked her down to the tram she took to her brother-in-law's in Otoka. The next day she came to take sheets, blankets. There were tapestries hanging in the living room. Dragan asked her, "Would you like me to take down the tapestries and pack them up?"

"No, they are my handiwork. Keep them here as a memento."

In the small room where I'd spent the whole war there was a photograph of a lovely little girl. She took down the picture and put it in her suitcase. I felt the tears well up in my eyes.

"Are you going to take Jelena away from me?" I asked through the tears.

"Well, I'd like to," she said, brushing away tears herself, and then she put the picture back on the wall and asked, "Take care of it as if she is your own little girl."

"I will care for it, thank you so much," I could barely speak.

She left, and the photograph stayed behind.

Later she called and said, "They were upset that I didn't bring back Jelena's picture."

"Please, don't you worry. Wherever I go, her picture will go with me. If you really want it, when someone comes to Sarajevo from Belgrade send him here and I'll give him the picture."

Her daughter's picture hangs on that wall today.

RAPE IN GRBAVICA

TOLD BY ZDENKA PERKOVIĆ

The *Kovačići part of Sarajevo

October 1998

I earned my pension working at the Sarajevo military hospital. The ward I worked in dealt in treatment that had to be kept confidential. I maintained strictly confidential documentation. In my file my assessment was: "Follows orders, does her job conscientiously, uninterested politically, devout."

I was always faithful to Catholicism and did what I could to help others. Socialism was a nice idea, but the individuals who tainted it were not so nice.

Since 1934 I have been living in Grbavica in the area called Kovačići, and it was on the first line of separation right from the start of war operations in Sarajevo. The Serbian army had to make routes in 1993 that it could use to access the front combat lines. They explained to us that it wasn't so much that they were evicting us, as that they were going to move us into other empty apartments, whose inhabitants had fled. They moved me about 300 feet further down into an apartment that had already been stripped of its windows, doors, and flooring.

People assigned to a work detail moved us. It took a lot of effort. I borrowed things from my new neighbors, and somehow managed to get the apartment into good enough shape that it was possible to live there.

Officially I had been assigned to a work detail, but my job was swabbing the army cafeteria. Although I was seventy-one years old, the work wasn't hard for me because I was in good health. A neighbor of mine worked at the kitchen, too, a Serb named Zoran. He would slip me more food than I otherwise would have been allowed. Often at night he would knock on the door and leave a little container of food. Whenever he saw me he'd say, "Don't tell anyone I'm bringing you food. They'll kill me. You, as a Croat, are the enemy. Anyone feeding the enemy runs the risk of getting into big trouble."

One December day in 1995 I saw two unfamiliar young men approaching the entranceway to our building. They couldn't have been older than thirty. I went to hide at the apartment of a Serbian neighbor. They were looking for me. The neighbor peeked out a little later and said, "They've gone."

I quickly went down to Zoran's apartment and rang the bell. "Zoran, can you hide me?"

"Quick, come inside."

I only had time enough to stand behind the door when his doorbell rang. He had to open up for them.

"Where is that Croatian woman?"

"What Croatian woman? I don't know who you are talking about."

They came in and found me immediately. They took the keys to my apartment, pushed me out into the hallway and threw me on the stairs. I screamed. One of them grabbed Zoran by the chest and shoved him toward the bathroom. He was lucky that he banged into the closed door.

"You! Harboring Ustasha, Croats, and Muslims, are you? If we find her hiding in your house ever again, we'll slit her throat first, and then yours," they screamed.

Then they pushed me into my apartment and maltreated me both physically and mentally. One of them held a knife, the other, a pistol.

"How do you want us to murder you? Take your pick. How about we slit your throat? Or you'd rather be shot?"

"Sir, do as you wish. You are the ones with the guns and the power. If God wills it, so be it."

"God has nothing to do with this. I can murder you if I feel like it."

"Yes, sir, I know you can," I said, reconciled to my fate. I was in luck. They left quickly. I don't hold it against them all; there are always rotten apples.

Zoran couldn't let me hide in his apartment any more, but he did keep sneaking me food. When his wife died, the whole neighborhood scorned him for burying her at the Catholic cemetery. The Serbian Orthodox priest didn't want to go out and hold the funeral and there was no Catholic priest in Grbavica. They taunted him, "What kind of a Serbian Orthodox believer are you, burying that Ustasha woman?"

In December 1995 two Muslim sisters, seventy and seventy-two years old, were raped in Grbavica. All of us lived in fear. In January 1996 a young thug smashed his way into my apartment by breaking down the door.

"Give me whatever you've got to eat."

What he couldn't eat he packed to take with him but he wouldn't go. He sat on a chair and waved me his pistol in front of me. Two bullets fell out when he cocked it.

"See these?"

"Yes."

"If you don't do what I tell you to do, I'll murder you, and no one will know because they won't hear the shot."

From his behavior I understood he was going to rape me. I pleaded with him, "Son, in the name of God, I implore you on your mother's milk, spare me, please spare me!"

"I am no neighbor of yours. I am from over in Serbia. How would I have known your name, that you are Croatian, that you are Catholic, that you are an Ustasha, if your neighbors hadn't told me so? You Croatian women are the best . . ."

"What do you want with me? Can't you see that I could be your great grandmother?" I pleaded with him.

"Shut up!"

He sat on the chair and unbuttoned his pants. I wept and pleaded with him, asking him to spare me, but nothing helped. He abused me sexually in all imaginable ways. If he'd cut me to pieces, I think it would have been easier to bear . . . He was not drunk. He left at two o'clock in the morning.

Everything depended on your neighbors. In the same part of town there were Croats and Muslim whose apartments, thanks to their neighbors, were never trespassed by the military and nothing ugly ever happened to them.

There were Serbs in my neighborhood who helped me and others who helped me who weren't Serbs. They did everything they did in secret, and asked me not to say who'd helped me. They all moved away after reintegration but they should never have left.

During the war in Grbavica there were Serbian doctors working who treated us quite decently. They would examine us and prescribe medicine for us just the same way they treated the Serbs. I even received humanitarian aid where no one treating me differently.

And today, three years after the war, my neighbor Mira, a Serbian woman, helps me out.

TAKE WITH YOU THE
PEOPLE WHO ARE YOURS

TOLD BY DR. SEAD ŠETIĆ

Sarajevo

January 1999

I was born in 1942. I graduated from the School for Dental Technology in Sarajevo, and after that I worked for five years in Višegrad in dentistry. After that I graduated from the School of Dentistry in Sarajevo and there I settled down and worked. In March 1992 I left my job as an assistant professor at the School of Dentistry, left my family in Sarajevo, and went to Višegrad to help the people where I used to work. I was respected by people belonging to all three ethnic groups who lived in the area. My sister was living in Višegrad with her son, who was an engineer. I wanted to help them. They managed to get out, as did many others, thanks to the fact that I was there. I arrived in Višegrad on 24 March 1992, and I wanted to see what was happening and whether there was anything a person could do to prevent trouble.

From the moment when ethnically focused parties were promoted in Bosnia and Herzegovina, I was certain that this would lead to terrible suffering. I tried, through public efforts, to explain to people that the only way to live in those areas and to survive was to keep things the way they had been, that there had to be coexistence, because World War II had done so much harm precisely because of the divisions and fostering of ethnic hatreds. Because of that, for the last years before this war began I would go to Višegrad every Friday. War was inevitable at that point in the country that Tito had created and kept at peace for fifty years, which no one else in the world could have done.

The truth must be told. The door has just cracked open to let in the truth, but when the million hearts who know the truth open wide, everything will be known.

In late March three buses arrived in Višegrad from Serbia, from the town of Valjevo, packed with men wearing civilian clothes and brandishing Chetnik banners with pictures of skulls on them. When they started draping the Drina bridge with their banners, fifty of us stepped forward to stop them, and traffic was held up for about five hours until Pecikoza arrived. He was a Višegrad Serb who was president of the municipal executive council. He talked to them and urged them to go peacefully back to Serbia.

After that, preparation began for the sale of weapons in town. Every person who had 1000 German marks could buy an automatic weapon. Black marketers were selling them off of trucks.

Wanting to prevent the trouble that was brewing over the town, I gave a speech over loudspeakers in front of the Višegrad Hotel in which I begged people I knew and who knew me to continue living the way we had until then, that neighbors should only help their neighbors, never hurt them. I cautioned them that mercenaries would come who would stir up trouble and we all had to stand up to them. There were local Serbs at that assembly. They all applauded, and I displayed a portrait of Tito at the hotel. There was even a circle dance.

While the *Užice Corps of the Yugoslav People's Army was stationed here, there was some sort of stand-off. The people trusted that the Yugoslav army would protect them. When this corps withdrew, paramilitary groups arrived in mid-May, first Šešelj's men, and then Arkan's. They ransacked homes and carted everything away. First they demanded that people hand over weapons with the promise that nothing would happen to anyone, so people did as they were told. The people who refused to hand over their weapons were taken into the woods and probably executed. In the villages and in town only the poorest remained. They were sure that no one would bother them because they had done no one any harm.

In early April there was shooting around town. People began burning down Muslim houses and then that spread to the surrounding villages. When they started torching houses in Dobrun, people began to flee to the nearby towns of Goražde and Žepa. Shortly thereafter, the authorities called on the people to come back, saying that nothing would happen to them. They would be assigned to a work detail. That was all. About five or six busloads of men, women, and children did return. After a few days these people began disappearing at night. The paramilitary soldiers were taking them from their homes. Some were taken to the prison that was at the police station. There were always fifty or sixty people held there. When they took away twenty people at night whom they murdered, they would bring in the same number of new people. They took away a large number of girls, women, and men to the Vilina Vlas Motel, where they used them in various ways and later had them murdered.

Most of the Serbian inhabitants, or at least those who sensed the imminent trouble and who were honorable people and wanted to have nothing to do with it or watch it happening, left, at that time, for Serbia.

The people perpetrating the terrible things were drugged or drunk. Some of them were people who had been released from prison, from psychiatric wards, and there were foreign mercenaries among them from Russia, Bulgaria, and Romania. They wore uniforms with some sort of insignia and lapel pins on their chests. Some of them wore beards. Around the time they were searching for Murat Šabanović, who had blown up a nearby hydroelectric dam in an attempt to flood them out, I saw about 100 drunken soldiers shooting and cursing in front of the police station. They broke into a cafe and toted all the liquor out into the streets where they caroused, dead drunk. I did not see a single man from Višegrad in uniform. About 100 paramilitaries were stationed in the house of a man who was later murdered at the school.

The Višegrad municipality had numbered prewar about 40,000. At that time there were about 2,500 refugees who fled across the Drina River to the left bank, which was in Serbia, along a seven-mile stretch running from the village, where there was a turpentine factory, all the way to a village that included five hamlets. Uniform-wearing members of paramilitary formations entered these hamlets with armored cars and tanks. They searched from house to house, picked up people and brought them back to Višegrad in marching columns. In the neighboring village they searched us and took everything we had on us.

At the new soccer club playing field I found myself with a group of 2,500 people, 90 percent of whom were women, tiny babies, and ninety-year-olds. It was raining. We were all in the stands when a military helicopter landed and out of it stepped Serbian colonels Ojdanić and Jovanović. Immediately before it landed they threw out leaflets calling on people to hand over the weapons they'd been hiding, and that if they complied, they would not be harmed. Colonel Ojdanić walked around in a circle staring silently at the people, saying nothing. He got back into the helicopter and flew away. Colonel Jovanović remained on the soccer field in his Yugoslav People's Army uniform, presenting himself as commander of the White Eagle paramilitaries. He asked who was in charge among us. I stepped forward because the president of the municipality wasn't there. Jovanović asked me, "Do we know each other?"

"I am Dr. Sead Šetić," I introduced myself.

"I believe I know you, but you don't remember me," he answered with a smile. "Don't you play soccer?"

"I did, for Sloboda, the Užice team," I answered.

"That's where I know you, then. We were teammates."

"I am a doctor, a humanist, I work at the Krčag army hospital," I continued.

"I, too, am a humanist," said the colonel.

"Can you see how all these poor, innocent people have been brought here?" I asked him.

"Don't you worry, doctor. I'll release them all this evening. Nothing will happen to them in the territory under my control, between the old and the new bridges. But watch out, you have plenty of your local breed of vulture around," he added.

"Their homes have been torched. Do you give your permission for them to find places to stay in abandoned homes here?" I asked him.

"Yes, they may. Each will receive a quart of milk and two loaves of bread. Take with you the people who are yours and get going," he told me curtly.

I turned and looked at all the people. Appalled by the dilemma he was placing me in I said, softly, "All of them are mine, Colonel."

"Look, get serious. Take anyone who is with you and get out of here." He turned and told the major that he was to let me out and anyone with me, and no one would touch us.

I went over to a woman with two little girls who were one and two years old, and took them, along with an elderly women. I carried the children five miles on my back in a sack I tied up like a rucksack. Their father was in Austria, where they are all now living. They came to visit me in Sarajevo after the war. Their mother told the two, lovely big girls, "If it hadn't been for this doctor, the three of us wouldn't be alive today."

That evening Colonel Jovanović did, indeed, release all the people from the soccer field, but that same night they were caught and murdered by members of the paramilitary units. Of the 2,500 at the stadium that night, about 1,000 died. Some of them were taken to the new bridge, which was illuminated by powerful spotlights from both sides. For nights from the bridge you could hear mothers shrieking and screaming, "Don't take my child, kill me instead."

How could these insane idiots fail to see that you can't simply extermi-
nate an entire people? The native Americans were not exterminated. They
were murdered for centuries, but there are still Indians alive today.

In early May, when my sister's house had been shelled while she was in
it, I went off to see what had happened to her. I was walking down the street
wearing an officer's trench coat when frenzied monsters, members of paramilitary units, skewered a disabled man I knew with a bayonet right in front
of me. The man stood there, his eyes open wide, leaning back against a wall,
looking at me, hoping I could help him. I tried to shield him, and pushed
away the soldier who had stabbed him. The second soldier scraped a knife
horizontally across my neck, though he didn't actually slit my throat. Yet
another smashed me in the face with his gun and knocked out some of my
teeth. At that moment what saved me was my military ID showing I was a
reserve officer in the Yugoslav People's Army. All bloody, I pulled it out
and showed them. The lieutenant cursed the soldier who had struck me,
saying, "What are you doing?! He's one of us!"

I could tell my artery wasn't severed, so I asked one of them for a cigarette and spread the tobacco on the wound and bound it with a sleeve I
tore off my shirt.

Dragan Lukić showed up in the first days of the war. He was born in Bosnia
but he had been living somewhere in Serbia, in Belgrade they said. He had
attended secondary school in Višegrad. His teacher, Suljo, told me that one
day Lukić broke into his house and demanded his wife tell him where Suljo
was. The woman wouldn't say anything, so Lukić opened the door to the
bathroom and saw Suljo there, terrified.

"What's wrong, professor. No need to hide. You were good to me, I
won't do you any harm, don't you worry," Lukić told him. He let Suljo go
but there were others who wanted to murder him. There was a time when
I saved Suljo.

Among all the people who had come to town who were strangers to me

I ran into a familiar face: Drakulović. He and his wife had been teachers in the Višegrad commerce-track secondary school. After two decades it was discovered that he had faked his own diploma and his wife's. Because of that he was sentenced to four years in jail and he was serving his term in *Foča at the time the war broke out. He was released from jail then and declared himself a vojvoda, a military leader.

His bodyguard brought me over to him, and he said to me, "You are a good doctor and a good man, and your sister is a good woman so I won't blow your brains out right here on the street, though otherwise I would."

He let me go. He stayed on in the function of town manager.

A list was drawn up in Višegrad of people to be murdered, fifty of us. We had been identified from a video film taken of the bridge when we protested their draping the bridge with the Chetnik banners. The whole confrontation at the bridge was taped by a paralyzed Muslim who gave them the cassette in return for them letting him leave town. He is still living in Germany today. They went from house to house and murdered most of the fifty. Only six of us survived.

I hid for twenty days or so in the home of the late Pero, whose son was one of their commanders, figuring they'd never search his home. During that time Višegrad was like a ghost town and all you could see on the empty streets were drunken, wild members of paramilitary units. After a while, seeing that I had no other choice, I went straight to the police. At that point people were being taken off buses headed for Serbia, and anyone who didn't have a permit to go, or who was on one of the lists of people to be murdered, would be pulled off. Patrols on the Rzav bridge were in charge of this and they killed the people they took off the buses right there. I went to the police two days in a row and asked Chief of Police Tomić to sign a permit for me to leave town and go to a small town just over the Drina into Serbia. The telephone lines were down and I wanted to get to the nearest phone to hear how my family was doing back in Sarajevo.

The second day Tomić signed my permit, saying, "After all, you are a decent man."

There were several travelers from Višegrad on the bus with me when I left, 24 May 1992, but most of them were from Serbia. At the first checkpoint four bearded soldiers got on, one at the front, and three at the back. While three of them were inspecting IDs and permits from the travelers leaving Višegrad, the fourth stood in front of me for a few minutes, and then said, "Doctor, why, Father and I were just talking about you. Where are you headed?"

I said nothing, and he continued, "I know." He chased the other three off the bus and ordered them not to bother or search anyone. As he was leaving he said, "Good luck," over his shoulder.

I still don't know whose son that was.

At the next checkpoint a soldier got on and said, "Which one of you is Dr. Sejo?" My first thought was that the boy at the earlier checkpoint had told them to murder me here, because he hadn't wanted to do it himself. I was barely able to say, "That's me." He said something to the driver, waved to me, and left the bus. My permit only allowed me to go to a nearby village, but I made it all the way to Užice, further into Serbia, without a hitch. From there I went to *Titograd in Montenegro where an old friend from my days as a student sat me down after I'd been there awhile.

"Look, you have my summer house on the Montenegrin coast and you may stay there for the rest of your life if you please. But it is far better that you don't stay on in Montenegro. It isn't wise. They are picking up the Muslims here from eastern Bosnia. I think it would be wisest that I take you, while it's still possible, through Serbia to the Hungarian border."

His fears proved to be well founded. That thug I'd seen in action back in Višegrad, Milan Lukić, pulled Muslims off the train in Štrpci, brought them back to Višegrad and murdered them there.

For several days I didn't leave my friend's house, and then he drove me up to a place in Serbia near the Hungarian border. From there I got to Germany, and from Germany I made it back to Sarajevo.

TEARS IN THE EYES
OF A GIANT

TOLD BY MIRA JANKOVIĆ

*Bosanska Dubica

January 1996

I lived in Zenica with my husband, Milan, and our children, Nataša and Dragan, until April 1994. Before the war broke out Zenica was an ethnically mixed town. We socialized with people of all the different backgrounds. Our background was Serbian.

I was terribly disappointed in people during the war. Many people I had considered to be my friends had changed, and this had nothing to do with how much education they had. It was only the rare person who was consistent. I had an apartment. Whenever I went out onto my balcony I'd hear all sorts of repulsive things other people were saying.

"All Serbs are really Chetniks deep down! Even an unborn baby is already a Chetnik and all of them deserve to die!"

I shut myself in and didn't go out at all for fear of trouble. No one actually came into our apartment to harass us, but they often threatened me over the phone.

I saw that the Croatian-Muslim army was even recruiting foreign mujahedin into its ranks who did terrible things wherever they went. I was afraid that Dragan might be called up to serve in that army. Life in town had become unbearable with the arrival of the mujahedin. There was tension in the air even without the unkind words.

Milan and I were unemployed. At the start of the war they took my husband's truck that he had been driving for years. We had to go out for a work detail, and we had no rights. When no one else felt like guarding the garage and company, he would go and hold the duty shifts.

At first we lived from what little savings we had socked away. Once Zenica found itself in a blockade, all of its inhabitants, regardless of their religious affiliation, were in a very difficult position. Food was too expensive, and no one had money. There was no electricity or firewood. It was extremely cold in the apartment. From conversations with those Croats and Muslims who, regardless of the war, still communicated with us, we learned that some of them were living in straits much more dire than ours. We got by thanks to the financial support of members of our family working abroad.

We tried a few times to get out of town. We'd paid in advance, but had no luck. In the end we were relieved each time that we made it back to Zenica with our heads on our shoulders. No one returned the money we'd given them when the attempt failed. We kept inquiring about new connections through Muslims. We began getting provocative phone calls: "So when are you going to try to escape again?" We had the feeling we were constantly being followed.

Finally a confederation was signed between the Muslims and Croats that increased our chances of getting out through Žepče.

A boy who had already gone over that route drew us a sketch of how to get there, and said, "You shouldn't be paying people any more to get you out."

Milan and Dragan, with another three acquaintances, managed to get to Žepče in their second try. Žepče was under Croatian control. They all found a place to stay in the home of a Croat, a guy named Mate, who was the only person in Žepče whom Milan knew from before the war. They stayed there for more than twenty days, and all the while I had no idea where they were or how they were doing because the phones weren't working.

My husband sent me a letter by way of a woman I knew from Žepče and suggested that my daughter and I should join them. In order to bring as many things of ours as we could Nataša and I went back and forth to Žepče several times with orderly papers. We didn't dare to leave the apartment both of us at once because often enough other people moved right in as soon as someone left. Nataša went with a neighbor whose husband had made it out with mine, and I would travel with that woman's daughter.

Mate's wife cooked and washed for five complete strangers for almost a month. When the four of us arrived they greeted us full of love and warmth in their modest home. They shared with us what they had. The nine of us spent another seven days with Mate and his wife, until we left Žepče through an exchange.

Mate was a giant of a man, well over six feet tall. When we parted at the bus that would take us away, tears shone in his eyes.

TUZLA, ABOVE
THE HATRED

TOLD BY MILINKO PERKIĆ

Tuzla

November 1998

Before the war I used to be a wrestler. As a top-notch competitor I was a member of the Bosna team of Sarajevo. I still have the medals from the Yugoslav Championship displayed in my room. Although I am an engineer by profession, when the war started I was out of work. As of April 1995 I started working at the district jail as chief of security.

What always appealed to me in Tuzla was the prevailing spirit of interethnic tolerance, which I always felt at even the most trying moments.

On the day that had been celebrated, for decades, as Youth Day, 25 May 1995, in Tuzla, shrapnel from a shell fired from the Serbian positions up on Ozren murdered the youth of this town. It was the greatest tragedy ever to hit Tuzla. At nine o'clock in the evening, on the main square where teenagers had gathered, seventy-one smiles were snuffed out forever. Another 124 were wounded. There is no way to describe that moment when 200 of somebody's children were lying on the square in pieces, and the parents, relatives, and friends couldn't tell where their child was . . .

Shells rained down on the town for the next three days. The funeral of these innocent young people was held at 4:30 A.M., using outdoor lamps almost in secret. Tuzla didn't even have a proper chance to bid farewell to its children, for fear that the number of victims might be even greater.

That tragedy left its mark on all of us. People rarely speak of it. The impact of the catastrophe on my fellow citizens was enormous. I think that there was no one in town who didn't have someone of their own among those innocent victims. If it wasn't someone of nearer or more distant kin, then it was the child of a friend, neighbor, acquaintance . . .

After a month and a half the Tuzla corps of the army of Bosnia and Herzegovina captured the Ozren territory where the gun stood that had fired that shell. About 100 Serbian fighters were taken prisoner at precisely the site where that gun stood. All the prisoners were brought to the Tuzla district prison. The whole town knew they were there.

I organized extra security measures for the prisoners, fearful of retaliation from the townspeople. It was reasonable to expect that there might be large demonstrations out in front of the prison, or people trying to avenge the unspeakable tragedy. I feared that the parents whose children had been murdered by that shell, their relatives and neighbors, maybe even the whole grieving town, might come to the door of the prison for vengeance and lynching. If there had been a lynch mob it would have been understandable.

I lived in terror that day and into the night. No one came even to shout, curse, throw a stone, and certainly no one tried to enter the prison.

The men spent six months in the prison before they were exchanged. Even during the exchange no one reacted in any way.

For me this was one more proof that Tuzla had risen above the hatred that was everywhere around us.

The prison staff conducted themselves professionally to the maximum according to all the Geneva conventions, and even more. The prisoners received medical attention. Many at first, probably out of fear, didn't dare speak of their problems. One of the prisoners had earlier been a guard in the Batkovići concentration camp near Brčko. I noticed that the others were urging him with pointed looks to speak to me. At my insistence he finally told me, "I have been losing weight every day. I can't keep anything down."

I figured this was from an earlier wound. When I asked the medical staff I learned that this was a problem that might be fatal. We informed the corps, which arranged within two days for a special exchange just for him. He went back to his side so that he could receive the proper treatment.

It happened that Muslims from Tuzla inquired about individual prisoners. They brought them cigarettes in response to requests of the prisoners' family members. Although there had been great divisions in Bosnia, the real interactions among people were never stopped. When someone needed to see to something on the other side, for instance to deliver a message, they would always be able to find a Serbian friend to help, just as the Serbs had their friends among the Croats and Muslims.

The prison guards reported almost daily to me that Muslim refugees who had fled Zvornik were bringing cigarettes to one of the prisoners who had also been a guard at the Batkovići camp. They were Muslims who had been held at that camp and remembered him.

"He was good to all of us. He helped us whenever he could, brought us cigarettes and shielded us."

Everyone loved and admired that man. Foreign news agencies learned that he was there and often visited the prison. They wanted to talk to him but he avoided it, fearing the reactions of his fellow countrymen when he went home one day. He left through an exchange.

PLEASE, MAMA,
DON'T LET THEM TAKE ME

TOLD BY SENADA MEHMEDOVIĆ[†]

Refugee from Višegrad, interviewed in Sarajevo

November 1998

I was born in Visoko, central Bosnia, married Esad in 1974, and moved down to Višegrad in eastern Bosnia on the border with Serbia. Later we built our own home in Sase, a Višegrad outlying area, where we lived with our son, Edin, and our daughter, Azra, until the war.

In May 1992 when the war began, Esad came back from Sarajevo to bring home his pay. He was working in Sarajevo in the public transportation company as a field worker. He was supposed to go back the next day.

Panic erupted that evening; I noticed how my Serbian neighbors were turning the lights out in their houses, so I told my husband, "I'll turn out our lights to see what's going on."

After fifteen minutes an unknown car drove into the yard, and then someone banged on the door and knocked three times. I didn't know what was happening and then I saw that the neighbors had turned their lights back on so I did, too. When I opened the door a flour sack fell into the front hall. Something inside it jangled. When we opened it we found an automatic weapon inside, two pistols, and four bombs. We were mystified and scared. Esad was furious.

194

"Why did you open the door?!"

I called my neighbor and asked her what I should do.

"Hush, don't speak to a soul. Lock it up, we'll talk tomorrow."

I saw a lot of men in uniform the next morning through the window. When I stepped outside a soldier cursed my Muslim mother, swung his gun, and struck me to the ground with blows of the butt. When he got tired of hitting me he left the yard and I crept back to the house, black and blue.

Esad called our neighbor, a Serbian woman, to help.

She said, "I'll come over a little later."

Out of terror even she didn't dare to come by until dark. I figured that really serious trouble was headed our way and told Esad, "You'd better go off to the woods with the boy. I'll stay here with our daughter, come what may."

"I don't want to leave you," he said resolutely.

"You've got to! The Užice Corps forces, troops here from Serbia, are already picking up men and taking them away."

At the entrance to the house they said, "Don't worry, we won't hurt you. We are protecting you. We are just searching for weapons. Do you have any ammunition?"

The next night those soldiers left the village. I pulled the sack out of the house and took it to the woods.

The next day Murat Šabanović took over the hydroelectric dam. There was a lot of shooting and the town imposed a curfew. The people in charge wouldn't let me go anywhere because I wasn't from around there. They figured I meant trouble for them. Soldiers kept coming to our house, mal-treating and beating me.

When Murat let the water out of the reservoir at the dam there was a flood. The soldiers fled but the local people stayed. Murat retreated and fled to Sarajevo, but we stayed there on the right bank of the Drina.

Our Serbian neighbor, Zaga, told us, "Esad, you must get out of here immediately. You'll be murdered!"

I pleaded with him to go, but he refused.

"You have to take Edin away. He is sixteen, they'll murder him, too."

At 2:00 A.M. I finally convinced him to leave. I stayed behind with Azra, who was fourteen. I knew I had to hide her somewhere. I had no better idea than a storage pit dug into the ground.

The next day Milan Lukić, one of the Serbian paramilitary leaders, showed up with four men I didn't know and wanted to know where my daughter was.

"She's gone," I answered.

"You're lying. I need her!"

"She's gone," I dug in my heels.

"Don't lie to me. Bring her out or we'll murder you!"

"So go ahead and kill me. She's not here."

"Who drove away that Serb's car?"

"The army took it, but I don't know who it was from the army."

"I bet you do, but you just won't tell us."

Lukić was the first to hit me. They beat me for a long time but he was the worst, with the butt of his gun. When I fell they kicked me, stomped on me, swore . . . At one point I fainted.

When I came around I was in the woods and I was all bloody. I didn't know what had happened to me. I tried to crawl toward my house because I couldn't stand up from the pain. Stanko, a neighbor of mine, a Serb, came running over from where he'd been hiding in the woods because he was so horrified by what the paramilitary soldiers were doing. I could barely speak because my lower jaw was fractured.

"What did they do to me, Stanko?"

"Lukić and three other men raped you. Forgive me, I watched everything from the bushes but I couldn't help you. If I'd said anything they would have murdered me."

He helped me get halfway back to my house but he didn't dare go any further for fear they'd see him. He ran back even deeper into the woods.

Lukić was looking for him, too, as a traitor. That man made no distinctions; he tortured Serbs who wouldn't join him, too.

I kept on creeping toward my house from the woods on my hands and knees. At one moment I'd caught sight of Esad and Edin in the woods. I signaled to them that they must retreat further in. I had no idea where Lukić and his men were.

When I dragged myself home, Azra ran out of the storage pit but I told her, "Azra, stay in the pit so they don't see you. They'll murder you if they find you."

The next day Lukić was back at my house. He beat me again, cursed my Muslim mother from Visoko, and said, "Tell me where your daughter is!"

I moaned as they hit me. They shaved my head and carved a cross across my whole scalp with a knife.

For the next five days they beat and maltreated me every day. When I was able to go over to my sister-in-law's house I could see what they were doing down by the Drina River banks: they were slitting people's throats, gouging out their eyes, chopping off women's fingers whenever they couldn't pull off their rings.

A soldier saw me and said, "Halt! Come with me. Lukić wants to see you."

I froze. Lukić came over and whacked me in the shoulder with his gun butt.

"Now you are going to have your throat cut, but first tell us where your husband and your son are."

"They're gone."

"You're lying!"

He spun around, furious, that moment because they had just brought in the *imam, the local Muslim clergyman, and his son.

First, in front of all of us they slit his son's throat. Then they made the imam drink his own son's blood. Then they slaughtered three women. I stood and watched Lukić's assistant sharpening his knife.

"What are you waiting for," he asked me.

"I don't know. I'm waiting my turn," I answered.

Just then Tomić appeared. Tomić was the Višegrad chief of police, and he asked me, "Sena, why are you here?"

"I don't know."

Lukić's men turned around and saw Tomić. Clearly they were afraid of him because they all started running. Tomić took out his pistol and without a word he shot Lukić's executioner dead. He put me in his car and drove me home.

He told me, "You can't stay here. Get out of here while you can!"

"Tomić, I've got nowhere to run to."

There was no way I could go anywhere with Azra. There were soldiers everywhere around us, and there were even women serving with them who were very cruel. One of them kicked me in the stomach in front of my house and knocked the air right out of me. Neighbors of mine, Muslim women, were watching but they didn't dare come out of their houses to defend me.

After a few days Lukić came back to my house again.

"You're coming down to the river!"

He beat me on our way down to the Drina. When he stopped I looked up and saw Edin and Esad.

They shot Esad right in front of us with a pistol. Edin pulled free of the butcher who was holding him, flung himself on me, and held me tight around the waist. He plunged his head into my breast and screamed, "Help me, mama! Please don't let them take me!"

I turned to Lukić, "Kill me. Let the boy live."

"I will not. This way we'll kill you with grief," he answered, yanked my son from my arms and slit his throat.

Azra came out of the storage pit. She couldn't bear to leave me alone. Together we buried Edin and Esad. After the funeral my neighbor Stana came over, "Sena, run while you can! You can't stay here any more."

"Why should I? All my family's gone."

"Don't say that. You have Azra and you have got to protect her."

That same day Lukić showed up with his men at my house. They took Azra down to the school building where they'd locked up a lot of the people from the village. I ran down to Zaga.

"Lukić took Azra to the school! Save my girl!"

Zaga's husband, Rajko, and their son, Steva, raced off to the school and absconded with Azra at the last moment. The evildoers hadn't had time to do her any harm, but she came back completely beside herself with what she'd seen.

"Mama, the school is all bloody. They are raping little girls, gouging out their eyes, chopping off their hands, feet, breasts . . . They brought scissors and they are snipping off bits of people as if they were paper."

We stayed twenty more days in the house but nobody touched us any more. The people who had been doing the bestial things in our village were getting caught and some of them were escaping back to Užice. The town was left under the administration of local Serbs who were given orders that they were not to slaughter, beat, or abuse anyone.

At dawn the next day Steva came to tell me, "Sena, while the monsters are sleeping you have to go with Azra and report to the Red Cross. Then tell them you want to go to Visoko to stay with your mother."

I took Azra by the hand and we started out on our way to Višegrad. Zaga, Rajko, and our other Serbian neighbors came out of their houses. They said good-bye to us and wept.

On our way through the villages to Višegrad I wept, too. I couldn't shield Azra from seeing all the horrors we had to pass. From a distance we could see the old stone bridge in Višegrad. Frenzied murderers had fifteen-year-old boys and men on the bridge and they were stabbing them in the back and flinging them over the railing into the Drina and while they fell toward the water they were shooting at them.

We ran toward the new bridge, below which hung twelve naked men, their eyes gouged out, their tongues dangling, their chests and guts flayed, their arms and legs mutilated . . .

There weren't any more butchers on that bridge but we barely made it across. We slipped on blood up to our ankles, human intestines tripped us, there was so much blood, and eyes and human hearts . . .

We reported to the Red Cross that we wanted to be taken by convoy out of Višegrad. They asked us there to give up our rights to our property. All of us wrote that on ordinary paper and signed it. At times like that property doesn't mean much. None of us even believed we'd survive.

There were seven trucks under a tarpaulin and three buses at the place where the convoy was supposed to start. Any young men who, who knows how, made it this far and got to the truck and were about to climb into it were taken off and slaughtered next to the truck right there in front of all of us. The people who did this wore bushy beards and fur hats with Chetnik insignias, with gun belts slung over their grimy, bloody uniforms. Many of them were drunk . . .

The driver of one of the buses was a Serb from one of the villages near ours, Mlađo Pecikoza, and he recognized me.

I went over to him and asked, "Mlađo, please look after Azra, these men are going to want to pull her off the bus."

Without a word Mlađo took hold of Azra's hand, took her into the bus, and sat her down next to him. The inflamed madmen were pulling little girls off the bus and they tried to take her, too, but Mlađo wouldn't let them.

"What is this Muslim girl to you?" they hissed angrily.

He replied, "Don't insult her! She is a cousin of mine and she's going with me!"

I stood by the bus next to a woman who had a little girl, a baby, in her arms and held her three-and-a-half-year-old son by the hand. They were pulling little boys from their mothers. A soldier came over and grabbed the boy by the hand. The boy withdrew his hand into his sleeve, and, I don't know where the courage came from, I pulled the little boy to me so that the soldier ended up holding just his jacket. I clutched the child and held on to him and they shoved the mother onto a different bus. With this un-known little boy I managed to get on the bus.

In our bus, aside from Mlađo there was another Serbian man from Užice and a policeman, someone Murat Šabanović had held as a hostage down at the hydroelectric dam and had badly beaten. The man had been freed by my sister-in-law's son.

At Knježina we were told that we would have to wait for the Duke to come. A heavy-set, tall man appeared wearing a uniform with a gun belt, a large beard, fur hat, and shiny Chetnik insignia.

"God be with us," he said, raising three fingers in the Chetnik salute.

"May God help you," we all had to answer and raise three fingers, too.

In a sharp tone he called to the Serb from Užice, "I told you to take all the young girls and boys off this bus!"

"You've got it easy when I bring them to you. Go find yourself some out there in the woods, why don't you? Forget about these here," the man answered him firmly. He jumped onto the bus, cocked his gun, and aimed it at the Duke. Mlađo and the other policeman cocked their guns as well.

"You'd better watch your step, you'll have to come back this way again," the Duke threatened, infuriated.

"So I will, and then you and I will see, alone," the man from Užice said while Mlađo started up the bus.

They stopped the next convoy in a small village, took off fifty-six people and murdered them. They murdered a sixteen-year-old boy and my younger brother-in-law, who was thirty-five.

We went from there through the woods in the direction of *Olovo. At the next stop we went out into a large meadow. Blue with the cold, thirsty, and hungry, we lit a fire. Soon, we heard someone whistle. Someone cursed and shouted, "All of us will get killed! Get in the bus!"

Panic erupted as we all tried to crowd back into the bus. With the boy in my arms I saw an older Serbian man in front of me. Bullets were rico-cheting off the rocks between us. Instinctively I pushed the man aside so that the ricocheting bullets wouldn't hit him. I knew that all of us would be in trouble if one of the Serbs was killed, because from their curses and shouts I figured it out that some people they were calling the *Green Berets were firing at us. That was the first I'd heard of them. Later they explained to me that Muslim units called the Green Berets from Olovo had had information that people would be taken off the convoy by that meadow and murdered, so they were shooting to stop the Serbs from massacring us. The Green Berets murdered one blind man from the convoy at that spot.

They took us back to a place under Romanija Mountain where they counted us and made lists. We spent the night in the buses without windowpanes. It was cold and rainy. The other Serbian soldiers called Mlađo, the boy from Užice, and the policeman to come sleep in the hotel, but they refused, saying, "We brought these people here and we plan to deliver them alive."

They spent all night with us in the bus. When they fell asleep I felt bad for them and I took three blankets from an old woman and covered them.

The next morning troops came, and the man in charge of them was the man I'd pushed aside when the Green Berets were firing at us. They called our names. I could see two buses and a truck with Serbs on the other side, but we couldn't be sure this was the exchange.

"Lady, hey you, stop! Are you Mehmedović?" the man in charge asked me.

"Yes, I am," I said, scared.

"What's the boy's name?"

"Fudo," I said, using the first name that came to mind, because he had been quiet the whole time and hadn't even told me his name. Azra stood next to me and I held the boy in my arms.

"Please don't touch my children!"

"I won't, don't you worry," he told me, and turned to the soldiers.

"See this woman? If it weren't for her yesterday I would have been killed."

He handed me two bills of 500 *dinars each, I remember seeing Tito's face on them, and a carton of cigarettes.

"No, thank you," I said.

"You've got to take it," he ordered and shook my hand.

We said good-bye to the people who had brought us there. Mlađo started to cry, saying, "Take good care of Azra for me!"

When he got back to Višegrad, Mlađo and his three brothers were murdered by Lukić because they had protected and saved so many Muslims. The Pecikoza Serbian family was wealthy and well known. They had their own sawmills.

When we got to Olovo I started to scream when I saw how many soldiers there were. These were the Green Berets.

They asked me, "What's wrong? We are your army!"

"What do you mean, our army?! Fuck you and your green mother and Green Berets! It was Green Berets and Chetniks who slaughtered my sixteen-year-old boy!"

They took me to the police in Olovo where they forced me to tell them everything that had happened. Someone told them that Lukić had abused me the most. They wanted me to talk about that, too, but I didn't have the strength. They held me two days in prison where they beat me and wouldn't give me anything to eat. One soldier kicked me and another slapped me, saying, "You prefer those Chetniks to the Green Berets!"

"I don't like one or the other," I answered, grabbed a bottle from the table and smashed it over his head.

"You are going to get more beatings from me," he said, holding his head.

"Leave the woman alone, can't you see what she's like?" the other soldier told him.

My stomach was bloated from all the wounds Lukić had inflicted on me, so I thought I was pregnant. I'd weighed 190 pounds before the war. I had dropped to ninety pounds when I arrived in Olovo, and after those two days in jail I was down to seventy-seven.

Esad's uncle came to see me in jail. I asked him straight off, "Where is that little boy, Fudo?"

"Who?"

"I don't know what his first or last name are, I can only remember vaguely what his mother looked like, but please, look after my children."

Before they released me, they asked me to register Fudo, so that if his mother was looking for him she could find him.

They carried me out of the jail because I could no longer walk.

We spent four days after that in Olovo.

The second day a woman appeared at the door. She didn't look familiar. She told me that Fudo was her son.

I didn't believe her at first, but when I saw how the child flew into her arms I knew that she must really be his mother. She brought a big present. Her brother was in the Green Berets, but I didn't want to accept the gift because the Green Berets had beaten me. Fudo kissed me and went off with his mother. It was wrenching. I didn't even have the strength to ask what his real name was. For me he will always be Fudo.

I was evacuated to Visoko from there with Azra on our fifth day. First they took us to the *stadium, and then they were supposed to transport us to a village. I wanted to go to my mother's house. She lived in the center of town. When I realized they wouldn't let me do that I slipped off from the bus. A soldier shot at me but by chance he didn't wound me. I had wide sleeves which were hanging on me, and the bullet went right through the sleeve. At that moment my sister's son, my nephew, happened to see me.

"Aunt Sena, where did you come from?"

"Azra is on the bus and these fools are shooting at me!"

He took Azra off the bus and the next day he took us to my mother's. Everyone came running out of the house: my mother, father, brothers, and sister. They were shouting: "Where is Esad? Where is Edin?!"

"They're gone, they're gone! What's done is done," I kept saying over and over again.

They took me to the hospital in Zenica because of a nervous breakdown. There I had to undergo a very difficult gynecological operation because of injuries that Lukić had inflicted on me with a knife. For two months the doctors fought for my life.

If I were to find Murat today I would accuse him, and I wouldn't be afraid. It is his fault that our children and husbands were murdered! From up on the minaret, from the mosque, he sprayed the town with gunfire. Maybe all of us could have gotten away if he hadn't done that. He pulled his own family out before he let the water out from behind the dam, and he left us on the right banks of the Drina River.

When I wanted, after all that happened, to take my own life and end the misery, Azra asked me, "Mama, what would I do without you?"

She is nineteen years old now and she must never learn that my every night is wracked with my son's cries, "Help me, mama! Please don't let them take me, mama!"

BRANDY FOR
A GRANDSON'S WEDDING

TOLD BY MARA JOVIĆ

Refugee from *Glamoč, interviewed in Kladari

November 1995

I lived in Glamoč for a full eighty-two years. When the time came for the local Serbs to retreat from my native village before the Croat-Muslim army, I refused to go.

"This is where I was born. This is where I want to die."

"Grandma, there'll be no one here to bury you," said my neighbors as they left.

"I don't care what happens when I'm gone," I answered, and stayed behind.

There wasn't much in the way of shots fired when the troops entered the empty town. They found me at home, and asked, "Where are your children, old woman?"

"They got away before you got here."

"That was smart. And what will you do here all alone?"

"I wouldn't leave my hearth and home. If you don't like that, kill me."

"Nonsense! We don't murder old women, we are soldiers," one of them said. As they were on their way out another soldier said, "If only we'd all stayed home like this old woman."

The next few days no one troubled me. The soldiers looked to their work, I looked to mine. As the time passed it became clear to me that a person cannot live from defiance alone. There were strenuous physical jobs to be done in order to survive under those conditions, and usually it was the younger people in the household who had done them. I decided to request permission for passage into Serbian territory. I knew they'd be happy to issue it.

Since no one had robbed me, I decided to go out and dig up my valuables that were hidden in the yard, not too far from the house. When it got dark I went behind the house with a shovel and with every step it got heavier. The soil was packed hard and I was weak. Amid my miserable efforts to shovel even a little clump of earth I heard a voice behind me, "Ma'am, need a hand?"

Scared, I saw it was a Croatian soldier. He couldn't have been more than thirty years old. I felt better when I realized that we knew each other. I had seen him almost daily since that first day when he was in my house. That meant that I had a chance he wouldn't kill me. As to the valuables, "Devil take 'em" is what I thought.

"Give me the shovel and show me where to dig."

I showed him the spot and walked toward the house. His voice stopped me.

"Stay here, please. I don't know what it is I'm digging for and I would never take it out without you here."

I sat on a stump nearby. In no time, what with his strength, a plastic bag appeared and a five-gallon jug of brandy. He handed me the plastic bag. "Is that what you were looking for?"

"Yes, indeed. There are 700 German marks in here," I answered, handing it back to him.

"Not for me, for you, Grandma. I just wanted to help you, not to rob you."

"How about we share it," I suggested.

"There is nothing for us to share. Take it wherever you're headed. I am a refugee, too, from Ilidža near Sarajevo. I know what it means to have to leave your hearth and home."

"Well, then at least take the five-gallon jug. The brandy is twelve years old."

"Thanks, but I won't take that either. You probably set it aside for when your grandson marries. May God give him a long life. You go, find him, and tell him where it's buried."

He was that same soldier who had said, on the first day, "If only we'd all stayed home like this old woman."

A GIFT FROM
GOOD PEOPLE

TOLD BY LJUBICA VUJIĆ

A Refugee from Zagreb, interviewed in *Banja Luka

December 1995

I lived with my husband and children in Zagreb in Croatia until August 1991. Although I was home on maternity leave at the time, I was fired from the company where I'd been working even though I was a Croat, because my husband was a Serb. He had all sorts of problems at work and we were under a great deal of pressure to move out of our apartment. Because of this my husband took vacation time, and we took the children to Banja Luka in Bosnia, where he is from. Seven days later the bridge at Okučani that we had crossed to get there was destroyed. As soon as we left Zagreb on vacation, my husband was fired from the company where he had been working, and we lost our apartment. We had nowhere to go back to, even if we'd wanted to and been able to.

When the war started in Bosnia my husband was called up to serve in the army of Republika Serbia. He was killed in combat in 1993.

At that time we were living in the cellar of a building in Banja Luka that we had traded for some property we'd owned in Zagreb. The cellar was not fit to live in and I had no money to fix it up nor did I know anyone I could turn to for help. I had been left completely alone with small children, one of them a baby.

Comrades of my husband's from the unit he had fought in knew me only by sight. After he was killed these people were really wonderful to me. I never dreamed that they would be able to help, but they did everything they could possibly do. They got a hold of construction material and adapted the cellar where I remained with the children.

One day Captain Miroslav Radetić appeared at the door and said, "I have great news for you! You have been given an apartment. Now you can move in there out of this hole."

"That couldn't be true! There are so many Serbian women who have been living here for years, and they haven't gotten apartments," I answered, stunned.

"Well, it's true. Do you want me to take you over to see where it is?"

We got to the building, where I am still living today, and the Captain showed me the apartment. I was thrilled, although the apartment was in a total shambles. The electric outlets didn't work, nor did the plumbing. When I moved in I didn't know whom to call to help. I sat, completely overcome, in the middle of the empty floor, when a neighbor came in.

When she saw me sitting there, she said, "I know a house painter who could paint your apartment. Do you want me to call him?"

I accepted her offer joyfully, although I couldn't believe the man would agree to do the job for only fifty German marks when I knew people were usually paid at least four times that much. I didn't have even that much just then. The painter did agree to do the job for hardly any money, and he didn't mind waiting until I could pay him. He did all the work that was needed for me and got the building materials himself. Before he painted he rearranged the walls in the apartment, made some new partitions, fixed the wiring and the plumbing and did everything so that I could live in decent conditions.

When I could no longer hold my tongue, I asked him, "Why did you agree to do this for money that couldn't even be covering the cost of materials?"

He looked at me, surprised, and answered, "I can see that you are in an extremely difficult situation. I'll make up the difference somewhere else, when I work for someone who has more they can pay me."

For a year I did my laundry in someone else's laundry bucket, cooked in someone else's pots, sat and slept with the children on someone else's furniture. All my furnishings were given to me by neighbors who helped me selflessly.

My husband's comrades came by almost every Sunday to visit. They did all they could to ease my troubles.

When it was the anniversary of my husband's death they told me that they would put up the stone on his grave because they knew I didn't have the money to do it myself.

All that the children and I have, we got from the good people around us.

FORGIVE MY PEOPLE
FOR WHAT THEY DO

TOLD BY JUSUF HALILOVIĆ[†]

The Vogošća part of Sarajevo

November 1998

I moved to Vogošća with my wife, Zorica, and sons, Asim and Omer, in 1980. That was the spring Tito died. I remember how all of us in the house wept with all of Yugoslavia. I was thirty-eight years old at the time.

It was mostly Serbs and Muslims who lived in Vogošća then in roughly equal proportions. There were very few Croats. All of Vogošća was tied up in a factory that employed about 15,000 people.

I worked abroad for seven years, set some savings aside, and built myself a nice, comfortable home in Vogošća in 1983. My plan was to open up a restaurant with local specialties for the *Sarajevo Winter Olympic Games, but the municipality issued me a permit for a bakery. We opened in 1984.

I socialized with my neighbors Slavko and Mićo, both Serbs, and Ismet, a Muslim; we worked together and tried to ease Meša's situation. Meša, another Muslim friend, had cancer which had gone into metastasis, and we brought him morphium to help with the pain.

When the war started we made a pact among ourselves that we would

212

not fight on any side. If it looked as if we'd be forced to fight, we promised to flee the country instead. Asim and Omer left in April 1992.

Ismet and Slavko and a Serbian fellow named Srđan, whom we called Điđa, lived at my place and worked for me. During the battle on Žuč, Mićo and Slavko worked at transporting the wounded to Pale. Ismet's family was the first to leave Bosnia for *Čačak in Serbia.

When I saw that pensioners had no money for bread, I gave them flour free of charge, and pretty soon I was handing out loaves of bread as well.

People from the municipality informed me that the bakery was a strategically significant facility for the army and that I would not be permitted to leave the city.

Right in the middle of the worst bloodshed and slaughter of Muslims, Grujo, a Serb from Visoko, stood out in the street in a tattered uniform and called to me, "Juso, please forgive my people for what they do!"

Điđa had grown up with my kids. Right at the start of the war he was called up to serve in the military police. He often stopped in for coffee. Once while he was visiting, my wife, Zorica, reminded him, "Điđa, don't forget your gun."

"I haven't forgotten it. Leave it there under the bed. If you need it, Juso will know what to do. I have another one."

"Điđa, this is just going to mean headaches for us," I objected.

"Uncle Juso, everything going on around us is about looting and thieving. The only part that has to do with war is people jumping on the chance to grab as much as possible without going to jail. Nationalism is everyone's excuse to steal and murder. Don't be afraid. If it comes to that I will personally dig a trench in front of your house, which is, after all, my house, too, and I'll defend it single-handed. I know you love me like a son. My father sleeps alone at home and I am here with you."

The gun stayed at our house.

Meša died and we needed to bury him on 10 June. I had never buried anyone but someone had to do it. Serbian friends of mine helped out. Điđa and I wrapped him in a sheet and laid him in the coffin. We had to carry him to a graveyard in a Muslim village that Serbian troops were ransacking at that time. I was scared.

"Don't you worry, I'll protect you," said a Serbian friend, Đoko, who went with me to bury him.

"Those of you who know the Muslim rituals, do those, and if you cross yourselves, do that," I said at the graveside. Each of us prayed as we knew best for Meša. Đoko saw me home.

Điđa and Boro were killed the same day at different places. Boro was a commander of a special unit. He pulled Volkswagens out of the TAS factory at the bidding of Momčilo *Krajišnik and Radovan *Karadžić. His murder was an ambush and four other young men died with him.

One of my bakers was a Muslim man married to a Montenegrin woman. The day after Boro was murdered, men came to his apartment, had a drink, and then took the two of them outside. They murdered the baker there in front of the house, and took his wife to the bridge, slit her throat, and dropped her into the River Bosna. That woman showed up in Vogošća a month later with this big scar on her neck. She knows precisely who cut her but she still doesn't dare say who.

On 19 June 1992, Điđa was dispatched to pull women and children from a bus that had been ambushed in Semizovac. Điđa was murdered in the fray. He was twenty-two years old and I loved him as if he'd been my own son. I decided I wanted to attend his funeral in the Serbian village.

"Don't go there, they'll murder you. I won't be able to protect you. Better your wife Zorica goes since she's Serbian," Mića reasoned with me.

After the burial friends told me how someone spoke at his grave and said he'd fallen for his fatherland and that they would avenge his death. Điđa's father, Rajko, interrupted the man.

"Dear friends! I did not raise my boy Srđan for Serbia. I raised him to be a decent man. Look at this woman here." He stopped, and turned to Zorica. "She has a Muslim family: sons Asim and Omer, her husband is

Jusuf. Srđan slept and ate in their house. She did his clothes. He learned his trade with them. He happened to be here because of his army service. I do not want my son buried for Serbia but as a decent man."

Zorica and I wanted to tend to Điđa's grave, but Rajko recently had him reburied in *Bratunac.

One evening we were watching TV with Mića and Slavko. A guy named Cvrle showed up out in the yard wearing a camouflage uniform, armed with an automatic and in the company of another soldier.

"Hey, Jusuf, come out here," he shouted. "I've got something to ask you!"

Mića wouldn't let me go out. He went out, instead.

"What do you need Jusuf for?"

"Just tell him to come out. There's something I need to know."

"Ask me, instead," Mića told him.

Cvrle climbed up on a slope above the house and shot at the front door. He shot a whole clip into the house. You can still see marks left by the bullets that came through the windows in several of the rooms. Luckily no one was hurt. Zorica, woken by the shooting, had a nervous breakdown.

That same night Mića and Slavko decided they'd take their families and my wife and leave Vogošća. I couldn't join them because I'd been told by the police that I couldn't leave.

They told me, "If you try to run you'll never make it alive to the bridge. Stay in the bakery."

They took Meša's wife with them. The sixteen of them headed for Čačak in Serbia. On their way out they cautioned the deputy commander of police, whose wife and two children were in Čačak, that if anyone touched a hair on my head his family would be in jeopardy.

A fellow by the name of Gliša from a neighborhood on the edge of Vogošća, moved into my house in August under orders from the municipality. They forced me to sign a contract that he and I were trading homes.

Most of the time he kept me locked up in a room. I was a hostage in my own home. I probably never would have survived if I hadn't been visited and protected by my children's Serbian friends.

One day Gliša allowed me to take a bath in the bathroom attached to the bakery. Meanwhile I noticed that someone had drained the water from the bread ovens and it had flooded the room.

A man suddenly appeared brandishing a long knife, which he waved in front of my face, and shouted, "Admit it! You are the one who let the water drain out!"

"How could I when I've been locked up all this time?"

"I bet you found some way to sneak out!"

Slavko's sister spotted him from the terrace and called Željko: "There is a Chetnik in the bakery. He has this big knife! He'll hurt Jusa! Run quick!"

I grabbed up a gun that happened to be there. While we were standing there, eye to eye, Željko barged in with a pistol.

He pushed his way between us and snarled at the man, "What is that knife for?"

"Nothing."

"What, nothing? What's the knife for?"

"I brought it in to sharpen up the blade."

"Get out of here," said Željko and threw him out of the garage.

An hour later the same man was back, this time with an automatic.

"Where are you, you filthy creep, damn your mother!"

I retreated to the upper floor. I heard him screaming, "Come out here, you *balija, if you dare!"

It was Željko who came out. The man wasn't expecting Željko.

"What is your problem?" Željko asked him angrily. "What do you want?"

"The town of Semizovac fell," the startled Chetnik answered.

"As if we care! Get lost. I don't want to see you here," Željko told him.

The Chetnik left, his tail between his legs, sat in a brand-new Volkswagen stolen from the local factory and fled. Željko came, worried, into the house.

"If you want, I can get you over into Sarajevo, but I'm afraid you might be murdered by your own men there. You aren't even safe in Croatia. There's no life for you here, too many hyenas nosing around. I don't know where to hide you."

That night a policeman came and took me to a safe place to sleep, and the next morning I left in a van, holding a Serbian ID issued in a Serbian name, on my way to Serbia.

Željko was wounded in the chest not long after that. When he recuperated he left for Germany. He often called me from Munich. He's living there still.

I left on 22 August with 300 German marks in my pocket. I passed through twenty-eight barricades in the van. It took me twenty-four hours to get to Sokolac. A school friend of my son's made me practice over and over again so that I'd be able to tell anyone who asked when my Serbian feast day was, the name of the fighting unit I supposedly served in, whose funeral we were going to, and what Orthodox churches and monasteries I'd better know about just in case someone quizzed me on any of it at a checkpoint. They used to do that to catch people like me with fake Serbian papers. We made it to Zvornik over Romanija Mountain. At that point a soldier threw us all out of the van at the border crossing.

He addressed me with the question: "Do you realize that a vehicle hasn't been through this checkpoint for the last six hours. Where are you headed, Radoslav?"

"We are going to Banja Koviljača."

"What are you going to do there?"

"My wife and kids are there. We've been in the trenches since Day One."

"How long will you be staying?"

"We'll be coming back on Sunday."

"Listen, Radoslav, my friend, look me in the eyes. You don't come back on Sunday and I'll come get you."

"Hey, no problem. You can count on seeing me Sunday evening."

There were two policemen escorting us who had money coming to them in Čačak for their help to us to the tune of 7,500 German marks.

My wife and friends with their families were waiting for me, ready for us to proceed. There were sixteen of us in the group, and all of them Serbs but me.

We traveled all over Europe. I came back to Vogošća on 4 March 1994. The only thing left in the house was the bread oven, because it was too heavy for anyone to cart off.

FAREWELL TO MOTHER

TOLD BY ĐORĐE ŠUVAJLO

From Tarčin, a Prisoner in the Silo Camp,
interviewed in Bratunac

March 1996

I was born in the village of Tarčin, not far from Sarajevo, in 1962. The yard of our family's house where my sister and I grew up was right next door to a huge concrete silo, with only a wire storm fence in between us and the silo.

Before the war I lived in the same house with my wife, two daughters, and my parents. I was finishing work on my own house elsewhere in the same village.

In April 1992 three armed local men, Muslims we knew, came into our house. They didn't ask us anything, they didn't ask if we had weapons in the house, and they didn't search us. They just ordered Father and me to go with them. Mother was scared, so I kissed her on the threshold and said, "Don't you worry now, we'll be back in no time."

They took us from our house straight to the silo surrounded by guards, all of them local people. By the next day there were 109 prisoners in this newly set-up camp, Serbs, who never dreamed that first day that they'd be spending the whole war there.

It felt so strange to Father and me, this imprisonment right next door to our own house. The everyday brutalities of some of the guards made it all cruelly real.

After more than a month inside that dark, cold concrete silo, they let us go outdoors to walk around the yard. We couldn't take our eyes off our own front door. Mother soon appeared in the doorway.

She ran over to the fence and with a mixture of joy and grief at seeing us, she said, "Đoko, son, your wife and children are safe."

She didn't have time to say another word. She looked on in wordless horror at the guards as they beat us with their gun butts and dragged Father and me away from the fence.

Every time after that when we came out into the yard it always ended in Mother's desperate attempts at pushing us a little food through the fence, or telling us bits of news. The same scene was repeated over and over, until the cruelest of the guards raised their hands against the poor old woman. From that day when we had to stand there, helpless, while they struck my mother, Father and I decided to go out into the yard as seldom as possible. And when we did go out, we kept to the other side, as far as we could from our fence.

The days went by, turned into months, and then into years of uncertainty and expectations. For the three years and eight months we spent incarcerated, there was not a single humanitarian organization, not even the Red Cross, which came to visit the camp.

Once they'd organized themselves militarily, they took us out to dig trenches that lay right along the front lines with the Serbian army. The close proximity of the Serbian positions, or rather their trenches, seemed like an irresistible temptation to escape.

After more than a year of being held prisoner, one of the internees threw down his shovel in despair and bolted for the Serbian trenches. All of us watched, wordless. He ran right through a mine field. No one shot on either side and, finally, he reached the Serbian trench. Applause erupted among us, with shouts of acclaim. The guards, infuriated by our elation, and by the escape itself, grabbed the closest two prisoners, took them to a wall that was not far from there, and shot them right there in front of us.

When we went back to the silo, we were told that if anyone else attempted to escape, twice as many people would be shot among the people who stayed behind. Despite the threat, after several more months, another prisoner couldn't resist the allure of freedom so close at hand, and two more men were shot.

Two years of life in the camp were horrible enough to inspire yet another prisoner to try and get away. We watched in despair as he died, having stepped on a mine. The next moment the guards vented their rage on the man next to me in the trench, and on me. With cruel blows they shoved us over to the execution wall.

As they were cocking their guns, their superior officer's voice rang out, "Halt! Are you insane?! There's been enough killing! Take the prisoners back to the silo!"

We were still paralyzed with terror when they drove us off the wall with blows from the butts of their guns and herded us into the column of prisoners marching back.

A year after this incident there was a similar scene. This time, too, the man running was murdered, and this time, too, they put me up against the wall to shoot me. The only difference was that this time it was different guards pointing their guns. It just so happened that the same superior officer forbade the execution and saved our lives.

At the end of our second year of incarceration, we got up off the concrete floor we slept on one morning and went down to the part of the silo where there were improvised wooden benches and eating tables. The food, which we'd gotten used to, was always in meager supply, but that morning as I went to sit down I thought I must be dreaming.

In disbelief I asked the man next to me, "Do you see what I see?"

"I'm seeing it, but I'm not believing it," he answered, blinking.

I went over to the table and touched two painted Easter eggs. Next to each bowl of tasteless food each of us was greeted with the same surprise. Most of us only then realized it was Orthodox Easter because we'd lost all sense of time.

Later we learned that a Catholic man had arranged the surprise for us. He was the food supplier and that day he delivered the food to the silo in person.

After a thousand mornings when I could see my mother, if nothing else, at least through the crack between the door and the concrete silo wall, as she gave us, with her stoic constancy, the strength to endure the horrors of camp life, a morning dawned, and a whole day passed, and Father and I didn't catch sight of her. We comforted each other that she was probably feeling sick.

The next day when we went out in the yard we saw close friends carrying a coffin from the house and we realized that Mother had died. Father and I walked toward the camp gates without even asking anyone's permission. The guard opened the gate, and with another man he escorted us. They didn't stop us from saying our last farewells to Mother and burying her. They were there, by our sides, the whole time, and we went right back to the silo from the cemetery.

We were released from the camp almost two whole months after peace was signed in Paris. I was the last to get out, on 27 January 1996.

Camp

IT TOOK COURAGE
TO GO HOME

TOLD BY BILJANA MIKETIN

Vareš

November 1998

I was born in Vareš forty-seven years ago. I have a degree in business. Right now I am working at the Cantonal Health Insurance Office, at the Breza branch, which is fifteen miles from my home in Vareš. I am forced to work this far from home because of the extremist politics that have been in power in Vareš first on one side and then on the other, and have kept people like me, a Croat but not a nationalist, from holding their regular jobs. I didn't fit in with what they had in mind. Thanks to colleagues at my company I've got the job I have now.

During the twelve days that the Croatian Defense Council forces held Vareš, they picked my husband up, who is a Croat, and drove him by truck to dig trenches. When the evacuation of Croats from town was ordered, the Croatian Defense Council extremists forced me out of my apartment because the building was slated to be torched, despite the fact that one of their officials lived there. We were told that we were being asked to leave briefly, but that as soon as things quieted down we could come back.

I went with my family by car, borne along by the mass of people evacuating town. I caught sight of my husband on a truck. I stopped the car and called to him. He jumped from the moving truck and squeezed into the car. There were seven of us in there. Only when we had left the part under Croatian control and reached the part of the territory under Serbian control did we realize that we were, in fact, being moved out of our town.

The Serbian authorities in the territory just beyond town were drafting all men fit for military service. Men were not allowed to leave the territory. For three nights with my children, ailing parents, and husband, I waited for a moment when I could do something to slip my husband through the Serbian lines and get him away.

When we got to a nearby village I mustered my courage to approach an unfamiliar Serbian commander and ask him, "Where are you from?"

"Ilijaš," he answered, startled.

I told him that one of my grandmothers was from Ilijaš and that I'd often spent time there. I gave him some names of people he knew. My hope was to convince him that we had known each other from before.

He accepted the lie and said, "There will be a truck headed toward Kiseljak. Turn your car around and follow it."

I drove behind that truck to a checkpoint where we were stopped by Serbian soldiers. They wanted to pull my husband from the car, but in the end they gave up and let us pass.

At Kobiljača where you passed over from Serbian territory into Kiseljak, which was Croatian territory, we all had to show our ID cards. A Serbian policeman asked, "Who is Biljana Miketin?"

"That's me," I answered, reluctantly.

"Woman, what are you thinking? Where are you going?" he asked me angrily, probably thinking that because of my name I must be a Serb.

"What do you mean, where am I going? I'm going where my children are going," I answered. I didn't dare tell him I was no Serb.

Only when we got to Kiseljak and Croatian territory did I fully understand what had happened to us. People like me, who have never given much thought to nationality but have always believed that it was more important what kind of a person you are, did not prosper during the war. I saw that Kiseljak was not a way out into the world for my family, but rather that it was a kind of a concentration camp where I had to do my time in the service of somebody's interests.

The members of Croatian mobile forces called the Maturice who committed the massacres in Stupni Do took all the men fit for military service to dig trenches and fighting lines. The women were able to move about freely but movement was limited for the men. My husband quickly realized he was not likely to be able to avoid the front lines, so he chose to go back to positions where the Croatian Defense Council forces were more firmly in charge. He went off with a dozen Croats and that was where he stayed until the end of the war. Since he didn't belong to the Croatian Defense Council forces or the leading Croatian political party, the *Croatian Democratic Union, and he was a mining engineer by trade, he was assigned to a work detail; he dug trenches, unloaded sacks—in a word he toiled at the hardest physical labor. That was how those people fared who refused to support one of the big political parties.

Seeing what was going on in Kiseljak, in territory held by the Croatian forces, I tried in thousands of ways to get my family out but I didn't succeed until February 1994, when we got out by exchange. That the irony be even greater, the list for exchange included eight Muslims and four Croats: my father, mother, my child, and me. They exchanged us for other Croats who were trying to get into Kiseljak.

We went from Kiseljak to Tuzla. It took us a number of different routes to get there, but we managed, thanks to my sister's husband, Jasmin Imamović, who came to pick us up.

I came back to Vareš in May 1994. I was really unprepared for the wonderful welcome some people gave me, but I also experienced having old friends turn their heads away. The Army of Bosnia and Herzegovina was in the town, and the leading Muslim party, the *Party for Democratic Action, was in charge. At that time Croats were unwanted, even though

Izetbegović was publicly calling on Croats over the media to come back. The reality was different: every Croat who did come back to Vareš was put on a truck and transferred to Kiseljak, a nearby Croatian town, because the Muslim forces hadn't yet secured conditions that would make it possible for Croats to come back. We managed to hold our own and stay, thanks to friends. Some of them worked at the police station and would call me to warn me if police were on their way to take us away.

They always gave us the same advice, "Go hide somewhere."

We hid for three months in the home of some Muslim friends, or in cellars, or the woods. When I realized that we couldn't go on living like that, I went to the chief of police and said, "I came back to Vareš with my family and I have no intention of leaving town. If I am supposed to go through some procedure of questioning, here I am. Go ahead."

The chief of police, who must have gotten an order from his superiors to chase the Croats away, told me then, "Ma'am, you are welcome in Vareš. No one will bother you any more."

It was probably my courage in addressing him directly that helped make up his mind, or maybe it helped that my father had been president of the municipality for twelve years before the war. I think that it was thanks to Father's standing that we weren't maltreated or expelled from our apartment. After I went to the police that day, everything changed. We didn't have to hide any more. We could breathe . . .

Friends who visited me those first months and brought me the essentials, and those who hid us, were exposed to various unpleasantries, even serious risks.

Thanks to colleagues from Sarajevo I received permission to go back to work. Despite this permission in Vareš they wouldn't let me go back to my job in the welfare and social security office. That was where they had all the documents about people's years of work, which had been terribly devastated after the Croatian Defense Council forces left town. Knowing how important those documents were, I did all I could to protect them. Because of that I sneaked illegally into my company to file the documents. One day a young man came in and told me to get out.

"What kind of a tone is that to use with me?" I asked, appalled, knowing how much I'd helped his mother and aunt before the war when they were sick and had no health insurance. I found ways for them to receive treatment. He'd forgotten.

"I won't have Ustasha around here!"

I knew his father really had been an Ustasha in World War II and that ticked me off, so I told him, "Look, all of Vareš knows who I am and who my father was. And they also know full well who you are and who your father was. You shouldn't go around calling other people names that apply to you!"

When I refused to leave he brought in three other young men who literally carried me out in their arms. Even after that I still kept going in to my company. There is something stronger than fear: pride.

Džemo Kevrić, a member of the Party for Democratic Action, a disabled man who was missing a leg, wanted my job and he got his wish. But I did not end up out of work; my colleagues helped out again and offered me a job in Vogošća. For three months I traveled to work and back. After that they offered me the job in Breza, and I have been working at that job for the last two years.

In August 1994 my father died. Džemo Kevrić, who was already working at my job then, came to our house with two other men. In the name of the Party for Democratic Action they brought our family 100 German marks, some alcoholic beverages, coffee, and juice to help us out.

Muslims helped me bury my father. They drove his body from the Zenica hospital and dug his grave. Throughout the war it was most often people who were not of my ethnic group or my faith who helped me.

A childhood friend came to see me with a friend as soon as she heard I was back. They were the first Muslim women who came to visit. They saw that we had almost nothing in the house, because the armies who had passed through had helped themselves to whatever interested them. She noticed I had nothing to wear but the clothes on my back and offered to give me some of her clothes. She brought me her coat and gave my son her children's sneakers and pants, and said, "Don't think about those fools. No one can turn us against each other. They can't ruin our friendship."

When the police were forcing Croats to leave town, a policeman who was a Muslim came to see me. I knew him from before, because for awhile I'd worked in the Court.

He told me, "I'm glad you're back, Biljana. It's good that you've come home. If you need anything, just ask for me."

When I got firewood, the man who was a commander at the time in the police brought his gasoline-powered saw over and cut all our firewood for us, even though he could have gotten into trouble for it.

Our building was torched by extremists from the Croatian Defense Council. A total of eighty-four apartments burned. Friends told me, when we got back, that the house where my husband's parents had lived had not been squatted, but that it was in pretty bad shape. With the help of friends and neighbors I managed to fix it up and make it habitable. Every time anyone stopped by for a visit, he or she would bring a basket: one brought some glasses, another some plates, some appeared with a sofa, others with curtains . . .

YOU REAP WHAT YOU SOW

TOLD BY P. F.[†]

The Grbavica part of Sarajevo

October 1998

I was born in Višegrad to a bey's [Muslim noble] family in 1921. In 1960 I moved to Sarajevo and I live there today. During Tito's Yugoslavia I was a Yugoslav. Now I am a Muslim.

I was widowed in World War II, with a one-and-a-half-year-old son. Later he graduated from Sarajevo University and worked in the center of town.

When they divided the city in 1992 he couldn't cross the bridge on the Miljacka River and go to work. I stayed throughout the war in the part of Sarajevo called Grbavica that was on the territory of Republika Srpska, the Serbian part of Bosnia.

There were more Serbs than Muslims in my building before the war. During the war my neighbors didn't want to help me. They acted as if everything that was happening was my fault.

Rade showed up in Grbavica in June 1992. He was a soldier for the Republika Srpska army who had been given the use of the apartment directly above mine. A Muslim used to live there, but he'd fled at the beginning of the war.

The first time he entered the building, my neighbors and some of the other new tenants harassed me.

"What are you doing here? Get out of your apartment," they shouted at me.

"Why should I leave? It's my apartment," I replied.

Then even the children began to curse me. One little girl kicked me.

Rade later told me that at that moment all he could think about was his own mother. How would it be for her, how would she feel, if someone were harassing her? He leaped forward to protect me from the others, who were behaving like a pack of hyenas, which attack other animals that are wounded or old and feeble. First he slapped the little girl.

"From here on in you have to go and buy her and bring her anything she needs," he snapped, angrily, and turned to the adults. "If anyone so much as gives her a nasty look, I'll kill you all. That there is Igman Mountain. There are plenty of soldiers up there. Go and fight them, if you feel like a fight. Easy for you to go around bothering a sick, old woman. You are competing to see who can do her the most harm, as if you'll get the Nobel Peace Prize for your trouble. You've got plenty of *balijas* up there in the hills to wrangle with." He glared at the strongest-looking man, and continued, "Go nab one of them, cousin, if you can. Then you can wrestle with him all day long if that's what you feel up to."

Protected for the first time, I went quietly into my apartment. I only locked the door at night. Rade soon knocked.

"Hello, grandmother?"

"Hello, son."

"How are you doing?"

"I've known better days."

"You stayed behind?!"

"But where could I have gone, son? I was afraid, but I did stay . . ."

"You are a hero. Not even a hero. You are a miracle, grandmother. You have nothing to fear. You are under my protection," he said, simply, as if he were my own son.

He stopped by after that whenever he wasn't on the front lines. Once he found me in bed, all swollen because my kidneys were malfunctioning. He was upset when he saw me. "Grandmother, what's wrong?"

"Well, Rade, I'm in bed. I'm sick and I'm cold. I've no firewood for heat."

"Do you have some kind of an axe?"

"It's over there in the other room. Go right in and take it."

"I'll go out and chop you some firewood."

"Rade, you needn't go too far. Just go down in the cellar and chop off part of the wooden partition around my storage bin down there."

"Do you have a piece of cloth or something I can carry the wood up in?"

He came back quickly, carrying the firewood.

"Now I'm going to make you a fire. Be patient another few minutes. I had to break most of the boards with my feet because the axe was dull," he said, out of breath, putting the wood down by the stove.

He often brought me firewood in a sack from somewhere.

He was forty-three years old when the war began. He told me about everything. About Tito's times when we had lived so well. He had managed to finish school then, and get a job, to build a house in Buća Potok, but he had had to flee.

He told me, "That was the best system for me. I was able to get ahead with my own efforts."

He talked about his father, who was now ninety years old. He remembered how his father had always told him, "Son, never close a door with your ass. Wherever you end up, always do good to others if you can. I can remember three wars. And remember this, you reap what you sow."

People stared at me as if I were a monster in Grbavica. How could it be that there was still a Muslim woman here, they wondered.

There were almost no men in my building during the war. Sometimes they'd come back from the front. Rade ordered that the front door be welded shut. That way no one could get in to steal and abuse the tenants. He broke the lower pane of glass on the door and that was how we got in and out of the building. When the women from the building asked him what he was doing he explained.

"No one should come into the building at night any more. Take your boyfriends to the park or wherever you like. There will be no visitors at night. If I see anyone coming in who is not one of the tenants, I'll kill him."

They grumbled loudly at this, as women can, so Rade shot off his gun in the hallway. Not a single one of them had a complaint after that. Everything quieted right down.

When he went off to the front, he'd threaten everyone there.

"I don't want to hear that Grandmother here had any trouble with you. No one giving her nasty looks, let alone saying something mean to her, otherwise you'll have to answer to me. Heads will roll."

"We never do anything bad to her. Maybe we will now just because you said we shouldn't," they'd answer maliciously, but I never had a single problem. While Rade was here I was safe.

He often brought me food from the army mess hall. Beans, sometimes, other times rice, whatever there was. Once he heard two women commenting in the hallway, "Look at that. Bringing food to the enemy!"

"Shut up!" he snapped. "Did I ask you anything? I did not. Go in and shut your door. And not another word out of you!"

While he was on the front I often burned things from my apartment in the stove, even shoes, because it was really cold and I'd used up all my wood.

Looking at what was happening in the city, I often told him, "Eh, Rade my boy. Arkan is king, *Salkan is scum. Everyone alive is a crook."

From time to time three of Arkan's men would stop by to visit, see how I was managing and what I was doing.

"Grandmother, how are you," they often woke me up.

"I'm alive, children, don't worry. There, I'll get out of bed."

When I had coffee, I'd make it for them. Then they'd open their souls. All of them thought of me as their mother. They probably felt better when they sat with me and talked. They never came with weapons. One was in a black suit with black glasses, in camouflage, while the other two were in civilian clothes or sometimes in uniform. They told me that they were Arkan's men and that they were from Belgrade. One of them brought me my pension because I couldn't go out to get it. They were the escort for an elderly man, but I never heard who it was. When they left they would leave a piece of paper with me that had their first and last names on it to put on my door. Refugees who had moved into the building tore the paper up at night.

"It's bad enough, you living in Serbian territory. Now you are putting up Serbian signs, too!"

When the Serbs left Grbavica in droves after reintegration, no one gave me a hard time. They took with them their parquet floors, took the fixtures off the walls, and the electric plugs. They took everything they could carry. I watched them loading it all into trucks. They set off bombs that they activated in the apartments above mine. Six apartments burned, including the one Rade had been given. They wanted to place the blame on him.

I told them, "Rade didn't set them on fire. I know who did."

Rade saved all the documents and photographs from that apartment and after the war, through friends, he got them back to the owner who had returned. He was one of the last to leave Grbavica. He came to say good-bye to me. I cried.

"What will I do now, Rade? I may not live long enough ever to see you again."

The people who moved away from here aren't likely to come back. Some of them sold their old houses and land, and are living in other people's apartments. There is no force that could make them go back to the village. They've had a chance to see what pavement is like.

Now, three years after the war, I have been having real trouble with the Muslims who moved in from villages, and took part in the fighting. They often insult me. They ask me all kinds of questions that I have to answer, like, "So, why did you stay behind, Chetnik-lover?"

"I had to look after my apartment."

"Why did you have to look after it?"

"I didn't have anyone else who could."

"The bridge isn't so far away. How come you didn't just cross over?"

"I couldn't. I was sick and it wasn't easy for me to get around."

"Well, when the Serbs come back, you can greet them with open arms and go live with them."

After he left, Rade called me on the phone.

"Grandmother, how are you managing now?"

"Not so good, son. Now these people have come and they want to throw me out. They are even worse than the Chetniks were."

I feared for my son every time I heard a shell explode. I had no idea when it was that he left the city because we had no way of talking to each other. I didn't see him for six years. I thought he'd been murdered. He never took up arms. They called him on the phone and threatened him. He managed to get out of Sarajevo and to go to America. He came back this year. Now they hold it against him that he didn't stay and fight in the war and he can't get a job because of that. He visits me often.

Rade has been living in Lukavica in a Serbian house since the war ended. He drew up a contract with the owner and is paying him rent. He refused to move into an abandoned Muslim home. He says that neither he nor his wife would be able to sleep at night. The owner sold his house to someone else with Rade in it as his tenant. He said to the buyer, "While Rade is in the house, it is his."

Even today, when he sends me a package by way of other people, he always tells them, "Knock softly on the door. Don't frighten her. Wait, let her come to the door slowly, to open it."

For last Christmas he sent me a whole dinner. The package had every-thing in it: meat and pastries. I ask whomever he sends to visit me, "Can I kiss you for Rade?"

It's been almost three years since I saw him. He lives only three miles from here, but he is in Serbian territory. He can't come to see me even though that man could never have done anyone any harm. I have trouble getting around so I can't go and visit him. For the last two years I haven't even left my apartment. I am sick. I have bad kidneys and a weak heart. Both of us have telephones, but communication lines between the *"enti-ties" almost never seem to work properly.

The last time he managed to get a call through to ask how I was doing, whether I had enough fuel to keep warm, and if I needed firewood, at the end of the conversation he said, "If I knew then what I know now, I would never have been in the war. I would have fled abroad, the way so many other people did. I don't want anyone to ever go through this again. We were doing fine in peace and then off we went to war. For a bunch of thugs."

A HUMANITARIAN
AID WEDDING

TOLD BY SLAVKO NINKOVIĆ
Refugee from *Zavidovići, interviewed in Modriča

December 1995

The war hit when my wife, daughter, and I were in Zavidovići, where we had been living and working until that time. The town of Zavidovići was run by Muslim and Croatian authorities once the war began, and they took away all the weapons Serbs had owned. Because of that they took away a pistol I had a license for. It is difficult, during a war, to live in the territory where your own ethnic group is at war with the major ethnic group, and when you are stripped of all weapons you feel insecure. A friend of mine, a Croat, stopped by for a visit one evening. He took his pistol out with two ammo clips filled with bullets and put it on the table.

"You never know when it might come in handy. These are bad times. If someone tries to break into your house at night at least you have something to defend yourself with."

Even in war love overcomes all obstacles, and my daughter decided she wanted to get married in January 1993. A few days before, we started preparing for the wedding, within the limits of what we could manage at the time. That day an acquaintance of mine, a Muslim man, knocked on the door and brought us a package of humanitarian aid that the Serbs did not have the right to receive.

Once I got a call from a Muslim man named Fikret, a man I was not acquainted with. He explained to me that he had opened a small, private company in Zenica. One of the people working at the municipal offices had recommended me as someone who could keep his books for him. I was surprised by the offer, because I had heard his name somewhere, but I couldn't remember where. He said that he had been a teacher in Prijedor where some Serbs arrested him when the war broke out. He spent six months in the *Manjača prison camp. He made no accusations against anyone, and the whole story was told quite evenhandedly. Listening to him, I suddenly remembered a radio broadcast I'd heard on Zagreb Radio several months before this conversation, when this same Fikret had related the very same story. His consistency and the courage with which he resisted the pull to join the media war laid the underpinnings for our future association on a daily basis. We played billiards in a cafe owned by a Serb.

During the war I had a heart attack. I spent seventeen days at the Zenica hospital. The people who worked there belonged to all three religions. The senior consulting physician was Dr. Momir Dragić, a Serb. I was treated decently there.

Before the war I always used to go hunting with a Croatian man who was such an extremist that he refused, ever, to utter the word *Serb*. We avoided talking about nationalist topics, but everything else was up for grabs, and we always played off against each other. He had a summer place on a mountain that had come under the control of Serbian regular troops. After they retreated, he went to see what was left of it. When he came back, he immediately had my wife and me over.

"I heard all sorts of stories about the Serbs. It was said that they ransacked and robbed, burned, and leveled everything in their path. What I have experienced is that I found everything exactly as I left it in my house, and there was even an extra sack of corn there," he said, excited.

Ten days later I ran into him on the street. His head was bandaged.

"Good lord, what happened to you?" I asked him.

"I went back up to my summer place three days ago. I found the door kicked in and there were Muslims inside. Someone smashed me on the head and knocked me cold. They took away everything I had and what they couldn't take, they ruined."

I knew a couple of Croatian men who got many Serbs out of town, and never would take money for it. When I heard of this I went down to the police station and asked to speak to one of them, a man they called Dodo.

"I would like to leave Zavidovići with my family."

"When do you want to go?" he asked.

Two days later they told me that we could start packing. We went by truck to Žepče, which was under Croatian control. My daughter and son-in-law stayed there to live, while my wife and I went on to Modriča.

Most of the people living in Zavidovići were Muslims. In that part of the country the Serbs and Croats mostly did not fight each other. In fact, it is known that they even helped each other out in the fight against the Muslims.

In October 1993 without any problems, I brought my daughter from Žepče to Modriča, from where she went on to *Doboj to have her baby.

After a month she came back with her baby to Žepče and she is living there today.

BANJA LUKA,
A TORMENTED TOWN

TOLD BY R. R.†

Banja Luka

January 1996

In the course of my eighty-four years I have been through four wars and am now living under my fifth government, all the while never having left Banja Luka. You have to admit that means I must have impressive experiences of surviving. A life like that also shows you the bad people and the good people.

I ran a hairdressing salon in town and was in touch with Banja Luka residents of all ethnic backgrounds. The loveliest greeting is one used by the Franciscans: "Peace and goodness." It is the way I greet everyone I meet.

The cemetery of St. Mark's is near my house. That is where my parents, husband, brothers, and sisters are all buried. During this war I went to twenty funerals of murdered and burned Croats. That, for me, is devastating proof of what happened here.

As a long-time resident of this town my memories take me back to World War II, when the monstrous fabrication called the *Independent State of Croatia did unspeakable things to innocent Serbs, taking them to the *Jasenovac concentration camp. There were honest Croats then like Stipe

239

Radman, a parliamentary deputy who went to plead with Ante Pavelić, the fascist leader of Croatia, to spare the Banja Luka Serbs. That man kneeled and wept before Pavelić with his hand clasped, praying for mercy, hoping this would protect the Serbs. Jozo Lipovac and Knumbić also went personally to Pavelić, asking that he not persecute their innocent fellow citizens. Our house, too, protected Serbs . . .

I must ask the question: What happened in this war? Now it happened that citizens didn't dare raise their voices to protect others. I ran into veterans from the last war, partisans who had fought from day one in the 1940s and asked them, "Where are you now? Why aren't you protesting?" They answered, "We don't dare . . ."

There was no one in Banja Luka who raised their voice, even at the risk of losing their life, but in 1941 half of us did that, and my home was the first.

The Catholics of Banja Luka suffered terribly. This is a tormented town. Young boys were murdered who are buried at Borik. Mothers' tears were shed for them. As a mother I cannot bear the thought of mothers grieving for their children they've lost. It is unnatural.

When I got sick last year everyone did what they could to help. Caritas and his excellency Bishop Komarica, even the dairy across the street from my house. They sent me butter, cheese, and cream so that I wouldn't starve to death.

Bishop Komarica was a wellspring of goodness and he shared with everyone, regardless of their religious beliefs. He did everything, with the Orthodox bishop, to help people who were suffering. Once he put it so nicely, "Let's dismantle the walls and live as one."

There were Croats who lived on the first street behind the dairy, and the military police came and threw them out of their house. Their neighbor, a dentist, came to protect them, so they attacked him, too. At night he received threatening phone calls. They didn't throw him out of his house at that point, but not long after a group of people came who showed their documents, which said they were from Belgrade, and immediately they took all the men from that house to the front to dig trenches. People who were prepared to help others were threatened so seriously that they feared for their own lives and the lives of their families.

I know a case of an elderly woman who had been from one of the wealthiest Banja Luka families. After World War II all the houses they had owned and their family property were taken from them under Communism, and she was given an apartment. That woman, now at the age of 94, was thrown out of her apartment into the street. She wept to me about it over the phone, confessing that she didn't even have her coat or a pair of shoes. Mayor Radić objected to that inhuman act, but he had no authority to return her to her apartment.

My brother and I took in a couple with two children from Glamoč in the fall of 1995 when such a large number of Serbian refugees from western Bosnia arrived in Banja Luka. We put them up in my brother's house, which faces the same courtyard, and my brother moved in with me. I love those boys as if they were my own children. You seldom meet such well-behaved young people. We let them use a completely furnished house. The day they arrived I was carrying over bedding and cooking utensils from my own house to my brother's when I tripped and fell on the stairs. Five of them arrived, and my brother asked me to make them dinner. I went off and asked them, "Are you hungry?"

"We don't need anything ourselves, but if you could give something to the children . . . ," they answered.

I took them tomatoes, peppers, milk, bread, eggs . . . We are like one family, even today. When it was Christmas, I prepared dinner for my own family the first day, and had them over the next.

In earlier years I would make my neighbors a special Christmas cake and I'd bake a silver coin in it, but this year I baked in a dinar. I hope they weren't disappointed. No one mentioned it.

There was a man from *Mrkonjić-Grad who was an acquaintance of our tenants from Glamoč. He came to visit but his real intention was to evict my brother and me. He sat down on a stump in the yard. Not knowing what had brought him there, I picked figs and gave them to his daughter, and said to him, "You enrolled your little girl at the music school. If she needs any help, please feel free to ask me."

Our tenant from Glamoč, when he understood what the man was after, told him, "You will have to murder me first. I would never let you evict these people from their home."

I like to walk around my town because all my memories are gathered here. But, sadly, I no longer meet a single familiar face. Only the houses look familiar.

Across from the cathedral a Dr. Ćurić lived in a marvelous house. He was a famous gynecologist. He loved this town and his work, and he was so dedicated to his work that he rarely went to church, even though he was religious. All during the war he would come to visit and tell me that better times were coming. He stopped by whenever I was sick. When the terrible evil and the persecution of the Croats began, his neighbors, Serbs, told him that he didn't have to worry about a thing and that he could turn to them if he needed anything. He was a man who had never lifted a finger to hurt anyone, and his only fault was that he had a nice house and a fancy car that people wanted to take from him. They chased him from his house and expelled him, on a ferry with so many others, across the River Sava into Croatia. Mayor Radić did succeed in protecting the doctor's huge art collection and preserving it, first at the Cultural Center and then in the museum, and then he asked that the doctor be informed that his collection was safe.

When he crossed over into Croatia, where he was interviewed by Croatian television, the doctor said, "Banja Luka residents would never do this to me. I was expelled by Serbs who were, themselves, expelled by Croats from their homes."

THE WALLET

TOLD BY AGAN AVDAGIĆ

*Bosanski Novi

January 1996

Bosanski Novi is the town where my predecessors have always lived. I spent a full eighty-two years there. There wasn't a single war, and in my time I've been through three, which forced me to leave. I am fortunate that I am telling you this story, today, in my own home.

I had many friends among the Serbs and Croats with whom I used to go hunting and fishing. In one period I acted as president of the municipality.

I always felt myself to be a Serb, even though my name is Muslim. During World War II terrible things happened to Serbs in these parts. Today I still hold on to an ID from that time that says I am a Serb.

When this war began, my advanced age allowed me to observe how my friends were behaving. Many turned their heads when they met me on the street. I know that some of them did it out of fear so that no one who might hold it against them would see, but there were others who had been carrying evil in them from before, but now they could flaunt it without fearing punishment.

243

I used to be the wealthiest man in town. At least thirty people of all the faiths borrowed money from me to build their homes. I never took a dinar of interest, and they all returned their debts to me honestly, once they were able to. Some of them, when they went off to the war, left their families with the obligation not to forget me.

It rarely happened that people did me harm. Once a policeman checked my ID at the marketplace.

"What do you want with us? We don't want Muslims here!"

He slapped me. I went home. I forgave him and the others because they did not know what they were doing.

My house was searched several times for a radio transmitter because someone had reported me. They were, sometimes, rough and tactless, but I understood that. Every war brings with it cruelty.

A policeman, who confiscated my weapons that I had licenses for, asked me, "Have any Chetniks been in your house?"

"Everyone has come to my house, so Chetniks might have been there, as well. I was arrested during World War II by the Germans and the Chetniks, and what are you going to do, now?" I answered calmly.

I have great respect for all the Serbs who, in these times of war, walked through town with their heads held high and talked with me without fear.

When unfamiliar Serbian fighters appeared in town they arrested all the Muslims and took them down to the train station. The soldier who was taking me, asked, "Do you have any money?"

"No, I don't. Everything I had was wiped out when the banks crashed or it has been stolen."

"How much do you have in your wallet?"

"I have seventy German marks," I said, and when I opened my wallet I noticed that I also had fifteen dinars.

The soldier took the money out and returned it to me, but he took the wallet.

I don't know whether someone intervened on my behalf or not, but the next day they let me go home. Most of the Muslims were expelled or disappeared.

After a week I saw my wallet on the terrace.

One night a policeman, a Serb, tapped at my window. I heard him whispering, fearful of the others who were ruling by force and weapons.

"Agan, if you are scared to sleep in your house, come over to my place. You'll be safe there. I am on duty tonight and I'll look after your house so that no one loots it or sets it on fire."

I couldn't leave the house because my wife was gravely ill with a weak heart. She was paralyzed and on her death bed. She died a few days later.

It happened that someone would come up to me on the street from one of the neighboring villages whose face I could only barely recognize, and they'd say, "Agan, are you needing anything? As soon as I get home I'll send it right over."

Lieutenant Colonel Stanić used to call from Belgrade, while my phone was still working, and ask, "Agan, do you have enough to eat?"

Why would I want to leave people like this?

TRICKED INTO
SURRENDERING

TOLD BY RAJKO BOGDANOVIĆ

Prisoner Held in Prison Camps in *Odžak,
*Bosanski Brod, and *Orašje; interviewed in Modriča

December 1995

I was born in 1948. Until the war I lived in and worked near Odžak, a village on a bank of the Sava River. In April 1992 we found ourselves surrounded by Croatian military units. We were all evacuated to the village of *Novi Grad, where there was not enough space or food for such a large number of people, so a delegation of us went off to negotiate with the Croatian side. We asked them to let us go over into Serbian territory. They made it a condition that we had to hand over the weapons we had.

At the agreed-upon time they even brought in television cameras to record our surrender. In Odžak, near the soccer fields, they searched us and took everything we had. That search and the theft were organized by our neighbors. They were the ones who beat us and maltreated us the most. They kept the men in Odžak at the camp, and they let the others go.

Our whole village was destroyed in combat. The state farm had over 100 tractors that were taken away to Croatia. For fifteen days we, the internees at the prison camp, loaded the food that was left in the village onto trucks and the trucks took all the food to Croatia.

The men who worked at the camp, whom I knew, were from our part of the country but they pretended they had never seen me before. I had worked with one member of the Croatian army for eighteen years at my company. He never even offered me a single cigarette, nor did he say a word to me. There were situations where someone we knew might come over during the day and offer us a smoke, and then when night fell that same person would pull a sock over his head and come and beat us up. They'd line us up at night in five rows, and one by one they'd pull us out of the lines and beat us. The next evening a different man would be doing the beating. All that time they were drunk and vented their rage on us; they even beat a seventy-year-old man.

Ibro was a prisoner at the camp. He had a son in the Croatian army. Ibro's son often came to the camp and beat his father! While he beat him, Ibro would tell him, "Son, you can smash every bone in my body, but you can't kill my soul!"

When representatives of the Red Cross came to the camp we weren't allowed to speak with them alone. Internees sat on one side of the table, and across from us were Croatian police and the representatives of the Red Cross, so we didn't dare tell them everything we wanted to. The Croatian authorities did not give them the lists with all of our names, instead they hid the men who were capable of digging trenches all day long in the woods, and only showed the Red Cross the ones who were old and feeble.

There was a Muslim who worked at the camp in Odžak. When he was on duty he wouldn't let us stand near the door.

"They are shooting out there. They might hit you. Keep clear of the door."

There were other guards who were nice that way, who told us, "While we are on duty you have nothing to worry about. We won't hurt you."

There were two Muslims working there, waiters. Whenever they could they brought us cigarettes, ćevapčići [grilled sausages], and bread, wrapped in a paper cone. They, too, feared Toma Džojić and Ante Golubović, who ran the jail.

When the front lines got closer to Odžak, before it was taken by the Serbian army, our camp was evacuated to the village of Novi Grad, where we spent three days, and then they moved us to Bosanski Brod.

The Croatian soldiers in Bosanski Brod were from Zagorje, the area around Zagreb. They had several units stationed there. The commander of the Zagorje units always pulled us off of digging trenches when the Serbian soldiers started firing so we wouldn't be hit. There were Muslims at that camp, too, who helped us out by bringing us food, even brandy. Our neighbors there also pretended not to know us.

When Serbian forces got close to Bosanski Brod they moved the camp to Orašje, where they maltreated us. The only food they gave seventeen of us to last for twenty-four hours was a single loaf of bread.

While I was digging trenches in Orašje on 5 November 1992, I was wounded in the left shoulder during combat with the Serbian army. They transferred me to a makeshift hospital that was situated in a convent in Tolisa. There were two other wounded internees with me. We had a doctor who treated our wounds and came around every six hours to check on us.

The doctor was helped by the nuns from the convent. Father Blaž, the priest, and the five nuns looked after us very well. They all behaved as if there was no war on at all. They brought us fruit and cakes every day.

If I hadn't been wounded, who knows how much longer I might have spent at the camp. Immediately after I was wounded they put me up for an exchange, and in November 1992 I was freed in an exchange, which numbered fifty-four Serbs who were exchanged for 125 Croats.

WHO IS AFTER US AND WHERE ARE THEY TAKING US?

TOLD BY JOLE MUSA

Mostar

November 1998

I spent my whole life in Mostar and graduated from junior college there. I left my native town only when I had to travel on business. I was the general director of the aluminum processing plant until 1987, when I was the first victim of the vicious political games.

Until that time I had held a number of key functions in the town administration and was a commander in the system of territorial defense. I admit that I could not fully understand my arrest and imprisonment in jail without guilt or a proper trial until this bizarre situation struck us all. From today's perspective, it is clear to me that none of this could have happened if people like me had been holding all the key functions. Now it is obvious that long before the *Socialist Federative Republic of Yugoslavia began, literally, to fall apart, those who were working toward that goal made all the right moves, eliminating individuals who might be able, thanks to the positions they held, to protest. In Mostar things certainly would not have developed as they did, which doesn't mean that I would have lived through it all.

Mr. Brajković, who was director of the aluminum processing plant after 1987, proved himself to be an extremist in his nationalist orientation in these times.

There were, in fact, two wars in Mostar. The first was in 1992, when the Yugoslav People's Army became a Serbian force and attacked the town. I held the function at that point of commander of the city's territorial defense, but I couldn't do anything because the Croatian Defense Council had surfaced as some sort of military force, which was better armed than what we call today the Army of Bosnia and Herzegovina, because Croatia was backing it, calling up men to serve and arming it. The fighting with Serbian troops didn't last long and there was relatively little loss of life. That part of the war mainly consisted of soldiers who were up in the hills shelling the city. The real war in Mostar began when Croats and Muslims went to war. With the arrival of the Croatian Defense Council, the legally elected municipal authorities, which included territorial defense, were suspended. The Croatian Defense Council formed a state within a state they called *Herceg-Bosna and with it they brought in a whole regulatory apparatus that, unfortunately, persists even today, and it is uncertain when we will see the end of it. At that time I was working near Mostar at the bauxite mine until the Croatian Defense Council mobilized all the men and equipment for the war in Croatia.

That war was not a civil war, though many like to call it that. It had specific features from one place to another, determined by the local milieu. It was entirely different in Mostar than it was in Travnik, or Prozor, or *Srebenica. When we read today what the politicians are writing we get the impression that everyone was fighting some kind of war of liberation and defense. It makes it sound as if there was no aggressor. As far as the Mostar situation I can say with certainty that the first aggressors here were the Serbian forces with the Yugoslav People's Army. After that, the Croatian Defense Council was the aggressor in Mostar, because it wanted to take over all of Mostar in order to bring about some idea *Tuđman had about introducing the *Banovina territories. The Croatian Defense Council in Mostar was a classic aggressive force, far more serious, with more serious consequences, than the Serbian troops had been.

The Muslims were the ones fighting a defensive war here. They were being chased from Bijelo Polje to Blagaj from a stretch of land sixteen miles long into a dead end that was about two and a half miles wide. Suddenly about 50,000 people, refugees from Nevesinje and Gacko, and their livestock with them, found themselves in Mostar without water, electric current, food, weapons, anything. Theirs was a genuine war of defense for survival. I don't know the situation, for instance, in Travnik. Perhaps the tables were turned there.

I watched the situation in Mostar develop from the first day in this manner and in practical terms I was on the sidelines. Mate *Boban, who was Number One for this region in terms of ideas, politics, and both civilian and military matters, thought of me and my popularity in the city. We didn't know each other at that point. He dispatched a member of the presidency to have me brought out to headquarters. The substance of the conversation with Boban came down to his offer that I could be mayor.

I asked him, "Mayor of what? Which city?"

"Of Mostar," he answered.

"What are you thinking of? Mostar isn't yours. Mostar is down on the boulevard, the front line. That is where it's heart is as a city. What you are referring to is only half a city. I am not half a man. I am so big you could give me Mostar and Čapljina to boot. That would be about my size." I joked about this intentionally because it was the last thing on my mind to enter into any sort of agreement with Boban.

When the talk got more serious, I told him, "Mate, if it's peace you want, and not war, then I must accept, on account of my Croatian people and the Muslim people; I must accept and I will without conditions, but I guarantee you and I'll sign my name to it that within three days there won't be any more war in Mostar. I'll go out onto the boulevard lines and I'll stand there and say, 'People, that's enough.' And I guarantee that I will stop the war in Mostar if that is what you want. If you want war, Mate, change your address. You and I have nothing to talk about."

"See you around," answered Boban, and that was our last encounter.

Then Brajković came along who bought what Boban said hook, line, and sinker, and the mess goes on.

Ever since then I have been branded, in a way, in Mostar, because my position was known. I presented it very explicitly in any media willing to broadcast it. I made a statement that there were 5,000 soldiers living in western Mostar who had occupied 5,000 apartments, and that it was time for them to go home, because there had been no combat in their home towns. Their homes were undamaged there, their chickens, cows, goats were being cared for by their mothers and fathers, while someone else's apartment in Mostar was like a second home to them. After that statement they tried to assassinate me, throwing a shell into my office, which I had left, thank goodness, a half hour earlier.

Two days later, precisely at midnight, two assassins shot from a nearby hill through the lit window of my living room with automatic weapons. I was watching television just then and my wife was asleep. I dropped to the floor and told my wife, "Lie still until they stop. Then get to the hallway."

At first all I felt was the heat of the bullet. It was only later that I realized I'd been wounded. I was fat, thank goodness, as I am now, and they told me at the hospital that my fatness was what saved me. The bullet hit me, ricocheting, but if it had struck me just half an inch further to the right, I would have been paralyzed in the arms and legs. Two doctors spent a long time removing the fragments. After the operation they asked if I wanted them to send me for further treatment to Split.

"Are you crazy? Split? The guys who just tried to would be sure to murder me on the way. Put me in intensive care among as many patients as possible, and I'll pull the sheet up over my head because it's no problem for them to come into the hospital and finish me off."

That was how it was until morning when the police came. I didn't know whose police they were because there were three or four different police forces in town. They were standing right next to me and I couldn't tell whether they were protecting me or I was under arrest. That lasted for some twenty days.

After that, whenever I came in to have the wound redressed I would be accompanied by a Nato Stabilization Force *(SFOR) escort. Their guards had been taking care of me about a month before the assassination attempt, standing in front of my house, but that night, a half hour before I was wounded, they went off somewhere.

I lived on the western side of Mostar, near the Rondo traffic circle. I was determined to stay in that apartment because to move out would mean admitting defeat, a lost battle, a lost war, and I couldn't allow that, no matter what.

From the start of Croatian aggression against the Muslims, the Croats were expelling people from the western side to the eastern side of the Neretva River, day and night. After about ten days they had expelled about 200 people from the neighborhood that was above my house toward the cathedral. There were women, children, the elderly being expelled. They went through our neighborhood. I went out to see what was happening.

The people who recognized me asked, "Jole, what is this? Who is after us and where are they taking us?"

I could do nothing else except bring about thirty of them into my apartment. There were women, men, and children, crying. I asked them to quiet the children so that no one would come and take me and them away. They stayed in my apartment all afternoon and night, and in the morning my younger son drove them to the homes of their relatives and friends, depending on whom they could think of.

The head of the Office of the High Representative, Mr. Garrod, offered me protection when I was wounded. He gave me security and the escort, which took me in when my bandages had to be changed. They repaired the damage to my apartment after the assassination attempt.

Earlier this year while he was mayor of Mostar, Safet Oručević, a Muslim, got me involved in building Croatian homes in eastern Mostar. Then I will move on to work on building Muslim and Serbian homes in the western part of town. That is a job that no one dares or wants to do, because it is obstructed, particularly in western Mostar, by the Croatian authorities. It is also clear why. They need refugees to fight the war for them, and after the war to vote for them in elections. When I started that work I was doing it more underground than legally, but now the situation is slightly improved.

I have a private company that was ransacked and looted by people who don't care for my political views. Unfortunately, that is what happens in this city to those who are not blind followers of the regime. The legal suit I started hasn't gotten beyond first base because everyone dreads it.

I had a lot of friends in Sarajevo whose support I expected, at least as far as work went, but all our relations over the last few years have gone no further than words of welcome, lavish dinners, and unfulfilled promises.

They are nothing like the citizens of Sarajevo, from whom I have experienced surprise encounters like one with a man I didn't know who stopped me on the street and said, "I am a Serb, and I feel much better when I see you around."

COFFEE, BEHIND BARS

TOLD BY B. L.[†]

Sarajevo

October 1998

The wife of a Croatian friend of mine left the Sarajevo neighborhood of Dobrinja with their daughter in May 1992, while he stayed behind, alone in their apartment. Dobrinja was under siege when I called him on the phone.

"What's up? How are you? Anything new?"

"It's absolutely awful here!"

"How are you managing? Can I help you with anything?"

"I'm getting by one way or another."

"Can you get out of your building? Maybe we could see each other, have a cup of coffee."

"I don't know if I'll be able to. Every time I try to leave the apartment I've got more chances of dying than living."

He did manage to make it over. He was beside himself. "I can't go back to that apartment. It's constantly being shelled. I don't know what to do. I've got no money because all I had is over on the other side, I'm out of cigarettes . . ."

"How can I help you?"

"I'm looking for a place to stay."

"Come stay with me," I urged.

"Thanks, but I have relatives who've offered to put me up temporarily. Everything is temporary around here."

"Any news from your wife?"

"Not a word."

I offered him cigarettes.

"Help yourself while we still have some. When they're gone I'll quit smoking, too."

When I hear him today tell of the pack of cigarettes I gave him when we parted, I understand what it meant to him. During those four years I felt what it meant to be out of cigarettes.

I was thirty-five years old when I was taken prisoner as a member of the Army of Bosnia and Herzegovina. Soldiers of the Republika Srpska forces surrounded us and called on us to surrender. We were in mountainous terrain where there weren't any natural shelters except caves, so we withdrew into one of the caves. I no longer remember exactly what happened. As we were leaving the cave, one of the other fighters snapped and either began to shoot, or to run. Their answering fire cut down four of our men. We pulled back into the cave but quickly surrendered with our hands up, without any further incidents.

Among us there were Serbs and Croats, though most of us were Muslims. A group of fighters from their side came over and asked, "Any wounded?"

There were eight. They offered them first aid on the spot: a bandage and a splint. They took us on foot in the direction of Kalinovik. We carried our wounded ourselves over the rocky, hilly terrain.

The men who had taken us prisoner stayed silent, while all the rest of them taunted us with curses, insults, and threats. At one spot we halted briefly to give them our background information. They searched us to see if we had any knives or bombs and took all the property we had: watches, chains, rings, money, cigarettes . . .

A young man lunged at the column, brandishing a knife at us, screaming, "One of you killed my best friend!"—

He stabbed three of us—one under the ribs and in the neck, another in the head, and me in the shoulder. All of us had leapt back, fleeing from death.

The crazed soldier grabbed one of our fighters, Zoran. In front of us first he stabbed him all over, smashed him with the knife handle, kicked and punched him, and then took him about thirty feet away, pushed him to the ground, sat on his chest, and slit his throat from ear to ear. In the gruesome silence all you could hear was the death throes of the dying man.

We stood there, petrified, until his commander spoke, "Let's go! Move as fast as you can so that the same doesn't happen to you."

A truck appeared soon after, which transported us to Kalinovik. They beat us the whole ride while we sat with our hands behind our backs.

In Kalinovik they beat each of us separately. Behind the building they threw us into the cellar where they maltreated us all night. Most of us had broken ribs, arms, legs, some even had fractured skulls.

The next day they drove us to an infamous jail in Foča that had been there since the end of World War II.

The prison was well guarded. We got three meals a day: a slice of bread with tea or soup. A doctor came to check up on the wounded every day, and he changed their dressings and treated them until their wounds healed. One of us had back pain so the doctor called for a medical examination. The next day the prisoner came back pleased with the doctor's careful treatment. He'd been examined and had been given medicine for his bad back.

There were Serbian prisoners in the jail, too, sentenced for murder, theft, and other crimes. We had no contact with them, but there was a guard always with us.

Jail isn't bad. People make it bad.

At first we were in solitary confinement. Later they moved us to a group room. The guards behaved decently and didn't maltreat us except for the occasional beating, hitting us, kicking us, smacking us with nightsticks. It was the other prisoners who maltreated us more, because the guards tolerated it, pretending not to see, looking the other way. When they took us to the showers, they beat one of the Serbs who was with us so badly that they broke his nose and lower jaw.

While we were working in the prison yard, four prisoners beat another Serb so brutally that they broke his arms, legs, ribs, lower jaw, and fractured his skull. The warden never let him back into the yard because he was maltreated much more badly than we were. He did live, and in the end he got out through an exchange.

Just before the exchange that took place in Kula, the guards behaved decently, handling their job like professionals.

The questioning in Foča lasted ten days or so, eight to ten hours a day.

The first examiner asked about the number of our fighters who had been taken prisoner, wounded, and killed.

"One had his throat slit after we were taken prisoner," I answered.

"Watch your tongue! See that hill? I can take you up there and you'll end up the way that man did. Do you want that?" he threatened, and went on. "Were you maltreated in any way?"

Our appearance spoke louder than words, so I said nothing.

"Why so bruised?" he insisted.

"I slipped, fell down the stairs several times, banged my head against the wall," I answered, sarcastically.

Clearly we weren't doing well at this conversation. He had the force, I had the lip.

The next day I had a different examiner in the room for questioning. He sat down across from me.

"Do you smoke?"

"I did."

"What do you mean, you did?"

"While I had cigarettes, I smoked. Not any more."

He put a pack of cigarettes down in front of me, and asked, "How about a cup of coffee?"

After all I'd been through I didn't know what to think. Was he provoking me or did he mean well? Was it possible that a person could offer me coffee and a cigarette when I might be killed any moment? Should I accept the offer, or not? Would I ever see coffee and cigarettes again? I decided, I'll accept, even if it's my last.

"Do you want coffee?" he asked, raising his tone.

"I do," I mumbled, barely audibly.

He brought me the coffee himself and put it on the table.

"Take another cigarette," he said, holding out the pack. When I helped myself he put it down on the table. "It will be here. If someone else comes in, serve yourself."

They were most interested in what life was like in Sarajevo.

Once we started working it got easier, even though the work we were doing was hard labor, cleaning the yard, trash, the jail cellars, parts of the furniture factory.

We were kept alive by our hope that we'd be exchanged, although they never hinted we could be for a single moment.

We did the hardest labor in the mine, but we had more to eat there, and half a pound of tobacco a month. There weren't any cigarette papers for us to roll the cigarettes with, so we used newspaper.

When we were on breaks we talked with the miners about women, drink, love: the usual things men talk about . . . With envy we watched them puffing at their cigarettes. When desire overpowered shame we interrupted the miner mid-sentence and asked, "Could you give us just one cigarette paper so that we can remember how that looks?"

The man absentmindedly gave the seven of us a cigarette paper each and went right on telling us about his family, though I wasn't listening any more. I had zoned out, savoring that real cigarette, though it burned up pretty quick.

For days I weighed the right moment to ask the miner, "Gee, do you suppose I could ask you for a cigarette paper or maybe a pack of them?"

He didn't say a word, but the third day when I'd given up all hope, he put a whole pack of papers in my hand, and said, "Tomorrow I get paid."

A SOLDIER WEPT

TOLD BY BRACO STUPAR

Sarajevo

November 1998

I spent the war in Sarajevo, but it was twice as hard for me as it was for the Muslims in Sarajevo, because I was born in the municipality of *Pale, which during the war was under Republika Srpska control. Whenever shells rained down on the city from the Serbian positions, the Muslims who knew me would provoke, insult, and curse me. Thanks to people who earned my respect, who meant a great deal to me and gave me the strength and the incentive to survive, I kept my sanity. I was unlucky in that when a person needs his family the most, I had to be separated from mine for almost four years. My wife was six months pregnant when she went to Banja Luka, on 26 April 1992, with my father where her mother lived. She had our little daughter there, while I stayed in Sarajevo with my mother.

That was the last time I saw my father alive. He died in Novi Sad three years ago. I saw my daughter for the first time when she was three and a half. My family was the first Serbian family to cross the bridge and move back into Sarajevo to stay.

In general terms, to be a Serb in Sarajevo all those years meant to carry a terrible burden, while, at the same time, of course, having done nothing wrong.

I lived in the part of town called Alipašino Polje, about five miles outside the center. I walked to and from work ten miles every day, not to speak of carting home water and firewood. I had to walk even further to collect little twigs that I could use to cook a little dinner with. For hours I'd wait in line to fill a two-gallon jug of water.

Most of my neighbors gave me a rough time. The only way I could deal with it was by going in to work every day. The problem was that I had to come home at the end of every day, and the torment went on day in and day out. The tenor of their taunts was at the level of their ability to reason: "Where does he go every day? What a stupid job! The court! The country's burning! What good can courts do?" they'd grumble, not caring for the fact that my going to work was how I preserved my dignity. It's true that the amount of work at the court during the first year or two of the war truly was minimal. I went in regularly, even when there was nothing to do, even when plenty of people whistled derisively, cursed, insulted, and taunted me.

"You Chetniks had a choice. You could have left. If you stayed, you must be here on assignment! Traitors! You are sending the snipers signals for where to shoot at us!"

There were several Muslim families living in my entranceway who cultivated a very decent relationship with me. Vahid told the people pressuring me the most, "Don't be barbarians! Drop the clichés. See every man for what he is, not through the ethnic group he belongs to."

In June 1992 my sister, whom we all call Seka, had fled from the Sarajevo quarter of Stup. With her husband and two daughters she crawled for two and a half miles to Otoka, where she lived. That stretch included the line of separation, and Chetnik units from Ilidža had broken through the lines that day, so there was a lot of shelling going on. They barely made it across the Dobrinja stream and reached Otoka, which was under federal (Croatian and Muslim, rather than Republika Srpska) jurisdiction. After several days they found a place to stay. Seka worked in a pediatrics clinic as a nurse. They came to throw her out six or seven times with the explanation that she would have to leave the apartment since it wasn't hers. In November 1993 they forced her to leave that apartment, and instead they turned it over to a colleague she had been working with!

With nowhere to go, Seka came with her family to the Alipašino Polje apartment where I was staying with our mother. The authorities had already started distributing humanitarian aid at that point. We received a third of a loaf of bread per member of household. At that time of starvation it meant a great deal. When it was her turn in the bread line, a member of the commission, a man named Fehim, told her, "You Serbs have no right to this bread."

"How come? I came here last night and registered."

"You have no right! Go to Otoka on the Republika Srpska side and deregister there and only then may you register here . . ." The man made such a science of it all just so he wouldn't have to give her any bread. Vahid interrupted the awful scene, saying, "Fehim, enough nonsense. Give the woman her bread!"

It was a Saturday around noon. I hadn't been working that day so I was sitting at home. Vahid had left Alipašino Polje to go in to the central bakery, and he came back, carrying five loaves of bread: "Seka, these are for you. While I am in this house you will not be wanting for bread. I've got to do something to stop that creep. If he gives you any more trouble, tell me."

We did have more trouble with that commissioner. He disliked us because we were Serbs. Fehim was a real extremist, so much so that after I was wounded he even came to see me at home and told me, rudely, wanting to hurt me as much as possible, "I know how you were wounded. You were turning to run and they shot you for deserting."

Enraged, even though I'd been wounded in both legs, I got up out of bed and with my crutches I pushed him out of the apartment all the way down to the first floor, even though that wasn't the way I usually communicated with people. He reported me: that I was hostile, that I was against the government and all sorts of other things. The report made its way to the office of the local commune, where Bajro worked, in charge of security. Without a second thought Bajro tore it up, knowing me, and, apparently, knowing Fehim as well.

They picked a few of us men off the street when we were on our way back from the court and took us out to dig. They didn't even look at our first and last names. All that mattered to them was that they'd have enough men to dig the trenches facing the Trebević front. It was June, and a banner year for cherries. It seemed to us as if there were more cherries than there ever had been. And starved, longing for cherries like everyone else in that trench, I gave in. I climbed up one of the trees with Goran and threw cherries down to the men who watched us from a sheltered spot. That surreal moment, when I didn't mind that they'd brought me up to dig, was interrupted by a burst of fire from a "sower of death," as we called the infamous M-84 machine gun. Instinctively I jumped free of the tree. I heard Goran scream, "Mother! They've got me!"

I turned to see where they were shooting from. At first I didn't even realize that they'd hit me in both legs. I panicked. I managed to crawl over and drop into a cross trench. I crawled some 450 feet to the main trench. The men who were digging looked at me, frantic. Although we were still under fire, a Muslim from Višegrad ran over and carried me like a child to a room where sentry duty was transferred from one guard detail to the next. There they administered first aid, and then a vehicle came and rushed me to the hospital.

At first the situation in the hospital seemed to be total chaos. There were about thirty wounded people bleeding, some missing arms or legs, some already dead, all in a jumble. Anyone who has never seen a situation like that can hardly believe it is possible to organize things well and save lives. But that is how it was; everyone knew precisely what they were supposed to be doing. The people in the emergency ward had a professional, humane attitude in the true sense of the word.

First they took care of my left leg, then my right. Doctor Kapidžić operated on me twice because of gangrene in my right leg. If I'd been his own brother I don't think he would have been more caring than he was with me. Every morning he re-dressed my wounds. Although I was the only Serb in the room, he came right over to me during his rounds.

"How's it going, Cobra?" he'd ask, grinning as he switched the syllables of my name around in pig-Latin-like slang.

I spent more than a month at the hospital. Each time I came in for a checkup, after I got out he'd extend my sick leave another month. After three months I felt I could walk normally, but the doctor wouldn't allow me to work for eight months.

At one point I was on the verge of a nervous breakdown. I was gripped by despair, and kept thinking, "There's no more food, there's no more hope. My family is far away. I have never seen my little girl, and probably never will. Life like this has no point . . ." Asaf gave me warm, human, moral, and spiritual support.

In a situation when a man is marked by his nationality as Serbs were in Sarajevo, where most of the people thought and said, "All Serbs are Chetniks; I'm sorry, brother, but you, too, are a Serb," I experienced many moving moments when I didn't feel rejected at all. As far as my professional work was concerned I even experienced the upward mobility of success.

Eight months after I was hurt, when I was all better, Asaf called me to come back to work. He had been named a judge, so his position as chief administrator of court clerks was vacant. It was unthinkable to me that as a Serb in 1994, during the worst time of the war, I could be given this job. Asaf told the president of chambers that he stood behind me. The president accepted his recommendation. After that Asaf pestered me to study for the bar exam.

"Take the bar. Study. Don't waste your time," he urged.

"Asaf, I can't. I'm not up to anything. I have no strength. Who knows what tomorrow may bring."

"You have to study. You must! You must!" he kept repeating, until I finally agreed. While I studied he kept after me, "Time to take that test."

"I'll wait until the war's over."

"Take it now."

"I'd rather not."

When the war ended I took the test immediately and passed it before a committee made up mostly of Muslims, but with one Serb and one Croat as well.

Asaf and I are still inseparable. That terrible time, behind us now, only reinforced our friendship and cooperation.

For two months I went to the bridge every day after the Dayton agreement was signed, hoping I'd see the names of my wife and daughter on the list of those who'd been given permission to return. Finally the day dawned, 4 January 1996, when I saw, in the eighth and ninth slots on a list of ten, the two names dearest to me: Mira and Jelena Stupar.

Thirty of my friends came out that day, it was freezing cold, to the bridge to share with me the joy of their return. There were very few who didn't cry.

The first seven crossed the bridge. Then for the next two hours there was nobody. I went over to a policeman and asked, "What's going on? Will the others be crossing today?"

"They will, but we'll have to wait until Tuđman passes by," he answered.

It just so happened that Tuđman was visiting Sarajevo that day. As soon as he passed they reopened the bridge. A member of UNPROFOR carried my daughter over, and another pushed their bags on a cart. Behind them came my wife. The soldier who had crossed the bridge with my daughter in his arms, asked, "Braco?"

"That's me," I said, choking up.

"Here is your daughter," said the soldier.

"Give Daddy your hand," I said, unable to take my eyes off her. A lovely, big girl, three and a half years old, she flung her arms open wide.

"Do you love your Daddy?"

"Yup."

The soldier cried. I couldn't. I was frozen to the spot. My heart was bursting.

TRUST EARNED

TOLD BY M. P.†

A Judge, Mostar

November 1998

I was born forty years ago in Doboj. My father was an army officer; I spent my childhood and youth in Zagreb where I earned my law degree. I married a Muslim man and moved to Mostar at the age of twenty-five for love. Mostar may not have been my native town, but since the war I feel as if this city belongs to me.

The war began for me on 19 September 1991, when the reservists came to Mostar. I was at my job, a vantage point from which I could see everything that was going on, including the flourishing of the mood that led to the war. At that time I was living in what is called western Mostar, though I loathe the distinction between what became the western (Croatian) and eastern (Muslim) parts of the city. During 1992 I worked as a commissioner for the Croatian Defense Council authorities on the western shore of the Neretva. After this shore was freed of Serbian hostilities on 16 June 1992, I crossed over to the eastern part of town to help in reinstating some form of civilian life. I worked here until 9 May 1993. I happened to be in my apartment that day, perplexed by the erupting situation. You couldn't tell who was firing guns, or where they were firing from, or why. That was the beginning of the Croatian Defense Council's attack on eastern Mostar, which soon became the Muslim part of town. When I analyze the events from today's perspective, there were certain hints of it as early as a month before, and maybe even earlier. Now, of course, we know that it was all planned well in advance.

My job was the organization of the influx of humanitarian aid. I cared the most about making sure that people had enough to eat. Because the city used to function as a whole, it took awhile to set up separate services and utilities for the two sides of the river. It was only in April 1993 that eastern Mostar got running water. You could feel politics looming over everything. I even dueled with the director of water supply on a radio talk show on the topic of whether the fact that eastern Mostar had no running water was due only to technical problems.

I was lucky that my daughter was in a safe place as of 1992, with my mother, far away from Mostar, so at least I didn't have her to worry about.

That was when I began to negotiate my passage over to the eastern shore of the Neretva because my heart was pulling me to be with the people I'd been working with for ten years. The Croatian Defense Council gave me permission to move. The army would accept me because I was someone both sides trusted. I was going to check on what condition that part of the city was in because humanitarian organizations were on hand to help, but there wasn't a single humanitarian organization that would distribute aid without precise information on what the city needed.

I went over with UNPROFOR on 21 May 1993. A colleague was supposed to go along but he was not issued a permit, because the Spanish UNPROFOR officers were against it, since I'd be back in three hours' time.

I'll never know why it was that my name was not on the list of those to come back across the Neretva that day. In any case, the UNPROFOR authorities wouldn't let me return. Armed clashes erupted again, because the negotiations had not been productive.

I have never been sorry that I stayed: when I stepped out of the personnel carrier in front of headquarters, all the people who knew me from my work in food distribution were elated. They hugged and kissed me. They figured, If she's back here among us Muslims and she is a Croat from western Mostar, it must be that there won't be war. The relationship between these people and me hasn't changed. I stayed in eastern Mostar and did my job.

It was rough. For the first month I worked at my old job, organizing life in the city. I slept in the office where I worked, hoping every day I'd be able to go back to western Mostar. Only afterward did I learn that I had become quite interesting to the Croatian Defense Council because I was living in eastern Mostar. They figured I must have information of importance to them, and only when they threatened to lock my husband up if I didn't come back did I realize that that there was no going back for me.

My husband was arrested and taken to the *Heliodrom concentration camp where he spent ten months. They took people to the Heliodrom just because of their first and last names, of course, if they weren't Croatian. All these things are scars we will all carry with us for a long time to come . . .

We did all we could to set up civilian life in town, so that everything wouldn't be under the aegis of the army. I fought every day for survival in a town where there was no food, water, or electric current for a whole year. I belonged to a generation that had never dreamed it was possible to live this way.

My colleagues, though only a handful, managed to oppose the initiative to set up a *kangaroo court. Had such a court been established, there could no longer have been talk of democracy in this country.

A month after my arrival, a vacancy opened up on the bench. Until then I hadn't worked in chambers, and I didn't want to, but someone had the audacity to appoint me to the bench in the military court. I became a judge as a Croatian woman on 1 July 1993 in eastern Mostar during the fiercest clashes between the Army of Bosnia and Herzegovina and the Croatian Defense Council forces!

For all those six years no one attacked me for my work. My colleagues behaved very decently. They helped me out when I requested that I not be called upon to judge Croats. My child was somewhere abroad and my husband was being held in a concentration camp. We didn't dare try anyone in absentia at that point, not even members of the Croatian Defense Council forces.

From day one I was accepted and I had no problems, even when my views diverged dramatically from the views of the local government. That is what made this part of the city great, because no one pounced on the fact that I was a Croat to discriminate against me.

There were very few Croats or Serbs living in eastern Mostar during those years. Now they have begun to come back, but the ones coming back are mostly people from biethnic marriages. There is a major problem having to do with how many people can find suitable housing, since so many apartments were devastated. People have nowhere to come back to.

In this war I lost everything I owned, and acquired nothing. Only now, six years later, is there talk of finding a temporary solution to my housing needs, and that is only because I'll have to leave the apartment I've been staying in now that someone else is moving back.

I had the chance of going to Croatia, where I have an apartment and a house, but when I thought about how they respect me here, and that they need me, I decided to stay.

When there was talk in 1990 that people in biethnic marriages would have the roughest time of it I didn't believe them, but that is precisely what happened. This war brought up dilemmas for people they had never faced before. Whether they should follow their ethnic group or their beliefs. Some people felt crowded in the much larger country of the former Yugoslavia with their cosmopolitan beliefs, and now they feel really crowded.

I remember one young couple who got married in eastern Mostar in 1994. He was a Croat who spent the whole war in the Army of Bosnia and Herzegovina, while she was a Muslim. People from the neighborhood and his whole unit threw themselves into the preparations for the wedding so that they could celebrate it in style. They made a cake of two eggs, and decorated it with a paper cutout of the bride and groom. Someone lent the groom a suit . . . They live in Mostar today and have a baby.

Another wonderful example is a couple who were in love before the war. All through the conflict he was on the western side, a Croat, and she, a Muslim woman, was on the eastern side of the city. Despite the long time they were out of touch, and the tragedy that hit her family when a Croatian Defense Council shell murdered her sister's boy, that family had the breadth to embrace a Croatian son-in-law. They married after the war, despite the madness.

I didn't see my daughter for a year. I spoke with my mother for the first time after seven months through the efforts of an amateur radio operator from Italy. That was the first connection set up through ham radio operators and they helped me out so that I could tell my mother I was alive and well.

In June 1994 I left Mostar after working on an agreement between the Army of Bosnia and Herzegovina, and the Croatian Defense Council. I went to see my daughter and I had a Croatian Defense Council escort all the way to the border between Herzegovina and the Croatian border. The agreement was that I would be gone for a month and that I'd come back.

As the time for my return approached my family was surprised by my resolve, but I explained to them, "I don't know how long I'll stay on in Mostar, but I'll go back now because of the month that they made it possible for me to be with you. People did a lot, showing me this trust. I'd like to go back to thank them, and then I'll see." Many did not return when they had the chance to get out.

After an incident when a group of women blocked UNPROFOR from leaving town to protest the lack of humanitarian aid, UNPROFOR did start delivering food intermittently. I was living next door to a Croatian woman who had been living in the Muslim part of Mostar throughout the war. One of the members of the foreign humanitarian organizations found her on a list of recipients of aid and decided to visit her. They asked her what she got in the way of food. That was a time when people were starving and when food was distributed a maximum of twice monthly, because convoys seldom came through town. She answered that she had received a pound of flour, half a cup of cooking oil, two ounces of yeast, and one candle. The foreigner, hearing this, wanted to know, "Does this mean that as a Croat you were given more than the Muslims and Serbs were?"

"No, you can check if you want. I was given precisely the same amounts as everyone else," she answered with a smile.

No one drew distinctions when they gave out humanitarian aid. Not even those charities from the Islamic countries.

The target date for the beginning of a single system of courts for all of Mostar was 15 November 1998. As I record this it still hasn't happened. There are separate judiciaries in eastern and western Mostar, as with all the other local institutions.

By the nature of my work I was in regular contact with Konjic as well. I know that there were Croats who chose to stay there, too, in a predominantly Muslim community, and kept their jobs even though people always worry about what will happen later.

A PASSPORT

TOLD BY MIRSADA BOSNO

Sarajevo

October 1998

The hell in Sarajevo, with its brutality, darkness, coldness, hunger, and fear, cut short my youth when I was only twenty-five. My father's death during the second year that the city was under siege rocked my sense of safety and stability, and reduced life to a struggle to care for my mother, who was in very poor health. I was an only child, so I had to face that struggle alone. I could not get a hold of the medicine I needed for her and I knew I would have to get out somehow.

Every person who was in Sarajevo dreamed, one way or another, of leaving the city. I wondered whether I knew anyone who lived somewhere where they could help me. I remembered Dražena Peranić, a newspaperwoman I'd gotten together with now and then, but we'd never so much as had a cup of coffee together. I sent her a message by way of a friend who was going to Zagreb on business in the meager hope that he would find her. I asked her to help me find some way to get to Italy so that I could get my mother's medication.

I wondered what I had done to anger God. I was being cooped up here like a beast, I felt the authorities were persecuting me, that I had no way of getting out of here to see the light, a lit street, a store with food on the shelves. I didn't have to eat any of it, it would be enough just to see what things looked like in a normal city. To feel what it meant to sit and watch television, walk freely through the streets . . . And then all of it would melt into a single desire: to save my mother. She was all I had left.

My friend came quickly back to Sarajevo. He was smiling when he handed me a passport and press card.

"Dražena sent you these."

I stared at the passport. It had been issued in Ljubljana in Dražena's name. She lived in Zagreb, I lived in Sarajevo. I asked him, astonished, "What?"

"I called her as you asked me to and explained your situation. I asked her if she could take out some kind of press pass in your name. She tried but it didn't work."

At that point I hadn't even started working as a journalist yet and I wasn't writing.

"So, what did Dražena say? She sent me her passport! What is it that the two of you cooked up? I don't get it!" I asked, bewildered.

"She sent you her passport so you could get out of Sarajevo. That's what you wanted."

I stared, baffled, at her picture. She and I didn't resemble each other at all. She had dark hair, I was a blond. She had a broad face, my face was narrow.

"Why was the passport issued in Ljubljana?" I asked, still confused.

"You know that there is a war on between Muslims and Croats. You can't get any documents in Croatia right now. Dražena only just managed to get her Bosnian-Herzegovinian passport in Ljubljana a few days ago," he explained.

I didn't have time to think about her gesture. I needed to grab hold of the opportunity to go get the medication.

I decided I would try to travel on her passport, because, after all, the worst that could happen to me was that I might be killed. At that point I didn't stop to think about how I'd feel. My need to go guided me.

I studied her picture for awhile and in the end I decided to dye my hair black. Under wartime conditions I had trouble finding a working hairdressers' salon that had black dye. It took a lot but I did find some dark face powder and brightly colored lipstick. I worked on my makeup for seven days so that I'd look as much like her as possible. I figured that this was a time when everything was a mess anyway; everyone had changed their appearance in the chaos of the war. Lots of other people had pictures in their passports showing them with eighty pounds more weight on them than they now had; they looked nothing like their former selves.

Dražena was wearing large circle-shaped earrings. I focused on them as if they would make all the difference. I even found ones just like them and put them on. I was thrilled. I had to make it to the airport and fly out on a "Hercules" plane to Italy. The first checkpoint was run by UNPROFOR soldiers to whom I had to show my press card in order to secure a place in the personnel carrier that would take me to the airport. Only when I got in did I remember the incidents of kidnapping which had been happening on Kasindolska Street at the Serbian army checkpoint. It crossed my mind: "If they catch me there, my Muslim name or Dražena's Croatian one won't help much."

I lucked out and made it to the airport, which I didn't recognize because I had been imagining it in its prewar condition. Everything had been subordinated to the military, from the sandbags to the personnel carrier and the containers. It was filthy, cold, and weird. I was supposed to show my press card and passport and be issued a makeshift ticket, which would allow me onto the plane.

I kept repeating to myself that all that mattered was to get out of this alive. In my pocket was a long wish list, much of which was requests for spices, chocolate, and fancy Italian nylon stockings.

I stood at the airport checkpoint wearing those large earrings as if they would be my ticket to Italy. Luckily there were no mirrors. In order to make myself up, I had pulled a woolen stocking over my head, I'd thickened and darkened my eyebrows, I'd put on bright red lipstick and had used eye shadow to draw dark lines around my eyes. I looked like a caricature even to myself, because this was hardly a professional makeup job and I wasn't familiar with cosmetics.

Before I left I asked the small number of people who knew what I was up to, "Do I look at all like this picture?" and since none of them wanted to dishearten me, they all said, "When you put on those earrings the resemblance will be perfect."

The atmosphere among those who knew that someone was planning to leave the city was incredible; they all had the strength to convince the one leaving that it would be great, reasoning that if they'd survived the last two years in Sarajevo, they'd be sure to do fine as they left.

I had even convinced myself that I resembled Dražena and that I'd get through. I sat in the waiting room for the Ancona flight. Ancona meant salvation, the end to all my troubles.

An UNPROFOR soldier looked over each of us for a long time, and I had the impression that I was the only one he was really studying.

We finally got on the plane where the procedure for how to sit and use the bulletproof vest and helmets was to be explained to us.

We landed in Italy where we waited in the transit area for them to run an identity check for each of us. The procedure lasted quite a long time, and that frightened me again and sent me back in my thoughts to before the war when we all had passports that were acknowledged everywhere in the world and that we never had any trouble with anywhere.

Anxious, I was the first to hand over my, or rather Dražena's, passport. I was afraid I'd fail when I was almost there. Finally they called my name and I stepped into the airport building. At that moment I shut down completely. I couldn't say a word nor could I feel any excitement or even grief.

I felt nothing. I couldn't explain it to the friend who had brought me the passport and who was there with me. I said my first words that evening, at the pharmacy, when I asked for my mother's medication.

I didn't feel any urge to remain in Italy. Many asked, "Whatever is wrong with you? Could it be that you managed to get out and now you are going back?"

No one understood, and I had no desire to explain.

I spent only two days in Italy, far too short a time to begin thinking about peace.

I came home using Dražena's passport and press card without any problems. I brought home the odds and ends on the wish list and saw how much joy these things brought people.

Mother was saved, and my impulsive nature, not inclined to thinking, drove me to travel once more before I returned Dražena's papers, this time for fun.

It all unfolded as it had before: a Norwegian soldier glanced briefly at the passport and press card, bent over and wrote Dražena's name in the list of passengers. As he returned the papers to me, he said, "These aren't yours, but have a nice trip."

I was no longer as anxious as I'd been that first time. Even his words didn't shake me.

I got to Italy without a hitch.

Again I had a long wish list of requests and I had to stick within the fifty-pound limit on luggage.

At the cheap hotel where the journalists stayed, the scales went from room to room every morning for all the people traveling to Sarajevo. People passed on tips on how to cram a lot into as small a bag as possible.

It is human nature to want more than we can have. Even when I had no idea whether I'd be alive the next day or whether I'd even need everything I was buying. I figured somebody could use it.

There was a traitorous scale at the airport that showed that my bag went over the weight limit. I stuffed the overweight items into the bulletproof vest, and my handbag, in which women usually carry things like lipstick and handkerchiefs, was stuffed with salami and jars of spice.

The routine had changed—an electronic screening device was used to check every traveler. My suitcase and travel bag went through inspection. They asked me to remove everything that was wrapped in the bulletproof vest; there was a hush as they watched me pull out bags of instant coffee, cocoa, and artificial sweetener.

I panicked. I felt as if everyone suspected me of something; I couldn't tell why they thought me suspicious, whether it was because I was holding someone else's papers or because I was breaking the rules. They ran a metal detector up and down my arms and legs and it chimed like the church bells at Our Lady's!

My pockets were full of special safety valves crucial to installing gas piping. I laid them out obediently in front of the soldier. Here was yet another proof of my guilt.

The control device kept beeping, this time because of my boots. I took them off but there was nothing in them. They asked me to strip my socks, but they found nothing there. It took me several minutes to figure out that it was shards from bomb fragments in the soles of my boots. I lifted my boots and showed the soldier the damaged soles. They didn't understand that in Sarajevo I was running every day around on streets covered in bomb shards which no one cleared. That was when it dawned on me why my boots kept leaking. Angrily I cast off all my fear.

The head of the checkpoint tossed Dražena's passport over to me, but he kept her press card, announcing, "Young lady, you will never fly again."

I cursed in my native language, and he tossed my sunglasses, which had been part of the masquerade, after me.

Only when I sat down in the waiting room did I realize what had happened: with my cavalier behavior I had ruined Dražena. I had stripped her of her livelihood. She was a refugee from Sarajevo in Zagreb, a single mother with a small child and her job was her only way to survive. She had gone off as a reporter for the Sarajevo newspaper *Oslobođenje*, but had been lucky enough to find work with another agency. Now she wouldn't be able to work because I knew they'd destroy her press card.

I was swept by fear and panic. I was responsible for someone who had helped me with the very best of intentions, more than anyone else had ever helped me. Even someone who was my flesh and blood would have thought twice before being as generous as Dražena had been.

Everyone got onto the flight but me. I had to stay at the airport.

At the hotel I met an Italian who was intrigued by what was going on in Sarajevo. When I introduced myself I gave my own name, of course, without a second thought. That night I asked him, in tears, to help me. He tried to talk me into staying, as a refugee, in Italy or to go to Croatia. When I refused, he said, "You don't deserve anyone's help when you are so pig-headed and stubborn."

The next morning I spent two hours pleading with the man who had fixed my fate and Dražena's, but he was implacable.

After two hours the head of the U.N. High Commission for Refugees (UNHCR) took me aside and said, "I have heard of your case. This time we will let you through, but please, do not do this any more," and he handed me Dražena's press card.

I went through inspection once again, this time without a hitch. Twice they took us off the plane and back to the terminal building because there was something preventing our takeoff. Each minute something new kept happening, and the rules of travel kept changing. Because of that the travelers began to panic, and I among them.

The second time we were waiting to board the plane, a reporter from *Oslobođenje* asked if he could be let out of the transit area to use the bathroom, so he was escorted out by two soldiers. When he came back, he sat next to me and asked me, softly, "What's your name?"

"What business is it of yours?" I retorted sharply.

"That Italian guy I saw you with last night was asking if Mirsada Bosno got her press card back," he whispered in reply.

I was frozen with horror. So that meant that the fellow had come after me to the airport to see whether I had managed to deal with the problem and was trying to help me! The only mistake was in my name. When I recovered my composure enough to speak, I asked the reporter, "What did the soldier say?"

"That we give out no information about travelers," he answered, and continued, "The man is standing at the door and insists on seeing you."

Again I froze. I looked over at the doorway without a clue of what might happen next. Just as a soldier was walking out I caught sight of the Italian man looking for me. When our eyes met I waved, to show that everything was fine, and my gaze probably told him, "Please don't go asking anything more about me!"

He left and I got back to Sarajevo safe and sound.

My colleague took Dražena's passport and press card back to her in Zagreb, but they missed each other. She had had to go to Sarajevo urgently, and so she reported that her press card was missing so that she could get a new one.

Dražena told me that three months later she was at the Split airport waiting for a flight to Sarajevo and spied her papers under the glass of the counter. Delighted she took them and moments later by mistake showed the press card, which she had declared to be missing because of me. She was detained immediately, and released several hours later once they'd identified her.

THROUGH A MINE FIELD
TO MY LOVE

TOLD BY ZORAN SAMARDŽIĆ†

Refugee from Tuzla, interviewed in Bosanski Šamac

December 1995

Before the war I completed all the course work for my degree in geology and mining in my native Tuzla, in Bosnia. All I had was a few more exams and I'd be done. I had been in love for years with a young woman. Even the war couldn't destroy my feelings for her. My girlfriend managed to get out of Tuzla in time and got a job in Loznica, over in Serbia. I stayed behind in the city to take the remaining exams. We planned to get married as soon as I graduated.

I knew a lot of people from all nationalities, or at least I thought I knew them. I was shown just how mistaken I was by a good friend of mine, who completely changed during the war.

Even before the conflict actually broke out, the atmosphere was already pretty charged. *Green banners were unfurled all over town. Serbian, not Yugoslav, banners were unfurled on the Yugoslav People's Army tanks.

I believe that in time more healthy forces will prevail in my city because of us and our children. There are a lot of people among the Muslims and the Croats who think the way I, a Serb, think. I know that because we voted side by side. When I left town we said our good-byes over drinks. There were tears.

Recently I was watching a TV report on the Partisan cemetery in Tuzla. That is where the seventy girls and boys were buried who died when a Serbian shell hit the center of town. It happened after I left. I saw how they were all buried together, regardless of their faith, and that in the summer young people come to the grave by the thousands.

During the fighting around Tuzla there was a very difficult situation around distributing food supplies. There was no food, and what little could be found was not readily available to most people. You'd pay twenty German marks for two pounds of flour, fifty for two pounds of sugar, thirty for a quart of oil, and a pack of cigarettes cost between ten and twenty German marks. People had nothing to eat. There were about 100,000 displaced persons living in collective accommodations.

Suicide was rampant at that point.

A friend of mine named Sead, a Muslim, had dated a Serbian girl before the war. During the war he decided he wanted to marry her. He asked me if I would be his *kum [best man]. I was at their wedding. We shared all we had and helped one another out.

Sead refused to wear a uniform. He wanted to get away to his mother, who was living at the time in Vienna. He hid in the luggage compartment of a bus, but they found him there and arrested him. He was sentenced to a year in jail. A few days ago I got a letter from him. We correspond by way of my aunt in Germany. He writes that he and his wife have a son.

The only people who could leave the Tuzla area were the elderly, or those who were not fit for service in the armed forces. Everyone else had to find connections and bribe someone to guide them across the front lines. Once I'd graduated, I decided to leave town because of my girlfriend. I found my first connection through relatives. The arrangement was that five of us would show up at 5:00 P.M. at the local pharmacy. From there we'd follow a man on a bicycle. We walked behind him for ten miles through the woods to circumvent the checkpoints in the woods. While we were in the woods waiting to meet up with the next guy who would get us over to the other side, we happened upon Džemo, the deputy commander of the police. He had gone into the woods for the most ordinary of reasons—responding, as they say, to the call of nature. He arrested us and took all five of us down to the police station in the next village. As we were walking into the building, a policeman said to us, "Look, you've got nothing to worry about."

They were being nice to us. I took a bottle of brandy out and offered it around. No one refused a drink. I offered them cigarettes. One of the soldiers took out his own cigarettes and said, "We'll share what we have fifty-fifty."

They questioned us, using, at first, sterner tones but no physical abuse. When they brought me into the office, one of the soldiers searched me. He found the money I had in my inside pocket. With a look, he handed it back.

"Where were you headed?" the policeman asked.

"I was going to be with the girl I love. She is waiting for me over in Serbia. We've decided to get married and to try to go abroad. If you don't believe me, read her letters," I told them, showing them the letters. He didn't check them, but said, "Do you have any way of getting out of Serbia to go abroad?"

"I don't know, but I love her and I want to marry her. Where we end up living is much less important."

During the questioning I asked if I could use the facilities. A soldier went out with me. "If I'd been the one who found you I would have let you go," he said, sympathetically.

When the questioning was over, they told us, "Go back to Tuzla. You'll have to go along the main road and report to the police at each of the checkpoints along the way." As we left, all of them, laughing, chimed in, "Better luck next time!"

Džemo added, "I hope you get married soon!"

"I'll get married soon if you stay out of the woods," I told him. They all laughed. We shook hands and said we looked forward to seeing each other in better times and in a nicer place.

That same day, 28 Feburary 1994, firm in my plan to see my girlfriend as soon as possible, I managed to get out of Tuzla by another route, through another forested area, though I did have to cross a mine field to do it.

A CUP OF COFFEE
AT MUSTAFA'S

TOLD BY ANETA BENAC
Writer, Sarajevo

November 1998

During the war in Sarajevo there weren't many Jews left in the city. They were extremely well organized, probably because of the tragic experience they still carried with them from the Second World War. They got more than enough aid to meet the needs of their own, but they didn't stop at that. Instead, they helped everyone they could. All the other religious groups had too many people to look after for them to be able to secure adequate food for everyone else, and because of that there was real starvation in this town. During the war no one pestered the members of the Jewish community even though they, along with all the other citizens of Sarajevo, suffered the privations of the war. Many of the Sarajevans survived the war only because of the medicine they received, free of charge, from the Jewish Community Center. Often they couldn't have found the drugs anywhere else, and the Jews gave them out for free no matter what your beliefs were. Then some people started hawking at the marketplace the medicine they'd gotten free of charge. After that, when people heard that was happening they continued distributing the medicine free of charge but only with a prescription.

My husband and I ate at least fifteen times at the Jewish dinner hall. My mother went there much more often and brought us food from their kitchen. She still goes there to eat today. I'd be willing to wager that about 100 Jews were saved by eating at that hall, and everyone else who ate there belonged to one of the other ethnic groups. Under that good roof, all in one place, you could find hungry Croats, Serbs, and Muslims who lived in the neighborhood. A few times I received aid packages from them, and they were really wonderful. I lost eighty-eight pounds during the war, and my husband, Nikola, lost eighty-two.

My mother was an unstoppable dynamo. She just happened to make the acquaintance of General Jovan *Divjak during the war. He issued her a permit allowing her to get food at the mess for the Army of Bosnia and Herzegovina headquarters to feed my uncle, who was seriously ill. Instead of just giving her the one portion, they'd fill her whole bucket. She would trudge with that bucket from one side of town to the other, bringing food to all of us. She kept five of us alive with soup for a year and a half, walking at least ten miles a day.

My mother was a teacher and knew all sorts of people around town. Some of her pupils were the leading commanders in defense of the city. Once she went to see a member of one of the Sarajevo paramilitary units at his headquarters.

"I'm going hungry. Have you got any food at all here?"

"You used to whip me when I was little, when I was in your class," he said.

"I sure did," Mama admitted. "You behaved pretty badly."

"Well, still those were happy times, ma'am," he smiled, and turned to his soldier. "Take a look and see if you can't come up with some canned food for my teacher. Don't you worry, we'll find something."

The soldier soon came back with a bag packed with tins of canned meat.

Once she went to see Ismet Bajramović Ćelo.

"I was your teacher. Can you help me now? I have nothing to eat and I've no one left to turn to. I'm supplying three families with food."

"You sure weren't any teacher of mine," Ćelo grinned, "but I don't mind. Here you go."

If it hadn't been for good neighbors many more people would have starved to death. Whenever someone got an aid package they'd run to share it with their neighbors. Almost everyone did. Daily you could see young Muslim men helping by carrying water for elderly, retired women, Croatian, Serbian, and Jewish women who had been left behind when their family had fled the city or when their relatives couldn't reach them.

While politicians manipulated with the population, petty criminals, pitiful nobodies, had their moment of glory and became big time nationalists, no matter what nation they were from, to steal whatever they could get their hands on. Finally they, too, were "somebody."

My husband and I used to go to fetch water in different parts of town. Sometimes we'd go to the Brothers Seven restaurant, sometimes to the Bistrik neighborhood, sometimes down to Tito's Street in the town center, sometimes to the seminary near the center, depending on where there was water. For the last three years a hairdresser named Safet, who had his salon across the street from our house, used to give us water. Headquarters wasn't far away so there was running water. Half of Safet's family was murdered in the last war and in this one by Serbian soldiers, and yet he, a Muslim, helped us, Serbs.

One day when he saw my husband going off holding empty water containers, he said him, "Nikola, why don't you fill up on water right here?"

He always let us fill our canisters with water in his salon after that. He didn't give water to others because he didn't dare to let a line form. Thanks to Safet the hairdresser and Munevera, a woman doctor who lived in the next apartment building over, we were taken care of, at least as far as water was concerned.

Whenever we got a quart of cooking oil, we would trade it at the *Markale marketplace for cigarettes, matches, and batteries, which we needed so that we could listen to the news, because there was no electricity. We were always hoping to hear that the long-anticipated peace had finally come, because they kept holding negotiations.

It happened sometimes that we'd get beans in a package of humanitarian aid, but they needed to be cooked for a long time and we didn't have any way to cook them. It was awful to have food in the house and still be hungry.

One winter for several months we traded food we couldn't use at the marketplace for other things we needed, standing outdoors in the cold way below zero. We also sold our antique furniture at that marketplace, our artworks, silver, mirrors, chandeliers . . . In a word we sold all we had for a pittance just so we could survive. We used to dream about eating chicken.

My husband wrote six books during the war and published three of them. During the war I wrote poems. I published one volume during the war in Sarajevo. In November, Nikola was given a cash award for his work. That was the first time we'd eaten meat since the beginning of the war. I didn't even recognize the flavor. I had erased it completely from my memory. That experience was absolutely novel.

Time galloped by. When I run into an old friend I haven't seen for awhile, I can see that he's gotten old. I keep forgetting that it has been six years. It was all like one long, dark night, and only now life is picking up where it left off.

We came into the winter of 1992 unprepared. It was bitterly cold. At that point we hadn't figured out that we could burn our furniture, the parquet flooring, the wall-to-wall carpeting. At night, when the cold was the worst, while we still had some money we used to go off to visit Mustafa, who had a working gas stove at the International Center for Peace. We'd spend several hours there until we'd warm up, we'd have a cup of coffee and then we'd go home. We never took our clothes off at night but would go straight to bed in our coats, fur hats, boots. When we ran out of money for coffee we couldn't afford to go down and warm up at Mustafa's. Later, because we were writers, we got some financial support from America, to the tune of 500 German marks, which reached us, as I recall, by way of Slovenia. There was no one able to give us change for the 500 mark note. We showed Mustafa that we had the money, but that we couldn't pay because none of us had the change. Mustafa gave us coffee and said we could pay him later. We are still owing him, today.

AND SEVEN DAYS LATER

TOLD BY ADIL SULJIĆ

Displaced Person from Bratunac, interviewed in Sarajevo

November 1998

I was born in Bratunac in 1963, where I lived and worked until 10 May 1992. In late April 1992 strange things began to happen in Bratunac. Every day you could hear shooting on the outside of town and in the neighboring villages. Rumors began to fly. All the men fit for military service were being picked up.

We didn't know what to do. In terror we fled from our houses at nightfall and hid through the night in nearby woods. Two of my neighbors and I hid in a raspberry patch just up the hill from our street, because we had the best view from there down onto our houses. Our mistake was thinking they'd be after us at night, when it turned out they were picking men up by day.

One evening in early May we hid in the tall grass, about 300 meters above the house of my neighbor from where we could keep an eye on the whole street. There were only women and children left on the street. At about nine o'clock that night a car came down our street driving really fast. We were surprised because for weeks no one had been driving through the town except for the paramilitary fighters under Arkan with their jeeps, and new-comers with their fancy cars, who we were hiding from. They stopped in front of my neighbor's house.

"Do you have any idea who that is?" I asked him.

"Not a clue," he said, confused.

I went down the hill and read the license plate number on the old-model Mercedes.

"Do you know whose it is now?" I wanted to know when I got back.

"No, I don't."

I crawled back and peeked into the living room window. I could see his wife serving two men with coffee.

"As far as I can tell the situation looks completely normal. It looks to me as if your wife knows them," I told him and talked him into going down with me to look.

When he peeked through the window himself he recognized a relative of his on his mother's side, a man named Mehmed, who was with a man he didn't know. We went in.

Mehmed was born near Bratunac but he had been living in Belgrade where he had gotten married. He was talking excitedly.

"This morning we left my village to go back to Belgrade in Luka's car but they arrested us at the edge of town. They took us down to the police station and after checking our IDs they separated us. They kept me for questioning, and after they questioned Luka, since he's a Serb, they let him go. He didn't want to leave me there so he kept after the men, saying, 'Let the man go. He lives in Belgrade and he was going back to be with his family.' They questioned me for twelve hours. When they let me out, one of them grabbed Luka by the shirt and said, 'We have a little something to talk about with you,' and banged him up against the wall."

"I thought it was smarter for us to spend the night here, because it would be easier for them to murder us at night. We'll get up early tomorrow and then straight over the Drina. It is too dangerous to stay here," Luka explained.

They knew that every morning when the sun rose you could see corpses, who had been detained for questioning the day before, floating in the Drina River.

The next morning Luka did manage to get Mehmed across the Drina and Mehmed left for Belgrade. Luka came back to Bratunac to see if he could save someone else.

They were taking people off for questioning with meaningless accusations that they had a gun at home, or a rocket launcher. Someone they knew would go and look for them, and none of them ever came home. We were naive thinking we had never done anyone any harm, we had no weapons, we weren't organized and we had nothing to be afraid of.

The morning of 9 May people were working in the fields, sowing corn, when some sort of Civilian Protection people came and made them leave their fields, saying, "Go to your homes. You will be safer there if there is going to be shelling."

No one could imagine who would shell us, but people lost their ability to reason from fear.

The next day I hid up in the raspberry patch above the house with my neighbor. I watched them take the children, women, and men toward Bratunac, and they set some of the houses on fire right then. There was shooting going on all around us. Our street was empty. About 4:00 that afternoon three young guys in uniforms discovered us in the raspberry bushes.

"Come out and we won't harm you!"

When we came out with our hands in the air, they asked, "Is there anyone in those houses on the hill."

"We don't know whether they are empty or not."

Two of them went over to the houses and the third stayed with us. When we sat back down I asked him, patting my hands around my body so that he could see that I had no weapons, "Can I light up a cigarette?"

"Go right ahead," he answered, offering me one of his.

My cousin was curious.

"What is all this? Where are you taking us?"

"Believe you me, I haven't a clue. You are probably going down to the stadium. They're supposed to give you a lecture or something," the kid answered, his voice trembling. I looked at him more closely. He was crying.

The two soldiers came back leading an invalid.

"May I go down to my house and let my cow loose? She's tethered and she'll starve like that," my cousin asked.

"No need, you'll be back soon enough."

"Still, I'd like to let her go, just in case, so she has the freedom to graze."

They let him go. When he came back we walked down my street, which looked as if it had been deserted for ten years, not two hours. All the doors to the Muslim houses were wide open, many of them broken down, because probably each family had locked theirs behind them. Our Serbian neighbors were standing in front of their houses holding guns and saying nothing. Their women were standing next to them, watching us.

On the main street they said, "Now you have to walk in front of us as if we are herding you, otherwise the others will give us a hard time."

We walked that way for half a mile, and then they put us on a bus. That was when I saw a boy who had been wounded in the leg. I hadn't known him from before, but they told me that he'd tried to run away. They called to him to stop and he hadn't so they shot at him.

They took us to the stadium. It was packed with men, women, children, and the elderly. There were about 10,000 people there whom they had managed to pick up that day around town and in the villages along the Drina from Zvornik to Bratunac.

My mother is the only family I have. I could see her at the stadium but I didn't call to her. I figured it was better that she didn't know I was there. I knew they'd taken her off before because I'd heard every word and the shouting and the occasional gunshots for intimidation while they were searching my house.

I saw how many people, even whole families, were being led away from the stadium. The lucky ones had close family friends who were Serbs who were freeing them. Some of the people who were taken away were saved, and others were being taken to be murdered. There were plenty of people here who were saved with their whole families. Some people's neighbors helped them.

The women kept asking, frantically, "What's going on? What's going to happen to us?"

"You'll be fine, you are going to Kladanj," they answered curtly.

A young man with a sock pulled over his face ordered, "Take out all your gold, money, jewelry, and other valuables and put them down here in front of you." He told a mother for her little girl, "Take off that earring, don't make me slice off her ear!"

We all did what we were told without a word. There were a lot of people and many valuables, especially money, because everyone had taken with them everything they had, since that was all you could carry, and no one knew where they'd be tomorrow and if they'd even be able to go back to their homes.

At about 5:00 they began to take us out of the stadium. People from Bratunac and Arkan's paramilitaries were standing there, pulling people out. The elderly, women, and children were told to go to the right, toward buses and trucks, while they took to the left all the men they considered to be fit for military service.

They lined the men up against the stadium wall. Some tried to sneak over to the women and children's group next to one of their children, but they didn't get away with it. They pulled the children from their fathers' arms and pushed them into the group of women, and made the men go to the other side.

The weak and frail all went off in the trucks and buses, and they lined us up in columns and marched us over to the gym at the Vuk Karadžić School.

I could see into the dressing rooms and bathrooms from the corridor and they were all full of heaps of dead bodies, and there was a heavy stench from them.

About thirty-five people were lying on the left half of the gym floor, faces to the floor. I thought that they were dead, too, until the guards shouted at them to stand up. There were men among them I hardly recognized, they were so disfigured.

They pushed about 450 of us into the right side of the gym.

They ordered us to take everything out of our pockets and to take off our wedding rings, chains, and any jewelry we might be wearing, watches, lighters, and cigarettes. Whatever we hadn't left at the stadium we had to throw into a heap that grew to be pretty sizable. They pocketed the larger bills of foreign currency from the heap and left behind the change and the dinars. No one wanted to touch them.

Then the roll call began. They started taking groups of five men out and murdering them.

There were words exchanged when local people said something to one of the prisoners: "Remember that time you cursed my mother while we were playing soccer when we were kids? Come over here!"

That man would be murdered on the spot.

They beat up the school janitor, saying, "You reported me when you were on duty."

That same evening they brought Luka into the hall. Tersely they announced, "This is what happens to Serbs who help Muslims." And they put a pistol to his head and shot him.

We who watched all of that had to wash the blood and brains off the floor and carry the corpses out and load them into trucks that were taking them somewhere.

We were packed into the gym so tightly that nine men suffocated in the hall that night. One of them was a friend of mine, an athlete, only twenty-eight years old.

Something muddled my brain before dawn. It was so stuffy. Only when the morning air came into the hall and revived me did I see my cousin, who was sitting on a man. I asked him, "What are you doing?"

"Well, the guy's dead," he answered dully.

It was horribly close. They drew a line down the middle of the hall and no one was allowed to cross it. If someone lost their balance and stepped over, they would be murdered on the spot.

They made us raise the three-fingered Serbian salute and sing some Chetnik songs from the Second World War. Then the songs would aggravate them and they'd beat us even more.

Then they forced some men to climb up a rope and they'd put a chair or table underneath, and then they'd shake the rope until the person fell from it and smashed himself on the chair.

When they had no more ideas of how to choose victims, they'd throw a ball at us. The one the ball came to rest on, since there was no floor space for it to fall to, would be taken out and never came back.

They forced people to fight among themselves. They took out two men who had to hit each other hard so that the guards wouldn't hit them.

The local *effendi was so badly beaten I didn't even recognize him. They forced him to drink beer . . .

I was wearing a sweater of many colors, one of which was green. I had to conceal the sweater by zipping my jacket up to my chin because they might have murdered me, thinking the green was flaunting my pro-Muslim feelings.

The next two days they took some people out to be executed, brought in others, because they were busily "cleansing" Bratunac and the neighboring villages.

Anyone they took prisoners after 10 May was sent to Kladanj. We who were arrested that fateful day spent four days in the gym until finally we left.

The men who had been beaten the worst in the hall didn't come with us and were never seen again. They vanished without a trace.

A hundred and forty of us were driven in a truck covered with a tarpaulin all night. I can't remember how I managed to poke a hole in the tarp and put my mouth to the hole.

They took us to a recreational hall in Pale where they confiscated our shoelaces and our belts. Then they wrote our names in a list.

They had brought some weapons in the transport with us. Television cameras filmed us with their explanation that we were mujahedin with weapons who had been taken prisoner.

Later they informed us that we were going to be exchanged and that no one should cause any trouble.

They didn't beat us much there and no one was murdered because we were being guarded by policemen who had been in the police before the war. They told us that we had nothing to worry about, and they even welded bars over the door so that people couldn't just come in and maltreat us.

One day the guards were given permission to beat us when we went to use the bathroom.

I was the most frightened up on Pale when I fell asleep in an extremely awkward position: we were sitting in one another's laps with our hands on the floor. I dreamed that I was smoking and drinking coffee. When I woke up I realized that several minutes later I was still holding one hand as if I had a cigarette in it and holding the other as if I had a coffee cup. That was when I began to think I was losing my mind, because I heard lots of other men talking nonsense and hallucinating.

On the last day they tied ten of us into a group and we had to run the gauntlet of police chains and truncheons, and then all of us climbed up into a truck where we sat. Then we had to sing Chetnik songs and people threw stones at us.

The line of trucks halted by a stream. You couldn't see anything but a scrap of sky, a quarry, and earth-moving equipment.

In front of us they took down crates of beer from the two trucks, sat and drank. As I looked around the woods, the equipment, the stream, the earth, and the rocks, I figured this was where we were going to die.

Once they'd had their beer we set out again, and that was when I began to feel certain we were going to survive.

The rope I was tied with cut into my hands, and every time the man next to me moved it hurt terribly. For a month I had no sensation in one of my hands.

They exchanged us on 15 May in the town of Mala Vratnica near Visoko, and by then we already were looking a little better than we had three days before.

Seven days after the exchange I fell in love with a Serbian woman.

A LIFE WITH DIGNITY

TOLD BY D. V.,[†] Attorney

Refugee from Sarajevo, interviewed in Bosanska Dubica

January 1996

Sarajevo is the city where I was born, grew up, went to school, fell in love . . . I married there, started my professional life, and was a prominent member of the community. I lived in a two-story building in the Dobrinja neighborhood, out by the airport. Until the war I ran a road-building company. I had a lot of friends among Muslims and Croats. Regardless of the fact that the nationalist parties won the 1990 elections, their influence in Sarajevo was quite insignificant, barely there at all. It was a special city, and its people were special people.

While working in the Republican Department for Roads I traveled all around Bosnia and Herzegovina in the 1980s. Big changes began to happen after 1990 in the rural areas. It all depended on what party was winning. Everyone was changed, from the doorman to the president of the municipality. We didn't have any of that in Sarajevo. In the company that I ran for years there were 220 Muslims, fifty Croats, and fifty Serbs, and the ethno-national parties did not enter the company until the actual outbreak of the war. No one asked why I, as a Serb, was running the company. The topic of ethnicity served only as fodder for jokes.

On the eve of the war I started a private company with a Muslim and a Croat. The name of the company included the first initials of our last names.

There were no problems until early 1992, when the barricades went up in town and the first blood was shed. I was caught unprepared by the turn of events. You couldn't even get into the center of town. The first shells began to rain down on the city. There were eight families living in my apartment building, two of them Serbian, six of them Muslim. We put up bars over the front door for protection. All of the neighbors had weapons except me. My neighbor, a Muslim, gave me his pistol because he had another gun. In the long hours spent waiting, we played cards. The men agreed that if any of the national armies came and knocked on the door, we wouldn't let them inside. We weren't interested in armies. We wanted nothing but to protect our families. That was how things stood until 15 April 1992. That was when the *corridor was opened through Trnovo and Kalinovik to Gacko. This was the only way Serbs could get out of the city. A convoy was formed from Dobrinja and many people left town that way. I was torn: Should I go or should I stay? My wife dismissed all my doubts with the question: "How can we tell our neighbors that we are fleeing? This will probably blow over in a couple of weeks. How will we be able to come back and look them in the eyes?"

That was when I began to feel that we were not all of us quite as united as we had been at first. A neighbor, a Muslim, came from a meeting of the local cell of the Muslim party, the Party for Democratic Action, on 27 April 1992, and said, "They have drawn up lists for arresting and murdering the more prominent Serbs. It would be best for you if you got out of here in time."

I was miserable. I knew that we depend on each other because that is our fate. We needn't mingle socially, we don't even have to share anything. But we must tolerate each other. I had been left no choice, but I hope that the generations that come along will set to right what we did wrong.

My wife asked her brother and sister-in-law to send their son with us. He was only 15 years old.

"We are going to Belgrade. Let the child go with us. He shouldn't have to watch the horrors of war. If you don't want to go, at least let him leave."

A year earlier my sister's husband had fled Zagreb and come to Sarajevo. I found him a job at the airport as an aircraft technician. It was his first contact with the work because he had been a physical laborer at a hospital in Zagreb before then. He let me know that we had a plane for Belgrade that morning.

We packed up our documents and essentials and said good-bye to everyone. I gave our neighbor, a Muslim who later moved to Germany, the keys to the apartment, the garage, and our two cars.

My sister-in-law's son was waiting for us. There was a long line of cars waiting at the airport. Their owners had abandoned them there, running to catch planes. Two hundred of us wanted to get to Belgrade. To cross the line where you heard the words, "You will be on the next plane" meant you'd been saved. The army was making up the lists of the lucky souls who would travel. Women with small children, the families of army officers, the elderly, and the infirm were highest priority. We couldn't, all of us, fit into the planes they had, so they announced that the flight had been canceled. Noon passed. Half of the people who had come, left. Finally the plane arrived with 130 free places, and about eighty of the most persistent were there. The uncertainty continued, because junior officers began calling out names. We were enormously relieved when a senior officer came over and asked, "What do you think you're doing?"

"Calling out names."

"Whose? Can't you see that there are fewer people here than there are seats? Let them all get on board!"

The plane rolled down the runway. When it rose up above Sarajevo I looked down at my city, and thought, Could it be that I'll never see you again?

There is an old custom in Bosnia: when a good friend comes to visit, he is offered the honor of giving the youngest child its first haircut, thereby earning the title of "*šišani kum.*" This is a special tradition that brings him into the heart of the family. My wife is *šišani kum* to a Muslim couple. Her parents were in Sarajevo all through the war. In the second year of the war they met those people in town, who asked for news of us.

"They are alive and well. How are you?"

"Our son lost both his legs from an exploding shell. Now he is waiting for artificial limbs. Please give our love to them. All this will pass. Some day we will be able to be together again!"

I want to believe that the time will come back that Goran Bregović portrayed in the video film he made for his song about Sarajevo. I can see it now: you hear the muezzin's voice calling from a minaret, the chiming of bells from St. Mark's church, and there's the synagogue.

I called Davor, a Croatian friend of mine from Belgrade who lives in Sarajevo: "Why haven't you been calling?"

"Even dialing the Belgrade 011 area code makes me sick," he said.

I understood him. Sarajevo was being shelled from Serbian positions.

A year and a half later we talked again. He said, "I spent four months on the front in a Croatian brigade. Once I saw where this madness was headed, I deserted and paid 2,000 German marks to get across the airport. Thirty of us set out, but only four of us made it across the runways to Hrasnica alive. When I was running I had to jump over the dead bodies of the people who'd been ahead of me. Only now do I understand how crazy I was. I am gradually recovering."

This is a man with a degree in mechanical engineering. Now he is living alone on the northern Croatian coast, and he says, "I am fishing, even though I'm no good at it. It is what I make my living doing. I have no one here with me of my friends. I've sent you a letter."

In the letter I found a photograph from our last New Year's Eve that we spent together in Sarajevo. Davor and my wife are dancing Russian dances. On the back are the words, "To my brother and friend, to remember the days when we enjoyed a life of dignity. Bjelašnica, 31 December 1991.

THERE WOULD NEVER HAVE BEEN A WAR

TOLD BY PETAR PERANOVIĆ

The Village of Kolovrat near Tuzla

January 1999

I was born in the village of Kolovrat in 1934. During the war I lived in Slavinovići, a suburb of Tuzla. I was involved in the local communal government for seeing to the needs of refugees, supplying them with food and other necessities. I was commended by the municipality of Tuzla for my efforts during the war, although I never went to the front or held a gun.

In early February 1995 I got word from people in Slavinovići that there were groups of soldiers from the Army of Bosnia and Herzegovina break- ing into the homes of Serbs and Croats, including mine, so I hurried down there from Kolovrat. At about 11:00 in the morning I came upon two sol- diers I'd never seen before in front of my house, and there were two more of them inside, searching the house. They attacked me when I demanded that they leave the premises, but I did manage to get them out. After ten minutes or so about fifteen soldiers showed up at the door and wanted to come in. They cursed my Ustasha and Croatian mother and demanded that I abandon my home. I stood up to them at the door, so they attacked me with a carpenter's ax and a knife. We struggled in the doorway. I managed, fortunately, to wrest free the knife and the ax. They yanked off the door frame and tried to jab me with a piece of it in the stomach. I defended myself by grabbing a sharp piece of the wood with my hands, and cut the palms of my hands badly. Then my son and brother showed up. Also a TV reporter who filmed the entire incident, though the material has never been shown because the army confiscated the video cassette. The civilian police turned up, though they were not strong enough to stand up to the army. In fact the soldiers chased them down the street. They took me off to the hospital to suture up my palms. When I came back home that evening the military police was there and another television team.

The group of soldiers had expelled the owners from five Serbian and two Croatian homes. Mine was the eighth, but I defended it. That was a period when a huge number of Muslim refugees were pouring into our part of Bosnia from the areas where fighting was the worst in eastern Bosnia along the Serbian border and Drina River, and they were desperate to move into our homes.

That same evening the local Muslims, Serbs, and Croats got together and formed a commission that would represent all three ethnic groups in the struggle for realizing their rights.

After the incident we sought the help of the authorities: members of the police and the Second Corps. The deputy chief of security of the Second Corps came to our house at about 8:00 in the evening, but I told him, then, "Once the fighting is over, weapons are useless. I defended my home, and now I am asking you to return the homes to the other owners who were ousted."

The representatives of the municipality with whom we spoke promised to help us the next day. Commander Delić of the Second Corps would not receive us. At that point the people who had been making the trouble in Slavinovići asked to be received as well.

The next day we organized a street protest, and closed down the Tuzla-Bijeljina road. On the other side were the refugees from eastern Bosnia and the people who were supporting them. On our side were about 500 people. Croatian troops arrived from the front and they were with us. Special troops tried to open the road but we wouldn't let them by. A neighbor named Mustafa headed our group. We didn't let anyone pass until the municipal and cantonal leaders appeared. The blockade lasted all afternoon. We were prepared to defend ourselves physically. Everyone came, even Bešlagić, our mayor. I spoke and demanded that everyone be allowed back into their homes, especially those of us who were Orthodox Serbs, because they were likely to have a rougher ride than the rest of us. Everyone agreed that it was imperative that we do this, and one of those present suggested that it would be possible to move the squatters out in a matter of two hours. Some of the local Muslims sided with us. One neighbor swore, and said, word for word, "Their ancestors have been living side by side with ours for ages. We have to do the same, and so do our children. There is no force that can separate us at this moment. We must go on living together."

After his strong words, the other local people who had been unsure joined our cause.

When Mayor Bešlagić came with the municipal representatives and representatives of other parties, we organized a meeting in the library, where everyone put forth his or her opinion that it was essential to protect the civil rights of every individual. Those soldiers were, after all, following somebody's orders. Nothing like that ever happened by chance, which one could best see in the meeting itself. Thanks foremost to the inhabitants of Slavinovići, to all three ethnic groups, which had a strong feeling of solidarity and justice, the fundamental personal rights of the non-Muslim population were protected.

The media kept reporting on our incident. That evening I was visited by those foreign ambassadors who were stationed in Bosnia and could reach Tuzla. I told them what had happened, and foreign TV reporters and radio stations filmed and broadcast our conversations.

After a few days all the squatters moved out except from two homes. They crammed into a single room in Sava's place and stayed for another six months. He got sick and through the Red Cross I worked it out that he would be able to go and stay with his son in Bijeljina, and after two months there, he died.

After that the police cranked up their protection of citizens. We were masters of our own lives. We had nowhere else to go and we didn't want to move away. In conversation with Mayor Bešlagić, several days later, I asked, "Look, if it comes to the point that I have to go, I want to go like a man, not a bum. I do not want to end up hawking spoons and forks on a street corner. I want a commission formed to draw up a list of existing property. Then, worse comes to worst, we will be ready to divide things up fairly: each of us can join our own herd, no bloodshed. What's the point of fighting? Why should my child be persecuted? That's not what I want. If I can't live like a human being, I am out of here."

Bešlagić banged the table, the coffee spilled, and he shouted, furious, "Who are you to start ethnic cleansing?! I won't hear of it! The people of Tuzla are going to stay right here and live in Tuzla as they always have! You will never move away from here! This is a city for all of us!"

The UNPROFOR Spanish Battalion offered to protect us, but we didn't need their help.

A judge I knew urged me to sue the soldiers who had tried to break into my house. I refused. The soldiers had been expelled from other parts of Bosnia, Kladanj, Vlasenica, and Zvornik, which had seen massive campaigns of ethnic cleansing. They were just trying to find places to resettle their own families.

Later no one bothered us. Thanks to the local Muslims, we, the Orthodox and Catholics, managed to ensure our rights and stay in our own homes.

There were some minor incidents. In Sepetari, a neighbor I was acquainted with personally blocked the road with his car. I asked him, "Why are you doing this? We know each other! Are you crazy?"

"You are not using this road," he said fiercely.

"Look, don't be like that. I'll take my tractor and go around by way of the ditch. I don't have to go this way if it makes you feel better," I answered, smiling.

Other neighbors called the police, who came immediately and protected me, and stopped him from blocking the road.

In the neighboring village of Križani, there wasn't a single Muslim living before this war. There were so many Serbs there that we called one part of it Serbian Town. Now there are thirty new Muslim homes in Križani and Kolovrat, built on land that Croats sold when they moved away. There are only two Serbian houses left, which we have nicknamed our local "pepper." The Serbs started moving away when the war began and now, unfortunately, they are only left as a little spice for the neighborhood.

Our family never separated people. There were a couple of Serbian houses near us. When people began to starve and two pounds of corn flour cost twenty German marks, our neighbor, Mile, came crying to the house one evening: "Neighbor, I'll give you my house and all I have for twenty pounds of corn flour to keep my children fed."

We had four tons of dry corn kernels at that point and we gave almost all of it away for free to Mile and all the others. We didn't sell so much as a pound's worth. We owned a lot of land. We let people plant gardens on the land so that they'd have enough to eat.

When the Muslims who had been expelled from Bijeljina arrived, a family moved in next door. Every day I saw a little boy who was fast friends with my grandson. When I learned that he was a refugee, and this was at a time when a single egg cost five German marks, I came home and told my daughter-in-law, who was frying eggs, "And don't you forget to fry one for little Mućo."

"But I've fried them in pork lard and he can't eat pork because he's Muslim," she said, anxiously.

"Don't you worry about that, if the sin is to fall on anyone's soul let it fall on mine, just make sure he eats," I told her.

That child was at our house and ate there regularly, until one day I ran into his father.

"Ramo, there is something I've been wanting to tell you. I've nothing against your boy eating at my house, but I wanted to be sure you know: if you are religious that is your business. I don't believe in anything but my own hands and what I earn. Your child has been eating food at my house cooked in pork lard because we haven't any cooking oil. He's been eating bacon."

The man burst into tears, and said, "Thank you so much for feeding my boy. If it weren't for you he'd have nothing to eat."

Whenever I hugged my grandson, Mućo asked for a hug and a kiss, too.

We were always taught never to hate anyone. During the war we stayed the same as we'd been before. No one from our house carried a gun. We figured it was much more important to feed a child, because a child should live, and a gun kills. If only everyone had thought that way there wouldn't have been a war.

HANG ME, LET HIM GO

TOLD BY HAMID DEDOVIĆ

The Ilidža part of Sarajevo

October 1998

I stayed on in Ilidža when it became part of Serbian territory, because I didn't think what did happen could happen. Many Muslims were maltreated, some of them murdered, but I was saved by my Serbian, or rather I should call them Bosnian, neighbors. The evil was perpetrated by Serbs who came here from Serbia.

Six bearded men came into my house, Chetniks they were, wearing insignia of the White Eagles paramilitary group. From the moment they set foot on the threshold they started harassing my wife, my two daughters, and me. Our neighbor, a Serbian woman, came running in and said, "Don't you touch him. He's a good man!"

They lunged to smack her.

They took me to a place where they were collecting Muslims whom they were sending off toward Kula and Pale, where many of them were beaten and murdered. Red in the face, out of breath and very agitated, Boro, another Serbian friend, came running over to where they were holding us and stood in front of me. "Here, take me instead of him. Hang me, let him go."

Confused by his earnest concern, they let me go.

A Serbian policeman came by to tell me, "Look, try to get out of Ilidža. If they bring you back, they'll bring you to me. I'll see to it that no one harms you."

After a few days Boro told me, "I have to help you get out of here. I can't protect you from these Chetniks. They are bugging me, too." He helped me cross over from Ilidža to nearby Buća Potok.

I came into the home of a cousin who was married to a Serb. At that moment about half of the people living in that place were Serbs. They all helped me out financially because I had left Ilidža with nothing but the clothes on my back. Back there the people had even taken my shoes and kicked me in the rear. The Serbs living in Buća Potok gave me food and dishes, because my cousin's home had been looted.

Everybody looted and robbed in the war: the Serbs, the Muslims, and the Croats. War didn't bring us a lot of honesty.

ENJOY YOUR TRIP, MA'AM!

TOLD BY ZORA SAVIĆ

Refugee from Zenica, interviewed in Modriča

December 1995

I used to live with my husband and two daughters in Zenica, where our parents also lived. The war found all of us in Zenica. My husband was disabled and retired, and that was why he was not obliged to contribute to a work detail.

We spent more than two years living in impossible conditions, constantly looking for ways to get out. We had no money to pay our way out of town, as most people did in order to save themselves. To do that would have cost a lot because there were eight of us.

During the third year of the war I happened to meet a Muslim man I knew who told me he was working for the police. When I no longer knew whom to turn to for help, I went to see him at home. I complained to him about the situation I was in and he said, "Come see me at my office once you can get together photographs of all the members of your family. I make ID cards. I'll make new ID cards for all of you. You'll be able to use them to get out into Serbian territory through the town of Vareš."

A few days later, as he was seeing me off with my eight new ID cards with Muslim names, he told me, "You'll have to memorize all the information on the cards well, because if someone catches you and you confess who made you these cards, I'll lose my head."

No one but my husband knew who it was who had made the new documents for us. For a whole month I tested my family daily until they had memorized it all. I'd wake them up at night and ask them, "What is your name and where are you from?"

We decided to leave for Vareš only when all seven of them were able to rattle off the information at any time of day or night without a hitch. Of course, we were very nervous, but that was the only way we had of saving ourselves.

In Vareš at the checkpoint, the Croatian police came onto the bus and asked for IDs. The eight of us were sitting the way our new last names suggested, in several groups. The agreement was we didn't know each other.

The children and my husband's parents got through fine. My mother was sitting two rows ahead of me. When the young policeman asked for her papers, she plucked out of her purse her ID card with her real identity on it and handed it to him.

I sat there frozen. In a split second everything that could happen to us flashed through my mind. If they were to pull her off the bus, I would have to get up and go help her. That would set in motion a chain reaction and quickly all of us would be outside, with counterfeit documents to make matters worse. The policeman studied her ID for a while. Then he handed it back. He leaned over and whispered in her ear, "Not this one, give me your other ID."

Without a word Mother popped it back in her purse and showed him the other. While the policeman studied that one with interest, I couldn't believe what I'd just seen. I was terrified he was going to use this as provocation. When he had looked over the ID, he gave it back to Mother politely, and said, with a grin, "Enjoy your trip, ma'am!"

YOUR TYPICAL
JEWISH NAME

TOLD BY GORDAN KONRAD

Professor, the Grbavica section of Sarajevo

November 1998

I'm from Sarajevo, and was raised to think of myself as a Yugoslav. My wife is Serbian and we have two children. When the war began we were living in the Grbavica part of Sarajevo. I was an elementary school teacher.

Our last stroll around town was a visit to my mother-in-law, who lives in downtown Sarajevo, on 2 May 1992. After that we didn't see her until the war ended.

During the first days of the war, barricades started going up. People armed with machine guns came out of the offices of the local commune into the street and fired into demonstrations of crowds of people walking along Brotherhood and Unity Street. The next day, when things calmed down and when negotiations were under way, children went looking for and found the empty clips left over from these machine guns—the ordnance, cartridges, and knives; they brought them home and traded them among themselves.

When our apartment was searched we were all of us nearly killed because of an emptied machine-gun clip my child had brought home and stowed away.

The tenants in my apartment building guarded the entranceway to our building after 2 May. We had no idea who was guarding whom, or if there were neighbors among us who did have weapons in their apartments.

People started coming down from Vraca and the hills around Sarajevo and vandalized the stores. Inspired by their example my pupils took to roaming around Grbavica at night. You'd hear the tinkle of smashing glass. Crowds would rush in through the broken store window. You could hear their parents calling from their apartment balconies: "Be sure to get sugar and cooking oil."

At first the looting was timid. I watched a hungry old man who went into a store carrying an umbrella on a clear day just so no one would recognize him. At that point the stores still had their lights on. After a few minutes he came out carrying a bag, his umbrella open.

Those first days we took pictures of engineers and doctors carting food off from grocery stores. Thinking that it would all blow over in no time, I wanted to present my colleagues with evidence of what I'd seen and ask them how intellectuals could stoop so low. At that point I still didn't get it.

There were droll moments: a family dragging a frozen ox along the ice and up frozen stairs. The next day the electricity went out. They chopped the ox up with axes and gave it away as if they were a charity organization just so that it wouldn't defrost and rot. People carted the meat off in wash basins.

After robbing stores looters would blast them with explosives. At first others would rush out of their apartments and put out the fires. I didn't set foot outside my flat for five straight months. I spent only one day away from home, when Serbian soldiers dragged me off to training.

I witnessed at least forty robberies and the appropriation of automobiles. As the owner of a car was approaching his vehicle, someone would slug him from behind, take his car keys, and drive the car away. The man would be lying on the street and no one would help him out.

On her way home one evening, my wife happened to kick a cardboard box from her path. She heard a metallic sound inside. She opened the box and saw it held cans of fish. She brought them home. We were overjoyed. We had food for several days.

The anarchy had produced a weird atmosphere at that point. One day a van stopped in front of the supermarket and a man got out with a camera. The neighbors, delighted that this meant there would be no more robberies because television crews had come to film the broken store windows, began to come out from hiding into the streets. Two men armed with automatic weapons forced all the boys and children there to load into the van the things from the store, which hadn't been completely cleared out earlier. They put the camera on top of the pile of stolen goods and off they drove.

At first we guarded the entranceway to our building. Whenever I noticed someone I didn't know coming in, I would bang the metal stair railings so that the neighbors, whom I believed to be armed, would come down from their apartments and prevent any pillaging. Later I realized this was a game we were playing, as if we were kids. For a long time we lived in something very much like house arrest. The thieves who robbed apartments soon realized quite a few of the tenants were armed and wouldn't allow anyone, uninvited, to enter the building. This irked them. At night they'd shoot down from Vraca at any lit windows. And they shot during the day at any of the tenants who were entering or leaving the building. But what really mattered was that we didn't let them in.

I experienced the first attack on our apartment and harassment in June 1992. Three armed men barged into our place wearing bulletproof vests and pistols. The obligatory dagger was their calling card. First they checked my mother's ID. Last name: Konrad. Sounded Austrian. Points lost. Place of birth: Osijek, Croatia. More points lost. First name: Hildegard. Even more points lost. My mother had a facial tic, she'd had it since World War II. They jabbed a pistol in my stomach: "What are you hiding in those women's skirts? Where are your weapons?"

"This is my weapon," I replied, showing them my school records book with the names and grades of all my students.

"I used to work in a school, too. Now look at me," one of them said, and asked my daughter: "How old are you?"

"Fifteen," Mother said quickly, dropping her age by a year.

"Shame. If you were sixteen you'd make a swell nurse."

They liked it that my son's name was Russian-sounding: Boris. That put them in better spirits.

They finished searching the apartment and left.

Everyone ran out of food. Household pets began starving to death. We didn't dare speak loudly because there was no running water, and you could hear everything from apartment to apartment through the empty water pipes. We always kept the curtains pulled shut for fear of snipers. There were about 100 apartments in our building, but mine were the only children left. Everyone else had sent their kids off somewhere. There were people who, regardless of their ethnic background, brought my children an apple or a piece of chocolate every couple of days.

The day after my daughter's birthday, on 5 July at about 5:00 in the morning, a young man in a uniform appeared at the door. His accent sounded as if he had come from Niš in Serbia. He said, "What are you waiting for? Don't you know that all men who are not yet sixty years of age must report for duty? You have five minutes to get downstairs!"

Armed guards marched us in a line to an office building. I found several of my elementary school students there who had already been mobilized. They were all glad to see me. I couldn't recognize a number of my neighbors, because all of us were fifty to sixty pounds thinner.

My wife brought down my medical papers, hoping they would leave me alone when they saw I suffered from chronic ailments. I really did not want to be called up. I had no idea who I would be fighting for, or against. They confiscated our ID cards. Suddenly the greeting rang out: "God help us, Serbian Chetniks!"

The greeting confused me. I thought they must be kidding. They weren't. They lined us up and marched us back to Vraca. We were forced to run because a sniper was firing on us. At Vraca someone asked, "Anyone here in need of medical attention?"

I spoke right up.

"What's wrong with you?"

"I'm about to go in for three operations."

"OK, go see the doctor."

They took twelve of us to the Grbavica medical center, where I had been a patient.

Not knowing that it would decide my fate, I saw two civilians who were giving out people's medical files. I went over to the window and was given my file that included all my prewar diagnoses. I went into the doctor's office clutching my file, my heart pounding. Dr. Brajević pretended she'd never seen me before. She began, "Your heart is fibrillating. I see. No EKG. There's a kidney problem. You should do something about that gallbladder . . ."

She requested I be freed of any obligations for a month so that I might recuperate both physically and mentally and follow a strict diet. I had no problem with the diet since we had all been on a diet for months anyway. I spent another month in that office building. My students tried to cheer me up.

"Don't worry. You'll be assigned to some kind of light work detail in an office at the police station."

I heard them saying, "Let's figure out how to help our teacher!"

They figured out some way of getting their hands on my ID to return it to me, which they managed to do later. Thanks to Dr. Brajević I was never called up to serve in the army.

On the pavement out in front of our building the wind had been whisking a piece of paper around for a month, but it never blew away. I seldom set foot outside our apartment. Alone like a mouse, I would stare out at the marketplace through the window at life going on in the street.

One day my wife happened to pick up that piece of paper and read that a Jewish center was being formed in the building where the bank used to be and that there would be an effort organized to evacuate Jews from Sarajevo. She didn't know what to do. She wanted us to report to the Jewish center, but she didn't know what to do with my last name being German in origin. A Jewish fellow named Kafka who lived in our building took her down to the Jewish center. When she told my last name to a man named Rejmond who worked at the center, he grinned and said, "Your typical Jewish name."

He was just as welcoming to everyone who came in the door of the Jewish center to register, regardless of background. Rejmond was working to enroll as many people as he could. There were about 160 people on his list who dared claim they were Jewish, though many of them weren't. About two months passed until finally the center decided who would be able to leave. They drew up a list of about forty people who were approved and confirmed in Lukavica and had permission to leave Sarajevo. I was on the list with our two children. My mother cut my wife off with a single sentence: "You must go, too. I know what I'll do when I can't bear it any more."

My wife decided to stay with her, figuring this all was going to blow over by New Year's.

Finally we left for Belgrade through the city of Zvornik. Since I am hard of hearing I did not hear the snipers firing at the bus. At one moment I noticed that all the travelers were ducking and then a bullet zinged over my head. At the border near Zvornik, a soldier who was checking our papers asked, "What is this? Are these people all Muslims?"

We all fell silent. Rejmond explained patiently to him, "Apparently you aren't aware of the fact that you are Jewish through your mother's family, not your father's."

The soldier didn't know what to say to that. After an hour of waiting we continued on our way. Of all the travelers in the bus, I knew of only three who were actually Jewish.

I went to Germany with my children. In 1996 I came back to Sarajevo because my mother was dying. In April of that year, before she died, my mother had insisted that my wife go and see the children after four years. Her grandchildren didn't recognize her because she had lost sixty-six pounds.

". . . her sons . . . in the garden of her God"
The Jewish cemetery, Sarajevo

THOSE BARBARIANS
TOOK A PART OF US

TOLD BY RAMIZ PANDUR

Mostar

November 1998

I was born in Mostar at the beginning of World War II, in 1940. I am an artist and I have been working in Mostar for my whole life, where I lived through both wars. My gallery is near where the old bridge spanned the Neretva, and I have been working there for thirty-five years.

Just before the war I held a show of my work in Toledo, in Spain. Before I was to return to Mostar they told me, "Sir, don't go back. War is about to break out there. We will help you settle here. You will have an apartment, a studio, all you need for your work."

They had received me so warmly in Spain, but I missed Mostar. I couldn't stay. I had to take a taxi all the way home from Sarajevo because the buses weren't running.

Now that the war is over, Spaniards have come to visit twice, and have asked me, "Have you changed your mind?"

"I haven't decided yet," I keep saying, uncertain.

I am terribly disappointed in Yugoslav society. It hit me the hardest when people I'd known and trusted, most of them Serbs but some Croats, too, with whom I had lived and worked, with whom I had built the future, left Mostar without a word and abandoned us, stuck here in limbo.

There have been moments when I have wanted to leave with my family. But how can I go when everything I have is here: my home, my children, my work, my whole life . . . ?

The beginning of the horrors in Mostar was marked by shells that rained down on the city for days from Serbian positions, and then crimes were committed after the army entered the city. Many innocent Muslims were murdered in Borik. Among the Serbs perpetrating the evil there were people from Mostar, but there were also plenty from Trebinje, Nevesinje, Bileća, and Gacko. Šešelj's paramilitary fighters came from Serbia.

An elderly woman in her nineties lived next door to me. I heard her calling her grandchildren and asking for water through the window. I could see her feet through the keyhole. She was out flat on the concrete floor. I couldn't open the locked door of her house.

The Chetniks were already in town. A Serb was living with his wife in the apartment of a Muslim woman in my neighborhood. I don't know how he ended up in that apartment. I asked him, "Look, you have to help me get her water somehow. She will die of thirst just feet from us. The Chetniks won't bother you."

"Absolutely, Ramiz. Let's go right now," he agreed, without a second thought.

Just as we were trying to force open the door, I noticed eight of Šešelj's men nearby. They had already walked past the building, but one of them turned and caught sight of us. I was holding soup and drinking water when I saw, with horror, for the first time in my life, what a drugged man looked like: he had no control over his stride. His legs akimbo, his feet slapped the ground as he walked. He held a machine gun, and four hand grenades dangled from his belt. I spoke first so he wouldn't ask my name, and said, "There is an elderly woman starving in here. I've brought her some water but we can't open the door."

"Step back. I'll take care of this," he mumbled and shot a whole round into the door. This only served to fuse the lock. He emptied another round into the door frame. The lock was bent out of shape but the door stayed shut. In a fury he kicked the door but missed the metal frame and smashed his leg right through the glass door panel. Blood oozed out of the six-inch-long wound above his sneaker, but he didn't notice it or feel anything.

My neighbor had already run away. When I saw that the man was crazed, I pretended I'd felt a stab of pain in my heart, and I moved slowly back about six feet, which was enough for me to slip into my house. He stayed there, trying to break down the door. I heard him shout, "Lady, are you a Serbian, Muslim, or Croatian?"

The poor woman was Muslim; she had a Serbian daughter-in-law, but she was completely senile. Oblivious of what was going on, she said, "You Serbian piece of shit."

"Listen, old lady. I didn't come here to heal you. How about this for a greeting from Šešelj the Duke," he said, activated the four hand grenades and tossed them through the broken glass door panel. While the blasts rang out one after another, he bounded back to his colleagues, all bloody, his leg slashed, as if nothing had happened.

Once it got dark, I went out to see what had happened to the woman. I shone a flashlight into the hallway and saw her in a pool of blood on the floor.

A man named Slobodan was the first to enter my house. The door swung open when he kicked it. There were several other men with him of whom one was known to be dangerous, but he behaved decently, at least that time. I kept songbirds in the house that all went beserk when the men came in. Slobodan said to me, "I have a bird in a cage in my car. Could you feed it for me?"

"Sure. Why not?" I answered.

They brought in a parakeet in a damaged cage, its head bowed.

"We have to search your house. Do you have any weapons here?" Slobodan continued.

"No, I don't."

"I know artists don't like weapons. I trust you," he said, and left.

His parakeet saved me for four days. Whenever Chetniks appeared at the door, I'd tell them, "I'm looking after Slobodan's parakeet."

Slobodan's father was a major in the Yugoslav People's Army. They lived in the western part of the town near the old soccer stadium. During the time the Serbs were fleeing Mostar, Slobodan said his good-byes, and went off to Nevesinje where his mother was from.

We lived on the *left bank of the Neretva, later to be referred to as eastern Mostar. When the Chetniks came to town a man famous in Mostar named Garo, whom I knew only by sight, arrived with them. My brother, an artist in Belgrade, knew him pretty well. He heard I was in Mostar and asked them to call me.

I stepped out of my gallery and couldn't believe my eyes: Garo was standing there in a Yugoslav People's Army uniform, surrounded by men in Chetnik garb, wearing the typical Chetnik fur hats, insignia, daggers, boots, and knives. Next to him stood the leader of the Chetnik fighters, a man who had once gone to school with me. Garo threw his arms around me. The leader disapproved but kept his silence, scowling. I saw from his face that he wasn't pleased to be talking with me at all.

Garo was amazed that I was there. "What are you doing here? What have you waited for until now? The Chetniks are pouring in from Trebinje and Nevesinje. You should get out of here."

"Can you help me cross over to the other side?" I asked him.

"You want me to get you to Belgrade? You have your brother the singer there, and your sister-in-law. Or would you rather go to Bileća?" he replied, answering with a question.

"My whole family's here. And besides I don't want to go to Belgrade. I'm afraid someone would pull me off the Bileća bus."

Snipers were shooting into town at that point. Garo told me, "Pack your things. I've told the snipers to hold their fire until you cross the bridge."

He escorted us to the bridge with his men, and said: "We can't go any further. The Croatian forces are over there."

That was how I got over into the western side of town where no one had figured out, yet, that we were being expelled. Even my closer relatives had no idea of how serious the situation was. We found a place to stay in the home of one of my in-laws, whose wife was Croatian, but even he couldn't understand us. We moved into my sister-in-law's mother's house. The only person living there was her sister.

It was hard for us. We had no money and hadn't been able to bring any of our things with us. I was for us leaving Mostar. I asked SDA [Party for Democratic Action] officials to issue us documents that would let us leave Bosnia.

"But where will you go, Ramiz? If you leave, there will be no more Mostar," they told me at the office.

They gave me some money and urged us to move into an abandoned Serbian apartment. The woman who had lived there went to school with my sister. Before the war she went off to visit someone and couldn't get back. Here we were lucky. She had quite a lot of food stored away.

It wasn't long after that that Croatian Guard Corps (HOS) fighters appeared, who were tracking down Serbs in western Mostar. A Serbian woman who was living in the apartment next door to where we were staying jumped onto our balcony one night. She was about fifty years old. Anyone who hasn't seen someone persecuted like that doesn't know what fear is. Three Croatian Guard Corps members had broken down her door. She managed to escape over the balcony. "Save me," she moaned, beside herself with fear.

"You stay here with us. We'll share your fate," we told her, trying to calm her down, though we were quaking with terror ourselves.

All of us were lucky that night, because they didn't come to our door. She spent the night with us and left the next day.

As soon as the Serbian troops withdrew from eastern Mostar, around 9 May 1993, I went back. The city was in ruins.

When my younger son, Dino, was wounded a second time I went to the Institute for Hygiene that had been made into a hospital. Dino was on a stretcher. The stench of blood was everywhere. There wasn't time, or water, to wash. They treated his wound. A bullet had passed through the left side of his chest and exited through his back. A Serbian doctor, who had come with four other colleagues from Sarajevo to help, bolstered my confidence.

"How have you treated the boy?" he asked his colleagues as he came over to Dino.

"We treated the wound."

"Take off the bandages and let me have a look."

He lifted Dino's arm and said, "Son, you were lucky. The bullet detoured all your vital organs and didn't damage a single one."

It took him a long time to recover. He'd been badly hurt.

The suffering in eastern Mostar continued with the Croatian attack on 9 May 1993. That day 5,000 shells hit the small area. We thought nobody would survive.

The struggle to live went on. I got involved in the work of a humanitarian organization. People were starving. You had to be careful with every gram of flour. I remember an eighty-year-old man who came to seek help. "I have two sons, both of them wounded. Could you please give me enough flour so I can fry them up some dough?"

I was in charge of the Humanitarian Center. I didn't dare give him flour in front of everyone. I told him, "Take a seat."

When the other people had gotten what we had to give them I handed him a small package that included a few ounces of flour. It was getting dark. Shells were blasting all around us, and the poor fellow tripped and fell in the middle of the street. I watched him sweeping up the spilled flour from the pavement, his hands shaking, and hurrying off into the night . . .

We managed to put my daughter-in-law and grandson in an ambulance as part of the last convoy taking Muslims from the western, predominantly Croatian, part back to the eastern, predominantly Muslim, part of Mostar where we'd lived until the Serbian forces first expelled us. In front of the bus I recognized a man who had been working as a photographer. Somehow he managed to get me on board, but he wouldn't let my older son get on. A soldier said, "Hey, you, off the bus."

They were holding the younger people back so that they could murder them.

I crossed over, but my son remained on the western bank. He barely managed to survive; he fled over rooftops to save his life. Often it happened that tenants in the buildings would report him to the people who were after him: "We saw him last night up on the roof." They probably figured this would give them points with the authorities. An attorney by profession, he practiced yoga and, fortunately, was a well-grounded person. He played the guitar. He used to blacken the windows in the apartment where he was hiding, pick up his guitar and practice, strumming softly. That was how he kept his nerves. My two sisters and an aunt who lived nearby were able to get food to him from time to time. Each time they'd agree where they would meet next.

After a year he got tired of always hiding out. He decided to cross two mine fields to reach eastern Mostar where we were.

A Croat I'd helped by giving him food brought him to the Croatian mine field. I had worked at a humanitarian organization while we were having the earlier problems with Serbian troops. For the year my son was in hiding, the man brought him potatoes from time to time, though he could have been killed for it. You weren't supposed to.

When they arrived at the line of separation, the man stopped.

"You'll have to go the rest of the way yourself. I can't help you beyond this point. Everything is under mines from here on in. I don't know where the mines are. Go for it."

My son walked slowly across the mine field in broad daylight. He could see the taut nylon triggers of the mines. At one point he wasn't sure whose territory he was on. There was not a soul in sight. He shouted, so that no one on the eastern side would shoot at him: "Are there any soldiers there?"

He couldn't figure out how to proceed. This stretch was where the largest number of clashes had been between the Muslims and the Croats. Just then one of the Muslim sentries caught sight of him and shouted, "What are you doing out there? You are smack dab in the middle of a mine field!"

"Tell me where I should step," he said, quietly.

"Go right. Now straight. Stop! Go left . . ." the soldier led him slowly.

He got across.

The ordeals of war are truly difficult to predict. We experienced all sorts of things. You always had to run through eastern Mostar to dodge sniper fire and the shells. Anyone who didn't run was shot dead. One chilly morning when I was going along the street I noticed two women making their way toward me slowly. I was amazed that they weren't moving more quickly. When I reached them I found they were a mother and daughter: one wore only underwear, the other was naked. At Rondo, a traffic circle in western Mostar, the Croatian soldiers had stripped off their clothes and expelled them to the eastern side. They had been beaten until they were black and blue. I brought them blankets to wrap themselves in until clothing could be found for them.

The next day, at a rare moment of calm, I ran into an acquaintance on the street and stopped to say hello. Halfway through his third sentence the man toppled to the ground. I never heard the sniper bullet that killed him instantly.

Diabetics were in big trouble. They had little need for insulin because they ate so little, but they couldn't get hold of medicines in pill form.

One day when I was listening to the radio I heard regular calls for volunteer blood donors to come to the Institute for Hygiene. The shelling was heavy that day. The corridors of the institute were crowded with the wounded. The staff was operating without anesthesia. I was the only blood donor who showed up. Others must have been afraid to leave their homes, because the sniper fire was so intense.

Because of Croatian propaganda they were portraying us in the world as if we were backward. Mr. Jerry Hume was in charge of the local UNHCR office. He did a great deal for this city. When he first came to the humanitarian center, I asked him, "Could we have some sort of spices? People are starving here."

"You have cooking oil," he answered curtly. His attitude drove me to ask him to come the next day.

"Why?"

"I have something to show you."

"I'll be here."

The next day I brought brochures of my artwork. I laid out the catalogues and explained, "Mr. Hume, I am only one of the many people of Mostar who have traveled all over the world. I have probably seen more of the world than you have. I have been invited to show my work in many countries. I've been on television, received awards."

He was astonished. He didn't know how to respond. All he could say was, "The Croatian troops won't let the humanitarian aid convoys through."

"In that case, buy the food from the Croatian troops," I snapped, angrily.

The next day, thanks to him, a convoy of seven trucks carrying food finally made it into eastern Mostar.

During the conflict with the Croatian troops, Zoran Mandlbaum, president of the Jewish center in town, seemed nothing short of a miracle. That man helped many others at the risk of losing his own life, and I was one of them.

Dino's fiancée, Senka, whose mother was a Croat and father a Muslim, spent six months in Croatia working for a woman because she hadn't been able to get a visa and go to England as she'd intended to. She longed for Dino and for home, and he missed her terribly. She decided to come back to Mostar. She wore a gold chain with a cross around her neck that helped mask the fact that she was Muslim, so no one searched her on the bus. A gentle young woman with a lovely complexion, she probably looked like a nun to them.

As soon as we heard that Senka was back in western Mostar I told Zoran. He got back to me the next day. "I'll bring you your daughter-to-be tomorrow. Be there waiting for her."

He brought Senka over by truck, crouching among the packages of humanitarian aid.

We were all thrilled when she arrived. We quickly held the wedding and it was broadcast on foreign TV stations: the shells were falling, we celebrated. Since there was no food available, we had to make do with aid from a humanitarian organization.

Senka's father spent a year in the Croatian camps of Heliodrom and *Dretelj. He had been a giant of a man when he was taken away, and when he came back he weighed eighty pounds.

Two days before the old bridge was destroyed, my studio was looted. They told me at the police station to make a list of what had been taken. I went down under the studio to the cellar that had old walls two feet thick and provided excellent protection from shrapnel. I was just starting to compile the list when I heard the shells; fifteen of them were fired at the bridge. The first missed and hit the museum. The second fell into a cave under the bridge. Thirteen of them hit their mark.

I heard every single shell that was fired. I peeked out through the cellar window when each shell blasted to see how the damaged bridge was faring. I was one of the few witnesses, if not the only one, to watch the bridge be blasted that first day from so close at hand.

For thirty-five years I watched that bridge every morning while I had my coffee. I worked all day long, and would rest my eyes by looking at it. I experienced the bridge in a particular way, as if it were alive. I lived with it; it was a part of me . . .

The next day all it took was three shells to send the entire bridge tumbling into the Neretva River.

After that horrendous barbaric act, the snipers started shooting. No one paid them the slightest attention. People walked slowly by where the bridge had stood, as if paying their last respects. Some cried, others walked to Tito Street, numb and silent, and returned home. It was awful to see them.

We, the people of Mostar, lived for our bridge. Those barbarians took a part of us.

HELP FOR
A WOUNDED "CHETNIK"

TOLD BY DRAGAN SIMIĆ

The Village of Vranjak near Modriča

December 1995

I was born in 1966 in the village of Vranjak, near Modriča, in northern Bosnia near the border with Croatia. I spent my whole life there. As a member of the Republika Srpska army I was wounded during an offensive led by the Tuzla corps of the Army of Bosnia and Herzegovina on 3 March 1994. Shrapnel hit me in the stomach and left hip. The injuries were bad enough that I couldn't move. With my last ounce of strength I managed to crawl a few yards over to the bay window of the house next to which I'd been wounded. My fellow fighters jumped over me, retreating from their positions on the run, and though they saw my pleading eyes they didn't stop nor did anyone try to carry me. The pain was far too awful for me to muster the strength to shout, but I was conscious the whole time. I could clearly see all my comrades withdrawing without a word, abandoning me, wounded. Scenes flickered by as if in a film. It seems as if the next minute I was seeing Muslim fighters charging up out of the woods, crossing through the yard and coming up to the house. I had plenty of time to activate the hand grenade hanging on my belt, but

I didn't. In a wince of bitterness at the way my comrades had left me, I gave myself up for lost.

Three of the enemy soldiers came over cautiously, pointing their guns. I lay there motionless and looked straight at them.

"Damn those soldiers for leaving someone like this," the first man said. He kneeled by me and ripped open my uniform to see where I'd been wounded.

"Call in and tell them we have a wounded Chetnik. They should come to get him," the second soldier said to the third, who had a two-way radio.

All the horrible stories I had ever heard about Muslim bestiality when they took a Serbian soldier prisoner flashed through my mind. I had been hearing stories like that all through the two years I'd been fighting. I couldn't believe my eyes. A jeep drove up in a few minutes and transported me to the Tuzla hospital where they accepted me without a word and took me immediately into the operating room. The narcotic was a blessing, because only then was I able to stop thinking about the men who had left me behind.

After all I've experienced I know that there is no force on this earth and no idea that could force me to pick up a gun again.

After the operation they transferred me from the hospital to a jail in Gračanica. I was held there with another man named Branislav, a Serbian fighter, who also had been taken prisoner but not wounded. We spent five months in that jail, held separately from the Muslim prisoners. During that time they did not maltreat us, except when they slapped me on 7 July and called me a Chetnik and tore off my epaulettes. Two Muslims whom I knew, Huso and Bego, happened to visit the prison. When they saw me, they asked, "How are you? Are you convalescing?" I didn't smoke but they always brought Branislav cigarettes.

Five months later the Red Cross visited the prison. They saw me and put me on their list for exchange. A few days later I left Gračanica and went home.

YOU'RE NO BETTER
OFF THAN ME

TOLD BY LUCA PRGOMET

Bosanski Šamac

December 1995

I spent decades in Bosanski Šamac with my husband, Ivan. We had three daughters while we lived there. The oldest was killed in a car accident ten years ago. When the war broke out, our second daughter and her husband got out of Šamac in an exchange and moved to a coastal Croatian town. There she had two children we haven't seen yet. Our youngest daughter is with us. Ivan weaves and sells baskets. This is our sole source of income.

No one touched us in Šamac after the outbreak of hostilities. We lived quietly and worked at our jobs. Simo, a Serb, often stopped by our house to visit and greeted us with the question, "Are you having any problems, my friends? Do you need flour or something else I could bring you?"

After the huge influx of Serbs from western Bosnia, on 1 September 1995 refugees from Glamoč knocked at our door. "They told us at the municipal offices that we might be able to stay with you."

Ivan, a contrary man, turned them away. He explained that the whole house had only two rooms. Two hours later the police moved Sava and her son and mother-in-law into one of the rooms by force.

It hasn't been easy for us with our new tenants. They abandoned their homes, saving their lives, but they had nothing to their name. It has been worst for Sava. She is torn between Miloš, who is often away, fighting, and Ljubica, who is twenty years old. The two of us quickly began getting along fine. Whenever Sava needs to leave the house, I look after Ljubica, who is disabled.

There is very little space in the house. It so happens that we can hear everything going on in the other room. Ivan's bad temper is worst when he is drunk, which happens often enough. One such occasion he lunged at me and began to throttle me. I called out for help until I couldn't breathe, and then I lost consciousness. Sava heard my calls for help from the other room. After hesitating briefly she broke down the locked door of our room at the last moment and managed to wrest me free of Ivan's furious grip. I came to and saw Sava's tearful eyes.

"You poor woman. You're no better off than I am. Your fate, too, is cursed," she said, placing cold compresses on my neck.

I'LL DO IT

TOLD BY MUHAREM BEGOVIĆ

Ilidža

October 1998

I lived in Ilidža and had plenty of Serbian friends. When the horrors started, the local people of the Eastern Orthodox faith really did nothing wrong.

On 10 May 1992 I went with my neighbors, Drago and Neđo, out in front of the building to have a beer. Drago had been an orphan from World War II. He learned his trade and finished his schooling at an orphanage. He straight away saw through the situation that was happening around us. We had only just sat down when a Renault 5 drove up and a man I knew by sight wearing a camouflage uniform stepped out. He asked all three of us for our ID cards. He patted the two of them on the shoulder when he saw they were Serbs. I sat there quietly, assuming this was a routine ID check. When he asked for mine, I stood up and pulled it out of my back pocket. He tapped me on the shoulder, too, and said, "Stand over there."

I stood fifteen feet away from my friends, and he went over to the car. I thought he was going to write something down.

"Get in here, you *balija*," he ordered, opening the car door.

He drove me to a camp where there were about forty armed men. There was a girl with them. They all maltreated me and humiliated me both verbally and physically until a man appeared who called me by name, and said, "Let him go."

I heard that Drago had gone with Vukašin Prstojević to their headquarters, where they had intervened for my release. They were threatened there: "If you keep helping Muslims, you are going to be in trouble, too!"

I went to find Drago, who started crying when he hugged me. After twenty minutes Vukašin came in, and I saw tears in his eyes. His son, Darko, asked me, "Uncle Muharem, what happened to you?"

I didn't say anything because the others had threatened me when I left and forbade me to speak of the abuse.

Until 24 May I was afraid to leave the house, afraid they would be taking me to the camp again.

Early in the morning on 24 May someone rang at the door. My two daughters were sitting at the living room table with my wife and mother-in-law. I opened the door to five armed men with hats, each sporting a white feather.

"Hand over your ID," they barked, checked it, and said, "Look, don't you be going anywhere. First we have to take care of the other apartments that Muslims have abandoned."

In the excitement my blood pressure went shooting up. My wife came over because it had been awhile that I'd been standing at the door. I told her, "Go back inside and don't come out, just hand me my nitroglycerine tablets."

I listened to them breaking into apartments on the floor above mine, until finally their leader appeared, a man named Jovo, and took me outside. I could hear Dr. Slavica Đukić, a prominent gynecologist, telling him, "Mr. Jovo, you don't have to come in here. Everything is fine here." She was standing in the doorway of the neighboring entranceway.

They took me through the neighborhood where I had lived for years. We all knew each other, at least by sight. I looked the Serbs in the eyes. I didn't know many of their names, just as they didn't know mine, but they all looked at me with such sadness. Steva, who ran the local video store, respected me as his elder. He felt so uncomfortable with what was going on that he couldn't bear it and looked away.

This time they took me to a children's nursery school. Before we entered, Jovo said, "Report to the room on the right."

This was the nursery school where my grandchildren had gone before the war. There was a girl at the door, her eyes brimming with tears, who had been a friend of my older daughter, Jasminka's. She could barely speak. "Come in here, Uncle Muharem. Mr. Jovo will be here in a minute,"

I saw Bora there, whose sister Mirka had gone to school with my daughter. "Uncle Muharem, what is wrong? Why are you so pale?" he asked, frightened.

"Bora, what is going on here?"

"Sit down, nothing bad will happen."

All I had time for was to tell him, "Bora, I've got my nitroglycerine in my right pants pocket. If I should be taken ill, please put a tablet under my tongue."

A man was sitting under the window with a bushy beard and a Kalashnikov gun in his lap. I went over to my neighbor, the tailor, and told him, "Neighbor, my nitroglycerine is in my pocket . . ." and then I passed out.

I revived in the bathroom where Bora was daubing me with water. His gun was against the wall.

"Uncle Muharem, I put the nitroglycerine under your tongue. Don't you worry. Nothing's going to happen to you," he soothed me.

"Bora, do you have a cigarette?"

He gave me a full pack of Morava cigarettes. I went back into the room where there were about eighty Muslims and Croats. As I stepped into the room, the bearded Chetnik howled, again, "*Balija*, where have you been?"

I passed out again. As if in a dream, I heard Bora's voice: "If you move anywhere from that window I will empty the whole clip into your chest!"

After that the bearded Chetnik calmed down.

After three hours of uncertainty, Jovo appeared again and lined us up, one by one, along the wall. Bora asked the men to let me stand second in line because I wasn't well. Jovo sat at a table, his head bowed, and demanded to see my ID. I happened to put it down on the table a little further from him, and he asked me, "Could you be so good as to move your ID a little closer?"

When he picked up the ID and saw that I was born in Travnik, he said, "Muharem, I know Travnik well. I served in the army there at the barracks. Do you know where the Slemena are? That is where the shooting grounds are where we had target practice."

"Sure," I said, talking about Travnik to calm myself down.

Jovo butted in. "Cut it short, Muharem. You have two options: you can be loyal to us, your brother Serbs, put on a uniform, take up ammunition and a weapon, and go to the front lines, or you can move out of your apartment. If you decide to leave town, there are two directions you may take: into Sarajevo or over the mountain to Kiseljak."

As he said this I took a look at the ID card of the man who had been first in line, and wondered why he kept that man's ID.

"Sir, would it be all right for me to consult with my family? I don't know which option to choose. All my neighbors have left. I stayed behind. May I go home now, and get in touch with you tomorrow?"

"No problem."

I went home. As I was explaining to my family the situation we were in, Vukašin and Darko came over. When they heard what had happened, Darko said, wiping his eyes, "Uncle Muharem, if you decide to go I will drive you."

"Darko, thank you, but you mustn't do that. You are a young man. They will say you're saving a Muslim. They'll murder you. You know how they threatened Drago when he intervened on my behalf."

Darko turned to his father. "Do you remember what it was like when Mother and my sister left? Uncle Muharem was out on his terrace. I saw him crying as he watched them," he said, still crying. "I will do it. I'll take Uncle Muharem and Aunt Šerifa, grandma and Lejla. Let them kill me!"

That evening we packed up our documents and our essentials. The next morning we sat in Darko's car and headed for downtown Sarajevo. There were armed men at the exit point from Ilidža, at an underpass where the corridor was. At the points where the bridge joins the shore there were machine gun nests. I shook with fear and my hair stood up straight to the sky . . .

Darko pulled to a stop. Two soldiers came over and asked to see his car registration and his ID. When they saw that his last name was Prstojević, one of them asked him, "Is Nedeljko Prstojević any relation of yours?"

Nedeljko was one of the commanders of the Serbian army. He had been taking money to make arrangements for Muslims and Croats to get out of Ilidža. When the authorities learned of his activities, they demoted him from his commander position.

"That man is no relative of mine," Darko replied, softly.

They didn't believe him. They screamed at him and cursed, "You traitor, you are helping *balijas* and taking money for it!"

Darko managed to rein himself in, and told them, "Gentlemen, this is my neighbor. Yesterday he was at our headquarters where they told him he has to leave his apartment. I am his friend and the only thing I could do for him was to drive him this far. Please let me go another 100 meters so that these people can get out of the car. If you find out I am related to that Nedeljko guy, shoot me then. I'll be back in a couple of minutes."

At the line of separation we got out of the car and took our four plastic bags of documents and the most essential things out of the trunk of the car.

None of us was able to say a single word. We set out on foot and I couldn't help but look back. Darko had closed his trunk, leaned against the car and was weeping bitterly, watching us walk away.

After reintegration we came back to our apartment. Vukašin Prstojević and Veljko still live in our apartment building with their families.

LIKE A SISTER TO ME

TOLD BY RADMILA HAJDER

Refugee from Glamoč, interviewed in Bosanski Šamac

December 1995

I lived in Glamoč, a small town on the Croatian-Bosnian border, the population of which, before August 1995, was mostly Serbian, as were we. My husband, Miloš, was a member of the Republika Srpska army. He was off fighting more than he was home. I managed to survive somehow, thanks to the fact that I was living in my own home on my own land. The Muslim-Croatian operation *Storm to capture western Bosnia in the summer and fall of 1995 forced me to abandon my native town of Glamoč, driven out in a column of refugees.

My whole world collapsed. I set out, in terror, for what was total uncertainty from the shelter of my family hearth. My exodus ended in Šamac, where the municipality, accommodating the refugees, placed me in the home of a Croatian woman named Marija.

"Marija, this woman will be moving into your home with her husband. You'll be better off not complaining. In another three days you'll be driven from your home anyway, and forced to move to Croatia," they snarled, and left.

There I was, left standing face to face with this strange woman, who was, after all, a Catholic. I expected her anger, her understandable indignation. But Marija smiled warmly, took me by the hand, and said, "You must be tired and hungry. Come in, let me give you some refreshment and something to eat." She set out all the food she had.

"I'm sorry I have so little to offer, but these are difficult times," she said, genuinely unhappy that she couldn't treat me to a nicer meal. There wasn't a trace of hatred or defiance in her voice. Marija shared all she had with me. When one of her Serbian friends brought her food or something else to help her out she was sincerely pleased to be able to ease the ordeal of these terrible times for me as well.

Miloš was rarely home so the two of us shared all the housework. I felt as if I'd come to stay with my own sister.

For days that awful sentence rang in my ears, "In another three days you'll be driven from your home anyway, and forced to move to Croatia."

When Miloš came back from the front, I told him, "Marija wasn't the one who expelled us from our home in Glamoč. If they come to drive her from her home, I'll move out first."

IF EVERYONE ELSE
CAN WAIT, SO CAN I

TOLD BY NEVENKA KEJŽAR

The Grbavica part of Sarajevo

November 1998

I moved to Sarajevo in 1947 at the age of seventeen from the town of Modriča, where I was born. I married a man named Ivan who was a military officer. He and I were Croats. When this war started, we were living in Grbavica, a section of Sarajevo, in an apartment building that stood right on the first line of separation between Grbavica, which was in Republika Srpska, and Sarajevo, which was under Muslim control. At first we got by somehow, living off money that we were able to take from our savings accounts in a Belgrade bank. Once we'd used that up, since we were no longer receiving my husband's pension from Belgrade, we took our meals at the Red Cross kitchen. Five days running we would eat rice with no salt or oil. I would go out and gather fruits and cook my own jam. It inevitably went bad, but I'd even eat it bad. I lost eighty pounds. When I first came into downtown Sarajevo from Grbavica after the war, my daughter didn't recognize me, and my grandson asked her, "Mama, who is that lady?"

The retired officers who were Serbs received their military pensions, but the rest of us didn't. My husband didn't dare set foot outside the apartment for two full years. I fought to keep us alive. Twice during the first two war years, when things were at their worst, I went up to Pale, to the Republika Srpska headquarters. There were even Serbs who didn't dare go there. No one ever asked for my ID papers except when I went through the checkpoint near Pale. Whenever I passed near the front lines I would always greet the soldiers, and they greeted me.

"How are you today, ma'am? How's the health?" they always asked.

Personally I can't complain about the behavior of a single Serbian soldier. No one ever did anything nasty to me. Other people weren't so lucky. It made all the difference what sort of neighbors you had. All my neighbors in my building figured I must be Serbian. Near the end of the war one of my neighbors kept inviting me over. I turned down her invitation as politely as I could, because I had heard that she had lured another neighbor, a Croatian woman, into her place saying she had a message for her, only to beat her up when she got her inside. When I finally did go to visit them, her husband, Ljuba, asked me directly, "Nevenka, I'd like to ask you something, and please, be honest in your reply."

"Ask away!"

"What is your background?"

"I am a Croat," I answered, looking him straight in the eyes.

"Don't think I meant anything untoward by asking. I have always respected your family. I respect you today as I did when we used to sit together at the Communist Party meetings way back when."

"Sure, Ljuban, I know you do," I answered, though I wasn't sure at all.

The rumor spread around the neighborhood: Nevenka is not a Serb! Luckily the war was nearly over when that happened, so I didn't have any problems.

No one bothered us, thanks to our good neighbors. When they came to the apartment asking Ivan to hand over his personal pistol they didn't say anything insulting or hurtful. Another time soldiers came in to keep watch out our window. They probably could have seen better from up on the

fifteenth floor rather than from our tenth floor window, but, still, they behaved decently.

Our building was on the front line. There were barricades and bunkers
out in front. Sixteen of the bunkers were set up around our four high rises.
There were lookout posts on top. We built barricades in the apartments to
shield us from gunfire. We still have some of the bullets that were shot into
our apartment.

I went up to Pale to visit Ivan's relatives and to call my daughter, who
was living over in Alipašino Polje, another section of Sarajevo. She was living under the Muslim authorities, and we were living under Republika
Srpska. It was really tricky for me to get from Grbavica to Pale, even though
it was a suburb of Sarajevo just as Grbavica was. There was no transportation organized. I had to stand there in the dark, fearful of being hit by sniper
fire, waiting for some truck driver to take pity on me and pick me up. When
I finally made it to Ivan's relatives' house, I found out that the electricity
was out and the phones were down.

"What can I do now?" I asked them. "I was barely able to get here."

There was nothing they could say. They shrugged silently. Just then a
neighbor of theirs, a policeman, stopped by.

"Could you please tell me where there might be a working phone I could
call my daughter from? I came all the way from Grbavica to Pale just to make
a phone call."

"No working phones, ma'am," he answered tersely, and then went on
after a brief pause, "except, of course, at the police station."

I went straight to the police station. A young man stopped me at the
front door.

"How may I help you?"

"My name is Nevenka. I've come up here from Grbavica," I introduced
myself, careful not to mention my last name, which would have betrayed
that I was a Croat more than my first name did. "Would it be possible for
you to allow me to use the phone to call my daughter?"

"Where does your daughter live?"

"In Alipašino Polje," I answered.

"What street does she live on?" he asked, curious. When I gave the address, he nodded. "I know the building. That is where Juka, the paramilitary leader, lives."

"Must be that she is at one of the other entranceways," I mumbled, disturbed by what he'd said.

"Here, let me give it a try, though the connections are really bad."

He tried dialing my daughter's number for ages. After awhile he asked, "Is it that you would like to move your daughter out of Sarajevo and over to the Republika Srpska?"

Seeing that he was not likely to get through, I quickly lied, "Exactly, that's what I've been hoping for. My daughter is married. She would first have to consult with her husband. That was why I came here tonight, to ask her."

"If I get through, you can go ahead and ask her. If she decides she'd like to, we'd be happy to bring them over to the Republika Srpska side," he offered kindly.

Fortunately, he wasn't able to get through. I thanked him and went back home to Grbavica.

My daughter, son-in-law, and grandson were assigned to work duty throughout the war in Sarajevo.

Although I am sixty-eight years old, I have never met a person my whole life like Cvija. Every other day she dropped by to visit us. Whenever I went to see her, she would be cross: "I don't know what to do with you now. You can't stay here, but I can't let you go home. What if they were to shoot you on your way? Can't you see the sniper fire on all sides?"

She helped everyone, with such an open heart. Both materially and physically. If anyone needed help to make a phone call, send a letter, go to the store, there was Cvija. Muslims didn't dare go out to the store or the marketplace in Grbavica to buy food. She would go for them and buy things, often with her own money, when she had any.

After Mustafa died, she helped his family a great deal. She organized his funeral and paid for everything. While Mustafa was alive, she visited him every day because he was ill. She'd bring him a little cheese, milk, or hot soup whenever she had some.

When Serbian fighters attacked the Maričić family one night, people living nearby said that they heard so much gunfire. They all thought there had been an attack on the entire neighborhood. His wife had a nervous breakdown. She called for help in vain. The neighbors heard her but didn't dare come to her aid. They beat her husband so severely that he had to be taken to the hospital. When they were brought back, they were asked where they should be dropped off.

"At the marketplace," the Maričićes answered. They didn't dare go back to their own place. Instead they went to Cvija's house and hid there for three months.

Cvija and I went to the police to request that the Maričićes be protected. I went to UNPROFOR, too. The second time UNPROFOR agreed to talk to me, a woman living nearby who worked there as an interpreter, asked, "Why have you taken up their cause? Why do you care so much what happens to them? Why do you keep coming here and bothering us?"

Just so their things wouldn't be completely looted, Cvija's nephew went to collect what things he could retrieve and stored them somewhere else, and my daughter helped him.

There was a friend of mine who would never let me leave her home unless I ate something. Whenever she stopped by to visit us she would always bring along an onion or a potato or two. That was a lot in those days. She helped other people in the neighborhood as much as she could.

There were Šešelj's men, White Eagles, Romanija fighters who were wreaking havoc in other parts of Grbavica. The parts hit the worst by their activities were the neighborhoods Vrace and Grbavica II. They left us alone because we were right out on the front lines. There were no barricades here that would guarantee them safe passage. And there were army buildings where we were, guarded by armed sentries. Even people living in neighboring buildings didn't dare come by to visit, because every time you stepped out of a building you were taking risks.

There was a family living in the neighborhood called the Zečevićes. The husband was a judge, and his wife was a lawyer. As soon as the war began the wife and daughter left Grbavica, and he stayed behind with his son. At the very beginning of the conflict the local Republika Srpska authorities called him and asked, "What are you waiting for? Why don't you leave?"

He came to visit and ask for advice. "I can't figure out what is best. They are summoning me to join the Serbian army."

He had barely gotten the words out when Serbian soldiers came in and took him away to make him don a uniform. When they left we called his son, Nebojša, who had just graduated from the university, to come to our apartment. We hid him in the pantry. He was shaking with fear. I gave him a glass of brandy to calm him down.

"Sit here and keep quiet," I told him. "No one will look for you here."

When Zečević came back, he said, "It looks as if I will have to go. What will I do with Nebojša?"

It was difficult to advise someone what they should do in a situation like that. All of us talked it over together and decided the best thing would be for the boy to go with him. They served as sentries on Banja Luka Street by night, and in front of the School of Agriculture by day. There was valuable equipment in there, instruments and other things, which were supposed to be moved to Banja Luka.

Zečević had graduated from Reserve Officers' Training and held the rank of captain. During the war they promoted him to active officer. He helped many Muslims and Croats get to Belgrade. At that point the authorities were checking on everyone who went into Serbia. Muslims were not allowed to cross over from Bosnia into Serbia. Zečević brought whole groups of people over the Drina River into Serbia and put them on Serbian buses, which drove them to Belgrade. He'd tell the driver, "No one touches these people. Leave them be all the way to Belgrade. You answer to me personally for every single one of them."

He noticed a Muslim neighbor of ours in Lukavica, where the man had been taken by Serbian soldiers.

"What is this man doing here? Are you out of your minds? This is the finest man in our building. Release him immediately," he insisted until they finally did release him and his neighbor Grga, a Croat.

Once we were standing out in front of the local store in a line.

"Nevenka, it's better if you don't use the word 'kruh' for bread, it is too Croatian-sounding. Better for you to say, 'hljeb' so that the pea-brains don't give you a hard time."

I never could get it straight. Whenever I made it to the front of the line I'd get flustered and instead of asking for 'hljeb,' I'd say 'kruh' when I asked for bread.

"Fuck the 'kruh.' It's not 'kruh,' lady, it is 'hljeb,'" the shopkeeper would bristle.

Once they asked me in line, "Lady, who is that officer to you?"

"My neighbor," I answered proudly.

He was the only man who refused to cut to a better place in line. The women at the cash registers would call to him, "Captain, step to the head of the line. You have special status."

"Gee, thanks, but if everyone else can wait, so can I," he'd reply.

In October or November 1992 he went with his son to Bijeljina. Soon after that they sent us a sack of flour, a sack of potatoes, onions, tomatoes, peppers . . .

THREE POTATOES

TOLD BY SUBHIJA DEDOVIĆ NINKOVIĆ

The Otoka part of Sarajevo

October 1998

I was born in Sarajevo and spent my whole life here. When the war broke out, my husband, Aleksandar, and I were living in an apartment on the sixteenth floor of a high rise in the Sarajevo neighborhood of Otoka. Ours was a mixed marriage, my husband being Serbian, and my background Muslim.

Those years were an ordeal I will never forget. My sister, who lives in Turkey, used to send us a little money now and then and we'd divide it up among the nineteen members of the family. Once each of us received twelve German marks. It meant a lot at the time. You could buy a half quart of cooking oil for that.

There was no electricity, no water, no firewood, no food . . .

Aleksandar often went with our neighbor, Ranko, up onto Žuč hill to fetch firewood, pushing a heavy warehouse cart. It would take him three hours to get to the hill. He would always say, "It's harder for me to climb up Žuč with an empty cart than to come down with a full one."

Aca, as we called Aleksandar, didn't even know how to chop wood. I saw that once when I went with them. He would collect branches and twigs

351

for kindling, and Ranko would chop them and teach him as they went. They brought the wood back together. The hardest part was carrying the three sacks of firewood up to the sixteenth floor. Once he got them up to our apartment, he'd have a dish of green porridge, rest for a few minutes, and then keep going, because he had twelve empty water jugs to fill. He'd take them and go off to wait in the line for water.

Food was a special problem. I had no flour at all. Although my leg hurt, I'd make my way with difficulty up Žuč hill with my husband to forage for plants. I had read that any weed that wasn't bitter could be eaten. All the nettles and orach, plants known to be edible, were gone. I picked whatever weeds I found. When I'd filled my sack, I'd bring them to a water pump and rinse them. I invented a recipe for green porridge. Later the whole high rise was cooking it. I'd chop up the greens and use the salt we used to use for the dishwasher. To all of that I'd add some bran. That was what we ate for months.

Jovanka, a neighbor of mine, had a daughter-in-law, Branka, who lived over in Ilidža and sent her packages of food. Whenever she got something from Branka she would set aside a part of it for us.

Our granddaughter turned fourteen on 4 October 1994. She asked twenty-four children from the building to come over for her birthday party. I had managed to set aside a half pound of butter and what with one thing and another I managed to eke out a cake. And with a can of meat I made little meat pastries. The children came and brought pencils and erasers for presents, whatever they had. Branka brought us three potatoes and two green peppers from Ilidža. When my grandson, Elvir, saw the potatoes he exclaimed, entranced, "Grandma! Are those real, those potatoes? Please, can I touch them?"

"Sure they're real, dear."

"You're joking, aren't you Grandma? I bet they're plastic. Where did real potatoes come from? Come on, let me touch them."

When I gave him the potatoes, he prattled on, excited, "They are real, aren't they! Please, can you make me potato strudel with one, mashed potatoes with the second, and French fries with the third?"

"Honey, I can't make all that out of three potatoes. I can fry them up as French fries and share them with all the children here."

"But Grandma, that's no fair. Are you crazy? They can have the cake. How can you let them have the potatoes! Don't let anyone have the potatoes!"

"I can't do that, honey. That wouldn't be nice."

"Please! At least don't touch them until Father gets home to take a picture with his camera, and then do what you like."

I made French fries nonetheless and gave a few to each child.

The children had a grand time. Before they all left they asked the birthday girl what her favorite present was.

"I liked Aunt Branka's the best," she said without hesitating.

I had given her a beautiful down jacket I'd bought in Poland before the war for 200 German marks. I was expecting she would say my present was the nicest and her answer shocked me. I blurted, "What???"

"But I did like it best, Grandma. Aunt Branka's present was the nicest."

"How can you compare three potatoes to a jacket?" I asked her, amazed.

To that Elvir replied, "Grandma, you're the one being silly. How can you compare an ordinary old jacket to potatoes?!"

WE WON'T FIGHT
WITHOUT HIM

TOLD BY SLAVIŠA ŠUĆUR

Sarajevo

November 1998

I was born in Sarajevo in 1961 and lived there all my life, as I hope to do for the rest of my days. This is my country.

My story is probably a little unusual because I became a hero of the Army of Bosnia and Herzegovina even though I'm a Serb, joining the movement of resistance to the evil that loomed over this city. The beginning of the war was a particularly difficult time both because of the amount of evil around, and because of the distrust among the people of different nationalities stemming from that evil. I quickly grasped the monstrous plot to destroy a country, Bosnia, which had been known for centuries for its tolerance, for the way people lived together so well and so successfully, regardless of what religion and ethnic group they belonged to.

The amount of evil that spewed forth on Sarajevo in the form of raw violence—shells, guns, and tanks—pushed me to the thought that the only adequate response, at that moment, that a person could offer was by the same means. That was why I decided to join the Army of Bosnia and Herzegovina. At the time it was not a simple thing to be a Serb in Sarajevo,

354

let alone to join the army as a Serb. Since I had been a tank gunner way back when I'd served in the Yugoslav People's Army, I reported to the First Tank Brigade, which was the first tank unit formed in Sarajevo. At that point they had only two tanks.

I earned the trust of my comrades-in-arms pretty quickly. That allowed me to get into a situation where I could show my will to defy the evil, to defy fascism.

In September 1992, one of the first times our unit was in combat, Brigade Commander Rifat, who had been an officer in the Yugoslav People's Army, entrusted me with the assignment of tank gunner. I handled the targeting just fine.

After that, in December, we were planning a move that would be vital to the survival and defense of Sarajevo. It was a battle for the Žuč elevation. When the strike was planned, Enver Šehović, brigade commander at that time and later killed, demanded that I and no one else be the gunner, since he himself had seen earlier how well I handled the gun.

That was an exceptionally tricky and responsible job, but I managed to pull it off. After that, the units of the Army of Bosnia and Herzegovina won that battle without heavy losses and took elevation 850 and Golo Brdo. That meant that they freed a large section of Sarajevo from direct hits and in fact prevented an attempt to slice the city in two.

After the first successful day of that strike, Enver Šehović summoned me to his dugout. I will always remember his words. "I am proud you handled your task with flying colors. I want to make the Army of Bosnia and Herzegovina a real partisan army, an army that will follow the tradition of anti-fascism. I am particularly grateful to you for fighting with us. Without people like you and the other Serbian fighters in this unit, I could never hope to put together such a fighting force."

At his urging I was given the "Golden Lily," the highest honor the Army of Bosnia and Herzegovina confers.

During 1995 the army released me for three months to join the cabinet of the president of the Bosnia and Herzegovina Assembly, where I worked at computer, translation, and correspondence jobs with foreign organizations.

When planning was under way for the major push in 1995, I had already received, for all intents and purposes, my demobilization papers from General Delić, commander of the army.

The commander of the 1st Corps called me then and said that the fighters of the 1st Knights' Brigade with whom I had spent most of my time in combat, and who were to spearhead this particular campaign, refused to go on the offensive unless I was the gunner. It is important to add that the unit was already pretty powerful, with plenty of tanks and plenty of gunners. Although I was basically finished with fighting by then, I decided to join them, touched by their confidence.

In all that I've done, I've always been critical of the negative things that went on in the Army of Bosnia and Herzegovina and in Sarajevo. I had become well enough known that I could, in some way, influence the attitude toward citizens of Serbian nationality who chose to stay in Sarajevo.

For me the Bosnia I fought for was a symbol of something the world is moving toward in principle, where people will be able, with a large dose of tolerance and trust, to live together regardless of faith, skin color, and all that often gives rise to wars and evil.

THE NINTH BROTHER

TOLD BY JURE ZEKO

Bosanski Aleksandrovac near Laktaši

January 1996

My ancestors were Orthodox, originally from Montenegro. My great grandfather moved to Bosnia where, choosing between Muslims and Croats, he opted for the Catholic faith and became a priest. His name was Zeko, quite an unusual last name—it means "bunny rabbit." My parents moved to Bosanski Aleksandrovac when I was two. All that I know is tied to the people around here and the way they think. I have never felt myself to be an outsider, nor did I ever think of people in terms of their ethnic background. I have friends of all faiths. My children have Serbian names, Dragan and Danijela, but I am a Croat.

My Serbian friends did not change during the war. They all hoped the ordeal would end as soon as possible, that the murdering, abuse, and looting would cease. My neighbors helped me and others as much as they could. There were other families that were generous to us. The Orthodox priest and his wife treated us throughout the war as their flesh and blood. My children spent more time in their home than they did with us.

From the first days of the war Serbs protected my house so that none of the newcomers would threaten our safety. It was risky standing up to the frenzied bands of outsiders who came to loot, and I pleaded with them not to, but they would never leave me be. The guards who patrolled the city stopped by my house pretty regularly.

I did not fight in combat because I have been disabled since childhood when a mower cut off my leg.

My neighbor, a widow, had an only son who was wounded. He spent six months in the hospital. She hadn't enough money to go and visit him. I gave her money, and she burst into tears and asked, "How can I repay you? I haven't got anything."

Sometimes she brings me an apple, pleased that I'm glad to see her.

When so many Serbs had to escape from western Bosnia in the summer and fall of 1995, one of them, a man named Đuro, arrived with his family and stayed at my house. I hadn't known him before. Đuro couldn't believe I was a Croat, and yet so willing to help him. When they left to continue on their way to Serbia, we kissed five times, not the traditional Serbian three. At parting he told me, "You have helped me more than anyone. Now that I've experienced this, this war is over for me. I will never take up a gun again, and no one will be able to force me to."

I have refugees staying with me again. The first of eight brothers came with his wife and four children and asked, "Is there room for us in your house?"

I took them in immediately. I offered them money so they could buy what they needed, but though they had no source of income, none of them would accept my offer. They all know where I keep my money but they have never taken so much as a dinar. Four of the brothers live in Bačka Palanka, and four are in Aleksandrovac. Sometimes it happens they all arrive for a visit, with their mother and father. Then the house is so full we lose count. I count as their ninth.

I'M GOING WITH YOU

TOLD BY N. S.[†]

Vareš

November 1998

I was born in Vareš, forty-eight years ago. I am married and have two sons. I worked in a company where my coworkers came from all possible ethnic groups and I never had any problems with that.

The war in Vareš began for me on 23 October 1993, when the Croatian Defense Council units they called the Maturice came to town.

I was drinking coffee with my husband in the kitchen that morning.

Glancing out the window he spotted some armed men outside. Then we heard a rifle butt pounding the door. My husband opened the door and found himself facing two soldiers in camouflage uniforms. "What is your name?" they wanted to know.

When he gave a name that was recognizably Muslim, they said, "Get your things. You are coming with us."

I was in my nightgown and bathrobe. They only came in as far as the hallway. My older son had just gotten up and came out of the bedroom in his pajamas.

"How old are you, boy?"

"Twenty," he answered, still sleepy, rubbing his eyes.

"You're coming with us, too."

Then my younger son appeared. They saw that he was still a child. He was only twelve. He sat down at the kitchen table. They didn't touch him.

I was wearing, as I always had, my jewelry, gold rings, bracelets, a necklace, earrings. They noticed it all and demanded, "Hand over your money and your gold."

We stared at them in disbelief.

"Quick. Give your wallets here."

"Look, please don't take our things. What will we do when you've take what little money we have?" we protested.

I watched them. One of them had markings on his face to camouflage who he was, and he never said a word the whole time. Since the Croatian Defense Council had been in power we had been receiving our salaries in Croatian currency and in German marks. I brought out all the money we had in the house. The unfamiliar soldier who was not hiding behind war paint took the German marks and offered half of it to his friends.

"I don't want any of it," the other man spoke tersely for the first time, bowing his head, probably because he feared we might recognize that he was a local man from Vareš.

"I'm not taking my gold jewelry off. These are precious mementos I cherish," I said.

I was lucky. They didn't insist. They took my son and husband out of the apartment as soon as they got dressed. As they were on the way out, one of them said, over his shoulder, "Lady, I recommend you lock the doors. I'm saying it for your own good."

I went into the kitchen. My younger son was crying. I put my arms around him to comfort him, barely holding back the tears myself.

"Son, don't cry. Everything will be fine."

"Mama, let me unclasp your necklace. We should hide it somewhere."

I slipped it into my pocket. Another fifteen minutes and someone pounded on the door again. When I opened I saw two new soldiers. By then I was a little steadier. "What do you want?" I asked them, loudly, not letting them in.

"What do you mean, what do we want?" they asked, a little surprised.

"How many times are you going to come? What is going on here?"

"You mean someone has already been here?" they asked, still standing at the doorway. "Did they take your money and your gold?"

"Yes, they did, but I wasn't sorry about that. I was sorry because they took my boy and my husband. I have no idea where they went or why."

"Let's get out of here," one of them said, turning and starting down the stairs. "Lady, lock your door. Don't worry," the other advised me.

"How can I not worry?" I said after him as he walked away down the steps.

I went back in, and just then I heard a siren going off sounding a bombing alert. I heard my neighbors going down the stairs and into the shelters in the cellar.

"Mama, are we going down to the shelters?"

"No, it's chilly down there. If they shell us, our apartment is down low so they aren't likely to hit us. Take a chair and let's sit in the hallway just in case," I explained.

From that moment forward the only people who could help me were Croats, because the other Muslims I knew were busy fighting to survive.

A few minutes later one of my neighbors came by when she saw that we weren't down in the shelter with the others.

"How come you're waiting up here?"

I shrugged. I could hardly speak for the tears welling up in my throat.

"Come on down with me. We'll be all of us together," she insisted.

"My apartment is low down in the building. The shells won't hit us."

"Come on, hurry up," she kept at us.

"Son, dress warmly. It is cold outside."

We went down to the cellar. Since there was nothing happening I didn't have the patience to sit in that dank cellar. I was tense.

"I'm going back upstairs," I told my neighbor. "I don't know where they've taken my husband and my son."

Meanwhile another neighbor joined us who told me, "They've taken them over to the high school."

I went back upstairs. The neighbor I socialized with the most knocked at the door. She was looking after her sister's children, who had gotten out of Sarajevo.

"Why don't you come over to my place. You'll be safer there."

"Thanks, but I'd rather stay here."

I couldn't sleep that night. In the morning I went out to see if I could find my son and husband. My neighbors worried and tried to convince me not to leave the building. I wasn't afraid.

"I'm going with you. I won't allow you to go out by yourself. Just give me a minute to get ready," my neighbor said.

Nearby the high school building we ran into a friend of ours. "Where are you going?"

"I want to find my husband and son. They've locked them up in the school."

"Don't go up there now. They aren't letting anyone near. You'll just have problems. Come back when the new shift takes over. The local Vareš men will let you in when they're on duty."

That same day the man who was director of the company where my husband worked before the war stopped by. "Can I be of any help?" he asked with sorrow in his voice.

"Thank you so much for coming. That is already help."

"I saw your son and husband. They were doing OK. Don't worry. This will get better. Someone brought your son a jacket. Why don't you put together some of his winter clothes so that I can bring them to him. It's cold."

I put together some of his winter clothes. He had brought a bag and I packed them in.

"Give them my love and tell them that we are doing fine," I said, seeing him off.

Two hours later another man came by. He had the bag of things with him that I'd sent to my son and husband.

"I'm bringing you back the bag. Why did you send them new things? They'll just take it all themselves. How about some older clothes and shoes? They took your brother-in-law's shoes."

"I don't have any older clothes or shoes."

"Well, in that case we'll manage."

Every day someone stopped by to let me know how they were doing. A friend of my son's who was working at the Red Cross came by to tell me, "They beat up your boy and then hid him from the International Red Cross delegation that came to visit, so that they wouldn't see his bruises. Your husband is doing fine."

My husband did what he could to keep from being separated from our son. For the first weeks they were together. Then they pulled aside a group of the prisoners, including my husband. "We're releasing you. You can go home."

"I'll leave if you release my son, too. Otherwise I'm staying here," he answered categorically and stayed locked up with our son.

During that time I was able to move freely around town. People I knew in Vareš, local people, greeted me on the street and sympathized with me. None of them ever said anything mean.

One day over the loudspeakers the Croatian authorities called on everyone in town to leave their apartments and abandon Vareš. Panic erupted. Some of the people decided to leave, others didn't want to. Some set out to leave and then came back. Only a few of us from the building decided we were not going to go. I stayed on in my apartment until 2 November.

Most of the Muslims—women, children, and elders—assembled on the street in front of the elementary school where they were protected by the Swedish UNPROFOR battalion. They spent several days in the open here. I didn't want to join them.

Over the loudspeakers on 2 November in the afternoon we heard the voice of the Vareš Croatian Defense Council president. He called on people to go back to their apartments. He announced that there would be further announcements in the eventuality that we had to evacuate. You could see women and children in front of every building with their suitcases, blankets, and bags as they gradually went back to their apartments.

My mother stayed there in the front of the high school, hoping to see what would happen to her grandson and son-in-law. She never went home. I don't know how she found so much courage and strength, for she was frail.

I couldn't sleep. It was raining. About 2 A.M. a car drove through the town and announced over loudspeakers that the Croats should all evacuate. It wasn't the voice of the president of the Vareš Croatian Defense Council.

Three days before that, they had started pulling together all the Croatian inhabitants of the outlying villages and bringing them into Vareš. People started streaming out of the buildings once again. A neighbor whose parents lived in Pula, up in Croatia, came over sobbing. "I'd like to leave."

"Do you know where you're going?"

"I don't. I'm scared."

"Well, child, you should go."

I was afraid that they might be setting us up if we stayed alone in the building. I woke up my son and my sister's son who had been staying with us. "Children, let's go down to the school where the Swedish battalion is on guard."

About 3:00 A.M. we were out in front of the school. At dawn people were panicking and running around frantically. A Swedish soldier who knew how to speak our language a little said, "Now we are going to walk slowly over to Ponikve."

They were stationed by a saw mill in Ponikve, about a mile and a half above town in the hills.

"What about the prisoners? My son is in there."

People began to grumble.

"No, you didn't understand me. We are staying here. Another two transporters are coming who will escort you."

I didn't want to go to Ponikve, but my mother talked me into it. "You have to get that child out of here."

Croatian soldiers had locked up about 200 prisoners in the school when they withdrew. UNPROFOR soldiers broke down the school door on 3 November and went in, but they didn't release the prisoners because they were afraid of what the Army of Bosnia and Herzegovina might do when they arrived.

UNPROFOR told all the civilians to come to the school so that it could protect them from any hostilities on the part of the Army of Bosnia and Herzegovina before law and order could be established. There were people of all three nationalities at the school among the civilians.

Three corps of the Army of Bosnia and Herzegvina met at Vareš. It was chilly. My husband came out of the school, went to check on the apartment, and came right back.

Three days later, on 5 November, I came back to the apartment from Ponikve.

I was afraid to be alone at home because every person who set foot in the building was looting. I started to quarrel with them. The police were sent over to draw up an official record of the looting. Then I had the courage to think, "If I had to suffer with the oppression of the other side, I needn't suffer with my own oppressors." I did what I could to protect my neighbors' belongings but I couldn't. One brother couldn't protect his other brother's apartment. You could hold your own with the looters only if you behaved the way they did. At that point my husband was assigned his work duty in the forestry offices. They called me in to take part in an inventory committee at the company.

In April 1994 fierce battles were fought over Goražde, where my husband's whole family—his mother, father, brother, and four sisters, with their families—was staying.

My husband got drunk in despair and said something against the Muslim authorities. They immediately sentenced him to sixty days in jail. At the company, he was guarded by the military police even though he was a civilian. He had never served in any army, not even the Yugoslav People's Army.

I submitted an appeal to a judge who was not from Vareš. Time passed and nothing was resolved. I was told that the appeal had been sent on to the higher court in Visoko.

I went to Visoko and found the president of the court, who was a Croat, though Visoko was mostly Muslim. I asked him, "Has my petition for appeal gotten to you?"

When he had checked through everything, I received my answer. It had not. I went back to Vareš and asked the judge, "What is going on? I went all the way to Visoko for nothing."

"Ma'am, do you genuinely believe that he'd be released if we'd forwarded your appeal to Visoko?" the judge asked.

"It is your job to send them my appeal. Whether they will release him or not is no longer your problem," I said, angrily.

Immediately they sent my appeal to the Higher Court in Visoko. After three days the answer arrived. He was to be released immediately!

He had spent about forty days in jail.

Now we are not doing so badly, but the life we are living now is not even close to the life we used to live in the Yugoslavia I loved and can never put out of my mind. I still keep a picture of Tito in my apartment. I never took it down and as long as I live I won't. My uncles continue to live in Serbia. Before the war, I traveled all over Yugoslavia. I never felt like traveling abroad. I lived in the finest country in the world. How dared they take it from me?

OUT OF NOWHERE, A FEAST

TOLD BY LJUBIŠA MARJANOVIĆ

The Village of Rudice near Bosanski Novi

December 1996

I was born in a village near Bosanski Novi in 1976. During the war I was a soldier in the Republika Srpska army. Twenty of us were taken prisoner in combat near the town of Donji Vakuf.

As I threw down my weapons and went over to their soldiers with my hands in the air, I was anxiously waiting to see what would happen. They, however, behaved very decently, following all the rules of war. They gave us cigarettes and offered all of us brandy. No one abused or humiliated anyone. They did not even speak of the war.

They took us from the combat zone into Vakuf where we spent three days. There we experienced what we had feared from the start: we were beaten by other, unfamiliar soldiers who kicked and punched us and thrashed us with metal rods day and night.

We spent the next four days in *Bugojno where they maltreated us in a similar way.

In a state of exhaustion after the torture, we were transferred to a camp that was in Novi Travnik. There the first surprise for me was the man in

368

charge of the camp, Hamdija Krupić, a Muslim I had known from before when he was a policeman in the town of Bosanski Novi, which some now called Novi Grad.

The first days we were there I was beaten by a man named Azo, who didn't recognize me at all, and he was goaded to by a man I knew.

Just about when I thought I wouldn't be able to take the torture any more, Krupić called me in for questioning. Since we knew each other, I figured he would go on with the torture. But something quite unexpected happened instead: when I limped into his office, Krupić said to me, softly, "Sit down. I won't beat you, don't worry. I just want to explain what it is you have to say to the others when they question you so they'll let up."

He took out a cigarette and offered it to me. And then he gave me detailed instructions on how I was to behave and what I should say and not say in order not to provoke the rage of those who would question me. He didn't ask me anything at all. After his instructions, things got a lot better.

A electrician from Novi Grad named Đeđo appeared about that time. He would always protect me when he was on duty, and almost daily he brought me a pack of cigarettes, even chocolates. One evening he drew me aside, pushed a plastic bag into my fingers and said, "Here. Take this and keep your mouth shut."

I was afraid to look into the bag until I'd had a chance to hide. He had brought me a surprise: roast meat and cake! When I gave out portions of the rare meal to my friends, they kept asking me, "Where is this from?"

"Out of nowhere," I answered stubbornly.

There were several more times that this surreal scene was repeated. The next time I asked Đeđo where he was getting the food in wartime.

"We've been celebrating so I just take some of the extra off the table. Everyone is drunk, so no one notices."

A few days later, Đeđo invited me into his office. He was holding clean clothes for me. "Take this and go take a bath."

Two times in forty days were holidays for me thanks to that man. Those baths made me feel like a human being.

A week before I left, the ones who had been violent since the start extinguished their cigarettes on my face. That was the hardest for me because I knew that if I survived the war I'd be reading that inhuman handwriting every morning in the mirror for the rest of my life.

Another man, Adil, was on duty with Đeđo. He was my same age though we had never met before the war. Whenever he could he would call me in to talk. That was the time when he tried to give me strength by saying, "You must have the strength to last. This won't go on forever. When things get tough for you, think of your family waiting for you back home, and the joy you all will feel when you come back to them."

Before I left the camp he and I exchanged addresses.

I MEAN TO SEE AN END
TO THIS EVIL

TOLD BY MARIN POLJAKOVIĆ

Vareš

November 1998

I was born in 1950 in Vareš, where my father, a Croat, is from. My mother is of German background. I have friends who are Jews, Serbs, and Muslims. My wife is Catholic, because she chose the faith, but she is Serbian by birth, and was born in Serbia. We are still doing fine.

I started working for the biggest Bosnian employer in 1971 as an electrician, and went all over Yugoslavia, and even to Africa and Asia.

Immediately before the war broke out I flew home on the last Yugoslav Airlines flight from Tripoli. By then the Yugoslav embassy had closed. I took a different flight from Belgrade to Sarajevo on 23 March 1992.

My wife was taken to the hospital on 5 June 1993 by an ambulance from Vareš, through Pale. An Orthodox priest took her in and let her stay at his house, and found accommodation for the driver as well. The next morning he went late to his service in church in order to see her onto the bus. That man helped so many people. He used to be a minister in Vareš and had a lot of friends there.

In May 1992 I contacted the secretary for defense of the Vareš municipality, who directed me to Civilian Protection where people were working from all three ethnic groups. The members of Civilian Protection were not armed. All the authorities relied on them for their needs, particularly to call up the population to join the armed forces. It was chance that they didn't call me up, until the Army of Bosnia and Herzegovina arrived in Vareš. Then even they got me involved in Civilian Protection, which is where I was arrested.

While I was in jail, early in 1994, my closest neighbor, a Muslim woman, visited my mother, knitted socks for her and consoled her, "Don't you worry, Marin will be out soon. I pray for him every evening."

The units of the Croatian Defense Council forces had burst into Vareš on 23 October 1993 and stayed in town for twelve days. During that time no one dared move about the town, but Civilian Protection kept working and distributed bread to the local Muslims.

Members of the Croatian Defense Council forces arrested and took Muslims off to the hall of the secondary school in upper Vareš. There were more than 300 people being held at that prison. They let a few go after several days; UNPROFOR freed some of them on the twelfth day, and some of them were murdered when they were arrested. It was horrible to watch members of your own ethnic group committing injustices against another group. I was against it and helped as much as I could. We got a hold of UNPROFOR through the parish priest to help get people to safety. The chief of Civilian Protection was arrested at that point, and a Croat got him out of jail and hid him.

Vedran, whose mother was Croatian, came to me to ask, "What can I do? I have a cross tattooed on my arm, and my father is Muslim."

"Come with me," I said. I took him up to a second-floor bathroom, gave him a couple of cigarettes, and said, "Lock the door. I'll bring you something to eat as soon as I have a chance. If you hear anything suspicious, run."

Later Vedran left for Kiseljak with quite a few of the people of Vareš.

A Muslim came to the Civilian Protection offices to ask for help. I didn't know the man. The deputy chief asked me, "What should we do with this man? You'll have to hide him somewhere."

I took him down to my cellar and hid him there.

The people who were in touch with those in jail were able to do the most. Ilija wore a Red Cross band on his arm. He'd go into the hall and collect messages, which he usually handed to me. I could deliver the messages only at night, and a curfew had been introduced. I had to seek out the families that were hiding in the homes of Croats. I did manage to deliver about twenty messages. The horror lasted for twelve days, but it lasted forever for those who lost their lives.

People in town were trapped by the evil happening to everyone. The men were taken to jail, and their families intimidated, their money and valuables looted. The members of the Croatian Defense Council forces were the ones who did this, who had come from Kiseljak, Rajić, Grude, from different parts of Bosnia. There were about 300 of them. The people of Vareš tried to help one another. There were many Muslims taken care of in Croatian homes.

The Croatian units retreated, and with them evacuated most of the Croatian population. On that first day, in the whole Vareš municipality, which had numbered about 20,000 before, with 9,000 living in the center of town, about 750 of us remained. My mother stayed.

I continued my work at Civilian Protection until they arrested me on 24 December 1993. I must have gotten on someone's nerves, probably because I stayed in town, so they came up with a pretext: apparently I had allowed some people to escape from jail. My first day in jail it was proven that I had nothing to do with it, but I stayed imprisoned for seventy-three days. I was released on 6 March 1994.

The prison was run by the Army of Bosnia and Herzegovina. They kept me with Croatian prisoners of war who had turned themselves in, and we were held in the basement of a building in Vareš. There were more than thirty of us there. The prison wasn't registered anywhere. They beat me because I was a special prisoner. They probably needed to keep as many people as possible available for prisoner exchanges with the other sides. One of the guards, who didn't know me, gave me cigarettes whenever he could. Those who helped us feared their superiors, because they would be taken off guard duty if their help was discovered.

There were Muslims held in the next room. Hodžić was chained to a post because he had thrown a hand grenade when the Muslim forces came and stole his food. He killed and wounded a number of people. Many beat him and ultimately they transferred him to prison in Zenica. He was released from there later.

Some of the guards behaved very decently. Some of the prisoners wept when they saw guards helping them, but other guards maltreated them. Abuse usually began after midnight when the drunken Muslims summoned individual prisoners by name and took them off to be interrogated, where they beat them. They even accused me of taking part in torching the village of Stupni Do. They asked me, "When were you in Stupni Do?"

"I've been there three times."

"When?"

"First, when my friend Ibro was harvesting plums and pears to make brandy, and we went to help. Next, when he distilled the brandy. The third time when he bought himself a sofa."

When I was arrested, Beganović was in charge of security. Today he is the director of Vilka, who ordered me, "Take everything out of your pockets."

I took out my wallet in which I had two ID cards in Arabic, from Iraq and Libya, which, in fact, were residence permits and which I was keeping as mementos, as well as my own ID card and ten German marks. When he had looked over everything, he said, sarcastically, "Well, well, this sly fox has passes for every army."

Those documents saved my life twice. In late November, when the Army of Bosnia and Herzegovina entered Vareš, late one night soldiers banged on my door with white bands around their heads. I opened the door and saw only one soldier, who asked me, "Do you live here?"

"I do," I replied.

"*Eselamu aleich*," he tried to greet me.

"You've got it all wrong," I snapped, angry.

"What do you mean, wrong?" he asked me, astonished, as two others came over.

"You don't need the 'e' and the 'u' in the first word, and you cut the second word short."

"How do you know?"

I took out my Arab ID just as I felt a blow to my back that knocked me over. The other soldier said, "Get your paws off the man. Can't you see he's a mujahedin?"

Later they sent me to repair something as a member of Civilian Protection, where there was a unit of the Muslim forces. Two Muslims who took me up to the place suggested, "Look, better we don't mention your name. They are all mujahedin up there."

When we got there they all were praying. There were local Muslims and foreigners among them. I was done with what I'd come to do in a couple of hours. I had no problems, because I showed my Arab ID card and kept my mouth shut.

In April 1994, after I got out of jail, a man in a uniform knocked at my door. When I opened up, he said, "Praised be to Jesus."

It was Šefko, the friend of mine I'd been in Libya with. At that point there was a ceasefire in effect between the Croatian Defense Forces and the Army of Bosnia and Herzegovina.

"Where the hell have you been!" I exclaimed, overjoyed.

"I got here with my unit, so I came to find you."

We talked until dawn, and for the next few days he'd stop by with his comrades for a bath, because where they'd quartered there was no warm water. We spent the evenings remembering Libya and life before the war.

In downtown Vareš in June 1994 a man wearing an Army of Bosnia and Herzegovina uniform stared at me fixedly for quite a long time. He was wearing sunglasses. I didn't recognize him until he spoke: "Is that you?"

I embraced the doctor who had taken care of us for two months at a construction site in Zaire.

"Let's go have a cup of coffee and catch up with news," he suggested.

I had a better idea. "I'd rather not go to a café. Let's go to my mother's house."

While Mother rolled out pastry, we had our coffee and talked about our families and what had happened to us during the war.

He stopped by plenty of times after that and was a big help to my mother when she fell ill. He found a military vehicle to take her to Zenica and put her up in the hospital.

Mother later told me that everyone in Zenica looked after her, even though the doctors were mostly Muslims. She remembered very attentive nurses who were Serbian.

When the work detail was introduced in order to foster the wood-processing industry, an engineer asked me, "Would you like to work? No salary, no nothing, but it might perk you up a little."

We got the equipment up and running. I am still working today, as an electrician, running the machines. We have gotten salaries since 1995. No one gives me a hard time, since now the majority of the population are Muslims. Politics and parties cause trouble, but ordinary people work together just fine, just as they did before the war.

The people who were in prisons and camps during the war, like me, had the option of going abroad to live. There are things that keep me here. I mean to see an end to this evil.

A MAN AND THE WRITING
ON THE WALL

TOLD BY S. M.[†]

Mostar

November 1998

I was born in Mostar, but when I needed help, what with the war going on, there weren't too many people prepared to make that sort of sacrifice. It will make more sense if I say I am a Muslim and I was living in what we refer to as the west side of town where, after the war started, Croats mostly lived.

My daughter, who had only just come of age, was taken away in 1993 to some jail that wasn't registered anywhere on the books.

In August of that year I asked a friend of mine, a Croatian man, to help me get my daughter out. He promised he would introduce me to a man who could. But then he didn't show up when he said he would. His brother came instead and asked me if I knew where the man was.

"Haven't any idea. I'm waiting for him, too," I answered, worried.

His brother went out to the front lines to search for him and found him dead, next to a trench. We never learned who killed him. He helped so many people.

My daughter was later saved, thanks to the goodness of a complete stranger who felt sorry for her and got her out.

A friend, a Croatian man who heard I hadn't left Mostar, came over to the house with food packages at a time when there was no food to be had anywhere. He wanted to know how he could help me out and whether I needed money.

On 30 June 1993 the Croatian troops collected most of the Muslims and took them off to the camp at the Heliodrom. That same day the Army of Bosnia and Herzegovina entered Bijelo Polje. It seems to me that there had been some sort of a deal going on over our heads between the Croatian and Muslim authorities trading who was going to be in charge of Bijelo Polje for who was going to be in charge of Mostar, and that we ended up being the victims of the trade.

Eight men came into my house, armed to the teeth. They asked for my wife's ID and saw that she was Croatian. My obviously Muslim name was all they needed to say I would have to go with them for an "interview." They were strangers to me, who had come from out of town. There was a bus parked in front of the building and we all had to clamber in, while they shouted at us and cursed.

I will never forget the horrific atmosphere down at the Heliodrom, where they were holding 10,000 people who had been taken from their apartments just because they were Muslims. It was sickening to see the buses keep pulling up with new prisoners.

In the classrooms of what used to be the Military Academy at the Heliodrom I ran into a lot of friends and people I had never until that moment known to be Muslims. We had lived in a city where until the war your name had not been a measure of your worth. Almost all the prisoners at the Heliodrom were Muslims. Here and there you could find a Serb who had tried to conceal his friends so they wouldn't be taken away. I saw fourteen-year-old children there and men as old as ninety. They hadn't let anyone bring their medications with them when they were brought in; the people suffering from illnesses were fainting.

That first day when I got to the camp there was a lot of harassment going on.

The next day some people I knew from before were brought in. They were from the lower part of town. One of them was a friend of mine, a Croat who had offered to help me.

He told us to quiet down. "Look, we have to live together. I don't know what is going on here. But calm down. There is no point to all of this. You must be patient and see what will happen next."

He saw how many sick people were there and advised us to demand to have a doctor in to see them. He fought to set up a medical commission that got hold of the medications people needed. They returned people who suffered from heart problems and diabetes to their homes. Of the 10,000 prisoners, they let 153 go who had some sort of medical documentation on them at the time. Some of them had the misfortune of being picked up a second time and brought back to prison. It all depended on what neighborhood you lived in, and what group was "operating" where you lived. Some of them left and went to another country because by then the "export" of Muslims from Mostar was already running smoothly.

At that time of year Mostar's famous heat wave always hits. Out in the open, temperatures climb up over 100 degrees Fahrenheit. The classrooms we were being held in were designed to seat about thirty students. There were 150 of us in each room. We had to sleep in shifts because there wasn't enough space on the floor. We spent three days like that. They released me because of my illness.

I met a nun at Caritas, one of the Catholic relief services, who had served abroad. She had a big heart and a marvelous spirit. She helped me out, and plenty of others, despite my Muslim name. She was especially thoughtful with the elderly, who could no longer look after themselves. She didn't care what their background was. What mattered to her was that they needed help. They all got the same treatment. I met her through a Croatian woman I'd known who was going around to visit the elderly and the seriously ill, mostly Serbs and Muslims, who needed medicine, care, and attention.

In May 1994, a month and a half after the fighting stopped, the first packages, thanks to the efforts of Zoran Mandlbaum, president of the Jewish Community Center, began to come over from Mostar's west bank to the eastern side of Mostar where mostly Muslims lived. They had been sent to us by Muslims, Croats, and Serbs. More than thirty trucks crossed over at that point to the other side, for seven days. It was the first humanitarian aid that made it over into eastern Mostar, where people had been starving for months.

In the fifth month of the conflict between the Croats and the Muslims, when it was at its worst, I happened to see a neighbor of mine, a Croat, sitting in front of the building, and I went out to chat with him. Thirty feet from the entranceway another neighbor, Mika, was repairing his bicycle, as always, in front of his doorway. He had taken it upon himself to warn his Muslim neighbors if something dangerous was up. So he'd sit out there all day long, tinkering with his bicycle. Just after I'd taken my seat to chat with the neighbor, three young men armed with daggers pulled up in a car and jumped out.

"Are there any Muslim scum here?"

Mika glanced quickly over at me, and then said, "Not a one. We shut them all up at the Heliodrom."

Everyone knew it was me they were looking for. I walked right by my Croatian neighbor, slipped him the keys to my apartment, and hid at his place. Through the curtains I saw Mika, who had saved my life with those words. He could have lost his own life saving mine. Whenever the thugs couldn't find someone Muslim, they'd make do with a Serb. They took a vote. Two were against the idea of picking up a Serb.

One of them even said, "We don't need Serbs. Serbs have it hard enough as it is, just being Serbs. I wouldn't be in his shoes for anything. What we want is a Muslim."

They went off to another building, looking for a Muslim on whom they could vent all their hatred, and only then did I fully understand the graffiti I had seen at the Rondo traffic circle in large letters: "Thank you, Mother, that I am not a Serb." It is still there today.

Mika, poor fellow, helped so many Muslims during the war. He always ended up in the wrong place at the wrong time. He saw so much and knew so much. He was there when they killed his wife, who was a sister of one of the better known people of Mostar. They took Mika away and no one has seen him since. We've never heard what happened to him.

A PROMISE KEPT

TOLD BY NIKOLA JOVANOVIĆ

Modriča

December 1996

I am forty years old. I lived in Modriča until the war broke out. I was taken prisoner while the war was on, as a member of the army of Republika Srpska, on 12 July 1993.

While they guarded us, fighters for Muslim-Croatian units behaved very decently. During the transport to prison in a van, we were brutally beaten by two policemen.

The abuse and beatings continued at Gradačac. We worked at hard labor, shaved bald, all day in the sun. We were given only one meal a day.

There were many of their prisoners in the jail who had been arrested around town when they got drunk, partied, and shot off their guns. They were beaten by the guards, too, and looking at them, I wondered, "If they are that rough with their own, what will they do to us?" The voice of a guard interrupted my reverie, "Don't worry, we won't hurt you."

Still, we lived in terrible fear.

While we paced around the jail yard, it sometimes happened that a prisoner, a Muslim, would come over to console us, saying, "If they move you to the Tuzla jail you'll be better off, because the conditions are better there and they won't work you as hard as they do here."

The local people who worked at the prison behaved much more decently with us than the strangers who had come from other places. I knew some of them from before the war.

One day, a dentist named Živko, a Serb, came to the jail on some sort of business. Circumstances had kept him in Muslim territory. We had known each other from before the war. When he noticed me, Živko nodded discreetly and walked by.

The next day a policeman, a Muslim whose nickname was Tom, came over to me when no one was watching, and tucked a pack of cigarettes into my pocket. I looked up at him, surprised.

"This is from Živko. He asked me to bring you cigarettes, and I agreed, but under the condition that only the three of us know about it."

I asked him, "Were you a policeman before the war?"

"No," he chuckled, "I used to smuggle foreign currency. Where did you live in Modriča?" he asked me.

When I explained where my home was, we figured out he knew a lot of the people on my street. There were Muslims and Croats among them who had moved to Gradačac when Modriča became a Serbian town.

The next day several Croats and Muslims who used to be my neighbors came to visit. The first visits astonished me. Later I learned that Tom had told them where I was.

One of these visitors was a goalie for the Red Star soccer team. Later he played soccer for Skubica. We were good friends before the war. When he saw me, he started to cry, and said, "When everything is so absurd, I guess it's better that you are here than killed."

We talked about what had happened to the people we knew. As he was going he left me cigarettes, and promised, "When I go to the front I will let your family know that you're alive and well."

When I got out of prison I learned he had kept his promise.

* * *

A man named Paljica, who had worked in Gradačac before the war, was in prison with me. A lot of people knew him, and plenty of his colleagues came to visit. Paljica's uncle, who had a flower shop in the quaint, old part of Sarajevo, used to come to visit, and he'd always visit with me, too. He brought us cigarettes.

A neighbor of mine from before the war named Bekan, who ran the Bosna Café, also brought me cigarettes, and whenever he left, he'd say, "After the war we'll all live together the way we used to."

Two months later they transferred us to the central military prison in Tuzla. We were in total isolation there. When we arrived there were eight of our military prisoners, and the prison was full, because there were people serving terms there who had been arrested before the war.

At first we got three meals a day, but later they gave us two. They stopped allowing us our obligatory walk. We had no work detail here. Sometimes the Muslims, also prisoners, came to our door and talked with us. They were always saying, "Now we hate the Croatian side much more than you Serbs."

One day Professor Mersad Galicij stopped by the prison. He was a Muslim who was chief of the Gradačac police, and he told us, "All the Chetniks have been released from Tuzla. I expect they'll release you any time now."

Three months later I got out of jail through an exchange of prisoners.

A SCHOOL FRIEND

TOLD BY ZDENKA KNEŽEVIĆ

The Grbavica part of Sarajevo

November 1998

I was born in 1938 in Bijeljina, where I spent my childhood. My mother is Polish, and my father a Croat. I graduated in Sarajevo from a school for geodesy, got a job, got married, and had a daughter named Ivana who turned twenty in 1992. We lived in the Grbavica part of Sarajevo.

We were all surprised because none of us believed it would come to war, until the first days of May when the war broke out. On 9 May Ivana crossed the Miljacka River with friends to go around and see her crowd, and to see what they were up to. The next day, as we'd agreed, I went off to meet her and come back with her. I brought no money, or any of my medicine, which is important because I suffer from thyroid problems; I had nothing with me but my ID card. I found her at a friend's house, where we spent the night. The next morning we headed for Grbavica to cross the Vrbanja bridge, but you couldn't cross it because it had been shelled. We headed then for the Brotherhood and Unity bridge. You could hear shooting from the vicinity of the mechanical engineering school. Suddenly, Ivana dropped to the ground as she was walking, and said, "Mama, I've been hit!"

I got her to the first tree along the promenade, and we hid behind it. The first bullet had gone through her purse, the second passed through her belly. Her pants were all bloody. I called out, helpless, "This child is wounded! Help!"

No one reacted. Soon a truck came by that picked up garbage. It pulled to a stop near us. A driver and the garbage man, a gypsy, were in the cab. They were about thirty years old. As if God had sent them. The gypsy got out and asked, "What happened?"

"She's been hit by a sniper."

"The dog probably won't shoot at me," said the gypsy and ran across the street to get to us. He took Ivana in his arms and carried her, running, across the street and helped her into the truck cab. I jumped in, too.

"Woman, why did you cross over here?" asked the driver.

"I couldn't get over the Vrbanja bridge."

"Don't you know that no one gets over, because the snipers always shoot? We couldn't cross there because they are shooting from the Marshal Tito barracks so that's why we came this way."

They were scared, too.

The emergency room was closest, but you couldn't get to it across Vojvode Putnika Street because they were shooting from the barracks. So we went to Vrazova, where the doctor cleaned the wound and sent her to surgery.

"We must operate immediately on your daughter. The bullet went right through her gut," Dr. Pelagić told me and hurried into the operating room. The operation lasted for hours. When it was done, the exhausted doctor concluded, "The bullet injured her small and her large intestine. We have done all that was humanly possible. She is young. For now she is doing fine. Her youth is what we are counting on. We'll have to see how she pulls through. We'll take her to the postoperative unit. She'll wake up in about five hours. Come back after 5 o'clock."

No one at the hospital asked us about our ethnic background. Although we are Croats, you can't tell that by our first and last names. The people were extremely generous, despite the difficulty of the conditions; there were a lot of wounded people there, and not enough food or bedding. Ivana spent two days in the postoperative unit. Once they'd moved her to intensive care, she was lying naked on her bed. A Muslim woman, who had also been wounded, got up from her own bed, took off her nightgown, and covered Ivana.

I realized when I stepped outside the hospital that I wasn't sure where I could go. Wherever you went in town, you could get shot at. I had no relatives, there was no way to get back to Grbavica . . . I remembered an old school friend, Halida, who lived up on a hill overlooking the hospital in a neighborhood called Breka. I had last been to see her ages before, only once, when her mother died. My clothes all blood soaked, I rang at their door.

"What happened to you," Halida said, shocked, when she saw me.

"Is it all right if I come in?"

"Whatever happened?"

"Ivana's been wounded."

"Come in, please do come in," she was so shocked she could hardly speak.

I spent the first two days there. When Ivana moved into intensive care there was a free cot next to her, so I asked the doctor if it would be OK if I could stay in the hospital. "May I sleep here? I live off in Grbavica. I can be of help to you and my daughter."

The doctor let me stay in the hospital. Halida gave me a nightgown, a blanket, and clean sheets. By the seventh day Ivana could eat stewed fruit and drink tea. There was no food at the hospital. I asked Halida, "Can you help?"

"What do you need?"

"There is no food at the hospital, and Ivana would love to eat something light if there is anything."

"Here, it will just take a moment. Sit down and catch your breath," Halida answered warmly and went into the kitchen.

"Ivana will be getting out of the hospital in a couple of days. I don't know where to take her. We can't get back to Grbavica to our place."

"Stay here with us."

It was, in fact, ten days before we left the hospital together. Halida and her husband put us up and we spent the next month and a half with them. Ivana and I had no money. Halida and her husband supported us, although their son was ill. They shared everything with us. We didn't dare leave their apartment because there was so much sniper fire everywhere. I managed to let my husband know by phone that Ivana had been wounded.

"Try to send us food if you can, and bedding, clothes, and money," I asked, knowing it would be impossible.

"I can't even leave the building, they are shooting so much," he answered, miserable.

Luckily, a friend from his job called. Her daughter was leaving Sarajevo. When she heard what had happened she told my husband, simply, "Ivo, send them to me. I have plenty of space."

In early July I rang at Melita's door. I had to introduce myself because we'd never met. I asked her, "Is your offer still good?"

"Come right in," she grinned.

We stayed with Melita for three months. We didn't have a penny to our name. We got a small amount of food from humanitarian aid. Melita brought home three of Ivo's salaries and we used them to buy food.

When I heard they were organizing a group of wounded, ill, old, and disabled people to leave Sarajevo through the Red Cross, I went and signed up Ivana, who needed to leave the city with me as her escort. We had been waiting from July to November to leave Sarajevo.

Two thousand people got into a convoy on 11 November that set out for Belgrade, and another one just as large left for Split. We chose Split as our final destination. It took us ten hours to get to Kiseljak, traveling through countless checkpoints. We arrived at dinnertime and there was food on the table. The starved children from Sarajevo were shouting: "Look, there's bread, there's salami, there's bananas!"

After peace was declared we came home.

My husband served throughout the war on a work detail. He dug trenches on the first combat lines. When he brought food to the others who were digging, he passed a house where a boy lay who had just been murdered. A relative of the boy's came running over and kicked my husband because he felt my husband was one of the enemy. The father of the boy who'd been killed stopped the relative. "Leave the man alone. He did nothing wrong."

THE TUNNEL

TOLD BY ALEN POKRKLIĆ

Sarajevo

October 1998

I spent three years in the Army of Bosnia and Herzegovina, in Sarajevo, at tasks that did not require the bearing of firearms. My sister happened to be out of town in May 1992 when the fighting began, and for a full three years I had no word from her. When she managed to get in touch with me, I learned that she was working in an international organization in different places.

I was overjoyed when she announced she'd gotten married in the town of Makarska on the Croatian coast. I could tell by the name that my brother-in-law was a Croat.

We kept hoping, in Sarajevo, that the war would end with the next political agreement. Hunger, the cold, and so many victims among the people I had loved kept me very high strung. Knowing that my sister was well and that she might be able to help me out only sharpened my desire to get out of Sarajevo, because I could no longer see an end to the suffering.

The tunnel that had been dug under the airport, no matter how dangerous, was my only chance, but you had to keep going if you made it to the end alive. My brother-in-law, whom I'd never met, understood how I felt. When he heard, he said, simply, "Look, try to make it as far as Konjic. The rest is up to me."

I got a hold of some papers through a few friends, at least to get me through the *tunnel. Then I typed up a travel request for a business trip to Zenica, and stamped it with a stamp I found somewhere.

Once I was on my way to the tunnel, all I had aside from my ID card were those papers in my pocket. I was wearing jeans and had a large mountaineer's backpack, which loomed over my head. As I stood at the entrance I saw a lot of soldiers; some were leaving town, others on their way back. They were all of them exhausted, worried, nervous. None of them passed up the opportunity to ask, "What are you taking that backpack for? How are you going to get through the tunnel with that?"

I was afraid of talking to them, because I was not on military duty at the time, and I was scared, since they were irritated, that they would make me join them fighting some battle; there had already been too many deaths in Sarajevo and I did not want to fire a gun. I muttered the occasional few words, and luckily, they were far too preoccupied with their own problems for me to attract their attention for long.

The tunnel was just over five feet in height. It was so narrow that even two children would have had trouble squeezing by one another. The ceiling was propped up by metal rods, and I was warned they were sharp, so lifting your head up suddenly might be fatal. With that backpack I could only get through by crawling.

Off we went. The soldiers with their hands in their pockets, and me with that big backpack. I joined into their lines, although I had no idea how much the tunnel twisted. They were in water and mud up their knees. I knew it would be a bad idea to stand up because the whole line would have stood up behind me. I made my way along on my hands and knees, and came out drenched and mud soaked.

People were often shot coming out of the tunnel at either end. I was lucky that they didn't fire at me when I came out.

I made it on foot into Hrasnica, the neighborhood nearest the tunnel, where a friend was waiting. I spent the night at his place and in the morning he drove me to a hill. "Go uphill until you come to a checkpoint. Hitch a ride from there," he said as we parted, and left before I could ask him if he had any idea what it meant to me, after three years under siege on three little streets, to contemplate that, with a little luck, I might be able to get a ride for a full thirty miles.

My thoughts, and my feelings, were in total disarray. I found myself amazed at the thought that I hadn't sat in a car these last three years, and now I was supposed to hitchhike! My first question was, How do I get to the checkpoint?

Just then a group of boys interrupted my thoughts, pestering, in unison, "Pay us, and we'll carry that backpack for you!"

"How on earth could you carry it when it's bigger than you?" I asked one.

"Easy. I've been practicing. I do it every day, and I make money at it, too," the boy answered readily, and got the job.

I cared more that he show me how to get to the checkpoint than I did that he was carrying my backpack.

"How old are you?" I asked him as we climbed through a meadow where there was nothing we could hide behind.

"Twelve," he replied easily, just when the whistle of a bullet forced us to drop down into the grass. Automatically I reached out to pick a dandelion leaf growing by my nose, and then laughed and said to myself, "You don't have to pick weeds anymore for food, now there will be things to eat."

"Hey, do you have a smoke?" the boy asked as we lay flat again.

"Wait 'til we get to the woods and I'll give you one."

"Those guys are feeling peppy today," the boy said, looking toward the hills from where Serbian soldiers were shooting.

We finally made it to the woods and the boy got his hard-earned cigarette. He left me a few minutes later at the checkpoint and ran back to find his next customer.

That day there was a lot of shooting, so no one was driving on the road. It became clear, something I was dreading, that I might have to sleep in the woods.

So I was completely thrilled when a driver with a pickup truck gestured for me to jump into the back, without even fully stopping the truck. I managed to toss first my backpack in, then clamber in myself. Two springs were frantically bouncing around back there to the truck's rhythm while he made his way along the gravel roads and the dirt roads cut through forests. I spent two hours lunging about the back of the truck trying to avoid a dangerous encounter with the springs. "The shells didn't lose you your leg in Sarajevo, let's hope these springs don't smash it now." Still I was ecstatic to be out of that hell. I think I would have been every bit as happy if there had been five springs in the truck.

The driver stopped at the first military checkpoint, in the Igman foothills, but he didn't report I was there, and I was lying down the whole time so they didn't spot me.

The battle with the springs continued all the way to Pazarić, where I jumped down from the truck and made my way through the military barrier, because the guards were busy with other things.

A young man came over, "Need a cab?"

"Indeed I do," I answered, delighted.

"How far?"

"To Konjic."

In Konjic I found a good friend whom I got drunk with that night. He told me, "Your brother-in-law has been here asking about you and said he'd be back to pick you up tomorrow."

I spent that night at my friend's and my brother-in-law woke me the next morning with the words, "Get dressed! We are moving out of here now!"

He explained to me as he sped in a jeep toward Mostar, "We are going straight to Međugorje. A man I paid 1,000 German marks to for the service will take you into Croatia from there."

The heavy black clouds and the pouring rain and dense fog helped hide me from all manner of checkpoints on the road. We made it to Međugorje without a single stop. As we were about to enter the café where my sister was waiting, my brother-in-law told me, "You mustn't show any sign that you haven't seen each other for a long time. No kissing or outpouring of emotion."

The encounter was extremely odd: we tried to behave as if we'd last seen each other a half hour before. We each had a cappuccino and chatted about meaningless things, and all the questions we had been storing up for one another we kept to ourselves.

I was pulled away from the comfortable security of the conversation with my brother-in-law and sister by the worried look of the man who had come to get me. I had to leave with him. With no good-byes I walked out of the café and into uncertainty. The stranger threw me an ID and a list of background information such as what my name was, where I was born, and who my mother and father were, which I had to memorize in case someone stopped us and asked. We crossed the border without stopping. He flashed his high lights at the border guards, whom he clearly had made previous arrangements with. No one stopped us all the way to Makarska in Dalmatia.

My sister and brother-in-law drove me to his summer home the next day. I spent the next year recovering in the Croatian coastal resort town of Baška Voda. That was where I really got to know my brother-in-law, and met the woman who became my wife.

A LAST NAME SAVES THE DAY

TOLD BY STANA ZDILAR

Banja Luka

December 1995

Fifteen years before the war broke out, I was living in Sarajevo with my husband and three daughters. I worked as a production metallurgy engineer at a factory. During that time we had friends and acquaintances in all three ethnic groups. Until the war, Sarajevo had been a city where no one paid attention to one's religious background. It would happen that on Catholic Christmas, for instance, a Muslim, a neighbor of ours, came to wish us a Merry Christmas. I thanked him for his wishes, and explained that we weren't Catholic.

Our last name is unusual and sounds more Croatian than Serbian, so my husband wasn't bothered during the war by Muslims or Croats, but it did happen that some Serbian fighters led him off to be executed before a firing squad, even though he, himself, is a Serb. Luckily, the confusion was cleared up just in time.

The building where we lived stood right next to the airport. It was right on the line of demarcation from the start of the war. The Serbian barricades ran right along our garage, and on the other side, toward the airport, was a passageway controlled by the Muslims. Snipers from both of the warring sides were shooting constantly. For days at a time I couldn't get down to the garage to bring up firewood in order to heat the stove and make dinner or warm the apartment. The first four months of the war we couldn't go into the street, or even move safely about within our own apartment building. We spent most of the time with our Muslim neighbors in the cellar.

There were never any divisions among us. We never had coffee without them, and they didn't have coffee without us. We shared all our food, while we had it. They were never hostile toward us. The neighbors even turned off their television so that the anti-Serbian rhetoric wouldn't make us feel bad. During our long stays in the cellar, the smokers were stuck with no cigarettes, and they'd roll up tea and smoke that.

Once when a neighbor, a Muslim woman who had left her apartment and gone to stay with a relative in Dobrinja, another part of Sarajevo, came back to take the food from her deep freezer, she was brought there by a cousin who fought in the Muslim Green Beret forces. She came down into the cellar and gave my husband a carton of cigarettes.

Our building stood in something of a no-man's land, but because of the proximity of the Serbian and Muslim barricades it looked likely that one of the two armies would ultimately take it over. So we had a system worked out. If the Muslim army arrived, one of the Muslim neighbors would answer when they knocked. If the Serbian army were to come, I was supposed to open the door. And so it happened. One day Serbian soldiers appeared at the door and asked me, "Are there any Muslims living in this building?"

"Naturally," I answered.

"We're going to kill them," they growled.

"No you're not. Those people have done no one any harm. We've been down in the cellar together all this time and we've helped each other out," I told them.

The day before there had been no shooting, so a married couple, our neighbors, went back up to their apartment. The Serbian soldiers suggested we should evacuate. We were talking down in the cellar because there was shooting going on outside.

"Please wait a bit longer. I need to bring down my neighbors. They are up in their apartment but they should go, too," I explained.

"Are they Muslims?" one of the soldiers asked me.

"Yes, they are," I answered, looking back at him.

"You must be crazy! You could get hit just because of them," the soldier snarled.

We left the building with our neighbors, following the soldiers. In all the excitement I left behind my bag in which I had all our valuables and documents. There were a lot of dead bodies on the streets from the shelling, so we had to hop over the corpses and run to the airport. Almost without thinking about what was happening all around us, we made it to Ilidža, another suburb of Sarajevo. They offered us a place to stay in Ilidža, but I couldn't imagine setting foot in a place where other people had lived and using their things. My husband was extremely ill and completely exhausted at the time, so they took him to Kasindol Hospital. They couldn't treat him properly there. He had leukemia. So they sent him to Belgrade where, sadly, he soon died.

My parents and brother, who lived in Duvno, were freed from a Croatian camp in that city through an exchange of prisoners. I found them in the town of *Sanski Most on 30 June 1993. The Serbian government gave us the use of an abandoned house with no doors or windows, and we began to repair it slowly.

My father was ninety at the time. He was completely exhausted by the torture he had suffered in the camp. My brother was tortured by electric shock and beatings, and he couldn't lie down for a month and a half, so he slept sitting. Our family house in Duvno was looted and torched. None of us had any income. All of us were out of work.

Our next-door neighbors in Sanski Most were Muslims. They saw we had nothing, so they'd give us a bucket of potatoes, beans, cabbage, whatever they had. They kept cows and every other day they'd bring over some milk.

The Serbs would stop by and ask, "Do you have enough to eat?" But none of them ever brought us anything.

The neighbor saw we had no firewood, so she brought that, too. While we worked in the garden, they would always come over and help.

When the Serbian authorities took control of Sanski Most, our neighbors had to leave. They came to say good-bye, and said, "We would like it best if the cows could stay with you."

The Serbian government broadcast over the radio that everyone who was moving out, and had livestock, ought to hand it over at a certain place. The authorities knew we had no livestock, so I was nervous about accepting our neighbors' lifesaving gift.

"I'd be glad to take your livestock and take care of it, but I'm scared that you might get in trouble for it. Better leave them in the barn."

When they left, the Serbian authorities came by immediately and took the livestock. Three weeks later we had to leave Sanski Most, too. That day I realized what the power is of a media war. I listened to the Serbian news all morning where they kept saying that the lines of defense were stable and that there was no fighting going on. While the speaker was saying this, the shells began to fall, and then the Muslim forces entered the town. We barely managed to get out of there alive.

I believe that our neighbors came back to their home in Sanski Most.

LIVING SIDE
BY SIDE IN TUZLA

TOLD BY ILIJA JURIŠIĆ

Tuzla

November 1998

In 1993 Tuzla was in an acute state of siege. We could only move about the city proper, which resulted in terrible starvation, and people were literally dying of it. I saw the elderly from the old people's home going through the garbage cans at dawn in hopes of finding some remnants of food. The joy in their eyes when they found a morsel was terribly sad.

I've known Hasib since 1977. He is from the town of Brčko in eastern Bosnia, and I am from Tuzla, which is more centrally located. Both of us were teachers, principals of schools, and then went to work in the organs of internal affairs, where first one of us and then the other worked as the other's boss. We retired at the same time, and when the war began we both of us volunteered to defend Tuzla. We were inseparable for decades.

We were part of the armed forces, but this didn't help us get hold of food, because there simply wasn't enough to go around. Days went by when all we could do was complain and comfort each other. In those terrible days reserve soldier Jusuf appeared at our office. He was working in the nearby village of Koraj at the time, and today he is a displaced person in Ćelić.

"Have you got anything to eat?" he asked us.

We were delighted someone had even thought to ask.

"We come by a little here or there," we said softly, embarrassed.

"Do you have any corn?"

"That's an abstract noun for us," we said spontaneously.

"Would you like me to bring you some if I can still find it in Ćelić and Koraj?"

"That will be too much for you in these difficult and nasty times. It is only human to admit to you that we haven't any. But if you should come up with a kilo or two, we would be very grateful," I told him.

He said nothing, and left soon after. A few days later the on-duty police officer informed me, "A package has come for you and Hasib. Come and pick it up."

We were astonished. A besieged city, no one could get out. Where had this package come from?

"What sort of package?" Hasib asked me.

"The times are so crazy, you don't think it's explosives, do you?" I answered.

At the doorman's cubicle we found a tied sack with a tag on it: "I am sending my friends corn so they can give it out to others, Jusuf."

There were about sixty-six pounds of corn kernels in the sack! A real wealth! We were confused, as if we were taking something that wasn't ours to take, and happy that our friend had thought of us. We hauled it by foot, because there was no gasoline, the eight miles to Božo's mill, dragging it on a sled across the snow, our treasure. There was no electricity in town, so you could only grind corn into flour at a mill.

While the mill rocks ground down the kernels into lifesaving flour, we figured how much would be left once the miller took his part. In the middle of our calculations, Božo interrupted us, saying, "There, it's done. I won't take my part. I see that you are good people and that you are in a difficult situation. It was an honor to help you out. Time for lunch!"

I leapt up and kissed him. It was incredible. Why, that man had given up almost seven pounds of flour, practically gave it to us! And what's more, he invited us, who'd been starving, to lunch! And he'd never even met us before.

We hurried back to town to delight our loved ones, taking care not to overturn the sled and spill the flour. Out in front of the sports center we ran into Alma, the wife of our colleague. Their daughter had been on a sled that had been hit by a car and she fractured her hip. She was lying in bed at home in a cast.

"Where have you two been?" Alma asked us.

When she heard all the things we'd been through that day, she burst into tears. "I'm on my way to see my brother," she said in tears. "I have nothing to bring him, because I have nothing myself. I'm so worried about him. He has no food or firewood . . ."

As she spoke, both of us simultaneously remembered an incident when their son had hidden a piece of bread under his pillow before he went to school, saying that he was afraid his sister would eat it while he wasn't home.

Hasib was the first to open his sack, and said, "Alma, take half of what is here."

Between Orthodox Christmas and Serbian New Year of 1994, while people were starving in Tuzla, and two pounds of sugar or a quart of oil was worth fifty German marks, I set out with Hasib and three other friends to visit Mijo, who lived in a village a good twenty kilometers outside of town.

We brought him a package with a little flour, oil, sugar, and coffee. When we got there we found he had laid out a wonderful table with all kinds of delicacies we hadn't seen for who knows how long, like cheese, *kajmak, eggs, and smoked meat.

Šljivo was a man who ran a restaurant that served game and that was open on and off during the war, and he arranged with Mijo to buy a ram from him. We all went out to help him catch the ram. The host chose two, and told us to butcher them both. "One for the restaurant, Šljivo will pay for that one, and we'll cut the other up into four parts," he said, simply.

"As we were leaving, Mijo, at his mother's signal, brought up a crate of apples, which seemed bigger at the time than any I had ever seen. His mother told us to take as many as we wanted.

We all of us pounced on the apples. You couldn't tell who was grabbing for more.

Hasib was in Mijo's house for the first time. I was surprised when the old woman pulled him aside. They were very conspiratorial. After we got back to Tuzla, Hasib told me that she had said to him, "I have known Ilija for ages. I am meeting you for the first time but I see that the two of you are inseparable. I feel uncomfortable asking Ilija, so I'll ask you. Do you have enough oil and lard at home?"

"I wouldn't be telling the truth if I told you that we do," Hasib answered.

"I'm going right down to put a little lard together for the two of you, but don't say a word to the others because I don't have enough for everyone," she said and packed us up each a pound of lard.

When the war was over my wife, two friends of ours, and I went to Hungary. On the Hungarian side we were stopped by police, who, seeing from our passports that we were from Bosnia, said that some people wanted to talk with us. They took us into a room where there was a mixed international team with a translator inquiring about public opinion in that part of the country. They explained to us that we had been selected as a group and they asked us if we would answer the question, voluntarily of course: "Is it possible for different ethnic groups to live side by side in Tuzla?"

"You are holding our passports in your hands, which you took from us without our permission. If you look inside you'll see that we are Ilija Jurišić, a Croatian man; Stoja Jurišić, a Serbian woman; and Atifa Kunosić, a Muslim woman. If we can drive side by side in a car, why couldn't we live side by side at home?" I answered.

THE MAN WITH A HAT ON HIS CHEST

TOLD BY L. S.[†]

Banja Luka

October 1995

To be born in Banja Luka and spend more than half a century here is to belong to it heart and soul. This is a city you couldn't help but love before the war, even if you were only passing through. Scattered around the banks of the shimmering, clear Vrbas River, it was a focal point for a number of different cultures and folklores that gave it its special feel. The faiths of Islam, Catholicism, and Orthodoxy were refracted in Banja Luka, as in a prism, and they illuminated it with light of all hues and all kinds of sounds.

The horror that, for all people of broad minds, struck this part of the world did not, sadly, bypass my city. Fortunately, we were never on the frontlines, but we felt all the other hardships that go with war.

During the swing to nationalism it was difficult if you were not, by birth, a member of the ruling majority. Although I was in that thankless position, I know full well that it happened in all the other towns of star-crossed Bosnia and Herzegovina. Work details were introduced everywhere, and I was included in one, despite my serious illness. My task, with my master's degree, was to clean the streets. There is no way to measure humiliation, but judging by the reactions of my fellow townspeople, and all of us knew each other, it seems to me that it was harder for all the honorable and normal people in the town to watch me cleaning the street than it was for me to do it. At that point it was dangerous to be out in public and greet someone who was not of the true faith. I watched my acquaintances and friends, when we ran into each other while I was at my new job, to see how they would behave. I never allowed my reactions to be inappropriate in terms of theirs, for their sake rather than for mine. If someone looked away when he saw me, I'd pretend I hadn't seen him. If a person mustered the courage to nod his greetings, I would respond the same way. If someone greeted me aloud and came over, I would greet him back. There were very few who had the courage to stand and talk with me.

I remember the day a colleague and friend saw me, for the first time, wielding my broom. He was an honorable man with a generous nature. He was in a hurry at the time, but without a second's hesitation he came straight over and began, "Hey, there. It would be silly of me to ask you how you are doing. I'm at a loss . . ." He struggled to find the right words, and found it harder and harder. I interrupted.

"Look, don't worry on my account. I'm fine. Imagine how rough it is for Serbs in Zenica."

He merely nodded, his eyes to the ground so that I wouldn't see the sheen of tears.

As I shoveled snow, a woman who knew me went by in a fur coat. She looked away and walked by me with hurried steps, even though the going was slippery. I said nothing and kept working. She went another twenty paces on, stood there, and after a few minutes, came back. She took off her glove and offered me her hand, saying, through her tears, "I'm so sorry. At first I didn't have the courage, but we cannot go on living like this . . ."

Ever since the day the Ferhad Pasha Mosque was blown up, every morning at precisely 7:00 I see an elderly gentleman, a native of Banja Luka, a man of the Orthodox faith, who, as he walks by the place where the mosque once stood, a spot of leveled ground, stops, doffs his hat, and, holding it to his chest, stands in silence for five minutes, bows, and slowly goes about his business.

Those who could not bear to watch my humiliation managed, after a year and a half, to have me moved from street cleaning to an office job. Every morning, my friend comes smiling into the room where I work with him. He asks, "How are you?" now because now it doesn't sound so ridiculous any more.

You must believe me, who spent a year and a half with a wheelbarrow and a broom on the streets of Banja Luka, that the people in this city deserve a better life.

I WILL NOT LEAVE MY TOWN

TOLD BY RATKO PEJANOVIĆ

Mostar

November 1998

I first saw the light of day in Mostar in 1944. All my ancestors going back 200 years were born there. I got married when I was twenty.

From the moment the war broke out, I felt it my obligation to remain in my city with my people. That feeling that they were a part of me overpowered all else.

The war found us confused, unprepared, as it probably did most people. Because I am a Serb and my wife is Croatian, there were two periods when we didn't suit anyone.

I worked as the leader of a fire brigade in town.

I left eastern Mostar on 11 May 1992. The Serbian police had issued a warrant for my arrest, with the explanation that I was an Ustasha, because I had moved the equipment and people over to the other side of town, and, of course, there's the fact that my wife is Croatian.

The members of the Croatian Defense Council forces who greeted me there and received me adopted a decision to have me removed as leader of the fire brigade, because as far as they were concerned, I was a Chetnik! My wife and I experienced all the stations of our nation's cross.

When the conflict broke out with the Croatian forces on 9 May in the morning, I was at my job, at the fire brigade in eastern Mostar. Because of the amount of work we'd had to do, I hadn't been home in six days. The city was burning, and in a single day we'd have seven or eight interventions. The shells that fell did not stop the firemen. Five of our men were killed, and fourteen were wounded while they were conscientiously doing their duty. On the seventh day, between two fires, I managed to slip home for a moment. I would never have made it even then had I not been in a traffic accident and bruised some ribs.

They informed my wife I'd been hurt, and, anxious, she set out to find me. We met about 150 feet from the house. I had never seen her in greater disarray. Even when she went to fetch water while people were dying in the streets, she would always be tidily dressed and fully made up. That was how people lived in Mostar. Defying death.

As soon as we stepped into the house, a neighbor of ours, a man named Mirza, who was a Muslim whom I'd known for ages, appeared at the door. The two of us had grown up together in this town. While my wife, Jela, was making our guest coffee, Mirza said, "Look, Jela, over on the other side of the river Croatian troops are picking up all the Muslims. We've decided we'll start picking up Croats on this side."

"Mirza, what are you saying?" Jela stuttered, confused, and dropped into a seat across the table. The atmosphere was sickening. We all sat there in silence until she burst into an angry tirade.

"Mirza, you should be ashamed of yourself! So you wouldn't stand in front of me to protect me the way my Ratko would protect your wife, Gara?"

"I didn't mean any harm," Mirza said, quickly retracing his steps. "What are you getting so worked up for? You'll go to jail for a week, and I'll see to it that you'll be back as soon as there is an exchange of prisoners."

Then my temper exploded. I told him angrily, "This is disgraceful! You are hardly offering her ten days' vacation in Hawaii! You are offering her prison, where some idiot might take it into his head to break her back!"

Mirza left, angry. We stayed sitting there, speechless. Jela burst into sobs, inconsolable.

I didn't know whom to turn to. Nor did I have much of a sense of whether the local government was working or not. For a while in this part of town there was no authority in charge at all. The civil government wasn't working, and the army had not had time to take shape. The Mostar battalion was not yet a part of the Army of Bosnia and Herzegovina. I wasn't sure where I might find support and understanding. I would have thought I could trust my neighbor Mirza until that morning, but it became clear that I was not a very good judge of character. In this war it became clear that many people clambered to success over corpses. It was the pathological side of human life.

As I wracked my brain thinking of whom to turn to, I decided to go and talk with my neighbor, Juso, who was chief of military security. At one moment I felt ashamed, going to him. Our common friends, who worked with him, saw me waiting outside and let him know. He stepped out of a meeting.

"Is there anything wrong, Ratko? Trouble?"

"Juso, I don't know what to say, where to start," I mumbled, embarrassed.

"Start from the beginning."

"Mirza, our neighbor and yours, stopped by my apartment," I started, and told him in a tumble of words what had happened.

"Who is out picking up Croats?" Juso was astonished.

"I don't know who is picking up whom and why. I saw that they were expelling Muslims from the western part of town. But I didn't know that you'd be doing that on this side. I was so surprised."

"Look, Ratko. Slow down. Tell me what happened piece by piece."

When I'd calmed down a little I told him the whole story.

"Wait for me here," he said, and went running off.

I didn't know where he'd gone or why. A half hour later he came back, "Go home and tell Jela to put on the water for coffee. I'll be right there. I went to see the chief of police and told him that tonight by 6 o'clock I want to have on my desk his statement and the statement of the man who troubled you, so I can see who is cooking up what with whom, and what they are up to."

My wife was waiting for me when I got back, her eyes swollen with crying.

"Calm down, Jela. Juso will be here in a minute. Put on water for coffee."

Juso came to the door minutes later. He called, laughing, "Where is that Croatian woman, we've come to arrest her and take her away.

"No one will be bothering you again. If someone should come by, call me. You know where to find me. I will arrange for a patrol to watch out for you," he said as he left.

Stolac

Sad to say, Juso died that year in July. His wife and children were expelled from western Mostar. Now they live in Germany. His mother is old and frail. Amid the chaos she lost her only child, and now she is alone. Jela and I looked after her until a relative arrived with his family, and they took over her care. We still visit her from time to time.

In October 1993 Jela and I had all the documents we would have needed to move out of Mostar. Our daughter has been living in Hamburg with her uncle since 1992. She wrote us a letter of guarantee so that we could get a visa. I wrote her back saying that I didn't want to leave my city, because it is my duty to fight for it in my own way, along with everyone else, for a better tomorrow. And Jela refused to move away and to go off to live in a foreign land.

THE MOST LOYAL
COMRADE-IN-ARMS

TOLD BY ZDENKA KRUNIĆ†

The Grbavica part of Sarajevo

October 1998

Through the opening of what we used to call, in more normal times, a window, a ray of sunlight shone in and nudged me to look out at the street at a rare moment of quiet. No one was out on the streets of Grbavica in June 1992 unless he had to be, always hurrying, usually running. From the building across the way, from her entranceway, Dana ran out and down the empty street. She stopped suddenly, retraced her steps, stared at the pavement, stood on something that she'd seen, and, after a few moments when she looked left and right, leaned over and picked up what she'd covered with her shoe and continued down the street at the same pace, until she disappeared into the middle entranceway. That odd scene lodged itself, unexplained, in the corner of my memory.

The months of war went by, when I'd see her from time to time, as she hurried, a tray in her hands, on which she was carrying bowls. She was always in a rush . . .

It never occurred to me that more than a year later, with my carefully expressed concern, I would stumble on her secret. "Where are you always going, when you know how dangerous the shrapnel and the snipers' bullets are? Every day I see people who weren't so lucky when they tried to run across a street. You live alone and I can't understand why you are tempting fate."

"During the first days of the chaos, my neighbor, a Muslim woman whom I only knew by sight, came to me and, sobbing bitterly, told me, 'Something terrible has happened to me. I can't speak of it. I have been abused so badly that I have to leave Grbavica. Can I ask you to look after my husband until I come back?' I thought this was for a short time, that she wouldn't be gone for more than a couple of weeks. The war took its toll, she couldn't get back, and I am here with that man . . ."

As she talked on, I couldn't tell what was worse in Grbavica, to be a Muslim or Croat, or to be a Serb who was helping them . . .

"That man, he is an intellectual. He is smart and he is a good man. He is sixty-three and suffers from multiple sclerosis: his lower extremities are completely paralyzed. He relieves himself in a potty on his seat. You know I worked as a nurse until I retired. It isn't hard for me to look after him, and I can't leave him alone. That would be a sin," she continued, softly.

"How do you manage for food?" I asked her, because all of us were more hungry than we were full.

"One way or another. My son is in the Republika Srpska army. I share between us whatever he brings. Whenever he comes, he goes over in his uniform to shave the gentleman . . ." She paused for a moment, and then went on, "The poor fellow also loves to smoke. I know that it's hard to believe, but I go out and pick up cigarette butts that I find on the street, when no one is watching. When I collect enough of them I shake out the crumbs of tobacco and roll it in newspaper. He craves cigarettes. When he smokes he's happy . . ." I believed her, but she didn't know that only now did I understand the scene I had watched so long ago.

"It was pretty bad last winter. Four or five times a day I'd bring him over whatever God sent my way. It would happen that out there in the dark, on the snow and ice, I'd be slipping along with the tray to his entranceway and the snipers would be shooting. It was worse when a shell would explode nearby and I'd lose hold of the tray. I'd spent a half hour groping in the dark to collect at least the dishes and the keys. When I'd get to the apartment he'd see by my expression that something had happened, and he'd ask, his voice warm with understanding, 'What's wrong, my child?'"

When she said, "He reads a lot, book after book," I knew that all the books she had borrowed from me and the other neighbors she had taken to him.

In the autumn of 1994, Dana told me what happened the night before. "A Muslim woman lives across the hall from me. At midnight I heard loud noises from her apartment. I heard men's voices threatening to rape, beat, and murder her. I slipped off to the police station in the rain and reported that someone was maltreating my neighbor. The on-duty policeman told me, 'Go hide. If they find out who reported them, you will be in big trouble.'

"The police got there before I got home. They had to break down the door to save her. The terrified woman stayed with me that night and the next. Around 7:30 in the evening someone rang at my door. When I opened it I saw three men armed to the teeth. They had the Chetnik insignia on their caps, and ammunition belts full of rounds on their chests, and long daggers in their belts. They asked me, 'Do you know who reported us last night while we were in your neighbor's apartment?' There were Muslims living in the two neighboring apartments. I thought, if I tell them it wasn't me, they will torment innocent people. I told them calmly, 'It was I who reported you.' When they asked, 'Why?' I answered them with a question, 'Why should you murder her? She is a human being, too.' 'If we didn't murder her last night, we'll murder you tonight!' one of them said, and the other pulled out his dagger. 'So, go ahead and slaughter me! What are you waiting for?' I shouted so that all the neighbors could hear. They shoved me into the hallway of my apartment, shouting, 'Why stick your neck out, what business is it of yours?'

"'I am not afraid of you. If you kill me, the three of you will die, too,' I answered brazenly.

"'What makes you think that?' They were surprised.

"'There are ways. Time is on your side this time because my son isn't here. He is fighting in the same army you are, but he has never done anyone any harm. If he couldn't help, at least he did nothing to hurt. All of Grbavica knows how many people he has lent a hand to,' I spat at them defiantly, because a person has only one life. I was afraid for my neighbor, who had hidden inside the apartment. Luckily they didn't come in. Instead they retreated when I mentioned my son. They were ordinary thugs who had come to loot, abuse, and murder people." With that she ended her story.

What had been Dana's secret, for me, was known by a lot of people in Grbavica. I realized that when I heard women on the street who called loudly to each other as Dana passed by them, her head held high, "Hey, look at that woman, a maid to Muslims!"

One afternoon Dana talked about her patient with sadness: "He showed me pictures from his album. He said, 'Look Dana, here I was in the army. There is a Croat on one side, and a Serb on the other. There were no differences back then.'"

"I know. There are still people today who don't care about someone's first and last name," I stammered, to comfort her.

She took a deep breath, and went on: "His wife cannot get in touch with him. Now he feels so terribly lonely, because my sister is ill and staying with me and I'm taking care of her so I don't have enough to time to dedicate to spending with him. A few days ago he asked me to get a hold of a kitten for him. I found a skinny little kitten out in front of the entranceway and I brought it to him. He was overjoyed and immediately became attached to it. He has called it Tommy. Whenever I come over I find Tommy lying on his chest and purring, and he is patting it."

Dana looked after him, tended to his needs, and fed him for twenty-eight months. His wife finally found him through the Red Cross, which allowed him to cross over the Miljacka River into Sarajevo in late 1994. When he left he made Dana swear that she would look after Tommy, who is, still today, the largest tomcat in all of Grbavica; it weighs nearly sixteen pounds.

Dana received a letter from Sarajevo dated 17 October 1994.

My dear comrade-at-arms,

I had to wait for someone to set off on the last stage of their journey so that I could write these words, because that is, after all, the quickest way for the letter to reach you. How is your health, my dear, and does your back still trouble you? How do you spend your days and nights? How are the master and the lady . . . She, poor woman, put up with quite a lot from me and showed herself to be noble and unselfish. I can see her before me now, pretending to be anxious that Tommy might run over her feet. Of course, everything that everyone did to help me was because you were in charge. Because over me (after the good Lord) my Danuška was watching over me, taking care of my every need . . .

My dear comrade-in-arms, it is so strange here without you. I would love to know whether our friends managed to find the connection they were hoping for. Write me a few lines. The best way to send them is with someone who is crossing over. I will never get over the fact that I couldn't bring my lovely books with me. Please give my regards to everyone I know there, and I send you, my comrade-in-arms and wonderful friend, greetings and boundless affection.

M. G.

M. G. died in Sarajevo three months after he left Grbavica.

After reintegration, when so many Serbs abandoned Grbavica, Dana told me, "I have lived here for fifty-eight years and I will never leave. This is where my grandfather and grandmother, parents and sister are buried. My whole life is in Grbavica."

YOU ARE A DISGRACE
TO SARAJEVO!

TOLD BY ŠABAN EFENDIĆ[†]

The Grbavica part of Sarajevo

November 1998

I was forced by the Serbian police in Grbavica to join a work detail in late May 1992. We were assigned to a variety of jobs. It was nicer to chop wood for a woman who had two sons in the army than it was to dig trenches at the front lines. The army was in a state of anarchy, so individuals did what they pleased, and the police tried to maintain some semblance of order.

My Serbian neighbors were ashamed when they watched what the other Serbs were doing, and they helped us in any way they could. I ran into Milan at the front door to the building. He was summoning all the tenants to a meeting. I asked him, "Should I go and get my father, too?"

"No, you needn't get your father," he answered.

My first thought was, So the Serbs are starting to hold meetings here, too! I was nauseated, and felt crushed and miserable that I was alive to watch all of this. I was a Yugoslav in spirit; I had been raised that way for thirty-eight years. I went into my apartment but couldn't muster the strength to tell my father what I'd been through.

416

After an hour the doorbell rang. Father went to the door and brought Milan in. He started explaining from the doorway, "We have just held a meeting of the retired people in the building. We've decided that we will set aside part of our pensions for you because you aren't getting your pensions from Belgrade the way we do. We were all of us officers in the Yugoslav People's Army and what is happening is not right. Here, this is your part."

Father received an amount that was larger than what his neighbor, a Serb, received for his pension. I was overcome with shame for doubting these people, and they had given me back my faith in life.

I spent the two summer months working off my obligation chopping down trees in the woods. They assigned people who had family in Grbavica to this task, which went on near the line of separation between the Muslim territories and the Serbian territories, saying, "You are free to run, but know, if you do, that your families won't survive."

It was heavy, difficult work, because I had never held a chain saw before. We cut down trees from dawn to dusk, and loaded them into trucks until 11 o'clock at night.

We were guarded by Serbs who had chosen not to fight at the front. They were punished by being stuck with us on a work detail. If that was a punishment.

While we worked they helped us out. The first few days they were suspicious because they'd been told we were prisoners of war. We had to obey every command to the letter. Mirko, a sentry, asked me after a few days, "Where were you taken prisoner?"

"They came to my apartment and took me out to do this, if that is being taken prisoner."

"Liars," he spat, in a rage. "They told us they took you prisoner in combat somewhere!"

"They didn't. Man, I've never held a gun in my life."

He was touched by what I'd said and we got along just fine. It happened once that Mirko was felling a beech tree and suddenly realized that the tree would fall right where he'd put down the guard rifles.

"Hey, Šaban, be a friend and run over there and move the rifles! The beech will fall down and smash them all!"

I ran over and brought him an armful of guard rifles.

That same evening we were coming down from Jahorina in the truck when one of the guards remembered, "Oh, now, where are those rifles? We've left them all up in the woods! We've got to turn around right away and get them. They'll kill us all down there if they see us coming back with no rifles."

We went back and all of us looked for them together, fumbling around the woods in the dark with only flickering flashlights to guide us. Once we'd collected them all you couldn't tell who was the happiest among us.

The man in charge was Captain Rosić, who asked us once, "Are any of you from mixed marriages?"

For a laugh I said that I was.

"What's your mother's name?"

"Nura."

"A Muslim?"

"Yup, a Muslim."

"So, what's your father?"

"My father's a Muslim," I answered, grinning.

The Captain was very serious at first, and then he burst out laughing. He spent that whole day with us and was very decent.

Once some Chetniks barged into our apartment and took off with a carton of cigarettes, some cooking oil and flour, and they ordered me to bring our television set by 6 o'clock that evening to an address they gave me.

"If you aren't there with your TV at 6:00, we will be here at 6:30 sharp," they warned, and left.

I had to seek the help of a friend of mine named Dane who worked high up in the police.

"You go straight home and don't worry about a thing. Don't take your television set anywhere. I will take care of everything," he told me.

That evening no one came to our door, and the next day Dane brought back everything they had taken from us.

I wasn't afraid to go out into the street in Grbavica, though all my friends, policemen, cautioned against it. They told me not to show them my ID card if I was stopped in the street. I was to tell whoever stopped me I was a Serb, or say I'd forgotten my ID at home, because then they'd have to bring me into the police and that way I'd stay alive. Otherwise there was no telling what might happen.

In July 1992 I went out to the marketplace in Grbavica. Around 7:00 A.M. a truck came from Bijeljina with peppers, tomatoes, onions, and other vegetables. I was fifth in line at about 6:30. After a few minutes there was only one woman in front of me, who had already paid, and there were some thirty people waiting behind me. Out of nowhere three armed men appeared.

"Let's see your ID cards."

I decided not to follow my friend's advice, thinking that by daylight, in front of all those people, they wouldn't do anything to me. I gave them my ID to inspect. When he read my name, the Chetnik howled, "You filthy Muslim! I'm supposed to be feeding you?"

He threw my ID onto the street, shoved me out of line and struck me. None of the civilians did anything. They were shocked. The men took two more elderly Muslims from the lines, "Out of line you go!"

When they'd moved on, the woman who had been in front of me stepped out of line, picked up my ID, wiped it off with her sleeve and handed it back to me, saying, "Son, come right back in. Forget those fools."

Then all the people who happened to be there and saw it all shouted together after the three armed men, "Get lost you thugs! You are a disgrace to Sarajevo!"

Dane bumped into me in the street, and asked, "Having any trouble? Anyone bothering you? If your life is threatened come right over, no matter what the time of day or night."

He took me by the hand over to a building, and pointed to an apartment on the third floor. "I'm living here, now. So if you need anything you know where to find me."

One morning I came in at 5:00 A.M. to find my mother sobbing. She told me how the night before three armed Chetniks had burst into the apartment, and couldn't make up their minds whether to slit her throat and my brother's, or to throw them off the fifteenth floor. Luckily they were saved by the police, who had been summoned by a Serbian neighbor. I realized it was time to go to Dane for help.

"You've got to get away. The place is teeming with scum and someone might kill you. I am against all this. I am fighting for some sort of Republika Srpska, and I am some kind of Serb, but I don't fight the way those scum fight. If someone at the front takes up a gun and shoots at me, I shoot back. That's my kind of war. Look, go home. Don't worry. I'll take care of it. I can't get you out tonight, so come by my place tonight, spend the night, and we'll cross over tomorrow."

On my way back from his place I ran into Ljubiša, a neighbor. He saw how awful I looked, and asked what had happened.

I told him the whole story. He insisted we go back to Dane's together.

"Dane, they can spend tonight at my place."

He moved us into his apartment and brought in seven hand grenades and several rounds of ammunition.

"Here is a hand grenade. If they figure out you're here and try to break in, I'll shoot as long as I have rounds and grenades. They can only get to you over my dead body. If they kill me, you know how to activate a grenade. Leave a spare just in case. It is better you kill yourselves than you fall into their hands."

He looked after us for two nights and a day until we were able to leave Grbavica.

Ljubiša lives in Sweden today. Both of us are overjoyed with every phone conversation.

It was the autumn of 1992 when we crossed over the Vrbanja Bridge, thanks to Dane's help.

My new neighbor asked me to buy some homemade brandy from someone for his daughter's birthday. A quart of brandy cost 100 German marks at that point in Sarajevo, so I preferred to go out of town and buy it for twenty. My neighbor gave me fifty marks. I earned a full thirty marks! I went right out to a street vendor selling *ćevapčići* to get some for a treat for my nieces. I was seventh in line. I looked at the sign, which said that a portion of *ćevapčići* cost twenty-five German marks. The girl who took orders waited to hear what I wanted.

"Two portions, please, wrapped in paper."

The *ćevapčići* vendor was reading the paper on a corner, drinking coffee. Just then, not too far away, a shell fell. He jumped and hissed, "Damn their mothers! Serbs like that should have their throats cut!"

He infuriated me. I said, "So, why aren't you in Grbavica right now slitting their throats? Plenty of Serbs there! Easy for you, sitting here making money, while other people die. You'd be like a chicken with your head cut off up there! I bet you'd like to slaughter all the Serbs in Sarajevo singlehandedly, you creep! Who are you that you'd slaughter all the Serbs!"

The people standing around the cart exchanged silent glances. I was the first to get my *ćevapčići* and go.

I walked over to my sister's, who lived near the Markale open market. They were across the street from the headquarters of *Ramiz Delalić Ćelo's brigade. The little girls, who were watching for me at the window, shouted joyously, "Here comes Uncle! Uncle!"

I waved to them. The soldier guarding the entrance to the headquarters across the street heard them calling me, crossed the street, waited until I was near him, shoved his gun into my ribs, and demanded to see my ID.

"So, hero, do you have your military papers?"

"Sure do."

"So you are Šaban Efendić, are you? How come those girls called you using the Serbian, not the Muslim, word for uncle?"

"What business is it of yours what they call me? Those kids speak Bosnian. Who cares?"

When he saw I wasn't afraid of him, he took a step back. "Hey, don't go getting sore about it."

This was trouble. A man stepped out of the building the soldier had been guarding and asked what was going on.

When I explained, he had the soldier replaced and said to me, tersely, "Sorry."

The little girls still shout "Uncle, Uncle" when they see me, and it doesn't bug anyone any more.

THE HODJA'S HUNDRED GERMAN MARKS

TOLD BY SLAVICA RISTIĆ

Refugee from Gradačac, interviewed in Modriča

December 1995

I was born in 1952 in Tolisa, in northern Bosnia. I lived in Gradačac from 1971 with my husband and two children, and when the war came we were expecting our third. My children were scared of soldiers, so I took them to my parents' house in a nearby village. We all thought we wouldn't be separated for long. People said that fighting would never break out in Gradačac.

The first time the town was shelled by Serbian forces on 14 July 1992, I was at my job. I worked as a grocery store cashier. I saw a Croatian journalist and an Arabic man through the store window who were starting to film the city with a TV camera ten minutes before the attack. That evening, Croatian television showed the footage, and the next day a Muslim soldier I knew by sight warned me that I should change the name on my service jacket.

Before the war we lived in a building with five apartments. After the first time the town was shelled, Croatian civilians started using the shelter in the building where we lived, and we found shelter in a cellar where Serbs were hiding. The Muslim and Croatian police registered us there, warning us that by the third evacuation all Serbs would have to leave town, because anyone who stayed behind would be detained. The Serbs were being taken from town to an isolation center that was in the village of Donje Srnice.

Our friend, a Croat, came one day and told my husband that someone had reported to the authorities that we had a secret radio transmitter. Now everyone suspected us of communicating with the Serbian soldiers who were besieging the town.

"What could I possibly be telling them, that's what I want to know!" my husband asked, surprised.

"Apparently they figure you're telling them where to shell. Be careful. I've heard rumors you are to be killed."

We moved from shelter to shelter every night, in fear, until one day a couple of policemen found us. I recognized them. One of them used to work for my company. They took us off to a hill where a jail had been set up in the basement of a school. The warden of the jail, a Muslim who had been a high school teacher before the war, questioned us for three days. They left my husband in jail, but didn't harass him, and this Muslim was so decent about it that he even kept him supplied with cigarettes. Other policemen questioned me.

"So why didn't you leave town?" they asked angrily.

"The first night we spent in the shelter someone looted our apartment. They took away our TV, what jewelry we had, and some of our furniture. We didn't have money anyway. Food is so expensive, a quart of oil costs thirty or forty German marks, so we've been selling all the rest of the things from our apartment in order to survive," I told them through the tears.

"Why are you crying?"

"It's so hard for me without my children. I haven't seen them in ages, and I don't even know where I'll be when I go into labor."

One of them took a picture of a little girl out of his pocket. "I left my daughter in Croatia somewhere," he said, with sadness. Then he turned to his driver. "Take the lady to her apartment so she can pick up what she needs, and then drive her to Donje Srnice."

After fifteen days of questioning, they transferred my husband to that same village, and after that we were always together, though we still weren't with my parents and our other children.

My time was near. Our biggest problem was how we were going to make it to the hospital, which was in Međeđa, a couple of miles from the village where we were staying. There was no fuel anywhere; the people from the territorial defense forces had taken all the fuel there was in our villages.

We lived near a wealthy farmer named Steva, who told me one day, "Don't you worry about a thing. I have a little gasoline stored away just so that I'll have it when your time comes and I'll take you to the hospital."

The birthing place was in a private home in Međeđa. I heard that Dr. Asim, a Muslim, was working there. He was originally from down in Montenegro. I was a patient of his before the war, so I was happy to have him be my obstetrician, knowing that I would be safe in the hospital if he was there.

Dr. Asim welcomed me warmly. He was by my side the whole time. When he heard the baby cry, he announced, "Congratulations on your healthy baby boy!"

The next day he congratulated my husband when he came to bring me and the baby home.

I came back from the birthing place in Steva's car to Donje Srnice, a town where Serbs and Muslims were living together, afraid of the shelling. Before the war Donje Srnice was purely Serbian and Gornje Srnice purely Muslim. The war and fear of the dangers drew people of different faiths together, because they felt safer that way.

The next few days, my Muslim neighbors all stopped by to see the baby, according to old village customs. They congratulated me and said that he was a fine-looking child and nicely developed.

We spent two and a half years in that village. We longed to be with our other children and lived in the hope that we'd manage to make our way to

Serbian territory. We signed up with the Commission for Exchange. The commissioner was a fellow by the name of Safet, a Muslim who had worked as an attorney for my old employer. One day he stopped by with several members of the commission. A *hodja [teacher] was with them. I was so glad to see Safet, hoping he'd be able to help us, but he was curt. The hodja, a man we'd never seen before, was by far the heartiest of all of them.

"I worked in Brezovo Polje," he announced, to strike up conversation.

"I have a relative who is married to someone there," I answered.

"What is your relative's name?" the hodja asked. When he heard the name he smiled.

"Ah yes, I remember them."

Then he fell silent for quite awhile. He saw that a cooking pot was on the empty table. We had been eating nettles. As he got up to leave the house, the hodja shook hands with my husband and slipped something into the palm of my husband's hand. The hodja looked him right in the eyes and said, "Well, my man, may your son grow up to be a fine fellow."

When they left, my husband opened his hand, and we saw he had given us twenty German marks!

We saw the hodja once more. We went to lodge our protest with International Red Cross representatives who were touring the area. We told them they were refusing to exchange me and my baby. When he saw us, the hodja came right over and said to my husband, "I have heard you are from Šekovići. My family, wife, and children were saved by a Serb, a man named Duško, when Šekovići was attacked by the Serbian army."

When we left, my husband and the hodja shook hands again. This time, he left my husband 100 German marks!

I often think about the goodness of that man Duško from Šekovići who came around to our newborn son through the hodja's handshake.

Even after two and a half years the Commission for Exchange refused to allow us to transfer over to Serbian territory. People who tried to sneak across illegally mostly didn't make it. Steva paid some Muslims to help him and his wife and son cross over, but the people they'd paid killed all three of them to steal their belongings. Many lost their lives trying to pick their way through mine fields.

My longing to be with my children overcame all fear, and we finally made it over, one night, in the pouring rain. I was holding the baby in my arms. We crossed through the mine fields following a Croat who took us through for a sum of money we'd settled on.

COLONEL RISOJEVIĆ'S PROTECTION

TOLD BY MILE JOSIPOVIĆ

The Village of Žabari near Banja Luka

January 1996

There were about 4,000 Croats living in the Ivanjska parish until August 1995. There are only eighty left now. The village of Žabari used to be all Croatian. After the Storm military operation in eastern Croatia and western Bosnia that expelled all the Serbs from their homes, a three-member commission came around to all the Croatian homes on 14 August 1995. They ordered all the local Croats to leave their homes by the next day. There were buses arranged to take us to Croatia. I ran into the members of the commission outside my neighbor's house just as they were explaining all this to him.

"Where are you taking him? Can't you see the man is ill?" I asked.

"He'll have to leave," they answered tersely.

"So does this mean that all of us will have to leave our homes?"

"Yes. Where is Sekula's house?"

We went together and met him at the stream.

"Thank God we've found ourselves a Serb," they told him. They took him aside. After a few words Sekula came over and said, "Mile, you are safe.

You are a retired army man. No one will touch you. You can go home freely."

Then Jozo, a teacher and a close friend of mine, stopped by.

"All of us are leaving tomorrow."

"But you can barely walk. Can't you stay?" I asked.

"They aren't letting me. My mother is in terrible shape. Can I leave her here with you, if the authorities agree to it? I am afraid she'll die when we are on the road."

"Of course you can leave her here."

The next morning my wife and I packed three bags of food and the basics and took them to Jozo. We took him to the station. We waited for the bus all morning. Jozo collapsed. He was seriously ill. We took him back home. His own home had already been looted.

All the Croats left town on 17 August. My friend with his dying mother left, too. Zora was the only one left. She had serious psychiatric problems. She wasn't capable of looking after herself. They ordered me to take care of her, and to move her into my house.

There were Serbs I knew living in the next village over. If it hadn't been for them we would have been expelled, too, by the third day, or murdered. The Serbian refugees from western Bosnia were ruthless.

Boro and Slobodan were officers in the Republika Srpska army. Boro came to inquire, "Would you like to stay, or will the two of you be leaving as well?"

"We don't want to go," we answered.

"If that's how you feel, then stay. These are my soldiers. We will be close at hand."

Two days after that, Slobodan stopped by. "Look, you are free to stay. We will protect you."

They brought a Colonel Risojević to our house, and he quartered fourteen soldiers here. My wife cooked for them and did their laundry.

They were nice to us. They brought us firewood and chopped it for us.

When Serbian refugees tried to have us kicked out, they came to our aid, day or night. They even went around the neighboring houses to tell people to leave us alone.

As soon as the local people left, someone from the neighboring village who had been in prison for three years in Croatia brought two unknown women to Žabari to pick a house for them to move into. They first picked a neighboring house, and then the next day came to my door. One said, "My son was killed in the war. I want to move into your house."

"I've made the house available to the 2nd Krajina Brigade. You will not be able to move in."

They went off disgruntled, threatening that I'd have hell to pay. When Colonel Risojević heard what happened, he took out a pencil and paper without a word, and wrote, "This house has been requisitioned for the needs of the 2nd Krajina Brigade." He signed it and I tacked up the note on the front door.

On 17 November I went off to visit Vlada, a Serb, who was eighty-four years old. He was living in my friend Jozo's house.

"Sit down, Mile. Have you done the autumn butchering yet?"

"No, Gramps, I haven't."

"Better not."

"Why, Gramps?"

"I hear that they are planning to rob you."

"Let them rob all they like. They can steal but they can't take my soul."

"Mile, look. You are a good man. I feel bad for you. You'll be murdered. There is a man named Anđelko who wants to kill you."

When the soldiers heard that, one of them went off to the nearest telephone to inform Colonel Risojević. He came in a minute and went off with me to Vlada's. Vlada didn't see well, so he asked me, "Who is that with you?"

"Colonel Risojević, Gramps. He is the commander in charge here."

"Ah, if I could only see General *Mladić I'd ask him what he thinks to do about these ailing old Croats. Does he agree with the idea that they all be killed, slaughtered?"

"Gramps, is it true that Anđelko is planning to murder Mile?" he asked Risojević.

"Sorry, son, it is true."

"Thanks, Gramps."

At the door, Risojević told me, "There is going to be a soldier on duty every day at your house."

Recently the soldiers admitted to me, "We stopped Anđelko out in front of your house armed with an ax three times when he was on his way to kill you."

This was a man I'd never seen. All I knew of him was that he was a refugee with a strange disposition.

An elderly Serbian woman lived up on a hill in an abandoned house over the village. Her closest neighbor, Franjo, a Croat, brought her firewood and stoked her stove, and I brought her food every day. On 20 November when I was on my way to bring her food, I stopped by Franjo's. I found him all bruised. He'd been beaten. "What happened?" I asked.

"They broke into my house last night. They beat me up and robbed me. I can't get up onto my feet, so I wasn't able to light her stove this morning. Please go help her out."

When I came into her house, the old woman was lying on the floor, uncovered and almost frozen. I hadn't the strength to lift her up onto the bed so I went off to get a neighbor, a Serbian woman. I asked her to come with me. When we got the woman into her bed, two shepherds happened by.

"This woman's suffering is a disgrace to us all. Your cows and sheep graze her land, but none of you has so much as brought her a glass of water or a piece of bread. For the last three months I haven't seen a single Serb up here seeing to her needs, except Sekula and his family," I said.

They all left without a word. I stayed to get her fire going. She was unconscious, slowly dying. She died two hours later. I lit a candle for her soul.

I asked Luca, a widow, whose husband had died in combat, "The old lady died who lived up on the hill. Can you help me? My wife has to cook for the army."

We bathed and dressed the deceased. We tidied one of the rooms and I brought in four stumps. On them I lay a door and we laid her out on it. The next day two Serbs and I dug a grave. We buried her and prayed to the good Lord. That evening we made a dinner and invited Boro and Slobodan. All of us raised a glass to the old woman's soul, may it rest in peace.

TOUCHED BY
HUMAN KINDNESS

TOLD BY ABIDA BJELICA

The Grbavica part of Sarajevo

November 1998

I lived with my husband in the Grbavica neighborhood on the outskirts of Sarajevo when the chaos started in May 1992. Our daughter,
Snežana, was living up on Koševo hill across the Miljacka River, which runs
through Sarajevo, and we couldn't get to her because the snipers shot the
bolder people who tried to cross the bridge. She had a baby during the war.
Our other daughter was living in Oxford, England.

The suburb of Grbavica came under Serbian control, and though my
husband is a Serb, it was tough for me as a Muslim. My brother happened
to be visiting us at the time, and for four months he didn't dare step out
into the street.

The Muslim snipers took potshots at me from their positions on Hum,
whenever I went out onto my balcony, assuming that if I lived in Grbavica I
must be Serbian. A Muslim neighbor of mine was killed that way. The snipers
were the real criminals, regardless of whether they were Serbs or Muslims.

A friend of mine, a Muslim woman, who was an old maid in her sixties,
was raped in a neighboring building. Young men in their twenties abused

433

her all night long. After that she didn't dare sleep at home, and no one would take her in. She came to me, her face wet with tears. "Bida, I'm scared to be alone in my apartment at night."

"Look, stay here with me. If they are destined to murder us, so be it. Sleep here."

As a war victim from the previous war, she received a disability allowance of twenty-five German marks per month.

An elderly woman, eighty-three years old, confessed to me that four Serbs first robbed and then raped her.

At first they were after only Muslims. Then they started maltreating the Croats. For men, the work detail was the worst. They brought men to the front lines along the Miljacka River to work, while Muslims from the other side sniped at and killed them.

Mr. Fejzagić lived alone in a two-bedroom apartment in the neighboring building. Although he was seriously ill, they maltreated him because he was a Muslim. They were after his apartment and all his belongings. Cvija was the only person in that entranceway who stepped forward to protect and help him out. Fifteen minutes before he breathed his last, he told her where he had hidden 1,200 German marks and asked her to take the money. She told me how she went right down to her neighbor, a Mr. Vasiljević.

"Our neighbor, Mr. Fejzagić, just died. He told me where he had hidden 1,200 German marks. I don't know what to do with the money. I want you to know that the money is here," she explained to him naively.

"Could you lend me half of it? Six hundred German marks? I need it urgently. I'll pay you back," he asked for the money immediately.

He has never returned the money. Even I insisted that he return it, but he always protests that he has no way of paying it back.

Cvija is an extremely honest person. I had a terrible time trying to convince her to take part of the money that was left over, when the two of us no longer had enough to eat. All she'd take was fifty German marks, and she gave it to me.

Fejzagić's daughter, Dada, who lives in London, sent me a letter in 1996 before I went to England to visit my daughter, urging me to convince Cvija that she should keep the money for herself. "I can't figure out how to convince Cvija that she should take that money, as an expression of my gratitude for all she did for my father and for me. I know that there are things that no money can ever pay for. I know that she desperately needs the money right now, but she still won't touch it. I'd like it to be my way of thanking her. I feel so foolish. She needs the money to survive, and I have all I need here. I sent her a letter and asked her, if she has some of Mother's or Father's things, photographs, documents, that she send them with you. If someone else moves into the apartment I don't want them throwing those things in the trash, because they are part of my life and theirs . . ."

When I was leaving to visit my daughter in Oxford, Cvija brought me the remaining 500 German marks and everything that she had managed to salvage from Dada's parents' apartment—documents, photographs, needlepoint—for me to give to Dada, which I did.

Cvija lived alone, and helped everyone she could. She had a neighbor from the building next door. He and his wife had been beaten up twice, although his life depended on regular dialysis for kidney disease. Cvija brought him the medicine he needed. His children had gotten it for him in Germany and couldn't get it through to Sarajevo, so they sent it to Belgrade and Cvija picked it up there and brought it to him.

After he'd spent four months in hiding in my apartment, my brother asked me if I could find him a way to get out of Grbavica.

In late August 1992, I went to see a man named Dobrica. He had proper military training and was from Serbia. He had an office in the building we nicknamed the "Shopping" high rise. Drunken, grimy Chetniks sat out in front all day long.

I tried to explain to him what it was like for us Muslims living in Grbavica. "It isn't easy. My husband is seriously ill. I wait in lines for hours to get milk. When my turn comes, they announce that anyone who isn't Serbian should step out of line. I don't dare show my ID. I go through this daily in all the stores."

"That couldn't be true. I don't believe it," he said, shaking his head.

"You are a high-ranking officer, you have your own office and secretary. You have no idea what it is like out there because you always sit in here. If you were to go out among the people you'd learn about the real state of affairs soon enough. Please, help me get my brother out. He wants to go to Mostar. That's where his children are."

"I'll do what I can to get him out of Sarajevo with the army. Can he crouch in a bus all the way to Belgrade?" he asked.

"Sure. He'd stand on his head the whole way if it would help. The only way he can get from Grbavica to his children is through Belgrade, then Zagreb, then down the Adriatic Coast and into Mostar."

"Come back tomorrow and I'll let you know what I've managed to set up."

The next day when I went to see him, he was in a bad mood. "I went behind the lines. The army isn't going to be going to Belgrade. He can't go there."

"What can I do, then? I'm afraid for him. They keep saying they'll kill him," I burst into tears.

"Would he be willing to cross over to the other side of Sarajevo?"

"He would. He'd be better off over there than here, that's for sure," I said, and mused aloud, "but no one can get across with all that sniper fire."

"Come back tomorrow with your husband and your brother, and we'll manage it somehow. Give your brother my regards and tell him to pack his things and take only the basics."

While we were waiting for Dobrica the next day we listened to the men sitting out there in front of the office talking among themselves about how the only good Muslim was a dead Muslim.

After a few minutes Dobrica called Kemo in.

"Give me your ID. I'm going to put a call through on my cellular phone to your men to hold their fire while you cross the bridge. No one will shoot at you from this side."

Kemo left the office in tears.

"What happened?" we asked in unison.

"I've never met a better man. I was touched by human kindness. He even assigned soldiers to carry my things to the bridge."

We said our good-byes near the bridge. He left, alone, with no idea of what to expect.

"May I get a little closer so I can see if he makes it across alive?" I asked a soldier.

"Better not. Someone might hit you. Wait over there."

My husband and I cried, terrified, when a soldier came running over and announced, panting, "He made it. You can go home now. He's all set."

After the war I learned that the Muslims on the other side of the river maltreated him once he got to their part of Sarajevo because they suspected him of spying. They couldn't understand why he'd spent four months on the Serbian side and why the Serbian troops let him cross over.

The unrelenting sniper fire meant that you could get around on the streets only at a run. For a year I ran in zigzags, and I was never hit by a bullet.

No one ever called me by my real name. They called me Dušanka, a more Serbian-sounding name I was given by chance when I was waiting in line at a tank truck where milk was being distributed. A soldier armed with a rifle said, "Anyone in this line who is not a Serb should get out."

Dušanka, a woman who worked with me at the School of Forestry, was standing there next to me. When she heard the soldier's words, she blushed with shame. She glanced over quickly and slipped me her ID.

I stared at her, trying to memorize all the information, because if they caught me lying, they'd kill me right then and there. I read it through ten times, but couldn't remember anything, I was so terrified.

"Dušanka, I can't remember any of this. Thanks anyway," I whispered and stepped out of line.

Dušanka lived alone, old and frail, in a little house by the Partisan memorial up on Vraca. Her son was in Novi Sad, and her daughter in Sarajevo. Tanks were lined up around the monument, one next to the other. Every day I brought her something to eat, hiding it from my husband so he wouldn't know.

Once she accompanied me back up to the main road. We had to pass by a group of drunken soldiers who were sitting on the sidewalk, passing a bottle back and forth. She couldn't abide their behavior because she had seen them looting.

"What is her name," one of them called out to her.

"Vida," Dušanka improvised on the spot to protect me.

"Why are you here," they asked, and a lot of other questions.

"I came to bring my friend here something to eat. You yourselves can see that she is frail and needs help. She has to eat," I tried to explain.

"Get out of here and don't come back," they snarled at me. At dusk Dušanka came into our apartment extremely upset. She announced as she came through the front door, "Look, Abida, you must not come by my place anymore!"

"Why?"

"They said that you're a spy, that you were counting tanks. They'll kill you if you show up again."

"Where is this that you've been going?" my husband, Ljuba, asked me, terrified. "You don't mean to say she's been going up there, do you?"

"I had to come down and tell you. I was so scared you'd come again tomorrow. I couldn't bear to have your death on my conscience," Dušanka said, sadly.

It wasn't long after that that Ljuba suffered a nasty heart attack from all the stress. I had to take him to Belgrade urgently for treatment. I couldn't get through the town of Zvornik on the Bosnian-Serbian border with a name like Abida and make it to Belgrade with him. Ljuba asked the local Orthodox priest to convert me. Since I'm not a religious person, I didn't care.

"Where was your wife born," the priest wanted to know.

"Mostar."

"Then, take her to Mostar. That is where she should convert to the Orthodox faith," the priest answered slyly.

"Look, I can't even cross the bridge to the other part of Sarajevo to see our daughter, let alone all the way to Mostar. I'm sick, and the war is raging over there."

When the priest saw there was no way around it, he went off to the local commune government to ask a few questions. "What should I do? He has to go to Belgrade for medical treatment. There isn't a hospital here."

"Find two witnesses. Say that you lost your documents. Make up two first and last names. Find witnesses to testify that those are your real names. When you get your new papers, go to Serbia," they answered.

No one was willing to provide false testimony. Everyone was scared. Ljuba happened to run into one of our daughter's friends, a policeman by the name of Ranko, and asked him what to do. "If I don't get to a doctor in the next few days I'm going to die. I can't travel through Zvornik with Abida because she's a Muslim."

"Uncle Ljubo, bring your marriage certificate with you. When they see that you've been married for forty years they'll let you through. She doesn't look Muslim."

"Ranko, I'm not afraid of decent people. A decent person wouldn't ask us what nationality we are anyway. I'm afraid of idiots."

We decided to go for it on 21 December 1992. I remember it was about 0 degrees Fahrenheit. Ljubo tucked our marriage certificate into his pocket. There were four of us in the car. We drove over Romanija Mountain. We gave our last 100 German mark bill to the soldier who drove. Another soldier sat on the seat next to me. I curled up in the back and kept quiet.

"Hand over your papers," demanded the soldier at the first checkpoint. All three of them handed over their IDs.

"Great, you are all ours," said the soldier, hopping from foot to foot with the cold. "What about the woman?"

"She's my wife," Ljuba explained. "I'm taking her to the hospital. She's very sick. Do I have to get her papers out, too?"

There was a long line of cars waiting at the checkpoint. They all honked like crazy to get across the border whenever one of the cars took a little longer. Ljuba intentionally took his time going through his pockets to find my papers.

"Oh, go on," the soldier waved us on.

We went through nineteen checkpoints like that on our way to Zvornik. It was the same tension each time.

"Free at last," my husband said, once we'd passed the last checkpoint in Zvornik.

My husband was a Serb, but still the Chetnik fighters in Grbavica couldn't stand the sight of him. He was always trying to get across to Sarajevo to visit our daughter.

"Why didn't you take up arms and join the fight?" they'd ask him.

Ljuba said nothing to all their jibes, thinking to himself, This is a looter's war. This isn't my war. Why should I take up arms when I refuse to loot and kill?

"None of us can live in isolation," my husband always used to say. "When this war is over, I will move over to the other side because I'm revolted by what some Serbs are doing. I am ashamed to call myself a Serb."

I LOVE YOU,
GRANDMA, MORE THAN
ANYONE, ANYWHERE

TOLD BY OLIVERA TOMIĆ

Sarajevo

October 1998

I was born in 1961 in Sarajevo, where I went to school. I was a little pioneer for Tito. I think Tito is the greatest man on earth. During his time we all of us lived in peace and dignity.

I was stricken with multiple sclerosis as a young woman and, not only that, during the war I broke my leg and was badly scalded. Despite my illness I earned my undergraduate degree in the South Slavic languages. I teach the Serbo-Croatian language and the history of Yugoslav literature. During the war I helped children who were having trouble with their Serbo-Croatian, and I was glad I could do something since everyone else helped me so much.

Mother and I lived alone in the Olympic Village in Mojmilo built during the Sarajevo Olympics. Our second floor studio apartment, which had been our oasis until the war broke out, became, after May 1992, a place of constant unrest. Our building was right on the line of separation. Crossing the street you walked right into a Serbian village. Our neighborhood was shelled every day and sniper bullets zinged around us.

In the earliest days of the war an armed soldier knocked on our door one evening. "You have been signaling to the Serbs where to shoot at us. I'm shooting a shell straight into your apartment."

Our neighbor, a Croatian woman who was married to a Montenegrin, appeared out of nowhere and told him, "Don't you disturb them. There is a sick girl in there. Don't go around frightening people with that gun," she snapped at him.

"What business is it of yours? I'll shoot at you if I feel like it," he snarled back at her.

"Be my guest, but I will not tolerate you going into their place and bothering them."

The soldier shoved his way in nonetheless, and said, "You are sending signals. If this happens again, I'm shooting you."

I burst into tears because I couldn't figure out how to prove he was wrong.

"Don't you cry, ma'am," the soldier said, and left.

The next morning my mother went down to the territorial defense offices and asked why we'd been badly treated.

"Don't we have the right to live in our own city?" she asked the territorial defense commander.

"My apologies. It will not happen again. I will apologize to your daughter in person," he replied.

Soldiers searched our apartment twenty-four times. They always brought two witnesses with them: a Croat and a Serb.

During one search I was home alone. Mama had gone to work. Five soldiers and one civilian policeman came for the search. Our neighbors, Anto and Duško, came in right after them.

"What are you looking for here? There is nothing of any interest to you in this apartment. There are no men living here. These two women live alone," our neighbors tried explaining to the soldiers. The soldiers ignored them. One was even rude. "Do you have weapons in the house?" he asked me.

"I have books. Books are powerful. And I have the good will to help people learn things. Anyone who needs help," I answered.

Mama was taken by two policemen to the headquarters of Ismet Bajramović Ćelo in 1992. She was accused of going off to Grbavica and bringing back baskets full of food. We had relatives up in Grbavica, in the hills around Sarajevo, and until the war broke out we had been in regular contact with them, but at that point even a bird would have had trouble getting to Grbavica.

Salko, at someone's orders, brought her in to the improvised police station. The inspector told him, "You leave, she stays."

"I won't leave without her. I brought her in and I'm returning her to her daughter."

The inspector went over to my mother, slapped her across the face, and said, "Talk."

Salko pulled his pistol out and said, "That is the last time you hit her. Try it again and I kill you."

The questioning continued but with no violence.

"Have you been out of the neighborhood at all this past month?"

"No, I haven't. My daughter was badly scalded by boiling water. She has second-degree burns. I am constantly at her side."

At that point they were keeping track of everyone's comings and goings in the neighborhood. When they checked and saw that, indeed, she hadn't left the area for a month, the inspector apologized and let her go home.

Salko said, when he brought her back, "Look, take care. It's better if you don't go out. Who knows who was trying to get rid of you here."

At the same time the police came to search the apartment. My friend's father came in when they did. "I heard they took your mother off for questioning. I want to help you. I came to see if you are keeping a diary. It might help in proving that you are not aiding the Serbian side."

One of the policemen searching the apartment stopped at one moment and said, "Someday someone will be ashamed of all this and be sorry for how it all happened."

"Uncle, we haven't got any weapons here, " I said, crying. "What kind of a country is this, when they take a woman off for questioning who has done nothing wrong, someone who helps everyone else?" I asked.

After this awful scene we had no more trouble. Mama kept working at her job and everyone thought we were Seventh Day Adventists.

There was so little to eat. We didn't know how we were going to survive. The first people who helped us, aside from friends who sent us packages with food, were members of the Adventist congregation, who had my mother deliver their mail for them. They sent me food and the medicine I needed, they even sent a car when I fell and broke my leg. We were often visited by Pastor Ivan and by a lot of people I am still in touch with.

A German man, an Adventist from Bremen, visited me during the war. He saw that I was having difficulty walking and could only manage using a walker. In the spring of 1995 he came back through UNHCR [UN High Commission for Refugees] and brought me an electric wheelchair, which was actually a small vehicle, and said, "Here is a gift for Women's Rights Day, 8 March. Now you can get around your neighborhood and Dobrinja."

The NT 99 TV news team came and recorded the arrival of my gift, because it was the first vehicle of its kind in Sarajevo.

During the war I met thirteen wonderful soldiers and Nurko Karić, commander of the Fifth Motorized Brigade. On his way to bring food to his soldiers, Nurko would call to me from the street and hand me up a lunch bag, a box of cookies, and a package of cigarettes for Mama.

Azerina, who was an amateur radio operator, often helped me get in contact with the rest of the family. Later she told me that it made her the saddest when she connected me to the family of my friend who later died of leukemia in 1995. I asked Milan, also an amateur radio operator, to help me reach my grandmother, who was terribly worried about me and lived in Serbian territory. He explained that he couldn't. They would take away his radio station and it was their only connection to the world. At that point it was strictly forbidden for them to contact Serbian colleagues. When he saw the tears in my eyes, Milan felt awful. He said, "I'll connect you, I'll connect you. Please don't cry. You want your grandmother to hear a cheerful voice, don't you? Not sniffling."

"Grandma, I love you the most in all the world," I told her when the connection went through. Because of the few sentences we exchanged, Milan lost his radio station.

Almir was only fifteen when the war began. He joined the Army of Bosnia and Herzegovina immediately. At that time Sarajevo had no drinking water. Whenever a tanker truck arrived with water, he would call my mother to the window.

"Hand me down your canister and I'll fill it up for you. Olja always needs fresh water."

When I broke my leg, Almir carried me down and put me in the car and drove me over to the wartime hospital in Dobrinja. Dr. Hadžir treated me and sent me to get my cast.

"Put her in a wheelchair, it will be easier for you," they told Almir, who was still carrying me. "Let her sit in the chair, let her sit," they tried to convince him.

"I won't hear of it. I brought her in and I'm taking her home. Just let someone try to put her in a wheelchair."

When the Markale marketplace was shelled, the amateur radio operators from Fojnica called me to see if my mother was OK, because we didn't know, at first, who had been murdered in the blast. They knew that she was a courier for Adra and that she was always on the move.

Menso, who lived in my building, did what he could to ease my wartime troubles. Whenever he got his hands on chocolate he would bring me some.

He dated my best friend, Azra, who was prepared to work her way through all the barricades to come see me. She wasn't afraid of shells or those vicious snipers.

"Nothing can keep us apart. War, snipers, shells," Azra said.

Once when we were out of food, cooking gas, electricity, wood, and water, Azra's mother stopped by. She saw we were barely surviving. After a brief stay she got up and left. She brought back bread she had baked herself, and a warm lunch. I remember it well: potato stew.

Sadly, after the war she fell ill from all the stress she had been under and now she is in a wheelchair.

Munira had land she had inherited from her father up on Mojmilo hill, and throughout the war she was exposed to unrelenting sniper fire and shells. Despite all that, whenever she could set foot outside her house she would go out to pick cabbage leaves, some tomatoes and Swiss chard, and bring them to me.

Mama went with the women in the neighborhood to pick edible plants. They brought back dandelion greens, clover, and coltsfoot so they could make us dinner. It was a real celebration at home when we had soup and dandelion greens salad for dinner.

Adem, secretary for the Association of Patients of Multiple Sclerosis, got hold of food and medicine for me when he could, and saw to it that I was examined by a doctor after 1993, when I became a member. After the war ended he arranged for me to spend fifteen days at a health spa.

Mile Plakalović, the fine man all of Sarajevo knew, spent seven days collecting money so I could spend ten days in the Fojnica spa. Aside from my time spent at the cure, which he paid for into the bank account of the association, he also sent packages to all the other members. He helped everyone in the association, and the money left over from his donation was used to pay a neurologist to make house calls to see the paralyzed patients.

Whenever we got a package from someone, Mama would always call our neighbors to share it with them.

"We have gotten a package with food, but we have to share it with others. Maybe they don't have anyone who can send them things. Give so that you may receive," she used to say.

When she brought people their mail, they would often give her a can of food if they had one, or something like that. Tončika knew that I had low blood pressure so she would give Mama a little coffee. "Take this so you can make Olja a little coffee," she'd say as my mother went off.

In 1993 I got sick of hiding in the bathroom every time we were shelled. I couldn't get down to the cellar because it was so difficult for me to move around. That day I said to Mama, "Let's go sit near the elevator shaft. Isn't it safest in there?"

"I'll take out the armchair for you and a chair for me so that I don't have to stand," she said, and agreed.

While we sat in the hallway of our building, Asmira and Salko were with us. The rest went down to the cellar. When the shell fell I saw only the flash and sudden darkness. I felt something sting me under my throat. It was a tiny, hot shard that tore the skin of my neck. I screamed. Asmira was also slightly injured. Asmira and Mama picked me up and carried me back into the bathroom.

I saw a pool of blood under Salko, who had been thrown by the explosion through the doorway of our apartment.

"Don't scream! Quiet!" said Salko. "I'm wounded, too."

I looked at Mama and saw blood trickling down her leg. Although she was wounded, she carried me into the apartment to find another place to hide. A boy from our entranceway, Vanja, ran through pelting shells to bring a doctor who lived next door.

"I don't dare go with you, with all that shooting," the doctor said, terrified.

"There are wounded, there are wounded," Vanja shouted, panting. "You have to help them!"

"I won't, we'll both die!"

Vanja dragged her along until he brought her to where we were. I had no idea that our neighbor, Ramo, was wounded, too. He was on the stairs leading toward the cellar. The doctor gave him first aid, and then Salko, and then my mother. Salko went off to the hospital. Dr. Alma extracted a large shell shard from my mother's leg. Since she couldn't leave me alone, two soldiers came to pick her up every day and took her in to have her bandages changed.

The next year a shell fell below the window to our apartment. I was sitting on my bed, and Adnan was sitting next to me. When he saw the blast, he pulled me down onto the floor and threw himself over me to protect me. A big piece of the shell flew right over our heads and lodged in the wall above the door. A smaller shard ricocheted off the ceiling and hit my mother in the eye.

Our apartment had central heating before the war, so we had no extra heating stoves built in. Suad got his hands on a little tin stove for us, and Savo made us a cooking stove that my mother referred to as the "dead horse" because it was on wobbly legs. It still kept us pretty warm. Fighters brought me chopped wood from burned door and window frames so I'd stay warm. All during the war soldiers of the Army of Bosnia and Herzegovina would call me to the window as they passed and toss in wood they'd picked up along the front lines.

Zoran found a bit of birch and told Mama, "I brought you something to help keep you snug. I'll come by later and we can have coffee."

Sadly, he never made it to that cup of coffee. He accidentally sat on a small mine when he stopped to rest. He did not survive the wounds.

We had a neighbor who was in the police. Somehow he managed to come by food. He always set some aside for us. His son, Alen, who was only four years old, knocked on our door when people were starving and brought me cookies. I cried when the little boy held out the cookie, and he, startled by my tears, just blinked.

A friend, Taib, sent us fifteen quarts of oil, beans, fish and canned meat, sugar, flour, and cigarettes. We shared it all with the neighbors. We lived in a neighborhood that functioned like one big family. If someone got hold of milk, he'd bring some over, because everyone knew I wasn't well.

When things got really bad, Mama called the Catholic church in Stup and spoke with Brother Stjepan, "We aren't Croats, but I am beside myself with worry because I don't know what to give my daughter to eat. She's terribly ill."

"Just tell me where you live. I'll have food sent to your door within half an hour."

And so he did. A Mr. Pašić came over and brought us a dozen cans of Italian meat, fish, and four pounds of dry milk.

"Whenever I have the chance to send you something, I will," he said softly, and left. They sent me a package from Caritas that I shared with a Croatian man. Ante Konjicija brought the package over. I remember that they made sure I had more than half the package.

In June 1993 a shell fell into my room. Janja, who was living in our building, was visiting twice a day to change the dressings on the places where I'd been scalded. Mama lay on one bed, recuperating from her shrapnel wound, and I was on the other, all bandaged up from being burned.

One evening a group of soldiers gathered and told us that we would have to take shelter, because they were going into action. Zeko and Moco came by. Everyone in the neighborhood knew them as troublemakers before the war and feared them, except me. They told me, "We've come to figure out where Olja will be safest."

They carried an armchair into the bathroom, carried me in there and settled me down, and then told my mother, "It's best if Olja stays here until we finish with this. We will come back to let you know that it's safe for you to come out. You should find a safe place, too."

Soldiers traipsed through our apartment all the time, because you couldn't walk down the street for fear of being hit by a sniper. We lived on the ground floor, so the quickest route to the combat positions went through our living room, then over the balcony, because the snipers couldn't hit you there.

One of Juka's fighters was always bringing me chocolate and cigarettes for Mama. When he went out to the Dobrinja front he came to say good-bye. He brought me a beautiful silver bracelet, and said, "Here, this is as a memento in case I don't make it back."

He called every day from Dobrinja to ask how I was doing. When he got back he jumped off the truck in front of my building to say hello.

I didn't know any of the soldiers from before the war except for Sava and Menso. I got to know them during the fighting, and made thirteen wonderful friends. When the Brotherhood and Unity bridge was finally opened up again, Mama went over to Grbavica to visit the aunt who'd raised her; all of us spent hours telling each other about what was going on before the war broke out and what we'd do after the war.

During the last years of the war I met a man whom I fell in love with. As soon as the war ended we got married and now he looks after me, because I always need help.

After we got married, my thirteen wartime friends escorted me from the apartment, the way brothers would escort a sister, to my new home.

THAT'S NOT THE WAY I THINK

TOLD BY KATICA ROMIĆ

Vareš

November 1998

I was born in Vareš in 1953. I married Krešo and he and I have two children, Maja and Branko, and by now I'm a grandmother. My daughter married Samir Sarajlić, who is now a member of our family, and they have a little girl, Emina. I work as a cook at a school.

I refer to myself as nostalgic for Yugoslavia because my heart still beats for the Yugoslavia I was born in and that all my emotions bind me to. Josip Broz Tito made it possible for us enjoy a wonderful, easy life. The fact is that during that time I lived with dignity, and now I'm not living—I'm vegetating. I felt as if everything that began happening was at a remove, even though it was going on in my own country.

My brother and brother-in-law, who live in Croatia, called me to tell me what was happening there. I didn't want to believe it was possible. The media said one thing, but the truth was something else entirely.

Sadly, the war came all the way to Vareš.

The war for me began when I saw the first soldiers in town wearing garish uniforms, black socks, and knitted face masks. All you could see were their eyes gleaming. They held weapons. They were fighters for the Croatian Defense Forces.

Up to when the war broke out I always declared myself on the census as a Yugoslav. When they told me that Yugoslavia was gone, I said I was Bosnian. My husband, a reporter his whole life, was offered a position by the Croatian Democratic Union, the Croatian nationalist political party, as one of their reporters. He declined because he preferred not to belong to any of the nationalistic political parties. Instead he joined the territorial defense office as assistant to the chief for moral guidance and was one of the founders of the Army of Bosnia and Herzegovina in Vareš.

From the start of the war my husband was committed to the Army of Bosnia and Herzegovina, thinking that this was the true solution. I stayed in town with my children and ailing father and went through unimaginable horrors from the very same Croatian community I belonged to, from neighbors, even from my own relatives, because I didn't see eye to eye with them. They forced me out of food lines. I lost my job. I was terrified and expected the worst. When, under edict by the authorities, I went to turn in our hunting rifle, double-barreled gun, and carbine, they arrested me on the street so that everyone would see how they were "bringing me in" to turn over my guns.

While my daughter and husband were in the army, I went to Dabravine to bring them something I'd cooked. I had to leave the food at the Stupni Do checkpoint, because my neighbor, a Croat, wouldn't let me pass. Fiko, a Muslim, would stop by the checkpoint and pick up everything that had been left there for the soldiers and he'd take it out to them on the front lines. He often brought my husband his mail, food, and clean clothes. They didn't let me see my husband for six months, and he couldn't come see us.

My father died on 9 October 1993. The Croatian Defense Council forces wouldn't let my Krešo come to the funeral because he saw things differently than they did. My father had been president of the local veterans' organization for fighters from World War II. Everyone knew what a good man he was. Serbs, Croats, and Muslims flocked to his funeral. There were World War II veterans there, but because they were so frightened of the Croatian Defense Council forces they were afraid to say anything. The men who had fought with him back then against Fascism were afraid, that day, to say their good-byes. They disappointed me.

The authorities were watching to see who would bear the coffin to the grave. It just so happened that the men were Serbs, Croats, and Muslims. At the head of the procession, Veljko, a friend of ours, carried a wooden pyramid and the years of birth and death. My father was not a religious man and wouldn't have wanted a cross or any other symbols. I only recently discovered that Veljko is a Serb. At the time it wasn't something that mattered at all to me. My father, whom everyone called Didika, was the last to be buried with a procession through town. At the time, Veljko said, "Didika is the last person I'd do this for."

My mother was buried thirteen years ago at the Serbian Orthodox cemetery, which lies right next to the Catholic graveyard. Nothing separates one from the other. The only difference is that the tombstones themselves face in different directions. My father had a bench made by Mama's grave and used to say, "With this bench I'm saving myself a place."

I buried Father next to Mother without a second thought, but it did get people grumbling since he was a Croat and she had been a Serb. "Have you seen what that woman is up to, again?" they fumed.

My parents had had a wonderful life together and loved each other deeply. Earth is earth; why shouldn't they be buried together?

The Muslims living in the village of Stupni Do were struck by a gruesome tragedy, an unspeakable massacre, motivated entirely by politics. This residential area, in fact a small village, lies next to Vareš, all but a quarter of a mile from the main square.

The Croatian Defense Forces surrounded Stupni Do on 23 October 1993. The local people, the Muslims, figured they'd stay put. They couldn't imagine anything bad was going to happen to them because they hadn't done anyone else any harm. The families hit the hardest were the Likićes and Mahmutovićes. The way I see things, time should be measured in terms of pre–Stupni Do and post–Stupni Do. The Croatian forces were probably figuring that by committing this crime they would so compromise the local Croats in the eyes of the Muslims that the Croats would flee Vareš and go to join their own kind somewhere else.

I watched the Stupni Do massacre from my balcony as it unfolded. It wasn't just me. The whole town watched. There was shooting from all sides. A rocket launcher was situated by the reservoir for drinking water. They crushed people as if they were ants in an anthill. Only ten fighters were killed, and all the rest were civilians: six members from the local civilian protection office, five children from the ages of one to thirteen, and seventeen civilians, most of them women and old people. I can only imagine what those people thought and felt. The people who lived in Stupni Do were our neighbors. We had daily contact with each other.

That senseless act of violence against those innocent people was what finally settled me in the conviction that this war, I don't know what other word to use, was disgusting, and that the Croatian forces were doing their utmost to provoke the Vareš Croats to leave town. I made my views public when I wrote an article about the Stupni Do massacre in the *Bulletin*, presenting my understanding of what lay behind the exodus of local Croats from Vareš. The local Croats despised me after that. "The Romić family cannot play the role of the Willy Brandt of the Croatian people," they hissed at me, incensed.

I still insist that if our goal is to rebuild decent relations, someone of the higher-ranking functionaries should come to Stupni Do and say, "In the name of decent Croats everywhere, we wish to make it clear that we are appalled by the crime that happened here." Only then could the honest people of Vareš sleep easily. Even today many local people treat me as a traitor because of the massacre.

I was persecuted the same way the Muslims were. I was kicked out of my house and found myself on the street in Vareš, under the protection of UNPROFOR soldiers.

We lived in a puddle of water and slept out in the pouring rain for three full days and nights until the weather improved. We made fires and wallowed in the mud like pigs. Many people were there longer than I was. It was just after the Stupni Do tragedy, and before the Army of Bosnia and Herzegovina had entered Vareš. Whoever came near us would say, "You filthy *balijas*, lie down so we can slit your throats!"

The people gathered there were all of them, like me, people who were against the politics of the time. There were Muslims and other nationalities as well. We were surrounded by gun-toting soldiers in uniform. They, too, kept talking about how they'd slaughter us.

My son, who was only twelve at the time, started to cry.

"Don't cry, I'm here. I'll see you're safe," I told him.

"What if Daddy comes and finds us all dead?" the child asked. Because of that moment alone, if this nightmare were ever to happen again, I would go as far away from here as I could get, to New Zealand, Abyssinia, to the end of the world and further . . .

Only a very few citizens had the courage to befriend us. Most of them treated us as if we had the plague.

After the war the Croatian Democratic Union campaigned for setting up separate schools for the Croatian and Muslim children, as if children can even be said to have an ethnicity. Children are children until they come of age, and only when they come of age can they decide where they belong in terms of ethnicity and otherwise. I cannot make peace with the notion that they categorize us in those repulsive nationalist ghettoes, because life has proven something different: in the war people helped me who were not of my same ethnic group at all.

At that point people were starving. I requested to be allowed to tend a small garden plot somewhere near where I lived so I could plant two rows of onions. We had so few vegetables in our diet. First I asked the Croats, but they turned me down. Someone explained that they would be planting grass to feed rabbits on the parcel I'd requested. Others were planting flowers. I took my cause to Suljo Likić. "Suljo, look at all I've been through. I haven't even got a place to plant two rows of onions. No one will let me use even the tiniest piece of land, and I have no land of my own."

"You go up to Stupni Do and ask anyone up there. They will all be glad to help."

Up I went to Šerif Likić, who was clearing land in the woods.

"Listen, Šerif, do you think there might be a bit of land somewhere I could use to plant a couple of rows of onions?"

"Here you go, right here! Freshly cleared land. Take as much as you like!" He was delighted he could help.

I asked Huso, president of the local Stupni Do commune, "May I use a small plot of land to plant some vegetables?"

"Here is where we keep the manure, and this is where the land is best. I'll turn it over once for you myself to get you started, and then you take it from there."

There were relatives of mine who wouldn't even give me a pound of flour because they saw things differently than I did.

Today, the brother-in-law of a good friend of mine, who was killed in the Stupni Do massacre, lives in my neighborhood. His wife survived the massacre but was raped by Croatian Defense Council forces. Her father was murdered and her mother had to watch it all. On top of all they went through, they are still suffering today without enough to eat. No one is seeing to their needs. Someone was really vicious and published in the newspapers a list of all the women who had been raped. I find it untenable that those who suffered the most are living so badly today.

Since the tragedy in Stupni Do, relations between me and the Muslims who survived the massacre haven't changed. We have stayed friends just as we were before. When people get talking over coffee about what they went through during the war, each time before they use the word Ustasha they turn to me and say, "Sorry, we don't mean you when we say that."

"You don't have to apologize. I'm no Ustasha," I say quietly.

KILL THEM AND
KILL ME, TOO

TOLD BY SEVDA POROBIĆ

Refugee from Srebrenica, interviewed in Tuzla

November 1998

I was born in Bratunac in 1958, and married a man in Srebrenica, where we lived until the war broke out, side by side with our Serbian neighbors. Because of the evil that happened, I had to leave my home in 1992. We went down to the town of Potočanska Rijeka, where I spent three years, and after that we had to leave there too, and we came to Tuzla.

One spring evening in 1992 a neighbor of ours, Stevo, came to us and said, "Get out of here while you can! No one will be able to help anyone else! I won't be able to do anything for you, and you won't be able to help me!"

"Stevo, what are you talking about?"

"We just had a meeting where someone important said, 'If you help Muslims you'll be murdered!'"

We realized he was right and that there'd be no one to lend us a helping hand when the shooting started from near Bajina Bašta.

I immediately took my mother, mother-in-law, father-in-law, and children to my sister's house in the nearby town of *Potočari. My husband and

I stayed behind because we had plenty of food that we wanted to keep an eye on. People were beginning to starve.

That autumn was awful because the Serbian tanks and armored vehicles started arriving, and the infantry started murdering whomever they found, house to house. They didn't leave anyone alive, young or old, mobile or paralyzed. They torched and destroyed everything in their path. People didn't have time to run away or hide. We had to leave our home at 1 A.M. We were lucky that we got away at the last moment and headed for the woods toward Tuzla. When we got to the outskirts of Tuzla, the Serbian army was right there, so we had to turn back. We hid in the woods near a stream, under some cliffs, for about a week, because we didn't dare come out. When the Muslim forces pushed the Serbian forces away from Srebrenica, our home in Porobiči was set on fire, so we, too, joined the rest of our family in Potočari at my sister's place, where we stayed until 1995.

When the international forces arrived in Srebrenica, they told us, "Don't worry, we have come here to protect you and keep you safe."

We trusted them, but they let us down. They told us the Serbian army would be coming and we would have to leave. Our men who were fighting in the Muslim forces wanted to hold on to Srebrenica and fight for it.

The Serbian soldiers, however, had an agreement with IFOR, the international forces, and put on IFOR uniforms, and on 11 July 1995 they walked right into Srebrenica and Potočari, and we thought they were the international forces.

They went from village to village, searching homes, attics, barns, and confiscating any weapons they found.

When our men recognized their old Serbian neighbors in IFOR uniforms, they fled through the woods toward Tuzla.

The women and children went down into Potočari, and Serbian troops surrounded the whole area, so no one could get out.

Only those men who managed during the first two nights to flee, made it out through the woods; some of them got across, some were murdered or committed suicide, some disappeared or were taken prisoner, and until this day no one knows what happened to them. Three thousand of our men were picked up in homes and brought to Potočari. None of them managed to escape. We still do not know what became of them.

When we came out of our houses, Serbian soldiers took us down to the factory that used to make batteries. That was where they separated the men and boys from their mothers and no one knows where they were taken.

That first day, right in front of us, they took babies and little children from the arms of their mothers. They'd toss a child up into the air and impale it on their knives as it fell back down. Then they'd ask the crazed mother, "How does that make you feel!"

No one dared say a word. Any mother who started crying would be killed in front of everyone.

The next day they brought some sort of machine and started taking up the littlest children again. If one of the mothers caught their eye, they'd ask, "How many children do you have?"

She would answer that she had one, two, or three.

"Bring them here!"

The mother would have to show her children, and they'd grab them and throw them in the grinder. The horrors we went through and survived defy description.

We watched while they took a child from its mother, cut off its ear, and asked her, "Any problems with that?"

She didn't dare say a word. Then they cut off the child's hand, and asked her again. They carved a cross on the baby's chest, and asked the mother, "Any problems with that? Now he's Serbian and not a Muslim. We have christened him. Time to take him to church."

No one dared say a word. If you were silent, they'd smash you with an iron rod, if you said something, they'd say, "What are you talking about? Don't you know we are Chetniks and you are balijas?"

They did horrible things: put out children's eyes, cut off their ears and fingers. I watched with my own eyes when they took a boy of nine from his mother and sliced the flesh off his left arm. They asked her, "Hungry?"

She didn't say a word, and they went on, "Tell us, tell us, otherwise we'll kill you."

"I'm hungry but I can't eat," she whispered.

"Eat this now."

She had to put it in her mouth but she couldn't swallow. She fainted.

They gave the children sandwiches that made the children turn blue and die. The mothers were frantic. They couldn't tell the children not to eat, that the sandwiches were poisoned. Some people killed themselves when they saw what they were doing to the men they'd led away.

Those of us who watched it went crazy. They picked out girls they liked, and chose the ones who had long hair and took them off into the woods. I was terrified for my daughter, Fuadina, who was fifteen years old and had long blonde hair. I didn't have any scissors so I had her lay her braid across a rock, and with another rock I cut off her hair. I found a tarpaulin and covered her with it, but it did no good. When they came over to my daughter they pulled back the tarpaulin. My mother-in-law moaned, pulled her granddaughter to her and said, "Kill me or take me with her!"

The soldier grabbed my mother-in-law so roughly by the arm that he dislocated her shoulder. Another grabbed hold of Fuadina and dragged her off while she struggled to get away. At that moment General Mladić came up and said, "The buses are here. Anyone who wants to leave can go. Don't take anything onto the bus, just give the children something to eat."

If a mother had some food and gave it to her child to eat, the soldiers would kick the child in the mouth and knock the food away. They'd smash the child's teeth at the same time, and the soldiers would push their boot into the child's mouth. "Here, this is meat, you don't even know what meat and bread are."

General Mladić was right there. He told us, "Don't be afraid," but he'd ordered his soldiers to do what they were doing.

Then he told the soldiers, "Two buses can go to Tuzla, and twenty of them should go to the Ljubovija bridge. You know the orders."

The people got on the buses, but they took some women and men off and held them.

I went back to the place where they had killed a woman. She had been wearing *Turkish women's trousers and I took them off her and put them on my son, Ramiz, who was only ten.

As we were getting on the bus, they took off one boy just six feet away from us, stripped him naked, cut off his testicles and gave them to his mother for her to eat.

When they came to us they asked me, "Is this a boy?"

"No, she's a girl."

I held him close and got him into the bus.

Our two buses went toward Kravice, and I watched the other twenty head toward the Ljubovija bridge on the Drina. We have never had any word of the people who were on those buses. Eleven people from my family disappeared, and twenty-two from my mother-in-law's family. My father-in-law was murdered, my husband, brother, sister, her two children, two brothers-in-law . . .

We arrived in Bratunac, where the army stopped the bus. Our driver told the soldiers, "Leave me alone! The more you hurt these people, the more you hurt me. Let me drive on. If you were so anxious to abuse them, why didn't you kill them back in Potočari? That way none of them would have survived to suffer like this!"

He jammed his foot on the accelerator and went on to Kravice.

We looked out at the heaps of dead bodies by the roads. Some of them had their hands tied behind their back. Some had been hanged. They were impaling some on spits so they could roast them. Others were being roasted, and others yet were being prepared. They were making bonfires, killing people, digging with bulldozers . . .

We were stopped in Kravice by two personnel carriers. One man got out and told our driver to step down from the bus, while we were to remain inside. The driver shouted through the door, "I am not getting out of this bus and I'm not giving you these people! If you want to do something to them, I'll drive the bus straight into the river. Better they die that way than in your hands!"

Another man came in and grabbed the driver by the arms, hair, ears, to yank him out of the bus. While they dragged him he kept saying, "I'm not leaving here alive. Kill me and them and be done with this horror for all time!"

He managed to pull free of them and kept driving. A few feet further on he was stopped again by Serbian soldiers, "Get out. Your sons are up there in the woods, they are calling you to join them!"

The driver shouted out the window, "I'm driving through, and I'll run down anyone from the Serbian army who stands in my way!"

We didn't stop until we got to Kladanj. There, he explained to us, "You can walk the rest of the way but stay to the middle of the road. The shoulders are all mined."

We thanked him. He started crying and said, "Time for you to go. Take care, and look after yourselves."

I don't know who that driver was. All I know is he was a Serb.

In Kladanj we were greeted by our own soldiers. God gave me the opportunity to dig in Grandfather Stjepan's field. In two days I earned enough in wages to buy my daughter pants because she had been under a blanket for fifteen days since she had nothing to wear. The fifth day Stjepan asked me, "Sevda, would you like a job with a friend of mine? She would pay you for it."

I was as delighted as if he had given me all of Tuzla.

Emina hugged me the first time we met, and said, "Don't you worry about a thing. You have come to the right place and I have found the right woman."

At first I couldn't believe her. In the evening her husband, Milenko, came home from work and Emina asked him, "Could you please drive Sevda to the school where she is staying?"

"I will, but you come with us, too."

Emina came into the room where thirty-nine of us were quartered, and left, shaking her head, "Milenko, I can't bear to see this."

There were twenty-two little children there, one cot next to another. We had only a foot of space between each bed. After an hour Emina came back and brought with her a whole van of clothes and shoes. She was crying, and said, "Sevda, come back to my place tomorrow to work."

The next day she brought all sorts of things for me. I've been working for her ever since. I have a father, mother, two brothers, but no one can replace Milenko and Emina for me. Since 1997 we have been living in Tuzla, in a house that Milenko inherited. Milenko said to me, "Sevda, here is a house for you. Take your children and your mother-in-law, and come and live here until you can go back to your own home. Anything that Emina and I can do for you we'll do." Ever since we've been staying at their house, Emina has been working with Ramiz, because he hadn't learned anything yet even though he was old enough for the fourth grade. Since then my boy has started learning. They look after me and my children. My boy Ramiz was training for sports, but riding in the bus was too traumatic for him. They took him there by car and drove him back. They took him to the department store and clothed him from head to toe.

I never bought coal and wood, it was always Milenko who took care of that.

Milenko would never drop in without asking, "Sevda, do you have enough money, food, and clothing for the children?"

He gave me a garden plot I could plant, saying, "Use it as if it were your own."

This year they offered to buy me a cow, and I burst into tears, and said, "Milenko, it is a disgrace the way you keep giving me things. None of what happened was your fault."

"You've said that now, but never again. Please. Take what I have to give."

Milenko offered my children two plots of land, and said, "I'll help you to build them at least a summer kitchen for starters. Your children are like family to us. While I am alive, Sevda, you shall not want. I will be here, God willing, to marry them off when the time comes."

FADIL

TOLD BY JOVANKA ŠOBIĆ

Refugee from Sarajevo, interviewed in Banja Luka

December 1995

I moved to Sarajevo from Bosanski Novi when I was twelve. I went to school there and that was where I got married and had my two children. In April 1992 I sent my kids out of Sarajevo to stay with family, planning to join them on 1 May. I was prevented by the attack on Skenderija and the traffic blockade. Those who had a lot of money were able to buy their way out. If people had good connections, they could get out of the city.

We lived in the neighborhood of Hrasno that was Muslim territory during the war. We were the only Serbs in the whole building, and in an apartment near us lived a Croatian woman who, while visiting for a cup of coffee in my apartment, clearly let me know we were not welcome in the neighborhood. Muslims lived in all the other apartments and worked at the factory where my husband worked.

For seven years before the war broke out, a man named Fadil, a Muslim, lived in the apartment next to ours.

Fadil protected us every day as soon as the war started. Whenever someone came banging at the door, he would say to us, "Don't open the door! They could kill you because you are Serbs! I'll do the talking."

466

Fadil was assigned to a work detail. He walked by a bakery on his way to work. He never came home without bringing us bread. We weren't able to get it ourselves because we weren't on the list of approved customers.

He knew my brother-in-law was a member of the military. If he had said anything about that to the authorities, we would have been shot then and there.

Our apartment was on the corner of the building, and when snipers fired, Fadil wouldn't allow us to go down into the damp and chilly cellar. Instead he invited us to spend that time in his safer apartment.

I was wounded on 31 August 1992. Shell shards injured my rib cage. Fadil was there by my side. He brought out two of his own blankets and covered me before they came to take me to the hospital. I spent a month and a half convalescing, and Fadil walked eight kilometers to visit me.

Dr. Nakaš, who treated me, said, "You are one in a thousand to survive a wound like this. The shell fragment passed right by your aorta."

When Alija Izetbegović came to make the rounds of the wounded, the doctor brought him over to me and said, "Jovanka is a true fighter."

"Whose fighter?" Izetbegović asked.

"She's Serbian. She lives in a Muslim neighborhood of Sarajevo and was wounded by a Serbian shell. And even though we're treating her, she is going home tomorrow."

I didn't say a word. The doctor was right.

*Haris Silajdžić also came to visit the wounded. He asked me cynically, "So whose shell wounded you?"

I felt horrible. I knew that the shell had come from the area of Grbavica that was certainly in Serbian hands. I knew that I was one more victim of the mindless war but I had no strength to say so.

The hospital staff behaved very decently. I feared the patients the most. A lot of them were from the *Sandžak, a Muslim part of Serbia, and they were the most extreme in their views.

Right before I was released from the hospital, in October 1992, my husband was hit by a sniper on the street. He was yet another victim of the mindless war. Both Serbian and Muslim snipers were shooting into the city. He was in critical condition after his operation. The doctors said he wouldn't make it. Fadil visited him in the hospital, too, and when he died Fadil was the one who organized the funeral. He found the people to dig the grave and a car to transport the coffin. Fadil and I and two of our neighbors from the building were the only ones to attend.

People from the Sandžak moved into two of the apartments on my floor.

One day a shell fell on the roof of our building. I was still frail, having just gotten out of the hospital and recovering from my husband's death, so I was one of the last ones to get down to the cellar. Fadil came in right after me, and asked, "Was Jovanka able to get down?"

All hell broke loose. The men from the Sandžak started cursing him, and threatened to kill him and me. They insulted him and called him a Chetnik. They lunged at me, but Fadil stood between us. I left. If I'd stayed I am sure they'd have killed me. After that, none of the neighbors greeted me or Fadil.

When I went off to request the documents I would need to leave Sarajevo so that I could receive further medical treatment, they told me, "Why don't you go over to the other side. We'll give you the papers you need to go."

Fadil helped me cross the bridge where snipers often killed passersby. He knew I had difficulty walking. On that day, I went to the municipality to pick up my papers. That was the day when Radovan Karadžić summoned all Serbs over the radio to come to one of three places in the city. He said they should start moving toward Ilidža and gather at the church, and he promised no one would be shooting. Fadil set out with me. When we got to the bridge they let him cross, but they checked through my ID and took me to the police station. He came back and went after me. He explained, "She won't try to escape. She was wounded and she is in terrible shape. I guarantee she was only going to get her papers at the municipality."

"Go home today, go to the municipality tomorrow," they said, and let me go.

There were a lot of Serbs taken to jail that day. They shot at them in the streets, because they had gathered in the streets and started walking toward Ilidža. Nine Serbs were killed, and dozens were wounded. Later the Muslims themselves admitted it.

WHEN DEATH STALKED
THE STREETS

TOLD BY STANISLAV ZEC

Sarajevo

October 1998

When I was a child during World War II and the time of the Independent State of Croatia, I used to listen to my parents tell of how it had been when they lived in Banja Luka. There it was the Jews who were in the worst danger. Time and time again I witnessed scenes that were a challenge even to my lively child's imagination: my father dressing men up in the Muslim women's costume—the baggy trousers, tunic, and veil—so that my mother, who was from Dubrovnik, could get them out of Banja Luka and down to Dubrovnik on the coast. From there they could escape the evil of Nazism that ruled in northern Bosnia. I was obsessed by the question, How does a man feel wearing a woman's trousers? I had no sense at that age of what it meant to fight for your life. As I grew, I came to understand those things more, but it was only in Sarajevo that I fully understood, when I had to survive on nothing but unsweetened tea.

When David Kamhi knocked at my door, I looked more like a walking skeleton than a man. I weighed barely 100 pounds.

"I've been looking for you for days. You've got to come down to the Jewish Benevolent Society. They have organized everything."

From that day a ray of light shone in the darkness of Sarajevo, and it is shining still today.

Of the people I saw at the Jewish Center not very many of them were Jews. Most of the people the center was helping were Muslims, Serbs, and Croats, and the first thing I thought of were my father's words: What goes around comes around.

No one ever asked me who or what I was. We received humanitarian aid every time, regardless of religion and background. The packages were really generous. There were clothes for all of us, from underwear to everything else we needed. When there was no fresh water in town, lines of people out in front of the Jewish Center doled out water. They saved the lives of more than a thousand Sarajevans who would have starved to death without them.

In the seven years I have been eating at the Jewish Center I have never heard an unkind word. It was the single place in our city of sorrow where they always greeted us with such remarkable smiles. Whenever I went into the offices at the center I felt completely safe, as if nothing bad could touch me there.

At a time when we were all reduced to the essential square meters we had to have to survive, we were able to learn from the Jews how to pull ourselves out of total spiritual darkness. Every Saturday was an experience. They often held dances and all of us danced and sang while shells fell outside. Someone who didn't experience this can't possibly know what the sounds of an accordion and a guitar can mean while death is stalking the streets.

If they write a book about Sarajevo some day there ought to be a special place in it for the La Benevolencija society. The names of the people who worked here should be written in gold.

In this war the people who were good at heart stayed that way. It was hardest to be a good person.

On every important holiday from Tito's time they put fresh flowers at his statue inside the Marshal Tito Barracks. It was such a dangerous spot to linger, what with the crossfire, but there were people who had the love and courage to pick the flowers, bring them there and place them at the monument. At every important anniversary Tito's antifascist comrades-in-arms gathered here.

When the starvation was at its worst, I ran into Dr. Nakaš.

"Why don't you come down to the hospital where I work? Do you have enough to eat? Come by every Thursday and pick up a package from me."

I never took the packages home. I always brought them over to the Baptists in my neighborhood and shared everything with them. We stuck together, pulsing as one heart, trembling as one soul.

Fadil Pašić, whose grandfather used to be the mayor of Sarajevo, used to stop by to check on me.

"Look, don't you let things slide and end up with nothing to eat. Come to me. I am here. Call and I'll bring you what you need. If someone's giving you a tough time, tell me and I'll take care of it."

I never heard a cruel word from Muslims, or Serbs, or Romani during the war. All I could hear was the doorbell ringing as friends stopped by.

The times were horrible, you could be killed just for smiling, but we were stronger.

When it was at its worst, Mile picked up his fiddle and sang us romances.

For a while there were 300 babies up on Alifakovac. Night after night I distributed powdered milk that Caritas had brought in for them.

Many friends kept in touch from Belgrade in all sorts of ways, checking up to find out how I was doing and whether I needed anything. Friends invited me during the war to come to Zagreb or Ljubljana or abroad. But the people of Sarajevo love their city. In the end a person has to have a clear conscience. How could I have looked my fellow Sarajevans in the eye after the war if they had had to ask me, "How could you leave for London, or Paris, and abandon your city?"

AFTERWORD

The six years given over to collecting the material for this book were a treasure trove of experience culled from hundreds of encounters and conversations, each of which was interesting and special, as are human destinies. Each of the more than 200 recorded testimonies has a story of its own. Another book could be written describing all those encounters if I were to talk of my own work on the project; but from the start I felt this should be a book about my interlocutors and the people they tell of. I will end it as it should be ended, with a description of the way I found the first story in the collection, "Can You Count on Your Neighbors?"

My efforts were crowned, in a sense, by discovering *Baljvine while I was in Sarajevo. I wanted to find someone to talk to in a village near Mrkonjić Grad but knew no one in the area. Brane Božić, a reporter from Banja Luka, had supported the project from its inception. His enthusiastic comment meant more to me than any compliment: "What a brilliant idea! Why didn't I think of that?" The day after I'd asked him for help, Brane sent word to me in Sarajevo to get in touch with Ostoja Dulić, a secondary school principal in Mrkonjić Grad, who would put me in touch with people in Baljvine.

Jacques Paul Klein and Daniel De Luce, from the Office of the High Representative, graciously arranged for me to have a car and driver in the final phase of my fieldwork, for all my travel outside of Sarajevo.

On a clear but chilly November morning I left Sarajevo, headed for Mrkonjić Grad. The driver, on our way through Zenica, Vitez, Travnik,

Donji Vakuf, and Jajce, explained whose army had passed through which town and when. The sights were much like what I had already seen on other trips: ruined, often torched, houses, and appalling destruction. At one point I gazed into the clear, green waters of a river, and recalled the words of a man who had taken me to the source of the Buna: "If rivers could talk, they would have plenty to say."

Ostoja Dulić, a literature professor, seemed pleased to be setting out for Baljvine with me, saying as we left that he wasn't at all sure he would know anyone there. As the road wended its way from the Vrbas River to Čemernica, some twenty kilometers outside of Mrkonjić Grad, the professor said, "I like the idea of your project. It took courage in this war to follow one's own mind. The humanity you are looking for, that's heroism."

I was delighted with the autumnal foliage, something I'd always remembered in Bosnia. We were on our way to a village where even at the craziest of times only normal people lived. After everything I had been through, this was my most thrilling day.

At the entrance to the village the pavement stopped and there were only muddy ruts where there used to be a street. We saw a dozen people who were hard at work at the first houses, rebuilding their homes from ruins. They explained to us that they were Serbs repairing the homes of their Muslim neighbors and that we'd find the first Muslim whose house was ready to live in, another 300 feet down the road.

In the heart of the village we found a mosque, its minaret intact!

A tall gray-haired man stood in front of the first repaired house. The professor introduced himself and explained I was from Belgrade and I'd like to talk to him. The man shook hands warmly, and said, "I am Salih Delić. Welcome to Baljvine, good people. Come in, we don't have to stand out here, it is hardly fitting."

I was startled. I glanced over at the professor and we, both of us, grinned. Our host had spoken words from the title of my book, and he didn't even know what we were there to talk about.

We interrupted the family at their dinner, but they urged us to join them as if we'd known each other for years. As Salih Delić related his story, his words filled my heart. When I asked him whether the Muslim boys ever married Serbian girls in the village, I noticed Ostoja grinning. No one else saw it. The professor had joined the conversation only when we got to the point in the story about the false alarm in the village. When Salih finished describing what had happened, the professor picked up where Salih left off:

> I'll tell you that particular event from my own perspective, by way of illustration. At that point I was wounded, and was in the Banja Luka hospital. A man named Drago Tešanović, from Baljvine, was in the room with me. His brothers, Mitar and Drago, visited him. They were a Serbian family. When they told him about the false alarm, Drago told them, "What are you doing visiting me? I am all taken care of at the hospital. Go right back up there and make sure all the Serbs go right back to the village. Someone might think the Muslims made the Serbs leave, and then the army could attack innocent people. I was with my goats when the army began to march our way from Bočac. That is precisely what nearly happened. Rumors fly, and the army is always ready."

When we'd finished our conversation I gave Salih my card. Seeing my last name, he said, "I'm so glad you are writing this book. It was a nice life we had in the time of your grandfather. And by the way, Baljvine has always had trouble with drinking water. You must have some influence. Could you tell the right person about our problem? Maybe someone could help us get water piped in."

After we'd talked, I wanted to see the whole village. There was a gaping hole in the ground not far from Salih's house where they were collecting rainwater. I wondered, indeed, who'd be willing to help them so they wouldn't have to wait for their water to fall from the sky. With their history and their lives today, the people of Baljvine deserve that.

We drove off to the Serbian part of town that was mostly repaired by then. A newly painted Orthodox church gleamed at the highest point of the village.

I was intrigued by the professor's smile back when he'd joined the conversation. When we were back in the car he told me, "Your question about whether the Muslim boys ever married Serbian girls took me back to the days when I used to go along to chaperone the seniors on their class trip. I watched for quite awhile how a Muslim boy from Baljvine was stoically resisting the unconcealed affections of a charming Serbian girl from the upper part of the village. I took advantage of a moment when the two of us were alone, to ask him, 'Tell me, one man to another, how do you resist the temptation?' He answered without hesitation, 'Out of the question. She is like a sister to me.' 'Whose schooling is that?' I wanted to know. 'Father's.' With that one word he had said it all."

When I got home that evening, exhausted, after traveling almost 500 kilometers, an acquaintance asked me, "Was one story worth such a long trip?"

Too tired to explain, I answered, "Read the book. You'll see"

Dr. Svetlana Broz

"For Peace" (written in alternating Latinica and *Cyrillic letters)

APPENDICES

APPENDIX I:
BOSNIA-HERZEGOVINA:
HISTORY, CULTURE,
ETHNICITIES

AMILA BUTUROVIĆ

The history of Bosnia's cultural and political development helps to explain the pluralism that thrived in Bosnia before the war and provides background to the testimonies in this book. During the fifty years of Yugoslav Federation, Bosnia was often referred to as "Yugoslavia in miniature." It was so named because of the way in which its society and culture thrived as a synthesis of the traditions of all of the republics and a realization of the goal of a common, though not homogenized, life.

Although the land referred to as Bosnia-Herzegovina had been inhabited since the Paleolithic Age, it was with the settlement of various Slavic groups in the seventh century that a cohesive social and political development of the region begins. The name itself, Bosnia-Herzegovina, comes from two different etymological, geographic, and historical entities that emerged as a single political unit after the fifteenth century. Unlike neighboring Serbia and Croatia, whose names derive from tribal affiliations, the name Bosnia is connected to a river—Bosna, Bosina, Bosana—around which strong and productive settlements evolved and the basic features of political administration were established. Herzegovina, on the other hand, takes its name after a political title, *herceg*, assumed in 1449 by the nobleman Stjepan Vukčić-Kosača, who held power over the southern region of Hum.

Medieval Bosnia

Much of the medieval history of Bosnia was marked by tense and uncertain relations with its neighbors, especially the state of Hungary, which had ruled over Bosnia to varying degrees through appointed local dukes, the *bans*. By the reign of Ban Kulin (d. 1204), Bosnia had gained a considerable level of independence. As tensions with Hungary did not cease, the state's military and political resources were primarily deployed to resist Hungarian advances on the one hand and Rome's campaigns against Bosnia's rejection of the Papal authority on the other. This weakened the Bosnian state's institutional grip on its own population. The gradual economic strengthening of Bosnia's feudal nobility in the course of the thirteenth and fourteenth centuries ensured a greater degree of economic power and independence from external forces but mainly led to the strengthening of individual noble families rather than the state organization per se. Under King Tvrtko I (d. 1391), Bosnia reached the peak of its power and influence: its borders expanded and its economic development intensified. At the same time, the external pressure from Hungary and Rome and the advancing Ottomans would occasion the weakening of the central power in favor of individual noblemen and facilitate the fall of Bosnia to the (Muslim) Ottomans in 1463.

From early medieval times on, diplomatic and other documents refer to the people of this land as "Bosnians," or simply as "Sclavs." However, other ethnic references are also present; Serbs, Croats, and, as of the thirteenth century, Vlachs, are all mentioned as the inhabitants of Bosnia. Located between Catholicism and Eastern Orthodoxy, Bosnia was both open to their influences and resistant to their domination. With the state consolidated around the king and feudal nobility, Bosnian identity became a matter of territorial and political association rather than religious or ethnic. In fact, various religious cultures and ethnicities inhabited medieval Bosnia without any one holding sway over others. Three Christian denominations were present: Catholicism, Eastern Orthodoxy, and a local form of Christianity organized around the Bosnian Church (Bosanska Crkva), whose followers were referred to as "good Bosnians" (*dobri Bošnjani*) and whose belief synthesized folk practices and Christian teachings. In addition, a neo-Manichean dualist teaching known as Bogomilism, which stood apart from all Christian denominations, was present as well. For a long time, because the Vatican referred to Bosnia as the land of dualist heresy and to the Bosnian Church as the center of heresy, Bogomilism was thought to be the official teaching of the Bosnian Church. Recent historical research, however, disputes that theory.

The *language used and shared by medieval Bosnians was a Slavic dialect that became the language of liturgy as well, even among the Catholic population. It is known as Church Slavonic and it was written in Glagolithic script. The Glagolithic script was also used in Dalmatia, where its pervasiveness and centrality is said to have been decisive in the shaping of Croatian national culture. In the case of Bosnia, a specific form of Glagolithic known as *Bosančica* was used by the Bosnian Church for liturgical and other purposes. In light of the extant church sources and the fact that the Bosnian *bans* also used *Bosančica* in their transactions and general correspondence, there is a good reason to believe that the Bosnian Church served an important role in uniting the culture of this otherwise diverse population. A sense of regional unity and political integration of that shared culture seemed ostensibly more important than religious differences. In fact, this culture left behind some of the finest examples of funerary art and architecture, apocryphal stories, and folk traditions of medieval Europe that still beg to be fully studied. The advent of the Ottomans, however, sealed the fate of both the Bosnian Church and of *Bosančica*, shifting the written culture of new Bosnian converts to Islam to the usage of the three official languages of the Ottoman state: Arabic, Persian, and Turkish. Significantly, it is Bosnian Franciscans who actively maintained the link with native literacy and promoted knowledge of the Bosnian language through both spiritual and literary education.

The diversity of medieval Bosnia's religious profile in which no teaching dominated the others speaks to the nuances of regional relations and
an apparent lack of will, or success, of Bosnian kings to impose religious
homogeneity over their subjects. Nevertheless, the presence of the term
Bosnian as the marker of political, cultural, and regional affiliations, amidst
this religious diversity, is an important reminder that religion was not the
most distinguishing factor among the different groups in medieval Bosnia.
This observation is particularly important given the central role religion
was going to acquire in modern Bosnian history as the marker of ethnic
differentiation among Bosnian people.

The Ottoman Period, 1463–1878

Among many complex issues associated with the centuries-long Ottoman
rule of Bosnia-Herzegovina, two can be singled out as decisive in changing
the dynamics of interreligious and intercommunal relations among Bosnian
people: mass conversion to Islam and the Ottoman policies of religious
grouping. As regards the conversion—an issue that has drawn considerable scholarly attention—the steady pressure from the Vatican and Hungary to convert Bosnians to Catholicism, a comparable lack of trust in the
Orthodox Church, and the relatively relaxed religious atmosphere in which
no central power dictated belief are said to be the most significant reasons
for massive conversion to Islam. It needs to be noted, however, that conversion was neither enforced nor did it happen all at once; rather, it was a
gradual process spread over a couple of centuries. Conversion also involved
inter-Christian transfers of religious affiliation, especially from Catholicism
to Orthodox Christianity. The reason for such conversions lies in the status of the two Christian churches in the Ottoman state; unlike Catholicism,
the religion of aggressive neighbor-states, which was perceived as an an-
tagonistic institution, Orthodox Christianity was closely understood and
accepted. Moreover, in the sixteenth century the Orthodox Church was

granted greater autonomy within the state apparatus, including the right to collect church dues from the Catholic population.

Not only conversion but also the categorization of the population by religion was to have a crucial impact on Bosnian society. Demographically speaking, Bosnia changed little during the centuries of Ottoman rule. Prior to the Ottoman occupation, there had been waves of Serb immigration into Bosnia following Serbia's fall to the Ottomans in 1389. In the early stages of the Ottoman rule over Bosnia, negligible groups of foreign administrators were settled there, and they were slowly assimilated into the local population. More prominent were frequent migrations of the Vlachs who, as nomadic herdsmen, were employed by the Ottoman state to safeguard the routes and border areas. In the sixteenth century, there was an important wave of migration of Sephardic Jews into Ottoman lands, following their expulsion from Spain. Many settled in Bosnian towns; there, they formed strong communities, integrated into the economic life of these towns, and kept alive their traditions and language (Ladino). In contrast, Ashkenazi Jews, who settled in Bosnia toward and after the end of the Ottoman rule in smaller numbers than the Sephardim, became more strongly intermixed with the local population. Finally, there was the immigration of the Roma population as early as the fifteenth century. Usually settled in towns, the Roma lived in their own quarters and only partly adopted the customs of local Bosnians once they converted to Islam or Christianity; for the most part, they kept their language and traditional trades.

With the demography only slightly altered during Ottoman rule, the Bosnian population was mainly divided along religious and economic, rather than racial or ethnic, lines. Because of their protected status under *shari'a* (Muslim) law, Christians and the Jews were treated, along with Muslims, as subjects of the sultan. Although the rural population maintained its sense of regional integrity, and its religious practice, whatever it was, was imbued with strong regional overtones, as they had done before the Ottomans, the urban Muslim elite directly partook in the shaping of the Ottoman court culture and politics. Despite the fact that many Ottoman documents initially referred to the population of this region as Bosnian people, indicating a sense of regional and cultural unity, the official state policy of treating population groups as separate millets, that is, as religious communities, became routine after the seventeenth century. Thus, evolving economic and class relations and the ostensible privileging of Muslims within the Ottoman structures gave rise to a more prominent differentiation of Bosnian people based on their religious status vis-à-vis the state. The internal marks of separation became more clearly religious, motivated by the Ottoman policies on the one hand and by the intensified influence of the Catholic West and Orthodox Russia on the Christian subjects in the Ottoman empire on the other. The rift between Christians and Muslims further deepened as the two churches, especially the Orthodox, strengthened a sense of religious distinctiveness and, as elsewhere in the Balkans, used that sentiment to stir rebellions against the Ottoman ruler. Despite the fact that Muslim landlords also rose against the Ottoman center, demanding more economic and political autonomy, they were named by local Christians as collaborators with the foreign occupier and traitors of their pre-Islamic Christian identity. This religious differentiation that fermented in the last two centuries of the Ottoman rule would prove to be decisive for the emergence of distinct ethnonational groups during the national awakening of South Slavs in the nineteenth century.

The Austro-Hungarian Period, 1878–1914

In 1878 the Austro-Hungarian Empire occupied Bosnia, leaving it nominally under the sultan's sovereignty until it was formally annexed in 1908. Fearing general unrest, Austria initially maintained the Ottoman laws, including the agrarian privileging of Muslim landholders. Gradually, however, the new colonial government began establishing control over the three religious communities with the aim of curbing political and ideological ties between Bosnia and the neighboring Croatia and Serbia. To that effect, Austria tried to promote a sense of unified Bosnian identity—*Bošnjaštvo*— among all the inhabitants, downplaying the religious rift that had already begun to establish itself. It also tried to cut off religious ties with the imme- diate neighbors by undertaking the following steps: in 1880 it reached an agreement with the Istanbul patriarchate to nominate Orthodox bishops and metropolitans; in 1881 it lessened the traditional Franciscan authority over Bosnian Catholics by nominating Catholic bishops and archbishops; and in 1882, cutting the ties with the supreme religious clerics in Istanbul, it founded an independent *Islamic establishment for Bosnia that was or- ganized around the Islamic community (*Islamska zajednica*) and headed by the office of the *Reis ul-ulema* (the head cleric). Significantly, this re- mains to date the central Islamic institution in Bosnia-Herzegovina.

As education and literacy among local population improved, so did their ties with national movements in Serbia and Croatia. *Bošnjaštvo* gained little or no appeal and, instead, political parties with strong religious overtones were established to represent the interests of different communities. Even the Workers' Party, which initially operated in a nonnationalistic way, gradually moved toward Serbian political goals. The zeal of national awak- ening, pouring in from Serbia and Croatia, accentuated religious differences and became instrumental in steering the sentiments of Bosnian Orthodox and Catholics into their respective national agendas. The Muslim question was unresolved: Where did they belong? How were they to be approached: through cooperation, assimilation, or eradication? Croatia and Serbia were in competition to expand their political and psychological control over Bosnia-Herzegovina, and that could be accomplished by winning the hearts of the majority group: Bosnian Muslims. Both Croatia and Serbia explored various options toward the Muslim question, varying from more inclusive attempts to erase the gap (e.g., the Illyrian movement), to the campaigns of "ethnic cleansing" carried out by the followers of Serbia's Radical Party during and immediately after World War I.

Bosnia-Herzegovina in the Twentieth Century

Between the two world wars, the newly established Kingdom of Serbs, Croats, and Slovenes, headed by a Serbian monarch, incorporated Bosnia-Herzegovina, and made a concentrated effort to break up its political and territorial integrity and any sense of unity. As the pressure on Muslims to make up their national mind intensified, they found themselves torn between Serbian and Croatian ideologies, and compelled to find a third route. Unwilling to change their status as landholders, yet aware that their historical and cultural experience was inevitably subject to historical change, leading Muslim intellectuals founded the Yugoslav Muslim Organization (JMO) in 1919 as a way of protecting the interests of the community. Although the JMO was initially formed to safeguard the socioeconomic status of Muslim landholders, its mission gained a stronger political goal of developing a distinct ethnonational consciousness among Bosnian Muslims. This was, then, the period when the path was set for an internal partition of Bosnia's multireligious society. The religious pluralism that had been celebrated as a regional expression of shared historical, cultural, and political experience was turned into a multiethnicity that emphasized lines of separation and different agendas, loyalties, and aspirations. The overarching tension between Croatia and Serbia took its toll on the dynamics in the Bosnian society. As the events during World War II would indicate, religious differences in Bosnia-Herzegovina could be successfully exploited to stir an ethnonational conflict in the service of Serbia's and Croatia's nationalist goals.

Although Tito's Yugoslavia of the post-World War II period reaffirmed the territorial integrity of Bosnia-Herzegovina by constituting it as one of the six federal republics of Yugoslavia, it paradoxically reinforced the internal divisions along ethnoreligious lines. The population of Bosnia-Herzegovina was not treated as one national group but as constituent populations defined by religious heritage. Such politicized treatment of religion was exacerbated by the exclusion of religious practice from public life and its careful monitoring by the Communist Party. This was not as much a matter of official atheism—as was the case in Albania, for example—but of the fact that national particularism was inextricably tied in with the issue of religious differences. Therefore, in order for the official policy of brotherhood and unity to work, both nationalism and any overt appeal to religious symbols and identities had to be carefully monitored. Deemed incompatible with the idea of unified Yugoslav identity, nationalism of any kind was strongly curbed, and religion, as a manifestation of nationalism, was excluded from public life. Nonetheless, in addressing the grievance of Bosnian Muslims not to be treated as Serb or Croat nationals, the Yugoslav government ironically introduced the term *Muslim* as a national category in the 1971 census (when some 21 percent of the population in Bosnia-Herzegovina declared itself as Croat, 40 percent as Muslim, and 37 percent as Serb). Emphasizing the specificity of their historical and cultural experience that dated back to the Ottoman times, the category "Muslim" was intended to distinguish Bosnian Muslims from *Bosnian Croats and Serbs, but also to distinguish them from other Muslim communities within and outside of Yugoslavia. Bosnian Islam thus gained the primary function of demarcating the distinctiveness of Bosnian Muslims in relation to Bosnian Croats and *Bosnian Serbs, rather than of asserting their religious links with the rest of the Islamic world. This move was meant to bring national equality to all three ethnonational groups of Bosnia-Herzegovina and to put an end to the national aspirations of Serbs and Croats over Bosnian Muslims.

At the same time, various polls and studies show that the Yugoslav idea of brotherhood and unity found the most receptive ground in Bosnia-Herzegovina precisely because it transcended national divisions based on religious lines and because it allowed Bosnians of all faiths/nationalities to partake in the shaping of a more inclusive and accommodating concept of identity and nationality. For the generation brought up in urban centers in particular, religion represented a vague cultural yardstick, and the important dates on different sacred calendars were transformed into joint cultural celebrations. Interethnic marriages were common, and territorial intermixing precluded the formation of ethnically homogeneous zones. In the countryside the situation was similar, although religion there played a more tangible role in the life of a community. However, given that religion was transmitted through practice rather than through doctrine—as has historically always been the case with much of Bosnia—religious values were remarkably flexible, mutually accommodating, and syncretic.

As Yugoslav political leaders drew and redrew the internal national map of Bosnia-Herzegovina, its people did their best to carry on in the way they always had—through coexistence and interdependence, and the sharing of space, opportunities, and resources. Memories of conflicts that had inflamed antagonisms between ethnic communities in the past, including WWI and WWII, were strong, but the long history of living together offered an alternative way of thinking about the past, in tension with that generated by political history. Bosnia-Herzegovina remained a highly integrated and intermixed society. With the breakup of Yugoslavia in 1991 and the resurgence of nationalist agendas throughout the region, Bosnia-Herzegovina was set once again on the tragic course of having to square its historical reality of integration and intermixing with the nationalist ideologies of separation and purity. While the population had until recently nurtured only a superficial connection with religion, selected religious symbols were manipulated to carry out extreme nationalist goals. During that seemingly complete disintegration, however, the parallel history of coexistence also asserted itself; the centuries-long value of aid to neighbors and friends remained an ethical imperative for many Bosnians. The stories and experiences presented in this book offer some of the most touching examples of this predicament, and suggest that history and memory need not negate each other.

Amila Buturović
York University
Toronto, Canada

APPENDIX II: GLOSSARY

ELLEN ELIAS-BURSAĆ, SVETLANA BROZ, AND LAURIE KAIN HART

Arkan. The nickname of prewar criminal and wartime racketeer Željko Ražnjatović, associated with the paramilitary group, the Tigers. Murdered in Belgrade, 2000.

Army of Bosnia and Herzegovina. Originally the army of the Muslims. Now the army of the Bosnia and Herzegovina (BH) Federation. Initially a multiethnic force created for the defense of BH in the fall of 1992. In accordance with the Dayton Peace Accords the BH Army, comprising three ethnic elements, is now being reorganized to meet European criteria.

Bairam. A feast held at the end of Ramadan. One of the most important Muslim holy days.

Balija. Derogatory term for Muslim.

Baljvine. A village near Mrkonjić Grad. Population 1,226, including 699 Muslims, 438 Serbs.

Banja Luka. NW, population 195,692: Bosniaks14.6%, Croats 14.8%, Serbs 54.6%, Yugoslavs and others 16%; now in Republika Srpska.

Banovina. A territorial unit used in the 1930s and during World War II.

Beard. During World War II, so many Chetnik fighters sported beards that the beard became synonymous with royalist sympathies. In the Bosnian war, fighters who wished to be thought of as Serbian extremists often wore beards.

Belgrade. The capital city of Serbia and Montenegro.

BH. Abbreviation for Bosnia and Herzegovina.

BH Federation. The entity representing Bosniaks, Bosnian Croats, and those Bosnian Serbs who do not live in the RS.

Bijeljina. NE corner near Drina River, population 96,988 in 1991: Bosniaks 31.2%, Croats 0.5%, Serbs 59.2%, Yugoslavs and others 9.1%; part of Republika Srpska (RS).

Boban, Mate. President of the BH Croatian Democratic Union and first president of Herceg-Bosna from 1991 to 1994. In 1994 he stepped down, when the peace deal was signed between the Bosniaks and Croats. Died of a stroke in 1997.

Bosanska Dubica. N along Sava River, name changed to Kozarska Dubica during the war, population 31,606 in 1991: Bosniaks 20.4%, Croats 1.5%, Serbs 68.7%, Yugoslavs and others 9.4%; part of RS.

Bosanska Krupa. NW corner near Croatian border, population 58,320 in 1991: Bosniaks 73.9%, Croats 0.2%, Serbs 23.7%, Yugoslavs and others 2.2%; part of BH Federation.

Bosanski Brod. N along Sava River and Croatian border, name changed to Brod during the war, population 34,138 in 1991: Bosniaks 12%, Croats 41%, Serbs 33.4%, Yugoslavs and others 13.6%; part of RS.

Bosanski Novi. NW at confluence of Una and Sana Rivers, name changed to Novi Grad during the war, population 41,665 in 1991: Bosniaks 60.2%, Croats 1%, Serbs 33.7%, Yugoslavs and others 5.1%; part of RS.

Bosanski Šamac. NE along Sava River, name changed to Šamac during the war, population 32,960 in 1991: Bosniaks 6.8%, Croats 44.7%, Serbs 41.3%, Yugoslavs and others 7.2%; part of RS.

Bosnia and Herzegovina. Population in the 1991 census: 4,363,521, including 1,902,956 Bosniaks, 760,852 Croats, 1,366,104 Serbs and 333,609 (7.6%) Yugoslavs and others. One of the six republics of the Socialist Federative Republic of Yugoslavia until April 1992, when a referendum calling for secession divided the republic, the Bosnian Serbs refusing to secede from Yugoslavia, the Bosniaks and Bosnian Croats insisting on secession. The war began.

Bosniak. The term preferred after the war for Bosnian Muslims, the majority BH community.

Bosnian Croats. People of the Roman Catholic faith and/or background who live in BH.

Bosnian Serbs. People of the Eastern Orthodox faith and/or background who live in BH.

Bratunac. E on Drina River, population 33,619 in 1991: Bosniaks 64.1%, Croats 0.1%, Serbs 34.1%, Yugoslavs and others 1.7%; part of RS.

Brčko. NE on Sava River, population 87,627 in 1991: Bosniaks 44.1%, Croats 25.4%, Serbs 20.7%, Yugoslavs and others 9.8%; part of RS.

Brod. See Bosanski Brod.

Bugojno. Population 46,889 in 1991: Bosniaks 42%, Croats 34.2%, Serbs 18.5%, Yugoslavs and others 5.3%; part of BH Federation.

Čačak. A town in Serbia proper, across the Drina River from Bosnia and the towns of Bratunac, Višegrad, and other eastern Bosnian towns. Refugees, Serbian and Bosniak alike, fled to Čačak to escape the fighting.

Čajniče. SE corner on border with Montenegro, population 8,956 in 1991: Bosniaks 44.9%, Croats 0.1%, Serbs 52.6%, Yugoslavs and others 2.4%; part of RS.

Caritas. An international Roman Catholic charitable organization involved in humanitarian aid and relief work.

Ćelebići. A jail/camp run by Bosniaks near Konjic.

Ćelo, Ismet Bajramović. A Sarajevo racketeer and criminal.

Ćelo, Ramiz Delalić. One of the founders of the Green Beret Bosniak paramilitary group. Later in open conflict with the Army of Bosnia and Herzegovina. A wartime racketeer. Arrested in 2001 for assaulting a police officer.

Ćevapčići. Grilled sausages served in a bun, sold by street vendors.

Chetnik. 1. A term used by many citizens of Bosnia and Herzegovina to refer to those Serbs who took up arms against members of other ethnic groups during the war. It is used to set these Serbs apart from the rest of the Serbian population, and thus constitutes an attempt to avoid sweeping statements incriminating the entire Serbian population for the atrocities of a few extremists. 2. A member of the Serbian royalist forces during both world wars, most often aligned with Fascist forces. 3. The name used by members of a number of the Serbian Paramilitary groups. They wore Chetnik insignia from the Second World War in order to intimidate the non-Serbian population of BH during the recent war. 4. Derogatory term for Serb.

Civilian Protection. An office in most small towns for organizing local defense during natural catastrophes and local unrest.

Cluster bombs. These bombs have anti-personnel fragmentation features that can send hundreds of shards of steel at ballistic speeds over a wide area, or shaped charges that can penetrate heavy armor. Many cluster bomb canisters carry hundreds of bomblets.

Coffee. In almost every testimony in this book there is reference to preparing and drinking coffee. This is one of the rituals of Bosnian daily life, especially important in wartime. The coffee is made in a small pot with a long handle called a *džezva*. It is prepared as follows: Fill the pot with water, and bring it to a boil. Pour some water off into a cup and set it aside. Stir in four or five heaping teaspoons of finely ground coffee. Hold the pot on the burner until the coffee in the pot boils. Remove it briefly, then return it to the burner a second time to boil, then remove it yet again, and, briefly, return it a third time to boil. Pour the water that was set aside over the coffee to settle the grounds, and spoon a little of the creamy coffee foam into each waiting coffee cup. Then pour the coffee into each cup and serve.

Communist. Refers in these testimonies to the government, or officials, of pre-1991 Yugoslavia.

Corridor. A stretch of land linking two bodies of territory.

Croat. In the testimonies related in this book, Croat and Croatian are used in two ways: (1) to refer to people who are Roman Catholic by faith or tradition who have lived in Bosnia and Herzegovina for generations, and are often referred to as Bosnian Croats; and (2) to designate those citizens of the Republic of Croatia who crossed over into BH to fight during the war in Croatian Defense Council forces, paramilitary groups or forces affiliated with the Croatian Army.

Croatian Army. The army of the Republic of Croatia.

Croatian Defense Council forces. The fighting force of Herceg-Bosna, also known by its acronym HVO.

Croatian Democratic Union. Also known by its acronym HDZ. The nationalist Croatian political party, which came to power in the March 1990 multiparty elections. HDZ held the majority in the Croatian parliament for ten years, from May 1990 to the elections in January 2000 following Tuđman's death.

Croatian Guard Corps. Also known by its acronym HOS. The first troops organized for the defense of Croatia, key to the formation of the Croatian Army.

Cyrillic. The Serbian alphabet—The Cyrillic alphabet is transcribed in this book into the following modified Roman letters: a b v g d đ e ž z i j k l lj m n nj o p r s t ć u f h c č dž š. Cyrillic is used, though not to the exclusion of Latinica, in Serbia, the RS, Montenegro.

Dalmatia. A part of the Croatian coast of the Adriatic Sea.

Danube River. Forms the border between Serbia and Croatia before it flows through the Vojvodina to Belgrade and then out to the Black Sea.

Dayton Accords. Peace agreement signed in December 1995 calling for a Bosniak-Croat federation and a Serb entity within the state of Bosnia-Herzegovina. (See Chronology.)

Dinar. The currency of pre-1991 Yugoslavia. New currencies appeared after 1991 in the newly formed countries.

Divjak, Jovan. A career officer in the JNA before 1991. Famous for his decision to defend Sarajevo with the Muslim forces during the siege despite his Serbian ethnicity rather than join the RS Army. He held the rank of general in the Army of Bosnia and Herzegovina until 1977, when he returned his rank of general to Alija Izetbegović in protest "against the promotion to rank of general of persons who contributed to the sufferings of others." For the last nine years he has headed a nonprofit organization concerned with the education of children orphaned during the BH war.

Doboj. N central, population 102,549 in 1991: Bosniaks 40.1%, Croats 12.9%, Serbs 38.8%, Yugoslavs and others 8.2%; part of RS.

Donja Mahala. A Mostar neighborhood.

Dretelj. A camp run by the HVO in Herzegovina, 1993–1994.

Drina River. For part of its course it defines the border between western Serbia and eastern Bosnia.

Džezva. A Turkish coffee pot with a long handle.

Eastern Mostar. Otherwise known as the left bank of the Neretva River. The predominantly Bosniak part of the city after 30 June 1993.

Eastern Orthodox Church. The body of modern Christian churches, including the Serbian and Russian Orthodox, that is derived from the church of the Byzantine Empire, and adheres to the Byzantine rite and primacy of the patriarch of Constantinople.

Effendi. A title of respect, especially for government officials.

Entity. Term used to refer to the postwar constituent political bodies of BH. There are two entities in BH: the BH Federation with its Croatian and Bosniak communities, and Republika Srpska, the entity of the Bosnian Serbs.

Ethnic group (synonym: nationality). In these histories this refers to one of the three cultural/religious communities comprising the majority of the BH population: Bosniaks, Bosnian Croats, Bosnian Serbs. There are other, much smaller, BH ethnic groups, notably Jewish and Romani communities.

Exchange. Each side took prisoners so they would have people to exchange for their own relatives and fighters imprisoned by their enemies.

Expulsion. When people are forced to abandon their homes, either by a hostile army or their own retreating forces.

Federation. See BH Federation.

Fit for military service. Men between the ages of sixteen and sixty were declared fit for military service in the spring of 1992 throughout Bosnia and Herzegovina. Women served as fighters, but generally volunteered rather than being conscripted. Men were not allowed freedom of movement. If they were living in territory under the control of their own ethnic group, they were called to serve in the armed forces. If in enemy territory, men and women were obliged to sign up for a work detail.

Foča. SW corner near Montenegro, renamed Srbinje during the war, population 40,513 in 1991: Bosniaks 51.3%, Croats 0.2%, Serbs 45.2%, Yugoslavs and others 3.3%; part of RS.

German mark. The currency of Germany until January 2002 (when replaced by the Euro). Used widely throughout BH as the wartime currency, despite the other forms of currency: kuna and dinar. At the time of the war, one German mark was worth about $0.60.

Glamoč. SW near Croatian border, population 12,513 in 1991: Bosniaks 17.9%, Croats 1.5%, Serbs 79%, Yugoslavs and others 1.6%; now in the BH Federation.

Gradačac. NE, population 56,581 in 1991: Bosniaks 59.8%, Croats 15.2%, Serbs 19.8%, Yugoslavs and others 5.2%; part of BH Federation.

Grbavica. A neighborhood of Sarajevo held by Republika Srpska forces during the siege, reintegrated into the BH Federation after the Dayton Accords in November 1995.

Green. Green symbolizes Islam and is mentioned in the Qur'an as the color of paradise (55:64), and as the color of the garment of the paradise-to-be-dwellers (18:31, 55:76, 76:21). Also, in 6:100 it is a sign of fertility (earth).

Green Berets. A Muslim paramilitary unit.

Haris Silajdžić. A politician in Bosnia.

Heliodrom. A prewar helicopter facility. The HVO ran a camp there, 1993–1994.

Herceg-Bosna. The temporary Bosnian Croatian authority, 1993–1995.

Hodja. A Muslim teacher. The term is often used to denote a leader/teacher of a group of sufis in the Balkans.

Holiday Inn. Built for the Sarajevo 1984 Winter Olympics. One of the earliest sites of violence in the spring of 1992 in Sarajevo when antisecessionist snipers fired from the hotel into crowds of people demonstrating for peace on the Sarajevo streets.

HOS. See Croatian Guard Corps.

Humanitarian aid. Packages of food staples (such as dried milk, beans, canned meat) distributed by relief agencies wherever they could reach the civilian population in areas of combat and siege.

ICTY. The International Criminal Tribunal for the former Yugoslavia based in The Hague.

ID card. Every adult in the former Yugoslavia held a card of identification with a number unique to that person designating date and place of birth, and other encrypted information. A person versed in the encryption could decode this data about the cardholder from the number.

IFOR. NATO Implementation Force.

Ilidža. Central BH, population 67,937 in 1991: Bosniaks 43.2%, Croats 10.2%, Serbs 36.8%, Yugoslavs and others 9.8%. A municipality of Sarajevo held by Republika Srpska forces during the siege, reintegrated into the BH Federation after the Dayton Accords in November 1995.

Imam. A recognized leader or religious teacher in Islam. Any pious Muslim may function as an imam.

Independent State of Croatia. A puppet state set up in Croatia on 10 April 1941 by the German and Italian Fascists; it fell on 8 May 1945.

Islam. A religion based on the teachings of the prophet Mohammed, professing belief in one God (Allah) and in Paradise and Hell, and having a body of law put forth in the Qu'ran and the Sunna.

Izetbegović, Alija. President of Bosnia and Herzegovina and head of the Party of Democratic Action (SDA) from 1990 to his retirement from the presidency in 2000.

Jasenovac Concentration Camp. A death camp set up in the town of Jasenovac along the Sava River by the government of the Independent State of Croatia during World War II and used for the extermination of thousands of Jews, Serbs, Roma, and Croats who resisted the Croatian fascist regime. The people murdered in the camp were brought there from all over Croatia and Bosnia.

Juka. See Prazina.

Kajmak. A thick cheese spread aged from the richest part of fresh cream.

Kangaroo court. An ad hoc summary trial designed to produce a guilty verdict, followed by execution.

Karadžić, Radovan. Before 1990 he worked as a psychiatrist at the Sarajevo hospital. President of the RS until the Dayton Accords forced him to retire from public life. The ICTY has indictments for war crimes outstanding against him. At the time this book goes to press he is still at large.

Kiseljak. Central BH, population 24,164 in 1991: Bosniaks 40.5%, Croats 51.9%, Serbs 3.1%, Yugoslavs and others 4.5%; now in the BH Federation.

Konjic. S central BH, population 43,878 in 1991: Bosniaks 54.3%, Croats 26.2%, Serbs 15.1%, Yugoslavs and others 4.4%; part of the BH Federation.

Kosovar. A person of Albanian ethnicity living in Kosovo.

Kovačići. A part of the Grbavica neighborhood of Sarajevo on the front line during the siege, held by the RS.

Kozarska Dubica. See Bosanska Dubica.

Krajina, The. A swath of land running along the border between Croatia and Bosnia and Herzegovina that was, in the eighteenth and nineteenth centuries, a military frontier between the Ottomans and the Austrians.

Before the war, much of the population in the Bosnian and Croatian Krajinas was Serbian.

Krajišnik, Momčilo. One of the leading members of the Republika Srpska government during the war. Now being tried for war crimes at the International War Crimes Tribunal in The Hague.

Krupa. See Bosanska Krupa.

Kum. A close friend of the family. Best man in a wedding or godfather at a baptism.

Laktaši. N central BH, population 29,832 in 1991: Bosniaks 1.4%, Croats 8.6%, Serbs 81%, Yugoslavs and others 9%; now in RS.

Languages. Bosniaks, Bosnian Croats, and Bosnian Serbs speak a fundamentally common language referred to, in the former Yugoslavia, as Serbo-Croatian. They are able to understand one another despite regional vocabulary differences. Many now prefer to use their own name for the language (Bosnian, Croatian, and Serbian, respectively), while others continue to use the term Serbo-Croatian. New terms such as BCS (Bosnian-Croatian-Serbian) are also in contemporary use.

Latinica. The alphabet used both in Croatia and the BH Federation: a b c č ć d dž đ e f g h i j k l lj m n nj o p r s š t u v z ž.

Left bank. See Eastern Mostar.

License plates. In the former Yugoslavia, license plates included the initials of the city where the car was registered. As cities were taken over by one side or another, these plates declared the driver's place of origin and were therefore a safety threat for the driver and passengers when they drove through enemy territory. The entities, too, used different alphabets. OHR (Office of the High Representative in BH), therefore, introduced plates using all the numbers but only those letters the Latinica and Cyrillic alphabets have in common, making it impossible thereafter to tell whether the car was from the Republika Srpska or the BH Federation.

Lily. A symbol of the BH Army used in its coat of arms and on the flag.

Line of separation. The line delineating the division of territory during war.

Manjača. A camp set up by Serbs in the spring and summer of 1992 in the area near Prijedor in northwestern Bosnia.

Marijin Dvor. A Sarajevo neighborhood held by Bosniak forces during the siege.

Markale marketplace. An outdoor marketplace in Sarajevo that was the site of several major mortar attacks. The most deadly was on 5 February 1994, when sixty-eight people were killed.

Maturice. A Bosnian Croat paramilitary unit, closely affiliated with the Croatian Defense Council forces, to whom the massacre in Stupni Do has been attributed.

Merhamet. An Islamic charitable society involved in humanitarian aid and relief work.

Miljacka River. Runs through the city of Sarajevo, and served as the line of separation between the Bosniak and the Republika Srpska sides during the siege.

Milošević, Slobodan. Elected president of Serbia in 1990, reelected in 1992. Elected president of rump Yugoslavia in 1997, he remained in that position until he lost the election in September 2000. In March 2001 he was arrested by the new Yugoslav government. In June 2001 he was handed over to the International Criminal Tribunal for the Former Yugoslavia in The Hague for trial.

Mine. An explosive device most commonly buried in the ground and triggered by weight and/or pressure.

Mine field. A site where many mines are planted in the ground, often along the line of separation at the front, to prevent the passage of army and civilians from one side to the other.

Mladić, Ratko. Before 1991 a career officer in the JNA (Yugoslav People's Army). Commander of RS army in 1992. Withdrew to Belgrade after the BH war ended. The ICTY has indictments outstanding against him. At the time this book goes to press he is still at large.

Modriča. NE close to the border with Croatia, population 35,613 in 1991: Bosniaks 29.1%, Croats 27.5%, Serbs 35.2%, Yugoslavs and others 8.2%; part of RS.

Mostar. S central BH on the Neretva River not far from the Dalmatian coast, population 126,628 in 1991: Bosniaks 34.6%, Croats 34%, Serbs 18.8%, Yugoslavs and others 12.6%; part of BH Federation.

Mrkonjić Grad. W central BH, population 27,395 in 1991: Bosniaks 11.9%, Croats 7.8%, Serbs 76.9%, Yugoslavs and others 3.4%; now in Republika Srpska.

Muezzin. The person who calls the faithful to prayer from the minaret of a mosque five times a day.

Mujahedin. As used in these testimonies, this refers to soldiers who came from other Islamic communities to fight side by side with Bosniaks in the war.

Muslim. A follower of Islam. In Bosnia the term was introduced on the 1971 census in its ethnic, rather than religious, sense. By referendum, following the Dayton Peace Accords, it was decided to replace Muslim with Bošnjak (Bosniak). The term "muslim" with a lower case "m" refers to an adherent of Islam in the religious sense.

Muslim teacher. Can signify an imam or preacher as well as a teacher and can be used as an honorific in a secular context for a wealthy merchant. The title implies that its bearer has been on the hajj or pilgrimage to Mecca.

Names. Many, though not all, names in these testimonies signal ethnicity. Examples of names generally recognizable as Bosniak: men: Asim, Edin, Esad, Fadil, Fikret, Hajro, Ismet, Jusuf, Muhamed (nickname: Mujo), Muharem, Mustafa, Omer, Safet, Sead, Sulejman (nickname: Suljo); women: Abida, Azra, Emina, Fatima (nickname: Fata), Meliha, Mersiha, Nesiba, Nura, Sevda. Examples of names generally recognizable as Croatian: men: Ante, Franjo, Ivica, Krešo, Mate, Tomo, Stipe; women: Ljubica, Marija, Zdenka. Examples of names generally recognizable as

Serbian: men: Dobrica, Jovan, Ljubiša, Milan, Milutin, Momčilo, Rade, Radovan, Rajko, Slavko, Srđan, Stanko, Steva, Zoran; women: Biljana, Dušanka, Mara, Nevenka, Slavica, Stana, Zaga, Zorica.

Nationality. See Ethnic group.

Neretva River. Runs from the Herzegovina mountains to the Adriatic Sea through Mostar, dividing the city during the war into Bosniak and Croatian quarters.

Novi Grad. See Bosanski Novi.

Odžak. NE on the Sava River, near the Croatian border, population 30,056 in 1991: Bosniaks 20.7%, Croats 54.4%, Serbs 18.9%, Yugoslavs and others 6.0%; part of RS.

Olovo. E central BH, population 16,956 in 1991: Bosniaks 74.9%, Croats 3.8%, Serbs 18.8%, Yugoslavs and others 2.5%; part of BH Federation.

Orašje. NE on the Sava River Croatian border, population 28,367 in 1991: Bosniaks 6.7%, Croats 75.1%, Serbs 14.9%, Yugoslavs and others 3.3%; now lies in BH Federation.

Orthodox: See Eastern Orthodox Church.

Otoka. A Sarajevo neighborhood.

Pale. A suburb of Sarajevo. The seat of Karadžić's government and the RH parliament until the Dayton Accords of November 1995. It is still an important site of Republika Srpska, but Banja Luka became the RS capital in 1997.

Paramilitary unit. A group of fighters acting independently of, or partially independent of, the official armed forces. Some were police units responsible to the ministry of the interior of their respective republic but seconded to the army. Others were volunteers.

Partisans. A guerrilla force, Communist in ideology, fighting the Germans in World War II throughout the former Yugoslavia, drawn from all the country's ethnic groups and commanded by Marshal Tito.

Party for Democratic Action. Known by its acronym SDA, it is the nationalist Bosniak party.

Pećanin, Senad. Bosniak editor of the Sarajevo weekly *Danas* and outspoken critic of Izetbegović's repressive policies. He published documents in his magazine in 1993 describing how Izetbegović's government had persecuted and murdered Serbs in Sarajevo, and for this was vilified and threatened by the Bosniak authorities.

Personnel carrier. A van or truck for moving troops from one place to another, usually armored.

Plavšić, Biljana. A professor of biology. She was elected president of the RS entity after Radovan Karadžić was forced to step down following the signing of the Dayton Accords in December 1995. She held the office until 1998. She has been sentenced to serve eleven years in jail for war crimes, to which she pled guilty in 2003, and she is now serving that sentence.

Pork. Those who adhere to the dictates of Islam do not eat pork. In BH pork is a staple of the cuisine and has recently become a cultural marker.

Potočari. A village outside of Srebenica where the United Nations quartered a Dutch unit in an abandoned battery-producing factory to guard the Srebrenica safe area. When the Serbs began to move into the area in July 1995, the local people fled to Potočari to take shelter with the Dutch troops. Ratko Mladić and his men came to Potočari, divided the men and boys from the others, sent the women and children away in buses, and there began the Srebrenica massacre, lasting for several days, of about 8,000 people.

Prazina, Jusuf-Juka. A prewar criminal, he ran a black market operation in Sarajevo during the war, and armed a unit that fought briefly to liberate the city. After conflicts with the BH army he supported the HVO, then moved first to Croatia and then to Belgium, where he was assassinated by his bodyguard in 1993.

Rakija. A strong, usually colorless brandy distilled from fruit, often plums but also grapeskins after the wine has been pressed out.

Red Cross. The International Committee of the Red Cross, also referred to as the ICRC, which came into detention centers and camps to make lists of prisoners in order to protect them.

Reintegration. The process, following the signing of the Dayton Peace Accords in December 1995, by which certain areas, most of them in and around Sarajevo, that were under RS control during the siege, reverted to the BH Federation.

Republika Srpska. According to the Dayton Accords, the Serbian entity in BH. The name was coined and used during the war before Dayton and refers to the Serbian state, formed in defiance within the territory of the universally recognized independent state of BH.

Right bank. See Western Mostar.

Roman Catholic Church. The Christian church that is characterized by a hierarchic structure of bishops and priests in which doctrinal and disciplinary authority are dependent on apostolic succession, with the Pope as head of the episcopal college.

"Rose." Shell mark in pavement.

RS. Abbreviation for Republika Srpska.

Šabanović, Murat. A resident of Višegrad who toppled the town statue of Ivo Andrić, Nobel prize–winning novelist, and later threatened to open the floodgates on a large hydroelectric dam near Višegrad.

Salkan. Salko Mutapčić, alleged to belong to a Bosniak paramilitary organization.

Šamac. See Bosanski Šamac.

Sandžak, The. A part of southwestern Serbia directly across the Drina River from Bosnia, largely Muslim in population.

Sanski Most. NW corner of BH, population 60,307 in 1991: Bosniaks 46.7%, Croats 7.2%, Serbs 42.1%, Yugoslavs and others 4%; part of BH Federation.

Sarajevo. Central BH, population 527,049 in 1991: Bosniaks 46.7%, Croats 7.2%, Serbs 42.1%, Yugoslavs and others 4%. The capital city of the Yugoslav republic of Bosnia and Herzegovina until 1992. It is completely surrounded by mountains, and lies along the banks of the Miljacka River. Besieged in April 1992 by RS forces and paramilitary units, and under siege until the Dayton Accords in December 1995. During the war Sarajevo neighborhoods fell under either Republika Srpska or Bosniak control. Fighting was waged from neighborhood to neighborhood. Often the front ran along a city street. During reintegration after the Dayton Accords were signed, most of the neighborhoods around Sarajevo that had been under RS control reverted to the BH Federation.

Sarajevo Winter Olympic Games. Sarajevo was the site of the XIV Winter Olympics in 1984. Olympic sites were key to the siege; the playing fields around the ice-skating rink, Zetra, were packed with graves; the housing built in Mojmilo for athletes was badly shelled.

Sava River. Runs from the Slovenian Alps to Belgrade, where it flows into the Danube. For much of its course, it serves as the border between northern Bosnia and southeastern Croatia.

School. During the war in many small towns and villages, the nursery, elementary, and secondary schools were used to quarter troops or detain prisoners of war.

Scorpion. A submachine gun.

SDA. See Party for Democratic Action.

Serbia proper. The Republic of Serbia, left in the rump Yugoslavia after the other former Yugoslav republics seceded in 1991 and 1992.

Serbian. In the histories related in this book, the adjectives Serb and Serbian are used in two ways: (1) They refer to people who are Serbian Orthodox by faith or tradition, who have lived in Bosnia and Herzegovina for centuries, often referred to as Bosnian Serbs. (2) There are also references to those citizens of Serbia who crossed over into Bosnia and Herzegovina from Serbia proper to fight during the war, either in paramilitary troops or as part of the Yugoslav Army.

Serbian Orthodox Christmas. 7 January, based on the Julian calendar.

Serbian Orthodoxy. See Eastern Orthodox Church.

Šešelj, Vojislav. Right-wing member of the Serbian government, one-time mayor of the Serbian town of Zemun, associated with paramilitary groups active in the BH war. Indictments were raised against him by the ICTY; at the time this book goes to press he is in custody, awaiting trial.

SFOR. NATO Stabilization Force in Operation Joint Guard arrived in Bosnia on 20 December 1996 after the IFOR mission ended.

Shell. A projectile shot from a gun or other launcher.

Shelling. An attack when projectiles are launched at a place, target, or person.

Siege of Sarajevo. Sarajevo was under siege by RS units and paramilitaries from April 1992 to November 1995 after the Dayton Accords. The city lies at the foot of a circle of mountains, making it an easy target for a siege.

Silos camp. Set up by Muslims in April 1992, closed after the Dayton Accords were signed in November 1995.

Skopje. Capital city of the Democratic Republic of Macedonia.

Slava. A saint's day, one of the most important Serbian Orthodox family celebrations commemorating the day, centuries before, when the progenitor of a family first converted to Christianity.

Sniper. A person who shoots at passersby and people in their homes from a hidden nest. In Sarajevo there were snipers in the surrounding hills and mountains who shot from afar, but there were also sniper nests inside the city, on the upper floors of high rises and other vantage points.

Socialist Federative Republic of Yugoslavia. Often known by its acronym SFRY. The official name for Yugoslavia from WWII to the end of Yugoslavia in 1991.

Spanish Battalion. An UNPROFOR unit stationed in the Mostar and Jablanica area.

Split. A major Croatian city on the Dalmatian coast quite near Herzegovina. As one of the larger cities in Croatia near the fighting, it was a magnet for refugees, and its hospitals treated many wounded civilians and soldiers from BH until the conflict broke out between Croats and Bosniaks in the spring of 1993.

Squatting. People were expelled from their homes through BH during the war and fled to other areas. There they found the abandoned homes of those who had already fled for the place they were moving to and they, too, became squatters.

Srbinje. See Foča.

Srebenica. S near the Drina River and Serbian border, population 36,666 in 1991: Bosniaks 75.2%, Croats 0.1%, Serbs 22.7%, Yugoslavs and others 2%; part of RS.

Stadium. There often were no large halls in small towns to assemble and detain large numbers of people, so the local soccer stadium was the site of mass atrocities.

Storm. A campaign waged first in the Krajina region of Croatia by the Croatian Army that resulted in the explusion of 200,000 Serbian civilians, followed by a joint thrust of HVO, Croatian Army, and BH Army units across northwestern Bosnia to push RH forces from that region.

Stupni Do. A village near the town of Vareš, population 261 in 1991, including two Croats, 217 Bosniaks, 35 Serbs, and 7 Yugoslavs and others.

Talić, Momir. Before 1991, a career officer in the JNA. During the war, general of RS forces. Indicted by the ICTY for war crimes, but died from illness in 2003 before his trial was completed.

Tešanj. Central BH, population 48,480 in 1991: Bosniaks 72.1%, Croats 18.4%, Serbs 6.3%, Yugoslavs and others 3.2%; part of BH Federation.

Teslić. Central BH, population 59,854 in 1991: Bosniaks 21.4%, Croats 15.9%, Serbs 55.1%, Yugoslavs and others 7.6%; part of RS.

Tigers, The. A Serbian paramilitary group active in the BH war, associated with Željko Ražnjatović Arkan.

Tito, Josip Broz. Commander of the Partisans during World War II. After the war he held the office of President of Yugoslavia until his death in 1980.

Titograd. The capital city of Montenegro, now known as Podgorica.

Travnik. Central BH, population 70,747 in 1991: Bosniaks 45%, Croats 36.9%, Serbs 11%, Yugoslavs and others 7.1%; part of BH Federation.

Tuđman, Franjo. President of Croatia from May 1991 to his death in December 1999. The key figure of the Croatian Democratic Union from its formation to his death.

Tunnel. The Sarajevan authorities dug an 800-meter-long tunnel under the runways of the Sarajevo airport during the siege to allow people to move in and out of the besieged city. A short segment of it remains today as a museum.

Turkish. This term refers to the Ottoman Empire and the architecture and culture it brought to the Balkans. Often used during the war as a derogatory term for Muslims.

Tuzla. E central BH, population 131,618 in 1991: Bosniaks 47.6%, Croats 15.5%, Serbs 15.4%, Yugoslavs and others 21.5%; part of BH Federation.

Ugljevik. Upper E corner of BH, population 25,587 in 1991: Bosniaks 40%, Croats 0.2%, Serbs 56.5%, Yugoslavs and others 3.3%; part of RS.

UNHCR. United Nations High Commission for Refugees.

UNPROFOR. United Nations Protection Forces had the mandate of supporting the delivery of humanitarian relief, and monitoring no-fly zones and safe areas.

Ustasha. 1. Often used in these testimonies to refer to those Croats who took up arms against members of other ethnic groups during the war. It is used to set these Croats apart from the rest of the Croatian population, and thus constitutes an attempt at avoiding sweeping statements incriminating the entire Croatian population for the atrocities of a few extremists. 2. A member of the elite troops of the Croatian fascist forces during World War II. 3. The name used by members of a number of Croatian paramilitary groups. They wore Ustasha insignia from the Second World War in order to intimidate the non-Croatian population of BH during the recent war. 4. Derogatory term for Croat.

Užice. A town in Serbia proper quite close to Bratunac, Visegrad, and other eastern Bosnia towns. Refugees, Serbian and Bosniak alike, fled to Užice to escape the fighting. Užice was also an important logistical center for Serbian paramilitaries.

Vareš. Central BH, population 22,203 in 1991: Bosniaks 30.2%, Croats 40.6%, Serbs 16.4%, Yugoslavs and others 12.8%, part of BH Federation.

Višegrad. SE corner near the Serbian border, population 21,199 in 1991: Bosniaks 63.5%, Croats 0.2%, Serbs 31.8%, Yugoslavs and others 4.5%; part of RS. Known as the setting for Ivo Andrić's Nobel prize–winning novel *Bridge on the Drina*.

Vogošća. Central BH, population 24,647 in 1991: Bosniaks 50.7%, Croats 4.3%, Serbs 35.8%, Yugoslavs and others 9.2%; a Sarajevo municipality held by the RS during the Sarajevo siege.

Vraca. A Sarajevo neighborhood held by the RS Army during the siege.

Wartime assignment. Each person who was fit for military service was assigned a particular post he or she must fill.

Western Mostar. Otherwise known as the right bank of the Neretva River, became the predominantly Bosnian Croatian part of the city after 30 June 1993.

White Eagles. A Serbian paramilitary group originally associated with Vojislav Šešelj, later led by a series of other commanders.

Work detail. People living in enemy territory during the hostilities were required to report for a work detail, often digging trenches on the front lines, also assigned to maintenance and other war-related jobs. This allowed the aggressor force to keep track of men fit for military service.

Yugoslav. A certain number of people in BH referred to themselves as Yugoslav in nationality rather than Croatian, Serbian, Muslim, or Bosniak (see statistics given for BH and each town).

Yugoslav Army. Also known as the JA, was the fighting force of Yugoslavia from 1992 to 2003.

Yugoslavia. The name was first used after WWI. The government of Yugoslavia between 1918 and 1941 was a monarchy, led first by King Aleksandar and then, after his assassination in Marseilles in 1934, by regent Prince Paul, who fled the country in 1941 after signing an unpopular nonaggression pact with Hitler. In WWII the Partisans battled Ustasha, Chetnik, and German troops. Marshal Tito, Partisan commander, was Yugoslav president until his death in 1980. In 1990, after ten years of rule by a collective presidency, multiparty elections brought Tuđman, Izetbegović, and Milošević to power, among others. After the secession of Bosnia, Croatia, Macedonia, and Slovenia in the early 1990s, the name *Yugoslavia* referred only to the rump state of Montenegro and Serbia. Even they dropped the name in February 2003 in favor of the name *Serbia and Montenegro.*

Yugoslav People's Army. Also known by its acronym JNA, it was the army of Yugoslavia before 1991. All young men served for a year in the JNA, and were often sent to a republic other than their own. When the fighting first broke out in 1991, the JNA was still an active force, but as the situation grew more tense following the secession of Croatia and Slovenia in June 1991, the Croatian, Slovenian, and, ultimately, Bosniak and Macedonian young men serving in the JNA deserted, leaving a force under the control of Serbian officers. In 1992, the name was changed to the Yugoslav Army.

Zagreb. Capital city of the Republic of Croatia.

Zavidovići. Central BH, population 57,164 in 1991: Bosniaks 59.8%, Croats 13.3%, Serbs 20.4%, Yugoslavs and others 6.5%; part of BH Federation.

Zenica. Central BH, population 145,517 in 1991: Bosniaks 55.2%, Croats 15.5%, Serbs 15.4%, Yugoslavs and others 13.9%; part of BH Federation.

Source for population statistics: Stanovništvo Bosne i Hercegovine: *Narodnosni Sastav po Naseljima.* Zagreb: Travanj, 1995.

—Ellen Elias-Bursać, Svetlana Broz, Laurie Kain Hart

APPENDIX III:
RECOMMENDED READINGS
AND FILMS

Readings

Banac, I. *The National Question in Yugoslavia: Origins, History, Politics.* Ithaca, NY: Cornell University Press, 1984.

Bringa, T. Being Muslim the Bosnian way: Identity and community in a central Bosnian village. Princeton, NJ: Princeton University Press, 1995.

Burg, S. L. and Shoup, P. S. *The War in Bosnia-Herzegovina: Ethnic Conflict and International Intervention.* Armonk, NY: M. E. Sharpe, 1999.

Cohen, L. *Broken Bonds: Yugoslavia's Disintegration and Balkan Politics in Transition.* Boulder, CO: Westview Press, 1997.

Cushman, T. and Mestrovic, S. G. *This Time We Knew: Western Responses to Genocide in Bosnia.* New York: New York University Press, 1996.

Donia, R. and Fine, J. Jr. *Bosnia: A Tradition Betrayed.* New York: Columbia University Press, 1994.

Glenny, M. *The Fall of Yugoslavia: the Third Balkan War.* Penguin Books, 1996.

Mahmutcehajic, R. *Bosnia the Good: Tolerance and Tradition.* Central European University Press, 2000.

Malcolm, N. *Bosnia: A Short History.* New York: New York University Press, 1996.

Nikolic-Ristanovic, V. *Women, Violence and War: Wartime Victimization of Refugees in the Balkans.* Central European University Press, 2000.

Pinson, M. *The Muslims of Bosnia-Herzegovina: Their Historic Development from the Middle Ages to the Dissolution of Yugoslavia.* Cambridge, MA: Harvard University Press, 1996.

Ramet, S. P. *Balkan Babel: The Disintegration of Yugoslavia from the Death of Tito to the War for Kosovo.* Boulder, CO: Westview Press, 1999.

Sells, M. *The Bridge Betrayed: Religion and Genocide in Bosnia.* Berkeley, CA: University of California Press, 1998.

Silber, L. and Little, A. *Yugoslavia: Death of a Nation.* Penguin Books, 1997.

Ugresic, D. *The Culture of Lies.* University Park, PA: Pennsylvania State University Press, 1998.

Woodward, S. *Balkan Tragedy: Chaos and Dissolution After the Cold War.* Washington, DC: Brookings Institution, 1995.

Films

Miss Sarajevo, director: Bill Carter. Distributed by the director: 3121 Lemitire Way, Sacramento, CA 95833.

Perfect Circle (*Savrseni krug*), director: Ademil Kenovic. Distributor: Parnasse International.

We Are All Neighbors, director: Debbie Christie. Granada Television, 1993. Distributor: Films Incorporated Video, Chicago.

Welcome to Sarajevo, director: Michael Winterbottom. Distributor: Buena Vista Home Entertainment, 1997.

Yugoslavia, Death of a Nation. Discovery Channel, 1995–1996.

EDITOR'S ACKNOWLEDGMENTS

I would like to thank Svetlana Broz for having gathered these testimonies and Ellen Elias-Bursać for bringing them to the English-speaking world; Amila Buturović and Alexander Kitroeff for their excellent contributions on the context of the war; at Other Press, Judith Gurewich (without whom this book would not exist), Stacy Hague and Bob Hack; Kevin McGrath, for introducing me to the project; the students of my classes in ethnicity and conflict at Haverford College for readings of testimony that have richly informed my own; and Philippe Bourgois for his invaluable critique and encouragement. I am also grateful to Haverford College for generous support from the Faculty Research Fund for research and travel essential to the completion of this book.

Laurie Kain Hart

Photos in this book are by the editor.